The Communicator's Commentary

Genesis

THE COMMUNICATOR'S COMMENTARY SERIES
OLD TESTAMENT

Lloyd J. Ogilvie

General Editor

The Communicator's Commentary

Genesis

D. Stuart Briscoe

WORD BOOKS, PUBLISHER • WACO, TEXAS

Library of Congress Cataloging in Publication Data
Main entry under title:

The Communicator's commentary.
  Bibliography: p.
  Contents: OT1. Genesis/D. Stuart Briscoe
  1. Bible. O.T.—Commentaries. I. Ogilvie, Lloyd
John. II. Briscoe, D. Stuart, 1930– .
BS1151.2.C66 1986 221.7'7 86–11138
ISBN 0–8499–0406–4 (v. OT1)

Printed in the United States of America

5 6 7 8 9 9 AGF 9 8 7 6

Contents

Editor's Preface

God has called all of His people to be communicators. Everyone who is in Christ is called into ministry. As ministers of "the manifold grace of God," all of us—clergy and laity—are commissioned with the challenge to communicate our faith to individuals and groups, classes and congregations.

The Bible, God's Word, is the objective basis of the truth of His love and power that we seek to communicate. In response to the urgent, expressed needs of pastors, teachers, Bible study leaders, church school teachers, small group enablers, and individual Christians, the Communicator's Commentary is offered as a penetrating search of the Scriptures of the Old and New Testament to enable vital personal and practical communication of the abundant life.

Many current commentaries and Bible study guides provide only some aspects of a communicator's needs. Some offer in-depth scholarship but no application to daily life. Others are so popular in approach that biblical roots are left unexplained. Few offer impelling illustrations that open windows for the reader to see the exciting application for today's struggles. And most of all, seldom have the expositors given the valuable outlines of passages so needed to help the preacher or teacher in his or her busy life to prepare for communicating the Word to congregations or classes.

This Communicator's Commentary series brings all of these elements together. The authors are scholar-preachers and teachers outstanding in their ability to make the Scriptures come alive for individuals and groups. They are noted for bringing together excellence in biblical scholarship, knowledge of the original Hebrew and Greek, sensitivity to people's needs, vivid illustrative material from biblical, classical, and contemporary sources, and lucid communication by the use of clear outlines of thought. Each has been selected to contribute to this series because of his Spirit-empowered ability to help people live in the skins of biblical characters and provide a "you-are-there" intensity to the drama of events of the Bible which have so much to say about our relationships and responsibilities today.

The design for the Communicator's Commentary gives the reader an overall outline of each book of the Bible. Following the introduction, which reveals the author's approach and salient background on the book, each chapter of the commentary provides the Scripture to be exposited. The New King James Bible has been chosen for the Communicator's Commentary because it combines with integrity the beauty of language, underlying Hebrew and Greek textual basis, and thought-flow of the 1611 King James Version, while replacing obsolete verb forms and other archaisms with their everyday contemporary counterparts for greater readability. Reverence for God is preserved in the capitalization of all pronouns referring to the Father, Son, or Holy Spirit. Readers who are more comfortable with another translation can readily find the parallel passage by means of the chapter and verse reference at the end of each passage being exposited. The paragraphs of exposition combine fresh insights to the Scripture, application, rich illustrative material, and innovative ways of utilizing the vibrant truth for his or her own life and for the challenge of communicating it with vigor and vitality.

It has been gratifying to me as Editor of this series to receive enthusiastic progress reports from each contributor. As they worked, all were gripped with new truths from the Scripture—God-given insights into passages, previously not written in the literature of biblical explanation. A prime objective of this series is for each user to find the same awareness: that God speaks with newness through the Scriptures when we approach them with a ready mind and a willingness to communicate what He has given; that God delights to give communicators of His Word "I-never-saw-that-in-that-verse-before" intellectual insights so that our listeners and readers can have "I-never-realized-all-that-was-in-that-verse" spiritual experiences.

The thrust of the commentary series unequivocally affirms that God speaks through the Scriptures today to engender faith, enable adventuresome living of the abundant life, and establish the basis of obedient discipleship. The Bible, the unique Word of God, is unlimited as a resource for Christians in communicating our hope to others. It is our weapon in the battle for truth, the guide for ministry, and the irresistible force for introducing others to God.

A biblically rooted communication of the Gospel holds in unity and oneness what divergent movements have wrought asunder. This commentary series courageously presents personal faith, caring for individuals, and social responsibility as essential, inseparable dimensions of biblical Christianity. It seeks to present the quadrilateral Gospel in its fullness which calls us to unreserved commitment to Christ, unrestricted self-esteem in His grace, unqualified love for others in personal evangelism, and undying efforts to work for justice and righteousness in a sick and suffering world.

A growing renaissance in the church today is being led by clergy and laity who are biblically rooted, Christ-centered, and Holy Spirit-empowered. They have dared to listen to people's most urgent questions and deepest needs and then to God as He speaks through the Bible. Biblical preaching is the secret of growing churches. Bible study classes and small groups are equipping the laity for ministry in the world. Dynamic Christians are finding that daily study of God's Word allows the Spirit to do in them what He wishes to communicate through them to others. These days are the most exciting time since Pentecost. The Communicator's Commentary is offered to be a primary resource of new life for this renaissance.

It has been very encouraging to receive the enthusiastic responses of pastors and teachers to the twelve New Testament volumes of the Communicator's Commentary series. The letters from communicators on the firing line in pulpits, classes, study groups, and Bible fellowship clusters across the nation, as well as the reviews of scholars and publication analysts, have indicated that we have been on target in meeting a need for a distinctly different kind of commentary on the Scriptures, a commentary that is primarily aimed at helping interpreters of the Bible to equip the laity for ministry.

This positive response has led the publisher to press on with an additional twenty-one volumes covering the books of the Old Testament. These new volumes rest upon the same goals and guidelines that undergird the New Testament volumes. Scholar-preachers with facility in Hebrew as well as vivid contemporary exposition have been selected as authors. The purpose throughout is to aid the preacher and teacher in the challenge and adventure of Old Testament exposition in communication. In each volume you will meet Yahweh, the "I AM" Lord who is Creator, Sustainer, and Redeemer in the unfolding drama of His call and care of Israel. He is the Lord who acts, intervenes, judges, and presses His people into the immense challenges and privileges of being a chosen people, a holy nation. And in the descriptive exposition of each passage, the implications of the ultimate revelation of Yahweh in Jesus Christ, His Son, our Lord, are carefully spelled out to maintain unity and oneness in the preaching and teaching of the Gospel.

The author of this volume, *Genesis,* will be familiar to many readers. Dr. Stuart Briscoe, Pastor of the Elmbrook Church of Brookfield, Wisconsin, is widely recognized as a vibrant communicator of God's Word. As a preacher, Dr. Briscoe has proclaimed the good news throughout the world. As a prolific author, he has taught the body of Christ with timely, relevant application of God's truth. Many will know in particular Dr. Briscoe's earlier contribution to the Communicator's Commentary—the well-received volume on Romans.

Stuart Briscoe's treatment of Genesis lives up to the challenge of this commentary series. He grapples vigorously with the biblical text, often using Hebrew definitions to enrich our understanding of the English translation. He delicately unravels the theological intricacies of Genesis, keeping in mind the varied concerns of Christian thinkers, past and present.

But, in spite of Dr. Briscoe's valuable exegetical and theological counsel, his "main thrust has been toward an understanding which will lead to application in modern life." He allows Genesis to speak clearly to us today, to address our contemporary concerns and needs. As he communicates the timeless truths of Genesis, Dr. Briscoe equips the modern reader for effective communication in preaching, teaching, and Bible studies.

I am in full agreement with Dr. Briscoe when he comments: "It would be very difficult to overemphasize the significance of Genesis for this or any other generation." We need Genesis today! As we search for new beginnings, we must confront life "in the beginning." As we seek renewal by God's Spirit, we need to be reminded of the world when it was newly created by this same Spirit. As we reaffirm our covenantal relationship with Christ, we are instructed by God's fundamental covenant with Abraham. Genesis shows us who we are. It introduces us to our God who is both Creator and Redeemer. It invites us into relationship with this God of Abraham, Isaac, and Jacob.

So, Genesis deserves a contemporary hearing. Stuart Briscoe provides this hearing with an inspired, Christ-centered voice. We have much to gain as we listen anew to the Word of God "in the beginning."

LLOYD J. OGILVIE

Introduction

What Does "Genesis" Mean?

The first five books of the Bible are often called the "Pentateuch," a word which in its original Greek form means simply "five books." Traditionally these ancient writings have also been known as "the five books of Moses" or the "five-fifths of the law." This is reflected in some of our modern Bibles such as the Revised Standard Version where the first five books are entitled "The First (or Second, etc.) Book of Moses commonly called Genesis (or Exodus, etc.)." For our purposes we are particularly interested in how the name "Genesis" first appeared on the scene.

In the Hebrew Scriptures the first book was called "Bĕrêšîth" which means "in the beginning," the expression with which the first sentence begins. Incidentally, in ancient times it was common practice to name a document after its opening word or words in much the same way that we sometimes name hymns such as "Rock of Ages" or "Standing on the Promises." In the third century before Christ a group of seventy (-two?) scholars met in Alexandria to translate the Hebrew Scriptures into the Greek language. Their work became known as the "Septuagint," or by the abbreviation LXX, and they called the first book of Moses, "Genesis," an Anglicized version of the Greek word *geneseos* meaning a number of different things including "origin," "history," or "genealogy." This word appears throughout Genesis on numerous occasions such as Genesis 2:4 and 5:1, and some scholars suggest that its usage may hold the key to understanding the whole structure of the book.

Who Wrote Genesis?

For many centuries nobody seemed to question the authorship of the Pentateuch, including Genesis, presumably because everyone was satisfied with the ancient traditional ascription to Moses. But in the seventeenth century this all changed through the writing of a brilliant Jewish philosopher called Baruch (later Benedict) Spinoza. In his book *Tractatus Theologico-Politicus* he insisted that the Bible was to be understood metaphorically and allegorically rather than literally. This led him, among many other things, to reject Moses' authorship of the Pentateuch, including Genesis, because it speaks of Moses in the third person and also describes his death, and therefore could not possibly have been written by Moses. Neither of these arguments has caused any great concern to those who recognize that many authors have written autobiographically in the third person, and some other books of the Bible appear to have been completed with a brief appendix after the demise of the author (see Jer. 51:64–52:34).

Spinoza's thinking, however, had triggered many avenues of critical study which began to flourish in Europe during the latter part of the nineteenth century. One of the foremost theologians at that time, Julius Wellhausen, building on the work of other scholars, developed the Graf-Wellhausen hypothesis which attributed the writings of the Pentateuch to numerous sources identified by the letters JEDP which, far from being written by Moses, had actually appeared over a period of several centuries. Subsequent studies led to a bewildering decimation and multiplication of sources until scholars were talking about J1 and J2 and L and B and H and S in addition to the original JEDP. The problem with this approach can easily be demonstrated when it is realized that it was not uncommon for some verses to be divided between as many as three entirely different sources separated by centuries.

What then is the answer to the question of authorship? In addition to the traditional titles of the books of the Pentateuch including the name of Moses, it should be noted that the rest of the Scriptures speak about the Mosaic authorship of the Pentateuch (see, for example, Josh. 22:9; 2 Kings 21:8; Matt. 19:8). Furthermore, while it is obvious that Moses is not mentioned in Genesis it is not unreasonable to assume that the Lord Jesus was making reference (among other things) to Genesis when he talked to the Samaritan woman (John 5:46) and the discouraged disciples in Emmaus (Luke 24:27, 44). It should also be noted that such is the majestic scope and tone of Genesis that one would assume it would take a Moses to produce it. Therefore, there does not seem to be any reason to depart from the traditional view that the author is none other than the man who "esteem(ed) the reproach of Christ greater riches than the treasures in Egypt" (Heb. 11:26).

When Was Genesis Written?

The answer to this question is of necessity tied to the date of the exodus. For obvious reasons Moses could not have written Genesis after his decease, and we know that he died forty years after the exodus at the time that the children of Israel entered the Promised Land. Scholars have suggested dates in the thirteenth and fifteenth centuries B.C. for the exodus and archaeologists have been busy trying to unearth signs of the Israelites' conquest of the Promised Land with a view to narrowing down the date. The weight of opinion seems to be moving toward the fifteenth century date which would in turn parallel the details given in 1 Kings 6:1 where we are told that Solomon who ascended the throne early in the tenth century started the temple building 480 years after the exodus.

Of course if it can be shown that Genesis was not the work of Moses but the work of an editor or redactor such as Samuel or Ezra, who collected and collated materials from various sources, the date would be much later. Numerous theories to this end have been propagated but it is not necessary for us to pursue them at this time.

What Was the Author's Objective in Writing Genesis?

The Pentateuch, written as it was for the Hebrew people, concentrates on the two major events of Jewish history—namely the covenant with Abraham and the exodus. In the covenant Jehovah took the initiative and declared that He would be Israel's God and they would have the unspeakable privilege of being His people. In the exodus God demonstrated in the most dramatic fashion that He was strong on behalf of His people and that He would indeed lead them into the land He had promised to Abraham and his seed. No doubt the people were as eager to have more information to fill in the details as Jehovah was eager for them to know. So Genesis tells the story of how the children of Israel arrived in Egypt in the first place. That filled in the gap between the covenant and the exodus but did not explain the details of how man came to be on earth in the first place, or why it was necessary for God to intervene in the human experience in redemption and blessing. The creation narrative met that need in the same way that numerous other details, recounted in Genesis and the other four books, explained the wonderful workings of God in the affairs of His chosen people.

What Is the Relevance of Genesis Today?

It would be very difficult to overemphasize the significance of Genesis for this or any other generation. For example, the themes of "origins" or "beginnings" are so striking when we remember that Genesis teaches about the origins of the universe, the origin of mankind, the origin of marriage, the origin of sin, the origin of death, the beginning of redemption, the introduction of judgment, the origin of the covenant, and so on. When we look at Genesis from the vantage point of God's self-revelation we are introduced to God as Creator, Companion, Judge, Merciful Savior, Protector, Guide, and Sustainer. We are shown mankind in harmony with God, nature, and each other, and we are introduced to mankind desperately at odds with God, himself, and his environment. These profound themes are presented in the first section of the book in uncomplicated, majestic language simple enough for the child to grasp, profound enough to tax the wisest philosopher, and flexible enough to contain the findings of the most brilliant scientist. In the second section the style changes as God's dealings with mankind are presented in specific instances which recount the lives of individuals as they struggled to live rightly before God in the circumstances that men and women encounter today and every day wherever they live.

What Is the Structure of Genesis?

One of the most common approaches to the structure of Genesis is to divide the book into two unequal sections. The first one includes chapters 1–11 and is often called "Primeval History." The second, containing chapters 12–50, is known as "Patriarchal History." The "Primeval History" section, as its name suggests, covers the dramatic events relating to the "first age" of man culminating in the tragic showdown between man and God at Babel. The "Patriarchal History" covers the lives of the "fathers" or "family rulers" through whom God's purposes for His people began to unfold. These men—Abraham, Isaac, and Jacob, plus the sons of Jacob (later Israel)—lived turbulent, exciting lives which serve as a magnificent vehicle for God's faithfulness and power.

It has been noted by a number of scholars, however, that the expression "these are the generations [Greek, *geneseos*] of . . . ," which is used on eleven occasions, may be what is technically called a "colophon"—a title placed at the end of a tablet. If accepted, this theory, which raises its own problems, would divide Genesis 1–37 into eleven sections based on the eleven tablets which were collated by Moses. The remaining material (chapters 38–50), known as the "Joseph narrative," according to this theory was probably preserved through the oral traditions and put into written form by Moses.

As the narrative of Genesis is so clearly an unfolding story of God's dealings with mankind in general, channeled through Abraham and his progeny in particular, it will serve our purposes if we base our study on the chapter divisions as reflected in the Outline. See pages 23–28.

What Is the Approach of This Commentary?

Commentaries on Genesis abound and I am deeply indebted to many of them. Some approach the study of this crucial book critically and on occasion give the impression that their attention to detail has obscured the forest in the trees. This is not to suggest that the Bible will not stand up to the rigorous inquiry of honest, reverent, critical scholars. Neither does it imply that our grasp of the deep truths of Scripture will not be immeasurably enhanced through the work of godly men and women skilled in the intricacies of Near Eastern thought, culture, custom, and language.

Others concentrate their study on exegetical matters endeavoring to discover for us what the text of Scripture is really communicating. That this type of resource is of great value is readily appreciated when we remember that we are dealing with a document almost four thousand years old which has been preserved for us in Hebrew, Latin, and Greek.

Other commentators have had a devotional objective in mind and have sought to draw from the ancient text lessons which would benefit their readers in their daily walk with God and man. Because I am painfully aware of my scholastic shortcomings and I am acutely aware of modern man's deep spiritual needs, I have approached this work with a profound respect for the findings of scholars, and where time and space have allowed I have drawn from their work. But the main thrust has been toward an understanding which will lead to application in modern life. It is noteworthy that the major part of Genesis deals with some very human people living in very understandable circumstances while the opening and briefer part deals with fundamental principles of human existence without which no one in any era could adequately live as God intended. Accordingly it is my hope that my readers will find in this commentary things that will enrich their experience of the God of Abraham, Isaac, and Jacob and encourage them to emulate the high points of the patriarchs' walk and to avoid the pitfalls into which their evident humanness led them. When all is said and done, as my old math teacher used to say, "Learn by making mistakes and if you can learn from the mistakes of others, so much the better."

An Outline of Genesis

I. The God of Creation: Gen. 1:1–31
   A. Some Preliminary Remarks
   B. Some Powerful Revelations
   C. Some Practical Realities

II. Man—God's Masterpiece: Gen. 2:1–25
   A. Man—a Natural Being
   B. Man—a Spiritual Being
   C. Man—a Practical Being
   D. Man—a Rational Being
   E. Man—a Moral Being
   F. Man—a Social Being

III. Disaster in Eden: Gen. 3:1–24
   A. The Conflict in Eden
   B. The Consequences on Earth
   C. The Conclusion in Eternity

IV. The Human Race: Gen. 4:1–26
   A. The Derivation of the Human Race
   B. The Dedication of the Human Race
   C. The Deviation of the Human Race

V. Life and Death: Gen. 5:1–32
   A. Coming to Grips with Life
   B. Coming to Grips with Death
   C. Coming to Grips with Life After Death

VI. The Character of God: Gen. 6:1–22
   A. God's Principles
   B. God's Perspective
   C. God's Pain
   D. God's Pleasure
   E. God's Provision
   F. God's Patience
   G. God's Promise

VII.   A Man of Faith: Gen. 7:1–24
    A.   Faith—a Response to Revelation
    B.   Faith—a Relationship of Trust
    C.   Faith—a Readiness to Obey
    D.   Faith—a Release of Blessing
    E.   Faith—a Resource of Power
    F.   Faith—a Rebuke to Unfaithfulness
    G.   Faith—a Reminder to the Faithful

VIII.   The New Creation: Gen. 8:1–22
    A.   The Entrance to the New Creation
    B.   The Enjoyment of the New Creation

IX.   Human Dignity: Gen. 9:1–29
    A.   The Protection of Human Dignity
    B.   The Prostitution of Human Dignity
    C.   The Promotion of Human Dignity

X.   Untied Nations: Gen. 10:1–32
    A.   The Formation of the Nations
    B.   The Frustrations of the Nations
    C.   The Future of the Nations

XI.   God and Abram: Gen. 11:1–32
    A.   The Call
    B.   The Choice
    C.   The Conclusion

XII.   Faith: Gen. 12:1–20
    A.   The Experience of Faith
    B.   The Extremities of Faith
    C.   The Expressions of Faith

XIII.   Facing Up to Reality: Gen. 13:1–18
    A.   Facing Up to Failure
    B.   Facing Up to Friction
    C.   Facing Up to Facts

XIV.   Getting Involved: Gen. 14:1–24
    A.   Abram's Involvement with Sodom
    B.   Abram's Involvement with Salem

XV.   The Promises of God: Gen. 15:1–21
    A.   The Promises of God Banish Fear
    B.   The Promises of God Promote Faith
    C.   The Promises of God Unveil the Future

XVI. Making Mistakes: Gen. 16:1–16
    A. Making Mistakes
    B. Making Mistakes Worse
    C. Making Something Out of Mistakes
XVII. Covenant: Gen. 17:1–27
    A. The Concept of the Covenant
    B. The Content of the Covenant
    C. The Consequences of the Covenant
XVIII. Big Questions about God: Gen. 18:1–33
    A. A Question of Divine Ability
    B. A Question of Divine Strategy
    C. A Question of Divine Integrity
XIX. The Significance of Sodom: Gen. 19:1–38
    A. Sodom's Society
    B. Sodom's Sin
    C. Sodom's Significance
XX. The Danger of Underestimating: Gen. 20:1–18
    A. Underestimating Personal Characteristics
    B. Underestimating Spiritual Considerations
    C. Underestimating Special Circumstances
    D. Underestimating Practical Consequences
    E. Underestimating Divine Control
XXI. A Time for Every Purpose: Gen. 21:1–34
    A. A Time to Laugh
    B. A Time to Mourn
    C. A Time to Heal
XXII. Faith's High Point: Gen. 22:1–24
    A. The Incident as a Test
    B. The Incident as a Triumph
    C. The Incident as a Type
XXIII. Coping with Death: Gen. 23:1–20
    A. The Experience of Dying
    B. The Experience of Death
    C. The Experience of Bereavement
XXIV. Commitment: Gen. 24:1–67
    A. A Commitment to Providence
    B. A Commitment to Principle
    C. A Commitment to Performance

D.   A Commitment to People
XXV.   From Womb to Tomb: Gen. 25:1–34
A.   Man in the Tomb
B.   Man in the Womb
C.   Man in the Middle
XXVI.   Pressure Points: Gen. 26:1–35
A.   Political Pressure
B.   Psychological Pressure
C.   Personal Pressure
D.   Parental Pressure
XXVII.   All in the Family: Gen. 27:1–46
A.   How Are Families Founded?
B.   Why Do Families Fail?
C.   When Do Families Flourish?
XXVIII.   Meet the Master: Gen. 28:1–22
A.   The Action of Jehovah
B.   The Reaction of Jacob
XXIX.   The School of Hard Knocks: Gen. 29:1–35
A.   The School's Founder
B.   The School's Curriculum
C.   The School's Graduates
XXX.   Relationships: Gen. 30:1–43
A.   Relationships Reflect Values
B.   Relationships Reveal Vices
C.   Relationships Refine Virtues
XXXI.   Settling Differences: Gen. 31:1–55
A.   The Reasons Differences Arise
B.   The Results Differences Produce
C.   The Resolution Differences Demand
XXXII.   The Main Event: Gen. 32:1–32
A.   The Night of Struggle
B.   The Moment of Truth
C.   The Hour of Decision
D.   The Day of Blessing
XXXIII.   Repairing the Damage: Gen. 33:1–20
A.   Willingness to Admit Guilt
B.   Readiness to Accept Apology
C.   Openness to Administer Forgiveness

XXXIV.   Violence: Gen. 34:1–31
    A.   The Roots of Violence
    B.   The Results of Violence
    C.   The Response to Violence

XXXV.   Spiritual Renewal: Gen. 35:1–29
    A.   Why Is Spiritual Renewal Necessary?
    B.   How Is Spiritual Renewal Experienced?
    C.   When Is Spiritual Renewal Possible?

XXXVI.   The Bitter Root: Gen. 36:1–43
    A.   Esau's Experience
    B.   Esau's Example

XXXVII.   Boys Will Be Men: Gen. 37:1–36
    A.   The Instillation of Worthy Principles
    B.   The Inevitability of Various Pressures
    C.   The Intricacies of Divine Plans

XXXVIII.   The Chain of Events: Gen. 38:1–30
    A.   Links in the Chain
    B.   Lessons from the Links

XXXIX.   Success: Gen. 39:1–23
    A.   Nothing Succeeds Like Success
    B.   Nothing Seduces Like Success
    C.   Nothing Sustains Like Success

XL.   Discouragement: Gen. 40:1–23
    A.   Some Reasons for Discouragement
    B.   Some Reactions to Discouragement
    C.   Some Resources for Discouragement

XLI.   Living in Two Worlds: Gen. 41:1–57
    A.   The Spiritual World
    B.   The Secular World
    C.   The Spiritual Person in the Secular World

XLII.   Leadership: Gen. 42:1–38
    A.   The Acceptance of Responsibility
    B.   The Reputation for Dependability
    C.   The Development of Ability
    D.   The Exercise of Authority

XLIII.   It's a Changing World: Gen. 43:1–34
    A.   Change Will Be Inevitable
    B.   Change May Be Uncomfortable

C. Change Should Be Profitable
XLIV. Putting Things Right: Gen. 44:1–34
    A. Relationships Must Be Evaluated Realistically
    B. Responsibility Must Be Accepted Individually
    C. Repentance Must Be Expressed Genuinely
XLV. Joseph's Revelation: Gen. 45:1–28
    A. The Need to Relate
    B. The Need to Reconcile
    C. The Need to Restore
XLVI. The God of Surprises: Gen. 46:1–34
    A. His Surprising Purposes
    B. His Surprising Practices
    C. His Surprising People
XLVII. Life Is a Pilgrimage: Gen. 47:1–31
    A. The Mentality a Pilgrim Develops
    B. The Difficulty a Pilgrim Encounters
    C. The Quality a Pilgrim Displays
XLVIII. The Ages of Man: Gen. 48:1–22
    A. Jacob—the Voice of the Past
    B. Joseph—the Mainstay of the Present
    C. Ephraim—the Hope of the Future
XLIX. Appropriate Blessings: Gen. 49:1–33
    A. The Men Who Were Disqualified
    B. The Men Who Were Distinguished
    C. The Man Who Was Different
L. When Things Get Worse: Gen. 50:1–26
    A. Joseph's Statement of Faith
    B. Joseph's Symbol of Hope
    C. Joseph's Show of Love

CHAPTER ONE

The God of Creation

Genesis 1:1-31

1:1 In the beginning God created the heavens and the earth.

2 The earth was without form, and void; and darkness *was* on the face of the deep. And the Spirit of God was hovering over the face of the waters.

3 Then God said, "Let there be light"; and there was light.

4 And God saw the light, that *it was* good; and God divided the light from the darkness.

5 God called the light Day, and the darkness He called Night. So the evening and the morning were the first day.

6 Then God said, "Let there be a firmament in the midst of the waters, and let it divide the waters from the waters."

7 Thus God made the firmament, and divided the waters which *were* under the firmament from the waters which *were* above the firmament; and it was so.

8 And God called the firmament Heaven. So the evening and the morning were the second day.

9 Then God said, "Let the waters under the heavens be gathered together into one place, and let the dry *land* appear"; and it was so.

10 And God called the dry *land* Earth, and the gathering together of the waters He called Seas. And God saw that *it was* good.

11 Then God said, "Let the earth bring forth grass, the herb *that* yields seed, *and* the fruit tree *that* yields fruit according to its kind, whose seed *is* in itself, on the earth"; and it was so.

12 And the earth brought forth grass, the herb *that* yields seed according to its kind, and the tree *that* yields fruit, whose seed *is* in itself according to its kind. And God saw that *it was* good.

13 So the evening and the morning were the third day.

14 Then God said, "Let there be lights in the firmament of the heavens to divide the day from the night; and let them be for signs and seasons, and for days and years;

15 "and let them be for lights in the firmament of the heavens to give light on the earth"; and it was so.

16 Then God made two great lights: the greater light to rule the day, and the lesser light to rule the night. *He made* the stars also.

17 God set them in the firmament of the heavens to give light on the earth,

18 and to rule over the day and over the night, and to divide the light from the darkness. And God saw that *it was* good.

19 So the evening and the morning were the fourth day.

20 Then God said, "Let the waters abound with an abundance of living creatures, and let birds fly above the earth across the face of the firmament of the heavens."

21 So God created great sea creatures and every living thing that moves, with which the waters abounded, according to their kind, and every winged bird according to its kind. And God saw that *it was* good.

22 And God blessed them, saying, "Be fruitful and multiply, and fill the waters in the seas, and let birds multiply on the earth."

23 So the evening and the morning were the fifth day.

24 Then God said, "Let the earth bring forth the living creature according to its kind: cattle and creeping thing and beast of the earth, *each* according to its kind"; and it was so.

25 And God made the beast of the earth according to its kind, cattle according to its kind, and

everything that creeps on the earth according to its kind. And God saw that *it was* good.

26 Then God said, "Let Us make man in Our image, according to Our likeness; let them have dominion over the fish of the sea, over the birds of the air, and over the cattle, over all the earth and over every creeping thing that creeps on the earth."

27 So God created man in His *own* image; in the image of God He created him; male and female He created them.

28 Then God blessed them, and God said to them, "Be fruitful and multiply; fill the earth and subdue it; have dominion over the fish of the sea, over the birds of the air, and over every living thing that moves on the earth."

29 And God said, "See, I have given you every herb *that* yields seed which *is* on the face of all the earth, and every tree whose fruit yields seed; to you it shall be for food.

30 "Also, to every beast of the earth, to every bird of the air, and to everything that creeps on the earth, in which *there is* life, *I have given* every green herb for food"; and it was so.

31 Then God saw everything that He had made, and indeed *it was* very good. So the evening and the morning were the sixth day.

Gen. 1:1–31

SOME PRELIMINARY REMARKS

I have never run the Boston Marathon but at this moment I think I know what it feels like to stand at the starting line knowing over twenty-six miles of grueling road lie ahead. I've never seen Heartbreak Hill but as I look at Genesis 1, I can't help feeling this marathon is starting at the toughest part of the race! Such is the scope of this first chapter, and such are the matters raised in it that it is no surprise that it has been the focus of attention for millions of people down through church history.

Luther said of this book, "There is nothing more beautiful than the Book of Genesis, nothing more useful," and he regarded the opening verses as "certainly the foundation of the whole of Scripture." Need-less to say, not everyone has approached the opening words of the Bible with such warm delight! Rather, the early verses of Genesis have become a veritable battleground where those who defend the faith have waged war with those who approach them with calcu-lated skepticism or outright antagonism. Brief excerpts from *Human-ist Manifesto I and II* will suffice to illustrate the point: "Religious humanists regard the universe as self-existing and not created . . . we begin with humans not God . . . we can discover no divine purpose or providence for the human species . . . no deity will save us; we must save ourselves."

It was in the nineteenth century that the struggle between those who accepted biblical views of creation and those who rejected them reached epic proportions. Bernard Ramm writes, "This deep-moving secularism—life without God, philosophy without the Bible, com-munity without the Church . . . was an irresistible tide."[1] The tide which was to sweep men's thinking into new channels flowed from rebellion against an authoritarian church, a newly found love affair with science, and an approach to Scripture which pitted reason against faith and insisted that reason won. The struggle continues to this day with profound consequences.

The love affair with science has produced inestimable benefits for mankind as anyone who has flown in a 747, visited a doctor, or used a telephone will heartily agree. The problem is not with science as such, because where science discovers truth it can only be benefi-cial. The problem lies in the attitudes which exist between some scientists and some theologians. Where scientists worship their sci-entific approach to an extent that everything becomes verifiable only in terms of scientific evaluation, or where theologians distrust scien-tists so much that they automatically dismiss their findings when applied to Scripture, only conflict can arise. Sad to say, the theolo-gians have not done too well in recent years. The devastating result has been that the man in the street has tended to reject or ignore fundamental truths about himself and his world.

How should we approach the problem? One approach is to accept science as gospel and regard the Bible as an ancient irrelevance. This approach is fair neither to the Bible's claims nor the well-documented limitations of science. Another approach is to be totally immersed in Scripture like a hippopotamus in a river, emerging only to snort at the latest discoveries of irreverent science. The problem with this attitude is that it suggests that all that man needs to know about life is to be found in the Bible and that everything discovered from other sources is at best irrelevant and at worst devilish. The third approach tries to work on the premise that "all truth is God's truth" wherever it is discovered. The obvious problem with this is that it is not always easy to determine what is true. This can be the case both for the theologian whose interpretation of Scripture may be conditioned and therefore erroneous and for the scientist who has similar problems with "total objectivity"—a myth if ever there was one! Without suggesting that there are simple solutions to this problem I have endeavored to work on the principle that Scripture rightly understood is the final authority and that science properly conducted and applied serves to amplify and elaborate on the gracious revelation God gives to mankind. With that in mind let us proceed to the text.

SOME POWERFUL REVELATIONS

"In the beginning God . . .", the opening words of Scripture, promptly place the emphasis where it rightfully belongs—on God. The interest in Genesis chapter 1 as it relates to the cosmos, to mankind, and to the natural sciences has been such that this emphasis on God has often been overlooked. This chapter should be read primarily as a revelation of the God of creation rather than a statement about that which God created. While it raises many unanswered questions about *how* He created, it provides many answers to questions about *Who* did the creating. We will take note of His attributes, His actions, and His affirmation.

1. His Attributes

Knowing God is at one and the same time the most noble and the most frustrating pursuit of man. Whenever mankind tries to figure out God the result is God made in the image of man. When mankind is open to a divine initiative in which God reveals Himself, the result is rewarding in the extreme. God has revealed:

a. His self-existence. It was *"in the beginning"* that God created *"the heavens and the earth"* (v. 1). The concept of the beginning of the universe is mind boggling. We even have trouble thinking about the beginning of something as familiar as a house. When did my house originate? When it was completed, or the first brick was laid, or the foundations were started, or the excavators came in with bulldozers, or the surveyors brought their instruments, or the architect drew his plans, or the developer had an idea, or some man somewhere had the first idea of a house? The answers to my rhetorical questions may not be important but, whatever the answers to similar questions about *"the beginning,"* the unapologetic statement of Scripture is that whatever and whenever the beginning was God was there, alive and well. In fact, what Genesis states implicitly the New Testament writers make explicit. For example, John recorded Jesus' words, "Father . . . You loved Me before the foundation of the world" (John 17:24). This immediately puts Him above and beyond the material world. It states that He is independent of all that everything else depends upon, that He is totally and utterly "other."

b. *His self-sufficiency.* The expression *"God created"* is most interesting because the Hebrew uses a plural word for *"God"*(ʾElōhîm) but a singular word for *"created."* Later in the chapter we read *"Then God said, 'Let Us make man in Our image, according to Our likeness . . .'"* (v. 26). Some commentators suggest that the plural words are used to give a sense of intensity and majesty to God (in much the same way that the Queen in her official pronouncements uses the "royal 'we'"). But a clear statement about the Trinity becomes apparent when the *"Us"* and *"Our"* and the plural *"ʾElōhîm"* are considered alongside the statement about the *"Spirit of God"* (v. 2) being active in creation and the New Testament teaching about the pre-existence of "the Word" and His creative activity (see John 1:1–10). The significance of the Trinity for us is that before there was a universe, there was a "wholeness" and a "completeness" about God in His "three person-relatedness" which made Him totally self-sufficient. Any suggestion that God needed the universe to be fulfilled or that He was less than complete without mankind totally misses the point of the Trinity in whom love and communication were perfected.

I have often asked men to tell me about themselves and they usually tell me about their jobs. Apparently identity is inextricably bound up in what they do. In the same way, when women are asked about themselves they often talk about their children. There is no doubt that human identity is discovered and displayed in terms of relationships and activities, and this has led some people to assume that God created the worlds to prove something to Himself and then created mankind to make it possible for Him to have relationships which in some way would complete His personhood. This line of thinking serves only to suggest that if God had not created He would have been less than He is and therefore the creation served to meet some kind of need in Him. God did not *have* to create in order to feel good about Himself; neither did He *need* mankind to relate to in order to discover His identity. The triune God was always and continues to be complete and entire—needing nothing. To understand this is not only to appreciate God more fully but also to recognize the wonders of God's grace in choosing to create all that is when there was no necessity for Him to do so.

c. His self-determination. The idea to create was God's and His alone. It was God who repeatedly spoke the creative word to bring material things into being and it was He Who, communing with Himself (not with the angels as some have suggested), brought forth man in His own image. Isaiah the prophet captured the significance of this when he asked rhetorically: "Who has directed the Spirit of the Lord or as His counselor has taught Him?" (Isa. 40:13). And the answer came loud and clear from John on Patmos: "You are worthy, O Lord . . . for You created all things, and by Your will they exist and were created" (Rev. 4:11).

2. His Actions

The key word describing God's actions in Genesis chapter 1 is *"created,"* and it is used in connection with *"the heavens and the earth"* (v. 1), *"great sea creatures"* (v. 21), and *"man"* (v. 27). If we take the first occurrence to mean God's action in bringing the universe into being, the second as a statement relating to the beginning of animal life, and the third to introduce human existence we can see the word is reserved to describe divine actions of the greatest significance. He is responsible for originating all things material, all that is animate, and that which is uniquely human. Having been introduced to the *"heavens and the earth"* in verse 1 we promptly focus our attention on the earth which is described as *"without form [Hebrew, tōhû], and void [Hebrew, bōhû; and darkness was on the face of the deep"* (v. 2). While the universe is profoundly significant, the focus of Genesis is upon earth with particular reference to the inhabitants thereof and God's dealings with them through His chosen people.

There are two words that describe the creative activity of God— "progression" and "power." The Hebrew words *tōhû wā bōhû*, used in the expression "without form and void," are so striking that it was apparently used to rivet the readers' attention on the condition of creation in its initial stages. That God created *ex nihilo* (a Latin term beloved of theologians meaning "out of nothing"), while not explicitly stated, is continually implied throughout Scripture, as in Paul's statement about God "who gives life to the dead and calls into existence the things that do not exist" (Rom. 4:17, RSV). Apparently creation progressed from a state of "nothingness" through a state of "formlessness" and "emptiness" to a condition where the "formlessness" gave way to "form" and the "emptiness" surrendered to "fullness."

The six days of creation (see vv. 5, 8, 13, 19, 23, and 31) are presented in such a way as to suggest a careful literary structure. On day 1 *"light"* is formed. On day 4 *"two great lights . . . the stars also."* On day 2 *"God made the firmament, and divided the waters."* On day 5 these were filled with *"great sea creatures . . . and every winged bird."* On day 3 *"Earth"* is formed along with vegetation. On day 6 *"God created man in His own image; . . . and God said to them, 'Be fruitful and multiply; fill the earth.'"* *Tōhû* is finding "form," as outlined in the first three days, and *bōhû* is finding fulfillment in the fourth through the sixth days. The God of creation is at work. Considerable debate has centered around the days of creation. Are they to be understood as literal days of twenty-four hours set in a literal week, or is there some other explanation of them? There was a time when reverent students of God's Word were sure that they could tell us when God created the world and even set a date for the creation of man. Archbishop Ussher of Armagh calculated 4004 B.C. as the date of creation and John Lightfoot, the Cambridge scholar, went further and narrowed it down to the week of October 18–24, 4004 B.C. and Adam's creation at 9 A.M., forty-fifth meridian time, October 23rd, 4004 B.C.! These conclusions sound quaint and naïve to our ears, but we should bear in mind that these men, writing in the early seventeenth century, had no knowledge of the findings of modern geology and cosmology.

Therein lies the problem. The natural scientist talks convincingly in terms of millions of years and evolutionary eras while the Bible believer looks at the six days and wonders what on earth to do. Bernard Ramm has looked into various theories and suggested ways in which these matters can be harmonized in his book, *The Christian View of Science and Scripture*.[1] While it will not make everyone happy, it can serve to make many wiser! It is not at all unreasonable to believe that *"day"* (Hebrew, *yôm*), which can be translated quite legitimately as "period," refers not to literal days but to eras and ages in which God's progressive work was being accomplished. Some who find this interpretation unacceptable suggest that periods of time were concluded with literal days in which the process of creation was fulfilled. Others suggest that Genesis is teaching that God revealed His creative activity in six days rather than performed the creation in such a period.

This leads to another matter relating to the days which requires our attention. Do the "days" describe a series of creative acts in chronological order or did the writer concern himself more with a literary structure? This question has arisen because of practical concerns such as "Could there be light on the first day when the sun and moon were not created till the fourth day?" In the same vein, "Could the vegetation of the third day have survived before the sunlight arrived on the fourth day?" and "How could there be *'the evening and the morning'* of the first three days without the benefit of the sun?" These considerations have led some to believe that the writer's intent was not so much a detailed chronology of creation as a logical explanation using pictorial language leading up to the final creative act—the arrival of man on the scene.

On one thing we can agree and that is that there is no complete agreement! But this fact should not be allowed to obscure the much more significant fact that reverent biblical scholarship and honest careful science can continue to lead us into an increasingly integrated and harmonious understanding of divine creation. The progressive creation which is shown moving from formlessness through form to fullness is also expressed in the progressively significant development of created things—mineral, vegetable, animal, and on to the pinnacle of creation: humankind. As we have seen, while the creation of the universe is of great importance to Genesis, there is a concentration on Earth and similarly, while all aspects of creation are significant, the focus is clearly on humankind. Genesis in a very real sense is the story of God's dealings with man and woman on earth. God is speaking to humankind about humankind.

What is He saying? The answer: *"Then God said, 'Let Us make man in Our image, according to Our likeness; let them have dominion. . . . So God created man . . . male and female He created them. Then God blessed them, and God said to them 'Be fruitful and multiply; fill the earth and subdue it'"* (Gen. 1:26–28). God is saying to man and woman that each is made in the divine image. This does not mean that God has the form of a man or woman but that each is in some fashion a reflection of God. Man and woman do not have their origin and, therefore, discover their identity in the animal, vegetable, or mineral departments, even though they have affinities with each of them. Humankind's origin and identity are in God. Attempts have been made to suggest that men and women are made in God's image in the sense that they have capabilities foreign to the rest of creation, and therefore those unique aspects constitute the divine image. But the reflection of the divine is seen not in some separate sections of man and woman but in man and woman as a complete entity. This is expressed, and taken a step further, in the statement that it was *"man . . . male and female"* who constituted the divine image. There was a time when the image of God was thought to reside in the male while the female was something else of an inferior nature.

This is clearly contrary to Scripture in that it is mankind in maleness and femaleness that constitutes the divine image. This has led some commentators to conclude that male and female relationships of fellowship and love are a reflection of the Trinitarian relationship while others suggest that it requires both male and female characteristics to adequately portray the multi-faceted aspects of the divine nature. We are all familiar with the biblical revelation of God as Father and we rejoice in the resultant sense of security and firmness, watchcare and provision which this analogy provides. (Unless of course we have been unfortunate enough to be abused by a father who did nothing to portray the divine image.) But to grasp adequately the intricacies of the divine nature as mirrored in humankind we must not overlook the feminine aspects. For example, when the Lord Jesus reminded His people that He had longed to gather them to Him like a hen gathering her chickens (Matt. 23:37), He was using a feminine picture to describe His tender, loving care for them.

Sometimes when things get tough it is more comforting to think of God functioning like a hen gathering chickens than as an imperious cockerel strutting and preening while uttering ear-shattering cock-a-doodle-doos. In much the same vein Zephaniah promised,

> The Lord your God in your midst,
> The Mighty One, will save;
> He will rejoice over you with gladness,
> He will quiet you with His love,
> He will rejoice over you with singing.
>
> *Zeph. 3:17*

It would take little imagination to see this as a beautiful picture of God caring for His children in a way reminiscent of a mother in the nursery quietly, soothingly singing a distraught child to sleep.

Without doubt all these ideas concerning the unique status of humankind bear looking into and all of them lead to a position far removed from many modern concepts of man which have led to confusion, despair, violence, and shame. Humankind was commissioned by God to *"have dominion"* (v. 26) and to *"fill the earth and subdue it"* (v. 28). Pascal said, "Man is neither angel nor beast." Far from being on a par with the beasts and yet, unlike the angels, stationed on earth, humankind stands under God, above creation, to order and direct it as God desires. From the very beginning of time God put humankind to work in the most responsible position imaginable.

To do this *"God blessed them"* (v. 28) and thereby added ability to status and equipped men and women to function as His agents on earth. The creation was a going concern with man at the helm. Paul and Elizabeth Achtemeier captured the wonder of it all: "Man, as created by God, is a glorious creature, beautiful in his form, lordly in his dominion over the earth, favored in his relationship to his creator. Far from being an insignificant speck lost in a vast universe, man is . . . the exalted and glorious high point of all God's good creation."[2] What a far cry from the sad, weary words of the Hollywood star Rock Hudson who said, "I spent so much time trying to figure out what life was all about, I still don't know. But now I don't give a damn."

Another striking feature of Genesis 1 is the repetition of the phrase *"Then God said"* which introduces each new creational act.

The significance of this is shown in the way that the biblical writers in both Testaments use these statements to underline the fact that God's creative word, stemming from His creative thought, was all that was necessary to bring things into being out of non-being. The writer of the letter to the Hebrews wrote, "By faith we understand that the worlds were framed by the word of God, so that the things which are seen were not made of things which are visible" (Heb. 11:3) and the psalmist wrote, "By the word of the Lord the heavens were made . . . For He spoke, and it was" (Ps. 33:6, 9). It is difficult to imagine a clearer expression of the sheer power of God demonstrated in creation. His sovereign control, His irresistible dynamic, and His irrefutable design for the universe are presented in language easily understood by children who have stood before their father's desk, recruits who have faced a drill sergeant's stare, or employees who have answered a boss's directive. But the analogy is so inadequate, for Genesis speaks not of recruits and children but of nonexistence which hears the powerful enabling Word of God and in the command discovers the will and the means to exist. A mystery supreme but a glorious insight into the omnipotence of the One in Whom "we live and move and have our being" (Acts 17:28).

3. His Affirmation

With great delight God surveyed His creation. Light was scrutinized and pronounced *"good"*; earth and seas lay under His all-knowing gaze and were found to be *"good"*; and grass, herb, and fruit were tested and affirmed as *"good."* Turning His attention to the boundless expanse of space and the myriads of galaxies, He approved the immensity and it was *"good."* So it went on until finally man, male and female, stood before Him and heard the sweetest word—*"good."* They basked in His satisfaction; they were all He wanted them to be. *"Then God saw everything that He had made, and indeed it was very good"* (Gen. 1:31).

SOME PRACTICAL REALITIES

God's seal of approval on His creation is highly significant for those who honor Him and the things that He has made. There have been times in church history when this simple truth has been over-looked. For instance, it did not take long before the early Christians were engaged in furious debate about the person of Christ. The Greeks believed matter was evil and that therefore a Holy God could not create matter. That would be indecent, and God could certainly not assume human flesh. Therefore, the first arguments about Jesus were not concerned with His deity but with the reality of His hu-manity! The Docetists, for example, could not accept that Jesus was God manifest in the flesh; so they propounded the theory that He was God but only seemed to be a man and did not really die for sin, for how could a phantom die?

This may seem to be far removed from modern concerns, but the goodness of God's creation must always be of major interest. For example, those who believe that God created a good earth will be open to thoroughly enjoy all that He has given them. At the same time they will be anxious to preserve it from the ravages of men who care nothing for what God has made and entrusted to mankind as His stewards. Clearly this can have profound ramifications on peo-ple's concerns about ecology and nuclear matters. Those who believe God created everything good certainly will not be indifferent to de-velopments which may serve only to pollute and ruin, exterminate and defile all that He has made.

On my wife's desk stands a grotesque piece of pottery. It has a long nose, bulging eyes, and pale, swollen cheeks. Made by one of our children in junior high school, it has proved to be a great conversation piece over the years. We often say to guests, "This was made by one of our children. Which one do you think it was?" With-out exception our friends look at it, laugh, and without hesitation say "Pete, of course!" Dave is serious, Judy industrious, and Pete humor-ous. When you know that, you have no difficulty knowing who made the mug, because the created reflects something of the creator. So it is with men and women who know they are created; they long to reflect something of His glory through lives of obedience and faith. Created people are willing people.

They are people who have a sense of wonder, too. They cannot look dispassionately at either man or material, for they see some-thing of the Creator's handiwork. No person is insignificant and no part of the created order is without meaning. They might not write poetry like Wordsworth but they understand him when he writes:

> To me the meanest flower that blows can give
> Thoughts that do often lie too deep for tears.

This sense of wonder makes created people worshipers. Not only in the limited sense of attending church or cathedral and singing praises, but also in the "daily round, the common task" where everything is done, however mundane, with the sense that it is being done with His materials, in His time, for His glory with the energy and skill His grace alone made available.

NOTES

1. Bernard Ramm, *The Christian View of Science and Scripture* (London: Paternoster Press, 1955), pp. 120 ff.
2. Paul J. and Elizabeth Achtemeier, *The Old Testament Roots of Our Faith* (Philadelphia: Fortress Press, 1962), pp. 25 f.

CHAPTER TWO

Man—God's Masterpiece

Genesis 2:1-25

2:1 Thus the heavens and the earth, and all the host of them, were finished.

2 And on the seventh day God ended His work which He had done, and He rested on the seventh day from all His work which He had done.

3 Then God blessed the seventh day and sanctified it, because in it He rested from all His work which God had created and made.

4 This *is* the history of the heavens and the earth when they were created, in the day that the LORD God made the earth and the heavens,

5 before any plant of the field was in the earth and before any herb of the field had grown. For the LORD God had not caused it to rain on the earth, and *there was* no man to till the ground;

6 but a mist went up from the earth and watered the whole face of the ground.

7 And the LORD God formed man *of* the dust of the ground, and breathed into his nostrils the breath of life; and man became a living being.

8 The LORD God planted a garden eastward in Eden, and there He put the man whom He had formed.

9 And out of the ground the LORD God made every tree grow that is pleasant to the sight and good for food. The tree of life *was* also in the midst of the garden, and the tree of the knowledge of good and evil.

10 Now a river went out of Eden to water the garden, and from there it parted and became four riverheads.

11 The name of the first *is* Pishon; it *is* the one which skirts the whole land of Havilah, where *there is* gold.

12 And the gold of that land *is* good. Bdelium and the onyx stone *are* there.

13 The name of the second river *is* Gihon; it *is* the one which goes around the whole land of Cush.

14 The name of the third river *is* Hiddekel; it *is* the one which goes toward the east of Assyria. The fourth river *is* the Euphrates.

15 Then the LORD God took the man and put him in the garden of Eden to tend and keep it.

16 And the LORD God commanded the man, saying, "Of every tree of the garden you may freely eat;

17 "but of the tree of the knowledge of good and evil you shall not eat, for in the day that you eat of it you shall surely die."

18 And the LORD God said, "*It is* not good that man should be alone; I will make him a helper comparable to him."

19 Out of the ground the LORD God formed every beast of the field and every bird of the air, and brought *them* to Adam to see what he would call them. And whatever Adam called each living creature, that *was* its name.

20 So Adam gave names to all cattle, to the birds of the air, and to every beast of the field. But for Adam there was not found a helper comparable to him.

21 And the LORD God caused a deep sleep to fall on Adam, and he slept; and He took one of his ribs, and closed up the flesh in its place.

22 Then the rib which the LORD God had taken from man He made into a woman, and He brought her to the man.

23 And Adam said:

"This *is* now bone of my bones
And flesh of my flesh;
She shall be called Woman,
Because she was taken out of Man."

24 Therefore a man shall leave his father and

mother and be joined to his wife, and they shall become one flesh.

25 And they were both naked, the man and his
wife, and were not ashamed.

Gen. 2:1–25

The stage having been set in the first chapter, the spotlight of
Genesis in the second shines fully on the man whom God created to
play a lead role in the drama of history. Shakespeare said "all the
world's a stage," and he added that the people on it are "merely
players." He went on to outline with keen insight and savage humor
the seven acts or ages man passes through, beginning with the infant and ending "sans teeth, sans eyes, sans taste, sans everything."
That's certainly one way of looking at man, but Genesis chapter 2
has much more to offer. Before we look into this chapter's teaching
on God's masterpiece, it should be pointed out that some scholars
talk about two creation accounts. The writer of Genesis uses a simple technique of introducing a subject in general terms and then
leaving most of it on the sidelines to concentrate on the part which is
of particular interest. This is certainly true of the first two chapters.
In addition it should be noted that the New Testament draws freely
from both chapters and on occasion quotes from both without any
differentiation. For example, the Lord Jesus' famous teaching on
marriage draws from both as follows: "But from the beginning of
creation God 'made them male and female' [see Gen. 1:27]. For this
reason a man shall leave his father and mother and be joined to his
wife [see Gen. 2:24]" (Mark 10:6–7).

MAN—A NATURAL BEING

The first thing we learn about the actual physical creation of man
is that *"The Lord God formed man of the dust of the ground, and
breathed into his nostrils the breath of life; and man became a living
being"* (v. 7). The simplicity of this description, when placed
alongside the complex theories and brilliant dissertations which are
the products of man's incessant search for discovery of everything
including himself, serves only to show that there is fundamental

truth here, elastic enough to contain all that future discoveries would reveal. The Bible states unequivocally that man, like the animals, comes from the *dust of the ground"* and, moreover, will return to it (Gen. 3:19). Coder and Howe in their book *The Bible, Science and Creation* have taken the trouble to calculate that "the human body is composed of about fifty-eight pounds of oxygen, two ounces of salt, fifty quarts of water, three pounds of calcium, twenty-four pounds of carbon, and some chlorine, phosphorous, fat, iron, sulphur, and glycerine."[1] Of course it is one thing to make a pile of all these common elements, but it is another thing entirely to make a man out of them. The big question is "How did we get from the pile of dust to the complex and wonderful creature called man?" The most controversial answer to the question is wrapped up in the word "evolution"—a word which is gospel to many and strikes horror in the hearts of others. From the nineteenth century, when Darwin's book *On the Origin of Species* was published, to the present time the debate has been perpetuated. It has often generated more heat than light and is so intense that it has even found its way into the hallowed halls of the Supreme Court of the United States of America. The original opposition to Darwin's theory, which subsequent events have shown was well founded, claimed that if mankind was led to believe that it was caught up in an impersonal, mechanistic universe in which only the fittest survived, all manner of callousness, cynicism, and cruelty would result. The debate quickly degenerated into a black and white polarization of views which stated either that everything was made purposefully by God or everything was the result of chance. The choice became one between purposeful creation leading to meaning for existence and chance survival in a hostile environment leading to meaninglessness and despair. Even in the early days of the debate there were believing and unbelieving voices of moderation, and today there are those who, while holding firmly to man being purposefully created by a loving God, are open to the possibility that God's methods could have been evolutionary.

The debate on how mankind came from dust to be as brilliant as Einstein and as creative as Mozart and as beautiful as Helen of Troy should not be allowed to obscure the fact that it happened and that the Scriptures unequivocally point to the masterly hand of the Lord God. To underemphasize man's "dustness" would be to divorce man from his God-ordained environment—earth. It may also lead him to become arrogant—a condition which can be quickly remedied when he is confronted with the inevitability of his demise and the subsequent processes which will return him to his "dustness"! On the other hand, to overemphasize the "dustness" is to miss the point that as well as being a natural being man is also a spiritual being.

Paul Tournier, in one of his books, tells how he as a resident of Switzerland was used to seeing the Matterhorn from the perspective where it leaned to the left. When he saw a poster depicting the mountain leaning to the right, he thought it was a mistake until he realized it was produced in Italy and was an accurate depiction of the mountain from that perspective. In the same way man can be viewed from different perspectives. He is natural but he is also spiritual.

MAN—A SPIRITUAL BEING

If the word "formed" gives the impression that God was something of a technician when He was making man, the word "breathed" gives a picture of delightful intimacy. When God *breathed into his nostrils the breath of life; and man became a living being"* (v. 7) God was not only portraying man's total dependence but also showing His desire for a relationship with man. The Hebrew word for "being" is *nepeš* and its Greek equivalent is *psyche.* The same word is used to describe other created beings in Genesis 1:20, 21, and 24, but there it is translated "living creature." *Nepeš* is also translated "soul" on a number of occasions, but the idea behind the word is linked to the throat or the neck and accordingly has the connotation of desire, hunger, appetite, and longing as in: "As the deer pants for the water brooks, so pants my soul [*nephesh*] for You, O God" (Ps. 42:1). All the living creatures of the created order live only because of Him, but man was created in such a way that his being or psyche would long deeply for fulfillment and satisfaction, and the creation account shows clearly that the fulfillment would come only from *"the breath of life."*

Whether or not we are to picture God breathing into man's nostrils in much the same way that lifeguards resuscitate drowning victims, or perhaps see the language figuratively, it is clear that the image presented is one of the closest possible contact and relationship between God and man. This closeness of relationship which sets man apart from the rest of creation is further illustrated by the specific commands which God gave to man. God said *"Of every tree of the garden you may freely eat; but of the tree of the knowledge of good and evil you shall not eat"* (vv. 16, 17) and in so doing showed that man was capable of relating to God at the deepest possible level of commitment and obedience. He was able to hear, understand, evaluate, and determine what God was saying and then decide what he would do about it! Man as natural being was able to live in tune with earth but as spiritual being was equipped to live in touch with heaven. To suggest, as some have done, that man is a naked ape and nothing more is to fall desperately short of the truth.

MAN—A PRACTICAL BEING

At one stage in the creation process *"The Lord God had not caused it to rain on the earth, and there was no man to till the ground; but a mist went up from the earth and watered the whole face of the ground"* (vv. 5, 6). At a later stage, however, *"The Lord God took the man and put him in the garden of Eden to tend and keep it"* (v. 15). Clearly God's intention from the beginning was to put man to work. It is true, as we shall see later, that work became drudgery, but initially work was something not only which God intended for man to do but also something that God engaged in Himself! *"And on the seventh day God ended His work which He had done, and rested on the seventh day from all His work which He had done"* (v. 2).

The creation order is perfectly straightforward—man is to work properly and rest adequately. It is significant that the Sabbath rest which was to become such a distinctive feature of the lifestyle of God's people was introduced by God Himself at the very beginning of creation. Man's ignoring of it may be far more detrimental to him physically, socially, and spiritually than he realizes. On an entirely different level it is interesting that Snow White's dwarfs may have been nearer the mark than many people in the modern work place, for they sang as they went to work and whistled while they worked!

MAN—A RATIONAL BEING

Rudyard Kipling's commentary on Genesis may not rank with Calvin's but he had a point when he wrote:

> Oh, Adam was a gardener, and God who made him
>   sees
> That half a proper gardener's work is done upon his
>   knees.

The other half, as far as Adam was concerned, required him to use his head, because the Lord God had a mammoth task for him. *"Out of the ground the Lord God formed every beast of the field and every bird of the air, and brought them to Adam to see what he would call them. And whatever Adam called each living creature, that was its name"* (v. 19). This cooperative action initiated by the Lord God gave Adam the opportunity to discover the intellectual capabilities with which he had been endowed. Some see the naming process as indicative of Adam's authority over the animals and this may be the case, but there is no doubt that when Adam gave names he was describing that which he had discovered through observation. Perhaps this was the birth of scientific observation and categorical analysis!

MAN—A MORAL BEING

However, there were limits to Adam's knowledge because the *"Lord God commanded the man [Hebrew, ādām], saying, 'Of every tree of the garden you may freely eat; but of the tree of the knowledge of good and evil you shall not eat, for in the day that you eat of it you shall surely die"* (vv. 16, 17). Adam like the rest of the animals was made from the ground. (It is no coincidence that ādām is the Hebrew word for "man," ădāmāh the word for "ground," and Adam the name given to man.) The common groundedness of man and animals is demonstrated not only in their physical similarities but also in similar behavior patterns. As Pavlov showed with his dogs and Skinner demonstrated with his pigeons, animal behavior can be modified by "reinforcers" and "punishments" in much the same way that human behavior can be conditioned.

When taken to its extreme, however, the thought of modifying human behavior through controls leads to the questions "Who controls who?" and "Who decides what is best?" and "How do we avoid such control being used in an unethical and immoral way?" and "Whose standards of morality are adopted?" We have no knowledge that dogs and pigeons ponder such problems, but we know that humans do and it is in this area of morality that man's uniqueness shines through. A keen sense of morality is surprisingly evident in all people. Even the most immoral persons have their own ideas as to what is right for them, and amoral people have been known to complain loud and long if they feel that they are not being treated fairly! This moral sensitivity should not be regarded as a late development in man because Genesis states that *the tree of the knowledge of good and evil*" (v. 9) was introduced right from the beginning and man's ability to respond to it was there as soon as anything was there.

The question is often asked, "Was this tree literally standing in the middle of the garden, and if so what was it like?" In fact there were two trees of particular significance—the one already mentioned and *the tree of life*" (v. 9). While there is no reason to assume that the trees were not literal trees, it is not necessary to invest them with the sort of special characteristics that would make them look as if they were the product of a Hollywood special effects department. The thing that made them special was that God had chosen to make them special. He could have pointed out a stone and said "Don't move it" or have shown them a brook and said "Don't jump across it." The universal lesson in this is that God alone determines what is right and wrong, and that the essence of doing right is doing His will and the nature of wrongdoing is contravening His requirements and ignoring His precepts. Man's moral sensibilities are God-given and His moral standards are God-ordained. This much is clear from the creation account.

MAN—A SOCIAL BEING

According to Genesis 1, when God surveyed His creation piece by piece He affirmed it as "good," and when He had finished His work He said it was "very good." But there was one fly in the ointment: *"And the Lord God said, 'It is not good that man should be alone; I will make him a helper comparable to him'"* (v. 18). For the first time God announces something is "not good," and it has to do with man's sense of isolation and his inability to reproduce himself according to the divine instructions. The *"helper comparable to him"* was absolutely necessary. There are as many opinions as to how long Adam was alone as there are opinions as to the significance of his mate being created after him. Some say that woman was clearly an afterthought, and others insist that when God looked at the man He had made He knew He could do much better so He made woman! One suspects, and sincerely hopes, that such comments are made with tongue in cheek!

This account of the beginning of man-woman relationships, however, is deeply significant. It is in the context of Adam's review of the animal kingdom that *"there was not found a helper comparable to him"* (v. 20). Man and animals had their origins in the ground (*ădāmāh*), but as one species after another passed before Adam's inquisitive and insightful gaze, it was clear that while he and the animals had much in common, they all had their mates, yet he was very much alone. So the Lord *"caused a deep sleep to fall on Adam, and he slept; and He took one of his ribs . . . then the rib which the Lord God had taken from man He made into a woman"* (vv. 21, 22). This beautiful, perfect woman was then presented by God to the revived Adam who immediately recognized that she was uniquely part of him. The estrangement and distance which he had felt so poignantly as he reviewed the rest of creation was gone. They were truly meant for each other!

Theologians and commentators through the centuries have had a great time working on the significance of the *"rib"* and some of the results have been somewhat fanciful. But it is safe to see the ideas of Adam giving of himself for her and of her coming alongside him in his alone-ness and limited-ness, when we realize that the Hebrew word for rib can also be translated "side." This "alongside" relationship receives more support when we consider the famous expression "helpmeet" or "helper corresponding to him." It is unfortunate that "helpmeet" has been used in such a way that its meaning has been obscured. The word *"helper"* occurs twenty-one times in the Old Testament and on fifteen of those occasions it refers to God helping man in one way or another—a fact which casts doubt on the common suggestion that woman as man's helper was in some way subordinate and inferior.

When man saw woman he was so excited that he exclaimed *"This is now bone of my bones and flesh of my flesh; she shall be called Woman, because she was taken out of Man"* (v. 23). The expression translated *"this is now"* is really an exclamation of delight meaning "at last," or as some commentators suggest maybe even "Wow, look at that!" Up until this point *ādām* has been used for "man" but now the word used is *'îš* and the word for woman *'išâh*—a connection as obvious in Hebrew as the connection between man and woman in English.

The summation of all this magnificent truth about the one-ness, related-ness, alongsided-ness of male and female is: *"Therefore a man shall leave his father and mother and be joined to his wife, and they shall become one flesh"* (v. 24). The words have a familiar ring, of course, not only because they are the basis for the Lord Jesus' exposition of marriage in Mark 10:7–9 but also because they are usually quoted at some stage of the marriage service. The social needs of mankind are to be met uniquely but not exclusively in the marriage bond. As surely as God built physical laws into the universe from the very beginning He incorporated societal laws, and as surely as we cannot ignore the former with impunity we cannot allow the latter to be disregarded and expect our society to survive unscathed. The "leaving" and "cleaving" may sound old-fashioned—and so it is—but it is still God's societal law. The *"one flesh"* relationship of *"a man"* and *"his wife"* may sound very restrictive to a society bent on such high-sounding but low-living ideals as "sexual emancipation." But the law stands today as surely as it did in the beginning, and when it is honored and practiced the result is the same—man and woman in loving, mutual respect and support live in harmony and openness. It will be for them as it was when Moses wrote: they are *"not ashamed"* (v. 25).

Some years ago I picked up a hitchhiker who, in the course of conversation, told me he was "trying to find himself." I told him somewhat facetiously that I knew exactly where he was; he was sitting next to me! He smiled rather warily but then we talked more seriously. He really meant that he was trying to find significance and meaning in his life. Like many other people I have met he needed to be told or reminded that man's meaning is found in his relationship to God, and nowhere is it better explained than in these early chapters of Genesis.

NOTE

1. S. Maxwell Coder and George F. Howe, *The Bible, Science and Creation* (Chicago: Moody Press, 1966), p. 85.

CHAPTER THREE

Disaster in Eden

Genesis 3:1–24

3:1 Now the serpent was more cunning than any beast of the field which the LORD God had made. And he said to the woman, "Has God indeed said, 'You shall not eat of every tree of the garden'?"

2 And the woman said to the serpent, "We may eat the fruit of the trees of the garden;

3 "but of the fruit of the tree which *is* in the midst of the garden, God has said, 'You shall not eat it, nor shall you touch it, lest you die.'"

4 Then the serpent said to the woman, "You will not surely die.

5 "For God knows that in the day you eat of it your eyes will be opened, and you will be like God, knowing good and evil."

6 So when the woman saw that the tree *was* good for food, that it *was* pleasant to the eyes, and a tree desirable to make *one* wise, she took of its fruit and ate. She also gave to her husband with her, and he ate.

7 Then the eyes of both of them were opened, and they knew that they *were* naked; and they sewed fig leaves together and made themselves coverings.

8 And they heard the sound of the LORD God walking in the garden in the cool of the day, and Adam and his wife hid themselves from the presence of the LORD God among the trees of the garden.

9 Then the LORD God called to Adam and said to him, "Where *are* you?"

10 So he said, "I heard Your voice in the garden, and I was afraid because I was naked; and I hid myself."

11 And He said, "Who told you that you *were* naked? Have you eaten from the tree of which I commanded you that you should not eat?"

12 Then the man said, "The woman whom You gave *to be* with me, she gave me of the tree, and I ate."

13 And the LORD God said to the woman, "What *is* this you have done?" The woman said, "The serpent deceived me, and I ate."

14 So the LORD God said to the serpent:

"Because you have done this,
You *are* cursed more than all cattle,
And more than every beast of the field;
On your belly you shall go,
And you shall eat dust
All the days of your life.

15 And I will put enmity
Between you and the woman,
And between your seed and her Seed;
He shall bruise your head,
And you shall bruise His heel."

16 To the woman He said:

"I will greatly multiply your sorrow and your
    conception;
In pain you shall bring forth children;
Your desire *shall be* for your husband,
And he shall rule over you."

17 Then to Adam He said, "Because you have heeded the voice of your wife, and have eaten from the tree of which I commanded you, saying, 'You shall not eat of it':

"Cursed *is* the ground for your sake;
In toil you shall eat *of* it
All the days of your life.

18 Both thorns and thistles it shall bring forth for
    you,
And you shall eat the herb of the field.

19 In the sweat of your face you shall eat bread
Till you return to the ground,
For out of it you were taken;
For dust you *are*,
And to dust you shall return."

20 And Adam called his wife's name Eve, because she was the mother of all living.

21 Also for Adam and his wife the LORD God made tunics of skin, and clothed them.

22 Then the LORD God said, 'Behold, the man has become like one of Us, to know good and evil. And now, lest he put out his hand and take also of the tree of life, and eat, and live forever'—

23 therefore the LORD God sent him out of the garden of Eden to till the ground from which he was taken.

24 So He drove out the man; and He placed cherubim at the east of the garden of Eden, and a flaming sword which turned every way, to guard the way to the tree of life.

Gen. 3:1–24

"Eden" (ʿēden) in Hebrew means "delight." Sarah used the word— "After I have grown old, shall I have pleasure?" (Gen. 18:12)—and David, lamenting the death of his predecessor, reminded the women that Saul had clothed them with "luxury" (2 Sam. 1:24). The man and the woman whom God had placed in Eden had everything for their well-being and enjoyment. It is tempting to try to locate the site of Eden because Genesis does give details of the site. (Calvin does a thorough but unsuccessful job in this regard in his famous commentary.) We are told that a river flowed out of the garden and then in some way divided into four rivers, two of which, the Tigris and Euphrates, we can locate but the other two do not readily yield to identification. Perhaps this is as well or we might be running tours to the site only to discover what we already know—that Eden, after the events of one tragic day, is no longer a place of delight!

THE CONFLICT IN EDEN

The first two chapters of Genesis show that God granted man and woman a unique status and a unique responsibility. Rocks were made to roll and rivers to flow but they were slaves to gravity. Flowers would bloom and trees would grow because of inbuilt genetic codes. Lions would roam and seagulls would fly in accordance with divinely implanted instincts, but man and woman while subject to gravity and genetics and instincts were given the uniquely enriching and challenging capability of choice.

Man's freedom to choose was not the freedom to choose of a Communist government where people can freely choose any of the one candidates! Man and woman had the whole of Eden to enjoy; they were to eat freely, in every sense, of the tree of life, but they were to leave the other tree severely alone on pain of death. This restriction was not restrictive. It was a gracious reminder that man was created to live in an environment of dependent obedience in the same way that albatrosses were created for air and whales for water.

Without preamble a strange character enters this idyllic environment—*"Now the serpent was more cunning than any beast of the field which the Lord God had made"* (Gen. 3:1). There are many things Genesis does not tell us about this creature, but there are two things we do know—one, that it was created by God and two, that it was subject to man. However, Scripture fills in some of the gaps in other places. For example, the aged apostle in exile wrote: "So the great dragon was cast out, that serpent of old, called the Devil and Satan, who deceives the whole world" (Rev. 12:9). We are led to believe, therefore, that the serpent was indeed a *"cunning"* (the Hebrew word can also mean "prudent"—see Proverbs where the word is used eight times, always in a positive sense) creature, but at the same time Satan was utilizing the serpent's own natural brilliance for his own nefarious ends. We must note, however, that the Genesis narrative gives no indication of any tempter other than the serpent, does not mention Satan, and therefore gives no explanation of his existence or origin. Calvin suggests that Moses' "homely and uncultivated style, accommodates what he delivers to the capacity of the people; and for the best reason; for not only had he to instruct an untaught race of men, but the existing age of the Church was so puerile, that it was unable to receive any higher instruction."

a. *The serpent and the woman.* The serpent approached the woman and said, *"Has God indeed said, 'You shall not eat of every tree of the garden?'"*, to which she replied, *"We may eat the fruit of the trees of the garden; but of the fruit of the tree which is in the midst of the garden, God has said, 'You shall not eat it, nor shall you touch it, lest you die'"* (Gen. 3:1–3). The Hebrew word used to introduce the serpent's statement is difficult to translate. Luther said, "I cannot translate the

Hebrew either in German or in Latin; the serpent uses the expression *aphkî* as though to turn up his nose and jeer and scoff." Some commentators see this approach as a questioning of God's word— "Has God said?" Others point more to a questioning of God's goodness—"You don't mean to tell me that God has deprived you, do you?" Either way there is a definite albeit subtle and disarming attack on the woman's love for and loyalty to the God who made her. She responds in a commendable manner pointing out that far from being deprived by a spoilsport God, she and her man have been wonderfully provided for, and she gives no indication of any feeling of restriction or deprivation. It should be pointed out that there may be a little coloring in her response in that she does add some things that we have not heard God actually said! On the other hand this may indicate a less than adequate grasp of what God had told her man. The serpent's response, *"You will not surely die"* (v. 4), flatly contradicts the word of the Lord. Some translators suggest the Hebrew allows for "You shall not die utterly" or "You shall not die immediately," pointing out that while there is contradiction it was presented in a subtle and ambiguous manner. Evidently by this stage in the sad proceedings the woman was so well and truly hooked that the serpent threw subtlety and shrewdness to the wind and stated, *"For God knows that in the day you eat of it your eyes will be opened, and you will be like God, knowing good and evil"* (v. 5). Opinions differ as to whether the word *'elōhîm* should be translated "God" or "gods" (see KJV) but the possibility of *"knowing good and evil"* independently of God was the draw.

The woman who by this time was captivated by the possibilities being presented to her turned to consider the tree in question. She *"saw that the tree was good for food, that it was pleasant to the eyes, and a tree desirable to make one wise, (so) she took of its fruit and ate"* (v. 6). "Good, pleasant, and desirable" are the operative words used to describe what she saw. Physical food, aesthetic satisfaction, and moral and intellectual advancement were the things she saw hanging on the delicate branches. Eden being the place of delight had no quarrel with anything that the woman saw, no argument with what the tree offered, no problem with what she desired to have. For all these things had been created by God and given to mankind, yet were to be had and enjoyed only in the context of obedience and dependence. The serpent was offering freedom and fulfillment, delight and discovery, advancement and autonomy. God offered these too, except the autonomy. To offer man autonomy would have been to make him other than man was created to be. You can't offer a bird free-floating flight without air, nor can you let a fish swim and swirl without surf. They, like man, have their God-appointed environments outside of which all are less than they were divinely appointed to be.

b. *The woman and the man.* One of the most remarkable things about this story is the utterly passive and docile role which Adam plays. The woman had at least made an attempt to answer the serpent; she had given some indication of considering the issues. But all we hear about Adam is, *"She also gave to her husband with her, and he ate"* (v. 6). Where he was during the serpent-woman confrontation we do not know, although John Milton suffered from no such uncertainty, stating unequivocally that he was "waiting desirous her return" and while waiting he "wove of choicest flours a garland to adorn her tresses." Poets are allowed such freedom while we can only ponder their imaginative interpretations! If he was nearby his silence is inexplicable; if he was not near, his apparent immediate, unquestioning acquiescence to his wife's suggestion is equally inexplicable.

In the same way there is no record of Adam having had any dealings at all with the serpent-Satan. All we know for sure is that he faced his wife and succumbed to her suggestion. Again Milton explains, "He scrupl'd not to eat against his better knowledge, not deceav'd but fondly overcome with Femal charm." This may say a lot for the woman's charms but it says little for man's competence! Whatever the reasons for Adam's transgression the results were catastrophic: *"Then the eyes of both of them were opened, and they knew they were naked; and they sewed fig leaves together and made themselves coverings"* (v. 7). The serpent, of course, had promised that their eyes would be opened and he was right about that, but he didn't tell them the truth about what they would be opened to. The knowledge of good and evil, which they now acquired experimentally and experientially as opposed to academically, was that good is doing the will of God and evil is the converse. The problem for man then and ever since was that the Pandora's box was open. There was no going back.

While the Genesis record of these momentous events is spare and lean, the New Testament amplifies them in detail. Paul states, "Just as through one man sin entered the world, and death through sin, and thus death spread to all men . . . by one man's offense many died . . . by one man's offense judgment came to all men . . . by one man's disobedience many were made sinners" (Rom. 5:12–19). He then goes on to describe Adam as "a type of Him who was to come" (Rom. 5:14) and in another Epistle he sharpens the contrast considerably when he states, "As in Adam all die, even so in Christ shall all be made alive" (1 Cor. 15:22). For the New Testament writer the action of Adam in Eden was of such magnitude that it required nothing less than the activity of the Second Adam, Jesus Christ, in Incarnation, Crucifixion, and Resurrection to remedy the ills and reconcile man to God. Well might Esdras, the inter-testamental writer, ask with horror, "O Adam what hast thou done?"

c. *The man and woman and God.* Some scholars have suggested that mankind was put on probation in Eden and that if they had passed the test they would have been introduced to a new standard of experience which would have delivered them from the necessity to confront tests like the one they had just failed. Others have theorized that mankind was in a kind of juvenile state and that the test they failed served only to teach them a lesson from which they emerged sadder and wiser! One advocate of this view said, "If ever there was a Fall it was a Fall upwards." Jesus Christ would have rejected this view. Speaking on the subject of divorce He stated the original creation ideal of marriage and then added that Moses permitted divorce because of the "hardness of your heart." This hardness of heart was a factor introduced into human experience after the creation and it was clearly not a beneficial factor. It was a product of what we commonly call the Fall although the term is never used in Scripture.

The consequences of their actions became apparent to man and woman as soon as they confronted the Lord. When they realized He was coming to meet with them they *hid themselves from the presence of the Lord God among the trees of the garden*" (Gen. 3:8). This exercise in futility has been re-enacted by mankind ever since and will still be attempted by many at the end of the ages. In response to the Lord's inquiry as to their whereabouts Adam replied, "*I heard Your voice in the garden, and I was afraid because I was naked; and I hid myself*" (v. 10). Their pathetic attempts to hide their newly discovered nakedness spoke of their sense of guilt and shame as clearly as their hiding in the bushes admitted to their state of fear. In one brief, swift action three of mankind's perennial problems—guilt, shame, and fear—had been introduced into what had been a place of delight and peace. These things which plague all relationships, however, were first experienced in the relationship between God and man and still need to be recognized as problems with a spiritual foundation, which accordingly, among other things, require a spiritual solution.

The fact that nakedness and fig leaves were so much a part of the shame felt by fallen mankind has led many to suppose that the original sin was in some way sexual. In fact, some older commentators seem to suggest that the forbidden fruit was sex although it is hard to see how they could make that position fit into God's clearly stated objective that mankind should be fruitful and multiply. It would be extremely difficult for them to obey that command without resorting to their sexuality! It might be safer to view the covering of their nakedness as an attempt to hide from each other the fact that they were made differently and it was God Who had made them that way. In this sense they could not look at each other without being reminded of God. As their desire was to be like God (or gods), any reminder of the true God would be an embarrassment. So they did what mankind has done ever since when confronted with embarrassing reality—they covered up! Their sexuality also showed they were made for each other but being like God suggested to them an independence of everything including each other. Better to cover up the reminders of that too!

Perhaps Adam and Eve were suddenly aware of the awful truth that having declared themselves independent of God they were now totally dependent on themselves and a new sense of inadequacy overtook them. They were aware for the first time that all they could count on was wrapped up in themselves and having rejected their spiritual dimension they were left only with the physical. Their bodies were suddenly all that they had and they were stricken with a sense of inadequacy and impotence. In the poverty of their independent ability the best they could do was to try and patch things up with fig leaves and in so doing they showed that the path to freedom which they had chosen had led to a pit of bondage from which they could not escape and they were ashamed. All that was left for them was to try pathetically to hide from themselves and each other what they had done.

Further questioning by the Lord elicited a reluctant, self-serving admission from Adam that he had indeed eaten from the tree but he was quick to explain, *"The woman whom You gave to be with me, she gave me of the tree, and I ate"* (v. 12). Man was showing God that while his conscience might be pricking him his wits had not deserted him. They were as sharp as his conscience was sore. "If You hadn't given her to me and if she hadn't eaten first I would never have partaken myself," appeared to be the thrust of his answer leading to the unspoken suggestion that he was not really all that culpable after all! Similar but more sophisticated views are in vogue today. One line of reasoning goes something like this: "Sure I do things that are wrong, but that's what I'm like and that's how I'm made. I was presented with a packet of genes that made me the way I am, so I can hardly be held responsible for what I do." Those who reason like this are called "naturists." Another line of thinking suggests, "The family into which I was born lived in an area that was the pits. The kids I ran around with were a bunch of hoodlums. To survive I had to go along with what they were doing. So don't try to make me feel guilty about the life I lived because I didn't have any options." The ones who think like that are called "nurturists." It would be futile to tell Adam that God did not give him the woman or that the woman did not give him the apple. Clearly he was right on both scores. Similarly it would be unwise to suggest that nature and nurture do not play a part in our development as persons. But when men and women stand before God, as did Adam, they will be asked to account for their actions on the basis of their human responsibility whatever the contributory or extenuating circumstances might be.

The woman's response to God's question was short and to the point, *"The serpent deceived me, and I ate"* (v. 13). She did not say, "The serpent whom You created deceived poor little old me and I ate." There was no prevarication, no excuses, but sad to say there was apparently no remorse either. The woman's deception explanation was utilized by the Apostle Paul when, writing to Timothy, he denied women the privilege of teaching and exercising authority over men and gave as his explanation, "For Adam was formed first, then Eve. And Adam was not deceived, but the woman being deceived, fell into transgression" (1 Tim. 2:13–14). Some commentators interpret Paul's statement to mean that the woman was easily

deceived, that women are more easily deceived than men, and therefore men should handle the teaching and the leading in the church.
Others take issue with this interpretation and point out that the
woman's deception is related to her coming on the scene after Adam,
which meant that she did not hear God's word firsthand and therefore being much less informed than he she was more readily deceived. The women in the Ephesian church about whom Paul wrote
to Timothy were like Eve in this regard. They had certainly not had
the opportunities afforded to the men and were therefore less quali-
fied. If they were engaging in authoritative teaching, as has been
suggested, they were probably speaking with formidable authority
from the depth of their ignorance and we all know how destructive
that can be. The resultant error and confusion was of major concern
to Paul and Timothy, and therefore they advocated the denial of
teaching opportunities to the women in order to get the church back
on track.

While there is no agreement on this issue in the church it should
not be hard to reach agreement that this passage does not teach that
because woman was deceived all women are stupid and inferior any
more than it teaches that because Adam was not deceived all men
are smart and superior. That being the case, great care should be
taken in all aspects of male-female relationships to show proper regard and respect for each other and to avoid all stereotypes which
would tend to elevate men to a superior status than women for no
other reason than they are men while relegating women to inferior
status for no other reason than they are women. For example, I have
been called into marital counseling situations where the husband is
abusing the wife sometimes physically but more often verbally and
perhaps even insidiously through disparaging attitudes and remarks.
Quite often the man excuses his behavior because of some ill-
defined sense of superiority which he cannot explain but for which
he finds some degree of misplaced justification in what Eve did to
Adam and what Paul apparently thought about Eve!

THE CONSEQUENCES ON EARTH

Students of the literary excellence of Genesis point out the fine
structure of Genesis 3. First the serpent approaches the woman; then

the woman approaches the man. Then God reverses the order, approaching the man and after that the woman. When He addresses the threesome He starts with the serpent, goes on to the woman, and ends with the man. We now turn our attention to what God pronounced to the serpent, the woman, and the man.

a. God's statement to the serpent. It is interesting to note that God does not address the serpent in the way that He addressed both the man and the woman. He went straight into His pronouncement which deals with the immediate consequences and the ultimate consequences of what he has done. It should also be noted that the first part of the pronouncement relates to the serpent as a beast and the latter to Satan although, as we have seen, he is not named in the Genesis narrative.

The serpent is cursed *"more than every beast of the field"* (Gen. 3:14)—something that anybody who has observed both people and animals' reactions to snakes will have no difficulty understanding. The serpent will also crawl and eat the dust. This has led some to believe that the serpent originally had legs but lost them as punishment. It would be better to assume, with Calvin, that in the same way that Satan lifted himself up and was abased so the serpent did and was now returned ignominiously to his former estate.

The second half of the pronouncement introduces what theologians call the "protevangelium"—literally, "a first gospel." The reason for this fine-sounding title for Genesis 3:15 is that it is seen to be the earliest promise of the coming Messiah, His suffering, and His ultimate triumph over the Evil One. The Lord God said, *"And I will put enmity between you and the woman, and between your seed and her Seed; He shall bruise your head, and you shall bruise His heel"* (v. 15). If at first it seems that interpreting this passage in such a far-reaching way is stretching the bounds of credulity, it should be remembered that Paul was apparently referring to this when he wrote, "And the God of peace will crush Satan under your feet shortly" (Rom. 16:20). The promised enmity between the seed of the serpent and the seed of the woman not only predicts the promised conflict between Messiah and the demonic forces but also gives the earliest hint to the uniqueness of Messiah's birth in the expression *"her Seed"* when it would be more traditional to talk of the man's seed. The all too common experience of serpents biting men on the heel before being crushed underfoot takes on striking significance when applied to the wounding of Christ through Satan's hostility and the crushing of Satan through Christ's humility.

b. God's statement to the woman. Turning His attention to the woman who has heard in the words to the serpent the first intimations of grace, whether or not she understood them, God said, *"I will greatly multiply your sorrow and your conception; in pain you shall bring forth children; your desire shall be for your husband, and he shall rule over you"* (Gen. 3:16). Despite the promise of blessing through woman and the process of childbearing, first there will be pain and anguish through the same experience. Death was the consequence of sin and the first indications of death that woman would feel would be pain in the very act of giving life. The awful irony of sins' consequences is that even the most blessed events are often tainted with the odor of death.

Death would also make its presence felt in the death of a marriage. While commentators differ widely on their interpretations of the woman's desire and the man's ruling there is no doubt that the consequences of sin promptly appeared in that most intimate of relationships—marriage. The question most often asked is whether these relational problems are prescribed by God (meaning they are God's punishment on woman) or whether they are words used by God to describe what will happen because of sin (meaning they are the inevitable consequences but not a punishment). It would be true to say that woman has had more than her share of abuse at the hands of men—not to suggest that she has always been without fault. The tragedy, however, is that not a little of this abuse has been excused by men who have seen in this statement a vindication for their domination of women. If we come to the conclusion that the lot of woman prescribed by God is to be dominated we should still seek to alleviate the consequences for her in the same way we seek to alleviate her pain in childbirth through anesthetic and give man a lawnmower to help with the toilsome labor of cutting the grass and weeds. If, on the other hand, as seems far more likely to me, we are being told that one of the awful consequences of sin is the abuse of women, we should do all in our power to seek to help women in any area of abuse and distress. Either way the callous and careless subjugation of women should be resisted, particularly by those who know how the Lord Jesus treated women during His brief life.

c. God's statement to the man. God's curse of the ground for man's sake is merciful. Man must not be exposed to the brunt of the curse but neither must he be excused. Honest labor for which he was created and which he knew God Himself had delighted to engage in would become toilsome and loathsome. Winston Churchill, standing in the wreckage of war-torn Europe, told the House of Commons on the 13th day of May, 1940, 'I have nothing to offer but blood, toil, tears, and sweat'—words strangely reminiscent of the solemn words spoken long before to a man standing in the wreckage of a glorious garden. Life would become a struggle for survival, a battle against a world strangely reluctant to yield its benefits.

Discouragement and disillusionment would prevail and man's wearisome struggle with the dust would end in futility, for his life would continue *"till you return to the ground, for out of it you were taken; for dust you are, and to dust you shall return"* (v. 19). What man might have been and how he might have been transported from this scene we can only conjecture, but what he became and what he heads toward is all too clear as a visit to many a factory floor or cemetery will readily testify.

Yet once again in the gloom a ray of light shines for *"Adam called his wife's name Eve, because she was the mother of all living"* (v. 20), suggesting that he had heard and understood the implications of the offer of hope in the promise about the seed of the woman. The loving care of the Lord for His erring children is seen in His provision of *"tunics of skin"* (v. 21) which some see as a type of sacrifice prefiguring the ultimate sacrifice which would provide a covering for sin, but others regard as a winsome picture of God's concern for all the needs of His people.

THE CONCLUSION IN ETERNITY

The tree of life was to be enjoyed fully by man in his dependence upon God, but when he chose independence he was no longer eligible for life. Death was his lot. The fact that God *"alone has immortality"* (1 Tim. 6:16) reminds us that man by nature was not immortal, but through his sin he surrendered something that would have protected him from the horror of death. Perhaps the experience of Enoch who was *"taken away so that he did not see death"* (Heb. 11:5) teaches us what would have been the normal transition for man from earth to glory if sin had not intervened. But it is clear that more than physical death resulted from Adam's transgression. Paul said the Ephesians "were dead in trespasses and sins" (Eph. 2:1), and he obviously was not talking about physical death at this point. He was referring to the alienation between God and man which had resulted in a great gulf being fixed between them. This we can call spiritual death, and its ugly characteristics are manifested in human experiences ranging from outright atheism to empty religious formalism. It shows itself in harsh antipathy to God, apathetic attitudes toward God, or empty protestations of worship which owe more to mindless superstition than knowledge of the Holy One.

Then there are the social consequences of death. When Paul told Timothy that "she who lives in pleasure is dead while she lives," (1 Tim. 5:6) he was showing that individuals who live for themselves are the living dead when it comes to healthy social relationships. It did not take long for Adam and Eve's deadness to show up in the fracturing of the beautiful relationship they had previously enjoyed. The wages of sin are also to be seen in the eternal condition of those who have not been reconciled to God. John in exile on Patmos wrote "And I saw the dead, small and great, standing before God . . . and the dead were judged according to their works . . . then Death and Hades were cast into the lake of fire. This is the second death" (Rev. 20:12–14). The physical, social, spiritual, and eternal consequences of death are staggering in their implications and clearly beyond the ingenuity of man to solve.

So man was banished from the garden *lest he put out his hand and take also of the tree of life, and eat, and live forever* (Gen. 3:22). Now he was free to be what he thought he wanted to be but, like many a man since, he discovered that when he got what he wanted he did not want it any more. What finally became of Adam we cannot say, except that he was not allowed to return to his original condition in the garden. The cherubim with the sword saw to that, but the promise of the Redeemer already made, the naming of his wife *"Eve"* (literally "life"), and the grace of God manifested even to the chief of sinners lead us to believe that even the guilty pair could overcome and "eat from the tree of life, which is in the midst of the Paradise of God" (Rev. 2:7). This of course is the message of hope we take to a world all too aware of the consequences of Adam's sin even where there is skepticism or even rejection of Adam's existence.

CHAPTER FOUR

The Human Race

Genesis 4:1–26

4:1 Now Adam knew Eve his wife, and she conceived and bore Cain, and said, "I have acquired a man from the LORD."

2 Then she bore again, this time his brother Abel. Now Abel was a keeper of sheep, but Cain was a tiller of the ground.

3 And in the process of time it came to pass that Cain brought an offering of the fruit of the ground to the LORD.

4 Abel also brought of the firstborn of his flock and of their fat. And the LORD respected Abel and his offering,

5 but He did not respect Cain and his offering. And Cain was very angry, and his countenance fell.

6 So the LORD said to Cain, "Why are you angry? And why has your countenance fallen?

7 "If you do well, will you not be accepted? And if you do not do well, sin lies at the door. And its desire *is* for you, but you should rule over it."

8 Now Cain talked with Abel his brother; and it came to pass, when they were in the field, that Cain rose up against Abel his brother and killed him.

9 Then the LORD said to Cain, "Where *is* Abel your brother?" He said, "I do not know. *Am* I my brother's keeper?"

10 And He said, "What have you done? The voice of your brother's blood cries out to Me from the ground.

11 "So now you *are* cursed from the earth, which

has opened its mouth to receive your brother's blood from your hand.

12 "When you till the ground, it shall no longer yield its strength to you. A fugitive and a vagabond you shall be on the earth."

13 And Cain said to the LORD, "My punishment *is* greater than I can bear!

14 "Surely You have driven me out this day from the face of the ground; I shall be hidden from Your face; I shall be a fugitive and a vagabond on the earth, and it will happen *that* anyone who finds me will kill me."

15 And the LORD said to him, "Therefore, whoever kills Cain, vengeance shall be taken on him seven-fold." And the LORD set a mark on Cain, lest anyone finding him should kill him.

16 Then Cain went out from the presence of the LORD and dwelt in the land of Nod on the east of Eden.

17 And Cain knew his wife, and she conceived and bore Enoch. And he built a city, and called the name of the city after the name of his son—Enoch.

18 To Enoch was born Irad; and Irad begot Mehujael, and Mehujael begot Methushael, and Methushael begot Lamech.

19 Then Lamech took for himself two wives: the name of one *was* Adah, and the name of the second *was* Zillah.

20 And Adah bore Jabal. He was the father of those who dwell in tents and have livestock.

21 His brother's name *was* Jubal. He was the father of all those who play the harp and flute.

22 And as for Zillah, she also bore Tubal-Cain, an instructor of every craftsman in bronze and iron. And the sister of Tubal-Cain *was* Naamah.

23 Then Lamech said to his wives:

"Adah and Zillah, hear my voice;
Wives of Lamech, listen to my speech!
For I have killed a man for wounding me,
Even a young man for hurting me.

24 If Cain shall be avenged sevenfold,
Then Lamech seventy-sevenfold."

25 And Adam knew his wife again, and she bore a
son and named him Seth, "For God has appointed
another seed for me instead of Abel, whom Cain
killed."
26 And as for Seth, to him also a son was born;
and he named him Enosh. Then *men* began to call on
the name of the LORD.

Gen. 4:1–26

I read recently of a man who traveled out to the West coast as a
boy in a covered wagon and returned as an old man in a Boeing 747!
Things had certainly changed in his lifetime. My mother was convinced that man would never reach the moon because as she saw
it God had set "the bounds of man's habitation" on earth. She was
wrong, of course, but at least you could understand her point of
view. My kids can't imagine how I managed to grow up without
television and when I tell them that television was in its infancy
when I was in mine they howl with laughter and say uncomplimen-
tary things about the Stone Age. But I don't let it worry me because
I know their children will probably be incredulous when they hear
that their parents never spent a vacation in space.

That assumes, of course, that man will not have destroyed himself
in the interim. No sober-minded person dismisses that possibility as
he views the ways in which man's ingenuity is being put to work.
Right at this moment there are submarines at sea carrying more
explosive fire power than the sum total of explosives delivered in
human history. Therein lies the human puzzle. Brilliant but brutal,
creative but catastrophic, ingenious but incorrigible, man is a bundle
of contradictions. This became apparent right at the beginning of
human history as the story of Cain and Abel clearly illustrates.

THE DERIVATION OF THE HUMAN RACE

*"Now Adam knew Eve his wife, and she conceived and bore Cain, and
said, 'I have acquired a man from the Lord.' Then she bore again, this
time his brother Abel"* (Gen. 4:1, 2). The word *"knew,"* which means
in this context "to have sexual intercourse with," is significant
because it speaks of sex in ways that have become obscured in contemporary thinking. To know a person in this sense contradicts the

modern idea that sex can be casual and satisfying. Rightly understood sex is knowing a person at the deepest level of intimacy in the
context of taking the time and making the commitment to thoroughly
know that person in all dimensions. The early chapters of Genesis
leave no room for doubt that this requires a relationship of perma-
nence—or to put it simply—marriage! It was "his wife" he knew
with the accent on the "his" and "wife." The sexual activity that
brought Cain into the world was the result of man and woman's free
choice; it was an act based on their own volition. Cain, like all those
who followed him, was therefore the product of sexual and volitional activity on the part of his parents. But he was far more than
that as his mother's exultant cry demonstrates, *"I have acquired a man
from the Lord"* (v. 1). The name Cain is related to the word for
"gotten" and the new parents were stating that they recognized the
divine activity involved in his birth. This reminds us that babies are
born for spiritual as well as sexual and volitional reasons. The birth
of a baby is a reminder from God that He is still not through with
mankind.

The account of the boys' births, although brief, does not neglect
the biological considerations. Genesis states that Eve *"conceived,"*
and although the ancient writers could not have known a fraction of
what modern man knows about the mysteries and wonders of fertility and conception the record is wonderfully balanced. This reminds
us that if we are to treat people properly we need to bear in mind all
the factors that led to their existence.

There is a certain poignancy about the naming of the second son,
Abel, because the name means "vanity" as in Ecclesiastes 1:2. This is
not the kind of vanity that keeps people in front of mirrors but
rather that sense of futility which so often pervades life. "Meaninglessness" would be a good modern equivalent. Perhaps there is a
hint of foreboding in the naming of the boy, a foreboding which
events would soon show to be well justified.

THE DEDICATION OF THE HUMAN RACE

It is encouraging to note that even though Adam and Eve's relationship had undergone tremendous strain in the events leading to
their expulsion they were still together and apparently committed

to raising a family. There was a *dedication to love* which became evident in the succeeding generations. *"Cain knew his wife, and she conceived and bore Enoch,"* (v. 17) and so the human race began to proliferate because men found women to love, produced children whom they loved, and so the mandate to be fruitful and multiply began to be fulfilled. Love was starting to make the world go 'round.

No schoolboy worth his salt has failed at some time to ask the question, "Where did Cain get his wife from?" It may not be the most profound question ever asked but it does address a fundamental question about the beginnings of the race. The important question it raises is, "Did the human race originate exclusively in Adam and Eve or were there other sources from which people like Cain's wife could have come?" Those people who hold to evolutionary theories of the development of different segments of the human race are hard put to account for the remarkable similarities which exist between all segments assuming they all developed from different sources under different circumstances. The factors that unite the Eskimos and the Masai, the Aucas and Aborigines are infinitely greater than those that divide them. They share a common physiology and demonstrate a common psychology. They are so similar physically that they are totally inter-fertile. All these factors point to a common source of the race. Paul, of course, was unequivocal on the point, insisting that the fallenness of the race is attributable to its solidarity in Adam in the same way that salvation is available to all men through the mediation of Christ Jesus our Lord. We should, therefore, not hesitate to tell our schoolboy inquisitors that Adam and Eve no doubt had other children besides those who are named and that Cain presumably married one of them—hardly the normal thing to do but under the circumstances perfectly acceptable!

The human race apparently set to work with a vengeance. There was a *dedication to labor*. Abel was committed to a pastoral lifestyle; he *"was a keeper of sheep"* while Cain, we read, was an agriculturalist, *"a tiller of the ground"* (v. 2). Cain turned to architecture and *"built a city, and called the name of the city after the name of his son — Enoch"* (v. 17). Later on other activities developed including the artistic labor of Jubal and the industrial endeavors of Tubal-Cain, the former being an expert on *"the harp and flute,"* the latter a highly skilled craftsman in *"bronze and iron"* (vv. 21, 22). While all this activity points to the development of a skilled civilization, it also poses problems for those who try to date exactly the civilization which is here described. But the dedication to labor is clear.

Some people are surprised to discover there was also a genuine *dedication to the Lord. "Cain brought an offering of the fruit of the ground to the Lord. Abel also brought of the firstborn of his flock and of their fat"* (vv. 3, 4). Leaving aside for the moment the well-known fact that only Abel's offering was acceptable we note that both men displayed some degree of gratitude to the Lord for what had been produced through their labor. After the sad events which led to Abel's death Seth was born, and under his influence and that of his sons *"men began to call on the name of the Lord"* (v. 26). The three fundamental areas of dedication through which the human race is blessed were firmly in place. But all was not well, for this was a fallen society.

THE DEVIATION OF THE HUMAN RACE

It is indicative of man's fallen condition that even when he dedicates himself to love, labor, and the Lord he is still capable of deviant behavior. Cain and Abel, for reasons not explained to us, determine to offer sacrifices to the Lord. Cain being the agriculturalist brought agricultural produce; Abel the shepherd brought animals from his flock. *"And the Lord respected Abel and his offering, but He did not respect Cain and his offering. And Cain was very angry, and his countenance fell"* (vv. 4, 5). It is tempting to read into the differing offerings some suggestion that one contained blood and was therefore acceptable and the other did not and was therefore unacceptable. But the text gives no indication of this but rather stresses the fact that the person offering was acceptable or unacceptable, leading us to believe that God was looking on the heart—the attitude of the worshiper—rather than at the specifics of his offering. Even in worship man is capable of deviant behavior and attitudes. Cain shows it and church history confirms it.

Cain reacted violently to his rejection, but not against the One who rejected him so much as against the innocent one who was accepted. Jealousy had raised its ugly green-eyed head and was about to prove that it is truly "cruel as the grave." It is possible for us to read this story of fratricide with some degree of indifference because we have become conditioned to violence, but we should bear in mind that sin had "entered" and was already "abounding" and would shortly "reign" (see Rom. 5:12–21) in the most gross way. The text by repeatedly using the word "brother" brings this into sharp focus. The man first born on earth killed the second man born on earth—his own brother! Love had become deviant. This is shown by Cain's response to God's inquiry about his brother's whereabouts. Callously, and untruthfully, he responded, *I do not know. Am I my brother's keeper?"* (v. 9).

Conjugal love quickly deteriorated too. Polygamy with all its attendant evils soon appeared on the scene through a reprehensible character called Lamech, who compounded his polygamous and murderous activities with an arrogance and belligerence frightening in their intensity. He killed a *"young man for hurting me"* (v. 23) and boasted about it in a song written for the occasion which he then performed for his wives. Man's deviant behavior toward the Lord is clear in Cain's reactions. He lied when reminded of the immensity of his crime: *"What have you done? The voice of your brother's blood cries to Me from the ground"* (v. 10). There is no indication of remorse, and when he was punished with banishment there was no acceptance but only complaint: *"My punishment is greater than I can bear!"* (v. 13). God graciously provided protection for him stipulating *"'Whoever kills Cain, vengeance shall be taken on him sevenfold.' And the Lord set a mark on Cain, lest anyone finding him should kill him"* (v. 15). But this elicits no gratitude and *"Cain went out from the presence of the Lord"* (v. 16). It should also be noted that while there is no record of man's deviant behavior toward labor in the text (unless we assume that the killing suggests that skills in metal work were already being turned to making weaponry), it was not long until the first signs of man's abuse of God-ordained work and God-provided raw materials began to appear.

The cause of all this is remarkably stated in Genesis 4:7: *"If you do well, will you not be accepted? And if you do not do well, sin lies at the door. And its desire is for you, but you should rule over it."* The word *"accepted"* means "lifted up" and contrasts sharply with Cain's fallen countenance but suggests much more than a brighter face. There is restoration for all who will turn to the Lord from the heart. The enemy *"sin"* crouches at the door of man's life like a wild animal waiting to devour him, but God's way is for man to overcome the forces of sin. Cain did not, and sin abounded and reigned. The same principle works today. The identical challenge confronts contemporary man.

I think of two brothers who were friends of mine from childhood. Born into the same family, fed the same food, reared in the same church, exposed to the same truth they were also susceptible to the same temptations. One from his earliest days began to show a genuine love for the Lord and a desire to order his life in accordance with divine principles. He disciplined himself in study and preparation, married wisely and well, and eventually became a singularly effective missionary in a primitive part of the world where very few white men ventured. Like every other man he was not exempt from sin crouching at his door, but he did well and was lifted up in blessing and honor before God and man. Meanwhile his brother who was less disciplined and less inclined to honor the Lord began to fudge around the edges. His business began to suffer, his marriage began to deteriorate, and eventually he became so gripped by the sin which lay in wait to devour him that he lost family, wife, and business and eventually sat desolate in a prison cell.

This sad chapter of Genesis, as is so often the case in Scripture, contains a bright note of hope. Seth (meaning "appointed") was born to Adam and Eve and his mother said, *"For God has appointed another seed for me instead of Abel, whom Cain killed"* (v. 25). The reference to *"seed"* suggests that she was trusting in the promise she had heard from the Lord about the serpent's bruising. Attributing the birth to the Lord's appointing shows that in the midst of the chaos God still had His people. It is still true today.

CHAPTER FIVE

Life and Death

Genesis 5:1–32

5:1 This is the book of the genealogy of Adam. In the day that God created man, He made him in the likeness of God.

2 He created them male and female, and blessed them and called them Mankind in the day they were created.

3 And Adam lived one hundred and thirty years, and begot *a son* in his own likeness, after his image, and named him Seth.

4 After he begot Seth, the days of Adam were eight hundred years; and he had sons and daughters.

5 So all the days that Adam lived were nine hundred and thirty years; and he died.

6 Seth lived one hundred and five years, and begot Enosh.

7 After he begot Enosh, Seth lived eight hundred and seven years, and had sons and daughters.

8 So all the days of Seth were nine hundred and twelve years; and he died.

9 Enosh lived ninety years, and begot Cainan.

10 After he begot Cainan, Enosh lived eight hundred and fifteen years, and had sons and daughters.

11 So all the days of Enosh were nine hundred and five years; and he died.

12 Cainan lived seventy years, and begot Mahalalel.

13 After he begot Mahalalel, Cainan lived eight hundred and forty years, and had sons and daughters.

14 So all the days of Cainan were nine hundred and ten years; and he died.

15 Mahalalel lived sixty-five years, and begot Jared.

16 After he begot Jared, Mahalalel lived eight hundred and thirty years, and had sons and daughters.

17 So all the days of Mahalalel were eight hundred and ninety-five years; and he died.

18 Jared lived one hundred and sixty-two years, and begot Enoch.

19 After he begot Enoch, Jared lived eight hundred years, and had sons and daughters.

20 So all the days of Jared were nine hundred and sixty-two years; and he died.

21 Enoch lived sixty-five years, and begot Methuselah.

22 After he begot Methuselah, Enoch walked with God three hundred years, and had sons and daughters.

23 So all the days of Enoch were three hundred and sixty-five years.

24 And Enoch walked with God; and he *was* not, for God took him.

25 Methuselah lived one hundred and eighty-seven years, and begot Lamech.

26 After he begot Lamech, Methuselah lived seven hundred and eighty-two years, and had sons and daughters.

27 So all the days of Methuselah were nine hundred and sixty-nine years; and he died.

28 Lamech lived one hundred and eighty-two years, and had a son.

29 And he called his name Noah, saying, "This *one* will comfort us concerning our work and the toil of our hands, because of the ground which the LORD has cursed."

30 After he begot Noah, Lamech lived five hundred and ninety-five years, and had sons and daughters.

31 So all the days of Lamech were seven hundred and seventy-seven years; and he died.

32 And Noah was five hundred years old, and Noah begot Shem, Ham, and Japheth.

Gen. 5:1-32

At first sight the fifth chapter of Genesis appears to be nothing more than a list of names interesting only to historians and theologians. But there is a recurring theme which is of profound interest to every human being. The theme is: "he lived . . . then he died." It is important to remember that man has been given only two things to master: "how to live" and "how to die." Despite his ability to conquer space and disease and other massive challenges it is ironic that he still struggles with the problems associated with living well and dying nobly.

There are two preliminary matters which need to be addressed concerning the fifth chapter. First, the longevity of these remarkable gentlemen and, secondly, the period of time which elapsed during their lifetimes. Methusaleh lived to the ripe old age of 969 and his forebear Jared lasted only seven years less. We hear occasionally of remarkable people living in remote areas of Siberia whose age far outstrips the life expectancy of other groups, and, of course, considerable attention has been paid to their diets and lifestyles to see if we can learn their secrets. Apparently a steady diet of yogurt has played a major part in their unusual health and vigor! But their lives are infant compared to the antediluvians.

Some scholars have suggested that the ages are not to be taken literally or perhaps that the life spans related not only to a person but also to the family that sprang from his loins. Others wonder if *"years"* were calculated differently in those long ago days. While keeping our minds open to what researchers may discover in these areas we see no reason to doubt that these men were probably an exceptionally hardy breed.

The other question relating to the time which elapsed during this period is important. Scholars like Ussher took these genealogies seriously when they tried to calculate the date of the creation. They assumed, understandably, that the genealogies were complete and that if they added up all the ages of the antediluvians they would arrive at an accurate figure for man's first appearance on earth. Modern science has shown their calculations to be inaccurate and modern research has shown that the lists are by no means complete. We now know that it was normal genealogical practice to omit whole generations so that the person who "begat" somebody else could as easily be his great, great, great grandfather (*ad infinitum*) as his father! Therefore we conclude that while these are real men who lived real lives of a stated duration we are not obliged to assume that the antediluvian period lasted for a period of time equaling the sum total of the ages recorded in Genesis 5.

COMING TO GRIPS WITH LIFE

The first two verses of the chapter suggest that this account was initially self-contained. The brief introduction which summarizes the earlier chapters underlines this thought. For our purposes the brief reiteration reminds us of the glorious beginnings of mankind (the word used in v. 2 is actually "Adam"). *"Created," "called,"* and *"blessed"* are the operative words but things had changed dreadfully and perhaps this is demonstrated by the juxtaposition of the phrases *"the likeness of God"* (v. 1) and *"his own likeness"* (v. 3) referring respectively to Adam and the way he was created and Seth and the way in which he was begotten. Life lived in the image of God is drastically different from life lived in the likeness of sinful man as the sad saga of Genesis has clearly outlined. It is only as modern man recognizes the difference that he can start coming to grips with life. So long as he sees himself independent of God or refuses to acknowledge his propensity to sin, modern man is doomed to repeat the fatal errors of his antediluvian ancestors albeit in more sophisticated and socially acceptable ways. Truly those who refuse to learn from history are doomed to repeat it.

But God had promised the seed of the woman would deal with the serpent and the consequences of his activity among mankind. The careful tracing of the arrival of this One is one of Genesis's major themes. We note that the Cainites having been introduced are promptly excluded from further consideration. It is the arrival of Seth and his progeny that requires our attention. Seth, as we have seen, is the "appointed one." But it is one of Seth's sons, Enoch, who dramatically grips our imagination for it was he who *"walked with God"* (v. 24). Adam hid from God, Cain went from the presence of God, but Enoch walked with God. This simple phrase is full of great meaning for believers of all generations. Micah the prophet said it well: "And what does the Lord require of you but to do justly, to love mercy, and to walk humbly with your God?" (Mic. 6:8). And perhaps John, the beloved disciple, had the same thing in mind when he reminded his flock, "If we say we have fellowship with Him, and walk in darkness, we lie and do not practice the truth. But if we walk in the light as He is in the light, we have fellowship with one another, and the blood of Jesus Christ His Son cleanses us from all sin" (1 John 1:6, 7).

The writer of the Epistle to the Hebrews drew from the LXX translation of "walked with God" when he (or she) wrote concerning Enoch, "before he was taken he had this testimony, that he pleased God" (Heb. 11:5). It is not uncommon to hear glowing eulogies at funerals which sometimes lead one to wonder if one has wandered into the wrong event. We do tend to say nice things about "the departed," but the difference with Enoch was that people said nice things like "he walked with God" before he departed. That is the ultimate human compliment.

Ernest Gordon was a company commander in one of Scotland's finest regiments—the proud Argyle and Sutherland Highlanders. His life had been filled with "fair winds and noble yachts, good companions and bonnie lasses, happy times and laughing days," but now he lay rotting in the infamous Japanese prison camp on the River Kwai. He wrote in his autobiography *Through the Valley of the Kwai* that dead bodies were as common as empty bellies. But in that camp he met the Lord and a remarkable transformation took place not only in his own life but in the whole of the camp. They started a church, an orchestra, a university, and a library, but Gordon attributed it all to his discovery of the Lord. Leaning over the rail of a Dutch ship which took him back to Britain after his release he said, "The experiences we had passed through deepened our understanding of life and of each other. We had looked into the heart of the Eternal and found Him to be wonderfully kind."[1] This is what it means to walk with God in whatever situation we might find ourselves.

COMING TO GRIPS WITH DEATH

Images of death are common: the wailing of distraught Arab women hugging the blood-smeared bodies of their sons, victims of the latest outbreak of fanaticism; the parades to martial music in Red Square as an elderly Soviet leader's ashes find their way into the walls of the Kremlin; the singing, weeping, dancing inhabitants of Soweto as yet another victim of beating and burning is carried to a simple grave; the pomp and circumstance as the remains of servicemen long lost on foreign fields are returned to Arlington cemetery draped in the Stars and Stripes; the pitiful gaze of emaciated Ethiopian children lying, fly-infested, waiting for death to release them from the misery which is, sadly, all that they have known. Violence and agony seem to be the order of the day. We have become so inured to them that we can eat our food while keeping an eye on the television as it conveys to our minds the hideousness of death at the same time our knives and forks convey sweet food to our bellies. Death in the abstract no longer moves us and we like to keep it that way.

But death is not abstract. Paul tells us that "death spread to all men" (Rom. 5:12), and he attributes this to Adam's transgression. The death that Adam experienced started the day he sinned (Gen. 2:17), although he continued to live for many years afterward. This death was clearly not physical death but rather a separation from the God with Whom he had known intimate fellowship. But subsequently Adam died physically (Gen. 5:5). Whether Adam and the human race would have died if Adam had not sinned has been debated by many. But it would appear that since death is called an "enemy" (1 Cor. 15:26) and death will be ultimately destroyed (Rev. 20:14) that it could hardly be regarded as part of God's original plan for man. Of course this position raises practical questions about overpopulation and ecology not to mention theological questions about man's eternal state.

COMING TO GRIPS WITH LIFE AFTER DEATH

The monotonous refrain *"and he died"* is broken in the case of Enoch. He, we are told, *"walked with God; and he was not, because God took him"* (Gen. 5:24). The New Testament called this termination of his earthly walk "his translation" as if to suggest that his walk down here had been so precious and intimate that God chose to deliver him from the pains of death and simply transfer him to a walk with Him on a higher plane. Perhaps in this account and that of Elijah's translation we are given clues as to how man would have been taken from earth to glory had not sin entered. Whatever the case might be there is no doubt that this ancient statement pierces the gloom of pervasive death with a ray of hope which, shining through the centuries, grew in intensity until Christ's glorious resurrection and its attendant promise, "He who believes in Me, though he may die, he shall live. And whoever lives and believes in Me shall never die" (John 11:25, 26).

On the other hand, it is a sobering thought that no hint of hope for life after death is mentioned for the other men of this chapter. This alone does not mean that they perished, but it does remind us that life after death for some will mean glory and for others judgment. Part of this awesome prospect is called "the second death" and is related to the "lake of fire" into which those who are not written in "the Book of Life" are cast (Rev. 20:14, 15).

It has been suggested that only those who view death rightly can hope to live properly. If this is true, great care should be taken to ensure that we understand death in its spiritual, physical, and eternal dimensions and accordingly embrace life in all its physical, spiritual, and eternal possibilities.

When I first met Jody Albrecht I was impressed not only by her obvious charm and poise but also by a quiet strength and gentle drive that I had rarely encountered before. It was some time after the initial meeting before I heard the unwelcome news that she was battling leukemia and had been for about seven years. The disease took its awful course and one day my wife and I visited her in the hospital and it became obvious that her remaining days on earth were few. We talked about her impending death quite openly but at no great length for two reasons. First, because she said, "Everything is in order and I'm packed and ready to go," and second, because she insisted on quizzing me about my radio broadcast, its outreach, the response we were getting, and if we had any financial needs. I was embarrassed to talk about money with a dying woman and told her that there was no way I was going to accept the check she was preparing to write for the ministry. "How could I walk away from your deathbed holding a check in my little sticky fingers?" I asked her. She smiled, put away the checkbook, and said, "All right, I'll mail it instead." Two days later she called long distance and said quite cheerfully, "I just wanted to call and say 'Good-bye dear friends' because I think I'll probably go to heaven tomorrow and I want to encourage you to go on with your work and keep on telling them the good news because it's true." She hung up and the next day as she had predicted she went to heaven. Here was a woman who knew how to live well because she had already discovered how to die nobly.

NOTE

1. Ernest Gordon, *Through the Valley of the Kwai* (Westport, CT: Greenwood Press, 1962), p. 244.

CHAPTER SIX

The Character of God

Genesis 6:1–22

6:1 Now it came to pass, when men began to multiply on the face of the earth, and daughters were born to them,

2 that the sons of God saw the daughters of men, that they *were* beautiful; and they took wives for themselves of all whom they chose.

3 And the LORD said, "My Spirit shall not strive with man forever, for he *is* indeed flesh; yet his days shall be one hundred and twenty years."

4 There were giants on the earth in those days, and also afterward, when the sons of God came in to the daughters of men and they bore *children* to them. Those *were* the mighty men who *were* of old, men of renown.

5 Then the LORD saw that the wickedness of man *was* great in the earth, and *that* every intent of the thoughts of his heart *was* only evil continually.

6 And the LORD was sorry that He had made man on the earth, and He was grieved in His heart.

7 So the LORD said, "I will destroy man whom I have created from the face of the earth, both man and beast, creeping thing and birds of the air, for I am sorry that I have made them."

8 But Noah found grace in the eyes of the LORD.

9 This is the genealogy of Noah. Noah was a just man, perfect in his generations. Noah walked with God.

10 And Noah begot three sons: Shem, Ham, and Japheth.

11 The earth also was corrupt before God, and the earth was filled with violence.

12 So God looked upon the earth, and indeed it was corrupt; for all flesh had corrupted their way on the earth.

13 And God said to Noah, "The end of all flesh has come before Me, for the earth is filled with violence through them; and behold, I will destroy them with the earth.

14 "Make yourself an ark of gopherwood; make rooms in the ark, and cover it inside and outside with pitch.

15 "And this is how you shall make it: The length of the ark *shall be* three hundred cubits, its width fifty cubits, and its height thirty cubits.

16 "You shall make a window for the ark, and you shall finish it to a cubit from above; and set the door of the ark in its side. You shall make it *with* lower, second, and third *decks*.

17 "And behold, I Myself am bringing floodwaters on the earth, to destroy from under heaven all flesh in which *is* the breath of life; everything that *is* on the earth shall die.

18 "But I will establish My covenant with you; and you shall go into the ark—you, your sons, your wife, and your sons' wives with you.

19 "And of every living thing of all flesh you shall bring two of every *sort* into the ark, to keep *them* alive with you; they shall be male and female.

20 "Of the birds after their kind, of animals after their kind, and of every creeping thing of the earth after its kind, two of every *kind* will come to you to keep *them* alive.

21 "And you shall take for yourself of all food that is eaten, and you shall gather *it* to yourself; and it shall be food for you and for them."

22 Thus Noah did; according to all that God commanded him, so he did.

Gen. 6:1–22

John Naisbitt in his best-selling book *Megatrends* suggests that the history of the United States can be told in the occupational changes from farmer to laborer to clerk. By this he means that we have moved from being primarily an agrarian society to an industrial society to an information society. He even goes so far as to suggest that "we are drowning in information but starved for knowledge."[1] He was not speaking about spiritual realities but his observations are not without significance to those who are concerned about the things of God. To put it simply, as we live in a veritable explosion of information about our psyches, our societies, our bodies, and our environments we are certainly not living in a parallel explosion of knowledge about God. Those who do profess to know Him often admit that they are drowning in information about Him yet starving for knowledge of Him.

This chapter, which can be studied from a variety of perspectives, yields much information about the character and nature of God which can be translated into practical experience of Him.

GOD'S PRINCIPLES

God made all manner of things, *"both man and beast, creeping thing and birds of the air"* (Gen. 6:7), and determined their sphere of being and their *raison d'etre*. All created things, therefore, reflect the "principle of existence" which in itself is exclusively the result of His sovereign choice. They exist only as He chooses and survive only where He determines. Creeping things creep and beasts are beastly; birds fly and men are manly. We may be tempted sometimes to regard men as beastly and some beasts as creepy but the principle obtains. This in turn leads to the "principle of dependence." Man for all his skills is incapable of making something out of nothing and therefore is dependent upon the creative energies of the great God to provide all the raw materials necessary for his survival and well-being. When given proper consideration this directs attention to the "principle of obedience" which simply stated insists that man functions properly only when he acts in accordance with the mandates of the Creator. But what if man is disobedient? This, of course, is the root of the human problem—the cause of human anguish and heartache. The "principle of consequence" follows quite naturally because God's commands cannot be disregarded with impunity any more than the natural laws of the universe can be disobeyed without consequences. Modern man needs to be reacquainted with these fundamentals of the divine nature and character because as it was in the days of Noah there is today a disconcerting trend toward disregard of God's rule and disobedience of God's laws.

GOD'S PERSPECTIVE

"Then the Lord saw that the wickedness of man was great in the earth, and that every intent of the thoughts of his heart was only evil continually" (v. 5). Before we consider "what" God saw we should note that Scripture teaches us *"that"* God saw. There was presumably a perception in the days of Noah that God was in some way divorced from His creation, was not intimately concerned with the details of man's lifestyle, and therefore should not be taken seriously. Nothing could have been further from the truth. Note God's perception of "increasing disobedience." Like a laser beam the eyes of the Lord were observing not only the activities of the man He had made but *"the intent of the thoughts of his heart"* (v. 5). It is one thing to note a person's action; it is an entirely different thing to accurately identify motive. The courts of the land are sometimes required to discern the intents of the heart and even ball game referees are required to determine whether actions were intentional or otherwise. This is tricky territory for all but God, but He judges rightly. He calls them as He sees them, but His vision of the seen and the unseen is 20/20 at all times. This is sobering in the extreme.

God also perceived "increasing deviance." The passage about the sexual activities of the *"sons of God"* and the *"daughters of men"* (v. 2) is notoriously difficult because we know what they were doing but we don't know for certain who they were. Some suggest that the *"sons of God"* were fallen angels (see also Jude 6, 7)—a suggestion that is not as strange as it first seems when we remember that the expression is a common one for angels. Others who cannot imagine such sexual activity assume that the men were of the anointed line of Seth and the women belonged to the line of Cain. This is certainly easier for modern man to believe, but while it puts less strain on credulity it puts more stress on the language being used, and it hardly accounts for the breed of supermen that apparently resulted. Whatever the solution may be we do know that such behavior was extremely displeasing to the Lord because it clearly deviated from His revealed will for those people.

87

Then God also perceived "increasing destruction." He *looked upon the earth, and indeed it was corrupt; for all flesh had corrupted their way on the earth"* (v. 12). Corruption and violence characterized the lives of the rapidly multiplying society which God had created, and He apparently decided that it was only a matter of time until it would self-destruct. So God Himself determined to act, saying to Noah, *"The end of all flesh has come before Me, for the earth is filled with violence through them; and behold, I will destroy them with the earth"* (v. 13). The judgment of God was announced and man failed to hear and to respond. Modern man either does not believe God exists or he believes that if He does exist He is such a nice guy that He would not be unkind enough to judge anybody or anything. This wishful thinking needs to be corrected by proper enunciation of Who God really is and what He has already said and done in human history.

GOD'S PAIN

It would be as incorrect to assume God's disinterest and non-involvement in human affairs as it would be to assume His callous harshness in judging His erring creation. In actual fact, God's deep distress is wonderfully expressed: *"The Lord was sorry that He had made man on the earth, and He was grieved in His heart"* (v. 6). The word *"grieved"* is related rather pointedly to the words for "sorrow" and "toil" (Gen. 3:16, 17) which were to be the unhappy lot of Adam and Eve after their transgression. In a very real sense God was not exempt from the pain and anguish which sin had introduced into His creation.

The thought that God was sorry He had made man is somewhat unnerving as any child knows who has been told by angry parents in a fit of pique that they are sorry "they had him"! But God is not piqued with man; He is grieved and distraught and is thinking in terms of grace even at the moment of judgment.

GOD'S PLEASURE

To understand God it is imperative that due consideration be given not only to His righteous indignation but also His grace. The heart of God constantly overflows in loving kindness and tender mercies to His children. But not all of God's children are interested in grace or moved by divine favor. God's pleasure comes from dispensing grace and discovering those who warmly and willingly receive it. In the midst of the abysmal, widespread moral and societal destruction of his day stood such a man. *"But Noah found grace in the eyes of the Lord"* because he *"was a just man, perfect in his generations."* In short *"Noah walked with God"* (Gen. 6:8, 9).

The words used to describe this remarkable man point to his relationships with his contemporaries as well as the communion he enjoyed with his God. *"Just"* relates to proper behavior manward while *"perfect,"* which obviously does not mean "sinless," refers to a wholehearted commitment to the Lord. One can imagine the delight with which the Lord watched His child Noah grace the sordid society of which he was a part. It is encouraging to remember that God has always had His witnesses and that at no time in human history have things become so dark that no ray of righteousness shone brightly for God.

Centuries later, at a particularly dark time in England's history, God raised up a man called John Wycliffe. J. C. Ryle, the Bishop of Liverpool, wrote in his book, *Light from Old Times*, "England seems to have been buried under a mass of ignorance, superstition, priestcraft and immorality."[2] Yet in this kind of environment John Wycliffe shone brightly. Known as the "Morning Star of the Reformation," even though he died about a hundred years before Luther was born, he was acknowledged in academic, ecclesiastical, and political circles as being "no common man." For over twenty-five years the things that he said and the actions that he undertook spoke loud and long to his contemporaries. It is a fitting tribute that even though his body was exhumed and burned and the ashes thrown into a stream thirty-one years after his death, his name lives on in the ministry of hundreds of Wycliffe Bible Translators who have reached out to the hidden tribes with the message of Christ. There has always been a Noah or a Wycliffe.

GOD'S PROVISION

The Lord took Noah into His confidence, explaining His deep distress at the human condition, outlining His proposed judgment, and then instructing him in the part that he was to play in the furthering of the divine plan. *"Make yourself an ark of gopherwood; make rooms in the ark, and cover it inside and outside with pitch"* (v. 14). Detailed instructions concerning size and structure were also provided in addition to specific details of the passenger list, food, and cargo. The details concerning measurement and design are tantalizing to some people, leading them to careful and occasionally not so careful study of the ark. I remember as a boy hearing a very detailed description of the ark, complete with artistic impressions, and being very reassured by the speaker that it really was seaworthy. His words carried great weight with me because he was a maritime engineer in the nearby Vickers Armstrong shipyards! Francis Shaeffer also did his homework and came to the conclusion that the ark (the word means "chest" not "ship"!) was "almost exactly the size of the 'Great Eastern' which laid the first North Atlantic cable."

It is interesting that references to a flood are to be found in ancient traditions and myths in all parts of the world. They vary dramatically in detail and credibility but they do suggest that somewhere in the human experience there was a common knowledge of such an event which became corrupted over the years. Reverent students of Scripture, however, remember the references of the Lord Jesus to Noah and are conversant with the explanation of the writer of the Epistle to the Hebrews: "By faith Noah, being divinely warned of things not yet seen, moved with godly fear, prepared an ark for the saving of his household, by which he condemned the world and became heir of the righteousness which is according to faith" (Heb. 11:7). The idea was God's; the responsibility to expedite was Noah's. The creative initiative belonged to God; the willing obedience belonged to Noah. Grace flowed from the heart of God; faith appropriated it in the heart of Noah, and the eternal purposes of God went onward to their relentless conclusion.

The idea was ideal. If one bears in mind all that God wanted to accomplish in this dramatic intervention in human affairs it is clear that His provision through Noah and his ark was beautifully suited to do all that His heart desired. Man has always been the beneficiary of divine provision. However reluctant he may be to admit it, man must eventually concede that the best ideas come from God and that they are never less than ideal. To believe this thoroughly is to know God more fully.

As we saw in the very beginnings of our study, God ordained marriage as the basic structure of society. But down through the centuries man has devised methods of deriving the benefits of the marital state without having to accept the responsibilities of connubial bliss. We now call some of these human inventions "alternate lifestyles," and of course that is a perfectly accurate description. But they also need to be recognized as illicit alternative lifestyles and in a strange way this apparently is beginning to dawn on the collective conscience of modern people. This is not because of a great spiritual revival in the hearts of the masses but rather because of the proliferation of sexually communicable diseases through sexual activity outside the realm of marriage. Some would see this as a specific judgment of God while others who would not wish to be quite so specific would agree that it is yet another reminder that the Lord knows what is best for us, and if we do it His way we will live under the warmth of His smile and the fullness of His grace.

GOD'S PATIENCE

Presumably the God Who had made the universe could have thought of other ways of judging the sinful and preserving the godly without enlisting the aid of Noah and requiring the laborious task of building the ark. But throughout history He has shown Himself willing and eager to enroll man in cooperative ventures with Himself. This speaks not only of His grace in allowing us to be His co-workers but also pinpoints His remarkable patience. Peter speaks of the "longsuffering" of God as He "waited in the days of Noah, while the ark was being prepared" (1 Pet. 3:20) but also points out that Noah, during that period, was a "preacher of righteousness" (2 Pet. 2:5). No doubt Noah's curious neighbors gathered around him to ask what on earth he was doing building a three-story "coffin," and apparently Noah was ready for their inquiries. He preached righteousness to them; God was patient with them; but repentance did not come and eventually the judgment fell. God warns before He judges. He delays the promised wrath. He longs for people to come to repentance. But His patience should never be abused; it should be cherished.

GOD'S PROMISE

The word *"covenant"* is of profound significance in Scripture and it first appears in the account of God's dealings with Noah. After outlining the sad news of impending judgment God told His servant, *"But I will establish My covenant with you"* (Gen. 6:18). God's self-revelation has come to us in many different ways. First He showed Himself in Creation as the psalmist loved to remind us: "The heavens declare the glory of God" (Ps. 19:1). The god of Creation can be desperately awe-inspiring. His "frowning countenance" shown in thunder cloud and overwhelming flood does not make for warm, intimate God-man relations. But His revelation in covenant does. Herein God shows Himself ready to meet with people, to promise a relationship with them, and to outline the details of behavior which will make this promised relationship warm and wholesome. Once this idea of covenant has been introduced in Scripture the theme persists right through to the new covenant, sealed in the blood of Christ whereby mankind is thoroughly reconciled to God. There are few things more encouraging to me than the thought that the God of Creation is the God of covenant. When I look into the heavens I am struck with the immensity of it all and the grandeur of my God. Humbled I bow in His presence and ask with the psalmist, "What is man?" (Ps. 8:4). Immediately I am reminded that the God of transcendence is immanent—He has spoken to me as He did to Noah. He has promised me that He will act on my behalf. To know this is to know Him even more intimately.

NOTES

1. John Naisbitt, *Megatrends: Ten New Directions Transforming Our Lives* (New York: Warner Books, 1983), p. 17.

2. J. C. Ryle, *Light from Old Times* (Welwyn, England: Evangelical Press, 1980), p. 2.

CHAPTER SEVEN

A Man of Faith

Genesis 7:1–24

7:1 Then the LORD said to Noah, "Come into the ark, you and all your household, because I have seen *that* you *are* righteous before Me in this generation.

2 "You shall take with you seven each of every clean animal, a male and his female; two each of animals that *are* unclean, a male and his female;

3 "also seven each of birds of the air, male and female, to keep the species alive on the face of all the earth.

4 "For after seven more days I will cause it to rain on the earth forty days and forty nights, and I will destroy from the face of the earth all living things that I have made."

5 And Noah did according to all that the LORD commanded him.

6 Noah *was* six hundred years old when the floodwaters were on the earth.

7 So Noah, with his sons, his wife, and his sons' wives, went into the ark because of the waters of the flood.

8 Of clean animals, of animals that *are* unclean, of birds, and of everything that creeps on the earth,

9 two by two they went into the ark to Noah, male and female, as God had commanded Noah.

10 And it came to pass after seven days that the waters of the flood were on the earth.

11 In the six hundredth year of Noah's life, in the second month, the seventeenth day of the month, on that day all the fountains of the great deep were broken up, and the windows of heaven were opened.

12 And the rain was on the earth forty days and forty nights.

13 On the very same day Noah and Noah's sons, Shem, Ham, and Japheth, and Noah's wife and the three wives of his sons with them, entered the ark—

14 they and every beast after its kind, all cattle after their kind, every creeping thing that creeps on the earth after its kind, and every bird after its kind, every bird of every sort.

15 And they went into the ark to Noah, two by two, of all flesh in which *is* the breath of life.

16 So those that entered, male and female of all flesh, went in as God had commanded him; and the LORD shut him in.

17 Now the flood was on the earth forty days. The waters increased and lifted up the ark, and it rose high above the earth.

18 The waters prevailed and greatly increased on the earth, and the ark moved about on the surface of the waters.

19 And the waters prevailed exceedingly on the earth, and all the high hills under the whole heaven were covered.

20 The waters prevailed fifteen cubits upward, and the mountains were covered.

21 And all flesh died that moved on the earth: birds and cattle and beasts and every creeping thing that creeps on the earth, and every man.

22 All in whose nostrils *was* the breath of the spirit of life, all that *was* on the dry *land*, died.

23 So He destroyed all living things which were on the face of the ground: both man and cattle, creeping thing and bird of the air. They were destroyed from the earth. Only Noah and those who *were* with him in the ark remained *alive*.

24 And the waters prevailed on the earth one hundred and fifty days.

Gen. 7:1–24

Noah's ark has lost none of its fascination. Despite political difficulties, not to mention severe logistical problems, expeditions still endeavor to climb the icy slopes of Mt. Ararat on the borders of Turkey and the U.S.S.R. in the hope of finding the fossilized remains of Noah's masterpiece. Whether or not they will be successful is open to question; in fact there is some doubt if they are even looking in the right place since some scholars suggest that the mountain we know as Mt. Ararat gained its name relatively recently.

The extent of the flood has also been subject to much debate. Was it a universal catastrophe or a local inundation covering parts of Mesopotamia? The language of Genesis certainly lends itself to a "universal" interpretation. We read: *"All the high hills under the whole heaven were covered. And all flesh died . . . and every man . . . only Noah and those who were with him in the ark remained alive"* (Gen. 7:19-23). Yet this interpretation is by no means trouble free. If the writer of Genesis meant that the waters reached a depth of fifteen cubits over the peak of Mt. Everest it is estimated that the water required to achieve that end would be eight times the normal water content of the world. Where all this water came from and where it disappeared to is a mystery to many people for which no satisfactory answer has been found. Furthermore it has been pointed out by geologists that while there is considerable evidence for numerous floods there is no uniform evidence for a flood of universal proportions. There are at least ten traditional arguments for a universal flood but there are an equal number of responses from those who hold to a local event (see Ronald Youngblood's treatment in his book, *How It All Began*[1]).

Whatever conclusion we reach concerning the geographical extent of the flood, we should not allow the debate to obscure the facts of God's judgment and grace which are powerfully demonstrated in this traumatic event. Neither should we overlook the remarkable life of the central figure—Noah. "By faith Noah, being divinely warned of things not yet seen, moved with godly fear, prepared an ark for the saving of his household, by which he condemned the world and became heir of the righteousness which is according to faith" (Heb. 11:7). There is much to learn from his faith life.   -

FAITH—A RESPONSE TO REVELATION

We know that "faith comes by hearing, and hearing by the word of God" (Rom. 10:17), but there are few more striking examples of what

that means than Noah. Out of the blue he was told about a cata-
clysmic flood and he believed God. He was informed that the end of
all flesh was at hand, and he believed that too. Told to build a ark
the length of one and a half football fields and to fill it with animals
because all the animals would be destroyed, he believed it! And
when he was invited by the Lord to *"Come into the ark, you and all
your household, because I have seen that you are righteous before Me in
this generation"* (Gen. 7:1) he took what must have been a very difficult step out of all that was familiar and understandable into a situation which was incomprehensible except to the eye of faith.

FAITH—A RELATIONSHIP OF TRUST

When Noah took his big step of faith into the ark, *"the Lord shut him
in"* (v. 16) suggesting that Jehovah was gently but firmly assuring
Noah that he had done the right thing and that he was indeed secure.
But Noah's faith had already been in evidence for a considerable period while the ark was being constructed. And his faith had to perse-
vere during the year-long flood because strangely there is no record
of God speaking to Noah during that period. He had to go on trusting
through thick and thin, whether he could see and understand or not.

FAITH—A READINESS TO OBEY

James reminds us that "faith by itself, if it does not have works, is
dead" (James 2:17). By faith Noah set to work building a mammoth
ark. He gathered *"seven each of every clean animal, a male and his
female; two each of animals that are unclean, a male and his female; also
seven each of birds of the air, male and female, to keep the species alive
on the face of all the earth"* (Gen. 7:2, 3). If the flood was universal
then the task of gathering animals from all parts of the globe is
mindboggling, not to mention feeding and cleaning up after them!
One ancient writer solved this problem by asserting that they all
hibernated so they only needed feeding once! If the flood was local
then the task was not as great but was still immense. Neither was
Noah overwhelmed with the responsibility thrust upon him. He
took that in his stride of faith too. And he was clearly not at all

deterred by the apparent incongruity of what he was doing. In other words his faith worked!

FAITH—A RELEASE OF BLESSING

The blessing Noah's faith released in his own life (in a very real sense he was saved by faith) also spilled over into his family's experience. *"Only Noah and those who were with him in the ark remained alive"* (v. 23). The faithful expression of his faith as he preached righteousness to his contemporaries "condemned the world" and that was a blessing, because the people were exposed to truth even though they chose to ignore it. Then there is the benefit we receive from his faith as we read the account and are led to examine our own faith. Like Abel, "he being dead still speaks" (Heb. 11:4).

FAITH—A RESOURCE OF POWER

Noah's power to live triumphantly among his unbelieving contemporaries was a triumph of grace and faith. No man could be expected to find in himself the resources to live as he lived. He had the power to take decisive action as his society drifted toward self-destruction. He exhibited the power to make incisive declarations to those who did not heed what he was saying. He kept on saying it nevertheless. He had the power to show an alternative attitude to that which prevailed among the people of his day. He walked a lonely road. Many years ago I saw a magnificent tapestry in a home for recovering alcoholics in Germany. It was a picture of a stream with a shoal of fish heading one way and a solitary fish swimming in the opposite direction. Underneath were the words: "Any dead fish can float down stream—it takes a live one to swim against it." Noah through his faith had resources of strength to be a live one!

FAITH—A REBUKE TO UNFAITHFULNESS

Noah was described by God as *"righteous before Me in this generation"* (Gen. 7:1). This was a delight to God but in all probability an irritant to Noah's society. It is impossible to please God without sometimes displeasing those who are opposed to Him. Paul said, "We are to God the fragrance of Christ among those who are being saved and among those who are perishing. To the one we are the aroma of death leading to death, and to the other the aroma of life leading to life" (2 Cor. 2:15, 16).

My dad often used to observe, "Isn't it strange that the same sun that melts wax, hardens clay?" He would hasten to explain to me that the sun's properties do not change but the properties of the different materials on which the sun shines are revealed by its heat. In the same way Jesus showed that the same seed scattered on different places will produce entirely different results. Not because the seed alters but because the seed reveals what kind of soil it has landed upon. Whether it be the sun shining, the seed landing, the word being preached, or the glowing testimony of a believer the same rule obtains. There are those who will warmly respond to the vibrant testimony of a godly man or woman, and there are others who will become infuriated by the same testimony from the identical person. This is a demonstration of what is inside the heart of the hearer and observer of the testimony and also an indicator of the spiritual destiny of those whose hearts are either warm or cold to the truth however presented.

All of us would much prefer being a "fragrance of Christ" rather than an "aroma of death," but unfortunately we are not free to choose which we will be because this is determined by the reaction of others to what we say and do. By building his ark Noah offered salvation to those who would respond in faith. To those who entered with him it was a blessing and a delight, but to those who refused it must have been the most awful statement of loss and dismay as it disappeared into the mists.

FAITH—A REMINDER TO THE FAITHFUL

The Lord Jesus said that in the days of Noah the people were "eating and drinking, marrying and giving in marriage" (Matt. 24:38). In other words they were just getting along with their lives, ignoring the strange little man in their midst who was building a massive boat with nowhere to sail it. Perhaps they had grown used to seeing him working and preaching, and as nothing ever seemed to happen they had chosen to assume he was wrong about his dire predictions. But the judgment fell and as the Lord Jesus reminded His hearers, "so also will the coming of the Son of Man be" (Matt. 24:39). Noah's faith and faithfulness are powerful reminders to God's people to look for the glorious appearing of the Lord Jesus. Noah still has something to say to God's people when they are tempted to settle into lives just like the unbelievers!

So the righteous judgment of the offended Lord fell. But in the midst of the horror sailed a man and his family secure in the serenity of a faith which had released the resources of grace. So has it ever been throughout human history.

Many centuries after Noah's voyage another man of faith set sail in very different circumstances. William Carey was a pastor and a shoemaker (presumably he thought that if tent-making was good enough for the apostle Paul, shoe-making was good enough for him). He had published a remarkable tract with the resounding title, "An enquiry into the obligations of Christians to use means for the conversion of the heathens," and followed it with deeply felt sermons seeking to awaken the churches to the needs of the unreached peoples of the earth. He had been roundly criticized for his efforts by church leaders but undeterred he set sail for India on the premise that he should "Expect great things from God; attempt great things for God." He had very little formal education but this did not stop him from teaching himself Latin, Greek, Hebrew, Dutch, and French before setting out for India where he subsequently learned Bengali, translated the entire Bible into Bengali, and helped in producing Scriptures and related materials in no less than forty different languages and dialects. During his forty years' ministry he buried his wife and all his children in India, but he persisted in his conviction that God had called him, that he should obey and trust Him, that he should use his God-given skills for the blessing of God and man, and that one day he would land safely on the shores of Glory as surely as he had previously landed in India and Noah before him had landed safely on Mt. Ararat.

One of the great advantages of men of faith like Noah and Carey is that they inspire others to learn what it is to trust and obey in order to discover the riches of blessing that are stored up for those who will launch out into the deep.

NOTE

1. Ronald Youngblood, *How It All Began,* Bible Commentary for Laymen Series (Ventura, CA: Regal Books, 1980), pp. 125–37.

CHAPTER EIGHT

The New Creation

Genesis 8:1-22

8:1 Then God remembered Noah, and every living thing, and all the animals that *were* with him in the ark. And God made a wind to pass over the earth, and the waters subsided.

2 The fountains of the deep and the windows of heaven were also stopped, and the rain from heaven was restrained.

3 And the waters receded continually from the earth. At the end of the hundred and fifty days the waters decreased.

4 Then the ark rested in the seventh month, the seventeenth day of the month, on the mountains of Ararat.

5 And the waters decreased continually until the tenth month. In the tenth *month*, on the first *day* of the month, the tops of the mountains were seen.

6 So it came to pass, at the end of forty days, that Noah opened the window of the ark which he had made.

7 Then he sent out a raven, which kept going to and fro until the waters had dried up from the earth.

8 He also sent out from himself a dove, to see if the waters had receded from the face of the ground.

9 But the dove found no resting place for the sole of her foot, and she returned into the ark to him, for the waters *were* on the face of the whole earth. So he put out his hand and took her, and drew her into the ark to himself.

10 And he waited yet another seven days, and again he sent the dove out from the ark.

11 Then the dove came to him in the evening, and behold, a freshly plucked olive leaf *was* in her mouth; and Noah knew that the waters had receded from the earth.

12 So he waited yet another seven days and sent out the dove, which did not return again to him anymore.

13 And it came to pass in the six hundred and first year, in the first *month*, the first *day* of the month, that the waters were dried up from the earth; and Noah removed the covering of the ark and looked, and indeed the surface of the ground was dry.

14 And in the second month, on the twenty-seventh day of the month, the earth was dried.

15 Then God spoke to Noah, saying,

16 "Go out of the ark, you and your wife, and your sons and your sons' wives with you.

17 "Bring out with you every living thing of all flesh that *is* with you: birds and cattle and every creeping thing that creeps on the earth, so that they may abound on the earth, and be fruitful and multiply on the earth."

18 So Noah went out, and his sons and his wife and his sons' wives with him.

19 Every animal, every creeping thing, every bird, *and* whatever creeps on the earth, according to their families, went out of the ark.

20 Then Noah built an altar to the LORD, and took of every clean animal and of every clean bird, and offered burnt offerings on the altar.

21 And the LORD smelled a soothing aroma. Then the LORD said in His heart, "I will never again curse the ground for man's sake, although the imagination of man's heart *is* evil from his youth; nor will I again destroy every living thing as I have done.

22 "While the earth remains,
Seedtime and harvest,
Cold and heat,
Winter and summer,
And day and night
Shall not cease."

Gen. 8:1–22

The judgment of God must always be seen in proper perspective. It is based on righteousness, presented in advance by way of warning with a view to repentance, and coupled with grace which leads to restoration and new opportunity. This is clearly demonstrated in Noah's experience. We now come to a consideration of this new opportunity as it was established in what we can legitimately call the new creation.

THE ENTRANCE TO THE NEW CREATION

"God remembered Noah, and every living thing . . . and God made a wind to pass over the earth, and the waters subsided . . . then the ark rested . . . on the mountains of Ararat" (Gen. 8:1–4). Noah and his party were about to embark on an exciting new experience of discovery. But they were aware that all they had was directly attributable to the gracious intervention of God. This was underlined by God's remembering of them. They were not likely to forget, either, that they had escaped the judgment of God only because the judgment had been meted out in such a way that they had not been destroyed by it. They had gone through the same things that their contemporaries had experienced except that they had been sheltered under the ark of God's providing, and it was at His command that *"the waters subsided. The fountains of the deep and the windows of heaven were also stopped, and the rain from heaven was restrained"* (vv. 1, 2).

These benefits accrued to Noah through faith and obedience which he had exercised over many years and which he continued to exercise as the ark grounded and the waters receded. He seemed to have been in no great hurry to open the window and look out at the new environment in which he and his family had arrived. Patiently he continued his life of faith and his careful attention to all that God had instructed him to do. It was thus that he entered the new creation. Nothing has changed for those who, today, experience a similar but far greater salvation. Paul describes the person who is in Christ as: *"a new creation; old things have passed away; behold, all things have become new"* (2 Cor. 5:17). Peter makes even more explicit use of Noah's story to make a similar point in 1 Peter 3:20–22. In the same way that Noah sheltered in the ark so we shelter from the wrath of God in Christ and find ourselves raised into newness of life in Him in much the same way that Noah and his family found themselves in the new world.

THE ENJOYMENT OF THE NEW CREATION

Noah could have settled down in the ark and rejoiced in the fact that he had survived the wrath of God. But the ark might have been getting a little musty by this time with all those animals around the place! So he decided to start enjoying his new situation rather than rejoicing in his past experience. There is a lesson here for many of God's people!

He shows us "the excitement of exploration." Utilizing the resources he had available, in this case a raven and a dove, Noah started his scientific exploration of the new creation. Modern man has a tendency to think that he is smart and all his forebears were just chugging along waiting for modern man to appear on the scene and get everything together. But Noah certainly knew what he was doing. It would be a long time before Pavlov would experiment with his dogs and Skinner with his pigeons, but Noah knew how to use animals to discover his world. It would be many centuries before modern man would articulate the "scientific method," but Noah showed that he understood how to make a hypothesis, how to experiment, and how to come to a conclusion. There was no way that he was going to trust himself to the new post-flood environment without the kind of evidence that would assure him it was time to move. This in no way reflected on his faith any more than being a man of faith suggests that rational inquiry is out of order.

Noah dispatched the raven *"which kept going to and fro until the waters had dried up from the face of the earth"* (Gen. 8:7). With all the death around, the raven found plenty to occupy itself so *"He also sent out from himself a dove . . . but the dove found no resting place . . . and she returned . . . So he put out his hand and took her, and drew her into the ark to himself"* (vv. 8, 9). He now knew that a raven could survive outside the ark and a dove could not so he drew his conclusions from that data. After a week he dispatched the dove again and this time she returned bearing the well-known olive branch. Now *"Noah knew that the waters had receded from the earth"* (v. 11). After another week the dove flew another mission from which she did not return and Noah had all the information he needed so he *"removed the covering of the ark"* (v. 13). Noah, the man of faith and obedience, was also a man of resourcefulness and intelligence which he channeled into a thorough exploration of all that God had for him.

The excitement Noah experienced was tempered with "the discipline of delay." While scholars do not agree on the exact duration of the flood it is reasonable to assume that from the time Noah and family boarded the ark to the moment of disembarkation, approximately one year had elapsed. On the one hand this may seem a short time for all the water to drain away (if the flood was universal and covered Mt. Everest the drain off rate would be in excess of well over 100 feet per diem!), but for Noah sitting in the ark wondering what was going on outside it must have seemed an interminable amount of time. Yet he showed great patience as he methodically went about his work trusting the God who had given him every reason to trust Him. Being over six hundred years old has definite advantages when it comes to patience, but in our shorter life span we need to learn it more expeditiously. In an age and culture which has produced instant replays, instant potatoes, instant coffee, same-day cleaning, and Polaroid photographs it is not surprising that we have learned to pray, "Lord, give me patience and give it to me now!" But in the economy of God, which has an eternal dimension, things don't always move as fast as we would like and we have to remind ourselves that delay has its own discipline, and discipline produces its own character. That which is gained easily is often lightly prized, that which arrives suddenly more often than not departs in similar fashion.

It is significant that Noah's first action on dry land was an act of worship. He enjoyed "the sweetness of sacrifice." *"Then Noah built an altar to the Lord, and took of every clean animal and of every clean bird, and offered burnt offerings on the altar. And the Lord smelled a soothing aroma"* (vv. 20, 21). Noah's resources for himself and his family were definitely limited, and the task of repopulating the earth was immense; so it would have been easy for him to rationalize that a sacrifice at this time might not be wise. Apparently he did not arrive at this conclusion. There has always been a segment of society which regards sacrifice as waste and can always find better uses for resources than to spend them in acts of generous praise and thanksgiving. But those who never learn the joys of giving become shriveled in their hearts even as they become bloated in their assets. The anthropomorphism of the Lord smelling an aroma should be seen as a delightful expression of divine satisfaction and approval— something that more than compensates for any criticism that the worshiper may be subjected to by those who are more materialistic in their views. Paul uses a similar expression to describe the Lord Jesus' self-sacrifice on our behalf (Eph. 5:2).

God's response to Noah's worship was to say in His heart, *"I will never again curse the ground for man's sake, although the imagination of man's heart is evil from his youth; nor will I again destroy every living thing as I have done. / 'While the earth remains, / Seedtime and harvest, / Cold and heat, / Winter and summer, / And day and night / Shall not cease'"* (vv. 21, 22). As a result of these stirring and welcome words Noah was introduced to a new sense of security. "The certainty of commitment" became a factor in his new life. While he had shown a remarkable commitment to the purposes of God he was being reminded of a far greater commitment—that which God exhibits to His own purposes and plans. Noah found himself caught up in these plans and as a result knew that he was safe in the sovereign immutable purpose of the Eternal One. It is worth noting that God's commitment was not based on man's worthiness. God's statement was made at the same time that His awareness and disapproval of man's unrelenting evil was reiterated.

Noah's experience beautifully illustrates that of the believer who "in Christ . . . is a new creation" (2 Cor. 5:17). This believer, like Noah, is invited to step out and explore the newness of life which is his "in Christ," rejoicing in God's grace, reveling in the bounty which is his in the new environment, resting in the assurance of God's benevolence on his behalf, and reflecting his gratitude in sacrificial service. In this way the new creation is enjoyed and explored to the full.

In recent years our church has been privileged to work with many hundreds of refugees from the Orient. I have observed that there is no standard way in which they respond to their new environment. Some appear to be totally overwhelmed by the newness and the strangeness of everything that surrounds them, and I have often wondered if they have been so traumatized by their recent experiences that they have felt incapable of making any more changes in their lives. On the other hand some of them seem to plunge into the new environment with such enthusiasm and verve that it appears as if they have been waiting all their lives to grab this opportunity with both hands. The former tend to settle into an ethnic ghetto while the latter branch out into a lifestyle of challenge and growth.

The same things could have happened to Noah. He could have become so attached to his animals and his way of looking after them that he declined to step out of the ark when told to, but instead he obeyed and the new life began. Perhaps more importantly for our purposes it is sad sometimes to see new believers who appear to be content to sit in their ark of salvation and never branch out into the new life which the ark has offered to them. Life is for living, and newness of life is no exception to that rule.

CHAPTER NINE

Human Dignity

Genesis 9:1–29

9:1 So God blessed Noah and his sons, and said to them: "Be fruitful and multiply, and fill the earth.

2 "And the fear of you and the dread of you shall be on every beast of the earth, on every bird of the air, on all that move *on* the earth, and on all the fish of the sea. They are given into your hand.

3 "Every moving thing that lives shall be food for you. I have given you all things, even as the green herbs.

4 "But you shall not eat flesh with its life, *that is,* its blood.

5 "Surely for your lifeblood I will demand *a reckoning;* from the hand of every beast I will require it, and from the hand of man. From the hand of every man's brother I will require the life of man.

6 "Whoever sheds man's blood,
By man his blood shall be shed;
For in the image of God
He made man.

7 And as for you, be fruitful and multiply;
Bring forth abundantly in the earth
And multiply in it."

8 Then God spoke to Noah and to his sons with him, saying:

9 "And as for Me, behold, I establish My covenant with you and with your descendants after you,

10 "and with every living creature that *is* with you: the birds, the cattle, and every beast of the earth with you, of all that go out of the ark, every beast of the earth.

11 "Thus I establish My covenant with you: Never again shall all flesh be cut off by the waters of the flood; never again shall there be a flood to destroy the earth."

12 And God said: "This *is* the sign of the covenant which I make between Me and you, and every living creature that *is* with you, for perpetual generations:

13 "I set My rainbow in the cloud, and it shall be for the sign of the covenant between Me and the earth.

14 "It shall be, when I bring a cloud over the earth, that the rainbow shall be seen in the cloud;

15 "and I will remember My covenant which *is* between Me and you and every living creature of all flesh; the waters shall never again become a flood to destroy all flesh.

16 "The rainbow shall be in the cloud, and I will look on it to remember the everlasting covenant between God and every living creature of all flesh that *is* on the earth."

17 And God said to Noah, "This *is* the sign of the covenant which I have established between Me and all flesh that *is* on the earth."

18 Now the sons of Noah who went out of the ark were Shem, Ham, and Japheth. And Ham *was* the father of Canaan.

19 These three *were* the sons of Noah, and from these the whole earth was populated.

20 And Noah began *to be* a farmer, and he planted a vineyard.

21 Then he drank of the wine and was drunk, and became uncovered in his tent.

22 And Ham, the father of Canaan, saw the nakedness of his father, and told his two brothers outside.

23 But Shem and Japheth took a garment, laid *it* on both their shoulders, and went backward and covered the nakedness of their father. Their faces *were* turned away, and they did not see their father's nakedness.

24 So Noah awoke from his wine, and knew what his younger son had done to him.

25 Then he said:
"Cursed *be* Canaan;
A servant of servants
He shall be to his brethren."
26 And he said:
"Blessed *be* the LORD,
The God of Shem,
And may Canaan be his servant.
27 May God enlarge Japheth,
And may he dwell in the tents of Shem;
And may Canaan be his servant."
28 And Noah lived after the flood three hundred
and fifty years.
29 So all the days of Noah were nine hundred and
fifty years; and he died.

Gen. 9:1–29

There were marked similarities between the original creation which greeted Adam and Eve and the new creation which Noah and his family entered. But there were grave differences too. Sin had entered and while it had been judged it had not been eradicated. God's instructions to Noah show that while man's status in the divine economy had not changed, his capacity for sin was not to be overlooked. His human dignity was still recognizable, but it was vulnerable to the attacks that man in his sinfulness could make upon it.

THE PROTECTION OF HUMAN DIGNITY

God's words to Noah were intended to remind him of man's unique and dignified position. He spoke of a "special commission." *"Be fruitful and multiply, and fill the earth"* (Gen. 9:1). Despite his awful fallenness, man was still to reproduce himself and fill the earth with his kind. God's purposes still incorporated man and he was to do what only man could do. God had chosen not to eradicate man and had decided not to replace him with another order of created being. The commission to man still stood. Man was still in charge of the animal kingdom and the agent of the divine rule, but a new note had crept in. Under Adam's rule there was no suggestion of tension between man and the animal kingdom. But for Noah there would be a difference—*"And the fear of you and the dread of you shall be on every beast of the earth . . . They are given into your hand"* (v. 2). In addition man was given specific permission to eat flesh— *"Every moving thing that lives shall be food for you. I have given you all things, even as the green herbs"* (v. 3). This may have been an implicit right before the Fall but it had not been stated explicitly. The relationship between man and animal was basically the same, but the differences were real.

God also spoke about "special creation" reminding Noah, *"For in the image of God He made man"* (v. 6). There was no dilution of man's dignity at this point either, but the same note of caution was sounded. Man, made in God's image, had shown himself capable of taking man's life, and this was totally unacceptable to God. Man had to be protected from himself. *"But you shall not eat flesh with its life, that is, its blood. Surely for your lifeblood I will demand a reckoning; from the hand of every beast I will require it, and from the hand of man. From the hand of every man's brother I will require the life of man. Whoever sheds man's blood, by man his blood shall be shed"* (vv. 4–6). While these verses figure largely in debates on capital punishment it should be noted that they serve a broader purpose. They certainly have something to say about retribution but they are saying much more. If an animal killed a man, killing the animal could hardly be regarded as retribution but it was required! The eating of blood with the flesh was also regarded as unacceptable even though the taking of the life of the animal was permissible. This passage is speaking of the inestimable worth of lifeblood, whether human or animal but particularly human, because life itself is the gift of God and must not be abused.

Then God reminded Noah of the "special covenant" which He had introduced in response to the loving sacrifice at the time of disembarkation from the ark. It was described as *"the everlasting covenant between God and every living creature of all flesh that is on the earth"* (v. 16). The extent of the covenant is seen in the use of *"everlasting"* and *"all flesh,"* and the fact that it originated with God and guaranteed that there would never again be a flood like that which mankind had just experienced. In addition the introduction of an unmistakable sign in the heavens—*"I set My rainbow in the cloud, and it shall be for the sign of the covenant between Me and the earth"* (v. 13)—showed the depth of God's concern for His covenant children. For God to speak

111

in this way to mankind was yet another indication of the unique relationship which man, even in his fallenness, enjoyed not only with a Creator but also with a covenant God.

Man has always displayed an innate sense of his own worth. He resolutely insists on being treated properly and consistently speaks of his high view of himself. But man's reasons for this sense of his own dignity have not always been valid. It is only in his relationship to God through creation, commission, and covenant that man has the right to regard himself as uniquely worthy of respect. It is only in terms of deity that man finds dignity.

THE PROSTITUTION OF HUMAN DIGNITY

It is at these same three points that the prostitution of human dignity takes place. The doctrine of special creation has been widely dismissed. The concept of a divinely imparted special commission has been diluted, and to a large extent the special covenant has been ignored.

The results of these attitudes are seen in "the cheapness of human life." Despite the clear prohibition of Genesis 9:6, human history has been stained with the blood of violence's victims, and the horrors of terrorism and visions of nuclear disaster do nothing to alleviate man's nervousness. When the United Nations Organization was founded at the end of the Second World War, one of its objectives was to put an end to the strife and tension which lead to violence and bloodshed. Since that time over 20 million people have lost their lives in warfare not to mention other forms of violence.

Another evidence of the loss of human dignity is "the casualness of human relationships." God had introduced the wonderful principle of covenant and in so doing had not only shown his commitment to mankind but had also shown man how relationships based on covenant and commitment were to be normative. The breakdown in this area can readily be documented and the seeds of this breakdown can even be seen in Noah's family. When Ham, one of Noah's sons, was inadvertently confronted with Noah's shame he apparently delighted in it, shared it with his brothers, and was roundly judged for it.

Respect for parents, the sanctity of marriage, and the cohesiveness of the family unit would rapidly deteriorate producing all manner of aberrations in human sociology and psychology not to mention spirituality.

Then there was "the corruptness of moral standards." The sad story of Noah's downfall is but the preliminary to innumerable sordid stories of human disintegration. *"Noah began to be a farmer, and he planted a vineyard. Then he drank of the wine and was drunk, and became uncovered in his tent"* (vv. 20, 21). What the Bible has to say on the subject of strong drink and drunkenness should be carefully studied because the impact of alcohol on human morals and the resultant fallout in heartbreak and death is well documented. That Noah's sons, Shem and Japheth, instinctively recognized something was wrong about their father's condition is shown by their respectful action, and the blessing they received is evidence enough that there is reward for those who hold a high view of human dignity and refuse to do anything to diminish it.

THE PROMOTION OF HUMAN DIGNITY

Noah's patriarchal curse on Ham and blessing of Shem and Japheth were prophetic in that they predicted the relationships between the tribal descendants of the brothers. The subjugation of the Canaanite descendants of Ham has been used by some to justify slavery and racial discrimination, but it should be remembered that One was to come who would accept the curse of all men and even become "a servant of servants" in order that freedom from oppression and opportunity for fullness of life might be available to all people. Those who follow the Suffering Servant seek to alleviate suffering and to elevate the downtrodden to a place of dignity in His name.

There is no shortage of opportunities to promote human dignity because there is no shortage of attempts to abuse and denigrate God's creation. Anyone who has sat and counseled a battered wife knows something of the anguish caused by a man who either has no respect for his spouse as a person, whatever her failings, or has so little respect for himself that he has capitulated his life to forces which serve only to destroy whatever self-respect he may have preserved.

Many people are outraged at the incidence of pornographic materials which employ children or humiliate women. The callousness of those who seek to profit from such traffic and the condition of those who allow themselves to be aroused by such material serve only to show how deeply fallen we are and how desperately concerned we should be to see the results of human fallenness reversed in the power of Christ. Racism and bigotry continue to raise their ugly heads and in so doing plunge their victims into increasingly unacceptable positions of oppression and indignity. The commitment of many of God's people to alleviate the deprivation of the underprivileged and the suffering of the abused is the only appropriate response to an understanding of man's inhumanity to man and the need to redress it in the name of the Lord.

CHAPTER TEN

Untied Nations

Genesis 10:1–32

10:1 Now this *is* the genealogy of the sons of Noah: Shem, Ham, and Japheth. And sons were born to them after the flood.

2 The sons of Japheth *were* Gomer, Magog, Madai, Javan, Tubal, Meshech, and Tiras.

3 The sons of Gomer *were* Ashkenaz, Riphath, and Togarmah.

4 The sons of Javan *were* Elishah, Tarshish, Kittim, and Dodanim.

5 From these the coastland *peoples* of the Gentiles were separated into their lands, everyone according to his language, according to their families, into their nations.

6 The sons of Ham *were* Cush, Mizraim, Put, and Canaan.

7 The sons of Cush *were* Seba, Havilah, Sabtah, Raamah, and Sabtechah; and the sons of Raamah *were* Sheba and Dedan.

8 Cush begot Nimrod; he began to be a mighty one on the earth.

9 He was a mighty hunter before the LORD; therefore it is said, "Like Nimrod the mighty hunter before the LORD."

10 And the beginning of his kingdom was Babel, Erech, Accad, and Calneh, in the land of Shinar.

11 From that land he went to Assyria and built Nineveh, Rehoboth Ir, Calah,

12 and Resen between Nineveh and Calah (that *is* the principal city).

13 Mizraim begot Ludim, Anamim, Lehabim, Naphtuhim,

14 Pathrusim, and Casluhim (from whom came the Philistines and Caphtorim).

15 Canaan begot Sidon his firstborn, and Heth;

16 the Jebusite, the Amorite, and the Girgashite;

17 the Hivite, the Arkite, and the Sinite;

18 the Arvadite, the Zemarite, and the Hamathite. Afterward the families of the Canaanites were dispersed.

19 And the border of the Canaanites was from Sidon as you go toward Gerar, as far as Gaza; then as you go toward Sodom, Gomorrah, Admah, and Zeboiim, as far as Lasha.

20 These *were* the sons of Ham, according to their families, according to their languages, in their lands *and* in their nations.

21 And *children* were born also to Shem, the father of all the children of Eber, the brother of Japheth the elder.

22 The sons of Shem *were* Elam, Asshur, Arphaxad, Lud, and Aram.

23 The sons of Aram *were* Uz, Hul, Gether, and Mash.

24 Arphaxad begot Salah, and Salah begot Eber.

25 To Eber were born two sons: the name of one *was* Peleg, for in his days the earth was divided; and his brother's name *was* Joktan.

26 Joktan begot Almodad, Sheleph, Hazarmaveth, Jerah,

27 Hadoram, Uzal, Diklah,

28 Obal, Abimael, Sheba,

29 Ophir, Havilah, and Jobab. All these *were* the sons of Joktan.

30 And their dwelling place was from Mesha as you go toward Sephar, the mountain of the east.

31 These *were* the sons of Shem, according to their families, according to their languages, in their lands, according to their nations.

32 These *were* the families of the sons of Noah, according to their generations, in their nations; and from these the nations were divided on the earth after the flood.

Gen. 10:1–32

As we have seen, the style of Genesis is to introduce the affairs of one man and follow them through to his demise and then to introduce his sons briefly before focusing on the one through whom God would work out His unique purposes through His chosen people and the eventual Messiah. Noah passed from the scene. His sons— Shem, Ham, and Japheth—stepped into the spotlight. Shem, father of the Semitic races, took center stage after the explanation of the activities of his brother Ham's descendants which were to have profound impact on the development of the human race.

THE FORMATION OF THE NATIONS

When is a nation not a nation? When the United Nations was founded fifty nations were involved. Forty years later more than three times that number were member nations. The impression is sometimes given that a nation is a nation when it produces a flag, starts an airline, establishes a mission to the U.N., and gets an invitation to the Olympics! But clearly there is much more to nationhood than that!

The sons of Japheth developed nations with unique identities. *"The Gentiles were separated into their lands, everyone according to his language, according to their families, into their nations"* (Gen. 10:5). They had their own territorial identity, there was a social identity in their clans or families, they had a historical identity which was carefully recorded in their genealogies, and they had distinctive cultural identity in their unique languages.

Nimrod, descendant of Ham, *"a mighty one on the earth . . . a mighty hunter before the Lord"* (vv. 8, 9), whose prowess was recognized by his contemporaries and whose exploits in building, developing, and expanding remind one of a modern-day entrepreneur, was also a prominent force in the division of the human race into its national groupings.

This chapter is a veritable gold mine of information for those who are interested in the geography of the ancient world and the ethnic divisions and dispersions of the ancient people. It should also be noted that the genealogies recorded are not intended to be complete and that the events of this chapter happened after the events recorded in Genesis 11:1–9.

THE FRUSTRATIONS OF THE NATIONS

Nimrod among other magnificent achievements had founded Babel. The people who gathered there all spoke the same language, and they set about the task of building the city despite the fact that their building resources were pitifully inadequate. *"They had brick for stone, and they had asphalt for mortar"* (Gen. 11:3). Their decision to build a *"tower whose top is in the heavens"* is therefore even more surprising but apparently their reasoning had been affected by their stated objective to *"make a name for ourselves"* (v. 4). Some people see this as the first organized attempt at humanistic society which would be convinced of its own ability to survive under its own steam and to promote its own interests and protect itself from all ills.

But God, Who had shown His interest and involvement in the affairs of Adam and Noah, not to mention many others, was not unaware of what was going on in Babel. *"The Lord came down to see the city and the tower which the sons of men had built"* (v. 5). Self-sufficiency and independence of God were again raising their heads and once again the Lord stepped in saying, *"Come, let Us go down and there confuse their language, that they may not understand one another's speech"* (v. 7). The result of this action was the dispersion of the people, the rejection by God of man's attempt to find security in man independent of God, and a divine rebuff to man's attempts to reach heaven and bring God down rather than to humbly look for God to take the initiative and reach down to His erring children.

There is an interesting pun on the name Babel. In its original form it can mean *"gate of God,"* but it can also mean *"confusion"* (see Gen. 11:9). It may be permissible to see something of the pun at work in modern attempts by man to reach into the heavens of his own accord, to unite to solve the world's problems on the basis of human ingenuity, and his untiring efforts to make a name for himself, only to meet frustration and confusion. Even the Secretary General of the United Nations, which perhaps epitomizes man's modern efforts and designs, stated in his 1984 report that the organization's *"majestic vision"* had been clouded, that it had been impossible *"to take any peace-keeping action at all"* in some situations, and he admitted that many people are concluding that something is *"wrong with the United Nations and with the concept of internationalism."*

The divine decision to *"confuse their language"* (v. 7) which on the surface appears somewhat innocuous has had profound and far-reaching consequences. Language is sometimes defined as "a system of arbitrary vocal symbols by means of which a social group cooperates." English-speaking peoples have decided that "mist" means something akin to "fog, vapor, etc.," but Germans have determined that "mist" means "dung or manure." It is not necessary to point out the possibilities for confusion! Neither is it hard to see why there is so much estrangement and tension in our world when we remember that many people know only one language, have little knowledge of other cultures, and are therefore ill-equipped to "cooperate" with other peoples.

THE FUTURE OF THE NATIONS

Jesus predicted that "nation will rise against nation, and kingdom against kingdom" (Matt. 24:7) echoing the thoughts of the psalmist who asked, "Why do the nations rage?" (Ps. 2:1). But the events of Pentecost project a reversal of the disintegration of national relations through Christ, reminding us that the gospel of the kingdom will be preached in all nations (see Matt. 24:14) and that eventually representatives of every nation will gather around the throne of heaven (see Rev. 5:9). Men's efforts at united nations may be more like untied nations. But eventually the Father will keep His promise and give the Son "the nations for (His) inheritance" (Ps. 2:8).

CHAPTER ELEVEN

God and Abram

Genesis 11:1–32

11:1 Now the whole earth had one language and one speech.

2 And it came to pass, as they journeyed from the east, that they found a plain in the land of Shinar, and they dwelt there.

3 Then they said to one another, "Come, let us make bricks and bake *them* thoroughly." They had brick for stone, and they had asphalt for mortar.

4 And they said, "Come, let us build ourselves a city, and a tower whose top *is* in the heavens; let us make a name for ourselves, lest we be scattered abroad over the face of the whole earth."

5 But the LORD came down to see the city and the tower which the sons of men had built.

6 And the LORD said, "Indeed the people *are* one and they all have one language, and this is what they begin to do; now nothing that they propose to do will be withheld from them.

7 "Come, let Us go down and there confuse their language, that they may not understand one another's speech."

8 So the LORD scattered them abroad from there over the face of all the earth, and they ceased building the city.

9 Therefore its name is called Babel, because there the LORD confused the language of all the earth; and from there the LORD scattered them abroad over the face of all the earth.

10 This *is* the genealogy of Shem: Shem *was* one hundred years old, and begot Arphaxad two years after the flood.

11 After he begot Arphaxad, Shem lived five hundred years, and begot sons and daughters.

12 Arphaxad lived thirty-five years, and begot Salah.

13 After he begot Salah, Arphaxad lived four hundred and three years, and begot sons and daughters.

14 Salah lived thirty years, and begot Eber.

15 After he begot Eber, Salah lived four hundred and three years, and begot sons and daughters.

16 Eber lived thirty-four years, and begot Peleg.

17 After he begot Peleg, Eber lived four hundred and thirty years, and begot sons and daughters.

18 Peleg lived thirty years, and begot Reu.

19 After he begot Reu, Peleg lived two hundred and nine years, and begot sons and daughters.

20 Reu lived thirty-two years, and begot Serug.

21 After he begot Serug, Reu lived two hundred and seven years, and begot sons and daughters.

22 Serug lived thirty years, and begot Nahor.

23 After he begot Nahor, Serug lived two hundred years, and begot sons and daughters.

24 Nahor lived twenty-nine years, and begot Terah.

25 After he begot Terah, Nahor lived one hundred and nineteen years, and begot sons and daughters.

26 Now Terah lived seventy years, and begot Abram, Nahor, and Haran.

27 This *is* the genealogy of Terah: Terah begot Abram, Nahor, and Haran. Haran begot Lot.

28 And Haran died before his father Terah in his native land, in Ur of the Chaldeans.

29 Then Abram and Nahor took wives: the name of Abram's wife *was* Sarai, and the name of Nahor's wife, Milcah, the daughter of Haran the father of Milcah and the father of Iscah.

30 But Sarai was barren; she had no child.

31 And Terah took his son Abram and his grandson Lot, the son of Haran, and his daughter-in-law Sarai, his son Abram's wife, and they went out with them from Ur of the Chaldeans to go to the land of Canaan; and they came to Haran and dwelt there.

32 So the days of Terah were two hundred and five years, and Terah died in Haran.

Gen. 11:1–32

We have now arrived at the conclusion of primeval history and the beginning of patriarchal history. Abram, a man revered by no less than three of the world's major religions—Judaism, Islam, and Christianity—now steps into the limelight. As is customary in Genesis there is a detailed, but incomplete, genealogy showing the thread of God's working toward the resolution of His plan for mankind. Abram's wife, Sarai, his father, Terah, and his nephew Lot are all introduced and will figure in the story. The crucial statement is that all these people, *"went out with them from Ur of the Chaldeans to go to the land of Canaan"* (Gen. 11:31). Why they left and what they left need to be understood.

THE CALL

The reason for this move is given simply as, "Now the Lord had said to Abram: 'Get out from your country'" (Gen. 12:1). It is not clear how the call came to Terah and Abram, or at what specific point in time they were told the details of God's requirements. But we know they were called and we know they went! As the details of the call become more clear we note that God called Abram, the son, rather than Terah, the father. God determined that His purposes would be fulfilled through Sarai who was barren rather than Milcah who was not. Those who struggle with God's calling of certain people to do certain things should remember that ultimately everything is dependent on God's sovereign initiative. He chose creation over chaos. He decided to make men, not machines. It was His decision to establish a system of divine-human partnership rather than divine dictatorship. Sometimes we feel that we can understand His choice, while other times it is not so obvious. Terah may have been passed over because he apparently did not have his son's persistence in that he never arrived in Canaan, choosing rather to spend sixty years in Haran until his death. Milcah certainly would not have had the problems Sarai experienced in having a son, but neither would God's power have been displayed so dramatically as it was in the birth of Isaac.

Ur was a well-developed city with approximately 250,000 inhabitants when Abram lived there. Their houses, which were built around pleasant courtyards, had two or three stories. Educationally the people were well advanced—they understood mathematics to the extent they could calculate square and cube roots and figure out geometric problems. Unlike many modern students they could do all this without calculators! The famous ziggurat was a monolithic structure which incorporated much of the amazing architectural sophistication of the better known, but much later, Parthenon in Athens, and the thousands of clay tablets which have been unearthed give fascinating details of the well-developed cultural, business, and legal aspects of life in Ur. We know that Terah, Abram's father, "served other gods" (Josh. 24:2), and the moon god, Nanna, for whom the ziggurat was built, was the main deity. The new moon was believed to be the crescent-shaped boat in which Nanna sailed through the heavens. Royal tombs in the city have shown that it was customary for large numbers of courtiers to be buried with their king along with all manner of musical instruments and jewelry which were designed to enhance life in the hereafter. The people had religion, but it was far removed from that which Jehovah would reveal to his chosen vessel, Abram.

THE CHOICE

The call of God invariably leaves the recipient with the necessity of choice. Abram's choice was between Ur and its refinements and Canaan with its much more primitive culture. It was a choice between an invisible God and one who graciously appeared on a monthly basis in splendid procession through the heavens, and it was a choice between the familiar and that which was unknown.

But behind these factors were two fundamental choices. To obey or to disobey; to trust or to distrust.

THE CONCLUSION

In matters of faith and obedience nothing has changed since Abram's day. God still uses people. He still calls individuals. He still expects reverential trust and filial obedience. And He still unfolds His plans for His people in ways which leave them "lost in wonder, love, and praise."

CHAPTER TWELVE

Faith

Genesis 12:1–20

12:1 Now the LORD had said to Abram:
"Get out of your country,
From your family
And from your father's house,
To a land that I will show you.
2 I will make you a great nation;
I will bless you
And make your name great;
And you shall be a blessing.
3 I will bless those who bless you,
And I will curse him who curses you;
And in you all the families of the earth shall be
blessed."

4 So Abram departed as the LORD had spoken to him, and Lot went with him. And Abram *was* seventy-five years old when he departed from Haran.

5 Then Abram took Sarai his wife and Lot his brother's son, and all their possessions that they had gathered, and the people whom they had acquired in Haran, and they departed to go to the land of Canaan. So they came to the land of Canaan.

6 Abram passed through the land to the place of Shechem, as far as the terebinth tree of Moreh. And the Canaanites *were* then in the land.

7 Then the LORD appeared to Abram and said, "To your descendants I will give this land." And there he built an altar to the LORD, who had appeared to him.

8 And he moved from there to the mountain east of Bethel, and he pitched his tent *with* Bethel on the

west and Ai on the east; there he built an altar to
the LORD and called on the name of the LORD.

9 So Abram journeyed, going on still toward the
South.

10 Now there was a famine in the land, and Abram
went down to Egypt to dwell there, for the famine
was severe in the land.

11 And it came to pass, when he was close to entering Egypt, that he said to Sarai his wife, "Indeed
I know that you *are* a woman of beautiful countenance.

12 "Therefore it will happen, when the Egyptians
see you, that they will say, 'This *is* his wife'; and they
will kill me, but they will let you live.

13 "Please say you *are* my sister, that it may be
well with me for your sake, and that I may live because of you."

14 So it was, when Abram came into Egypt, that
the Egyptians saw the woman, that she *was* very
beautiful.

15 The princes of Pharaoh also saw her and com-
mended her to Pharaoh. And the woman was taken
to Pharaoh's house.

16 He treated Abram well for her sake. He had
sheep, oxen, male donkeys, male and female servants,
female donkeys, and camels.

17 But the LORD plagued Pharaoh and his house
with great plagues because of Sarai, Abram's wife.

18 And Pharaoh called Abram and said, "What *is*
this you have done to me? Why did you not tell me
that she *was* your wife?

19 "Why did you say, 'She *is* my sister'? I might
have taken her as my wife. Now therefore, here is
your wife; take *her* and go your way."

20 So Pharaoh commanded *his* men concerning
him; and they sent him away, with his wife and all
that he had.

Gen. 12:1–20

Abram is not only one of the great Old Testament figures but also
one whose shadow is cast over the whole of the New Testament.
Many aspects of his character and his relationship to God warrant
our study, but Scripture places special emphasis on his faith life.

THE EXPERIENCE OF FAITH

The basis of his faith was "revelation." While Abram was still living in Ur, the Lord had spoken to him (*"the Lord had said to Abram . . ."*), and many years later when Abram arrived *"as far as the terebinth tree of Moreh . . . then the Lord appeared"* (vv. 6, 7). We also note that Abram moved as he did because *"the Lord had spoken to him"* (v. 4). Abram was under no illusions as to what he should do.

> *Get out of your country,*
> *From your family*
> *And from your father's house,*
> *To a land that I will show you* (v. 1).

How this striking piece of revealed information was conveyed to Abram we do not know but there is no gainsaying the resultant life-changing decision to trust and obey. The revelation was compelling and dramatic not only because of God's requirements of Abram but also because of God's promises to Abram.

> *I will make you a great nation;*
> *I will bless you*
> *And make your name great;*
> *And you shall be a blessing.*
> *I will bless those who bless you,*
> *And I will curse him who curses you;*
> *And in you all the families of the earth shall be*
>   *blessed* (vv. 2, 3).

It is hardly necessary to point out the force of the repeated "I wills" of this passage because they introduce promises of eternal consequence, worldwide scope, and monumental import. The man who was to become a great nation could not at that time be the father of one child. But God had promised! In marked contrast to a world that had come to ruin because it insisted on making a name for itself independently of God, this obscure man's name was to become *"great"* because God was promising to bring it to pass. To a man embarking on a perilous journey that involved famine and threats on his life God promised unique support and encouragement even to the extent of accepting full responsibility for Abram's well-being. And now the God who had promised to bruise the serpent through the seed of Eve, sharpened the focus on His revelation and showed that it would be through Abram that blessing would come to the whole world. This revelation on God's part necessitated "recognition" on Abram's part. In some way that is not described to us in the Scripture Abram arrived at the necessary conclusion "that what He had promised He was also able to perform" (Rom. 4:21). On that basis he moved in faith.

There is always a danger of looking at such men and divorcing what they did from what God may be asking His children to do today. This kind of recognition of revelation is all too often regarded as the peculiar reserve of intrepid missionaries who take steps of faith into the great unknown. But all God's children are expected to walk by faith.

"So Abram departed . . . and [he] was seventy-five years old when he departed from Haran" (Gen. 12:4). In the highly mobile society in which we live today, people move because they prefer the climate, or they have a chance of promotion, or they feel a change of environment may solve some of their problems. Without suggesting that these may not be valid reasons for moving on, it may be healthy for us to consider whether we have ever made a move in faith based on what God has been saying to us about His eternal purposes and the role He expects us to play in their fulfillment.

THE EXTREMITIES OF FAITH

Abram's faith was promptly tested. Quite apart from the cost of leaving home and country Abram soon confronted "the Canaanites [who] were then in the land" (v. 6). The Canaanites were to become a thorn in the side of God's people for many years to come, and their religious practices would be one of the great temptations to which God's people would succumb all too often. We know little about the attitudes of the Canaanites at the time when Abram met them, but they apparently would not be too enthusiastic about this new man on the block who seemed to think that he had a special corner on the property they were occupying. Modern history makes it easy to visualize the situation when we remember that ancient Shechem is now modern Nablus, on the disputed West Bank, the scene of much present-day tension between the Palestinians and the Israelis.

Abram was greeted by inhospitable living conditions when he began to traverse the land because *"there was a famine in the land, and Abram went down to Egypt to dwell there, for the famine was severe in the land"* (v. 10). It would be expecting too much of this man if we did not allow him to have some misgivings about what he had done in bringing his family into such invidious circumstances.

He was also very nervous about his own well-being because he had a beautiful wife and felt that his neighbors might be all too happy to dispose of him to get at her! So to his lasting discredit he told her, *"Please say you are my sister, that it may be well with me for your sake, and that I may live because of you"* (v. 13). In all fairness to Abram we should point out that his suspicions about the Egyptian roving eyes were well founded. We should also note that technically Sarai was his sister, or more accurately his half-sister. Abram showed himself to be not only an expert at the half truth, but also a vulnerable man who, like many others before and since, suffered from periodic failures of nerve. Both men and women have been intrigued that Sarai at the age of sixty-five was such a beauty! We have no definite answers to the question but it is unlikely that she had some special Middle Eastern cosmetic secret called "Oil of Delay"!

God intervened, perhaps because He saw the possibility of Abram losing his vision of God's purposes, and the unfortunate Pharaoh was subjected to *"great plagues"* (v. 17) which he astutely attributed to Abram and Sarai, and he promptly had them deported. The purposes of God were intact even though the reputation of Abram was decidedly tattered.

It should also be noted that Abram, by this time, was becoming prosperous and may have been discovering what every generation of man has had to struggle to relearn: *"the love of money is a root of all kinds of evil"* (1 Tim. 6:10).

Abram's faith was being tested at its extremities. His love life, his family life, his business life, his physical life were all being subjected to pressure, but he learned that even though his faith was at times shaky, his God was at all times steadfast.

THE EXPRESSIONS OF FAITH

When Abram stood under the oak tree at Moreh and heard God say, *"To your descendants I will give this land,"* he promptly, *"built an altar to the Lord"* (Gen. 12:7). Then he moved on to Bethel and *"there he built an altar to the Lord and called on the name of the Lord"* (v. 8). His propensity for building altars should be noted as it contrasts with his own preference for living in a tent. While his lifestyle was nomadic he was intent on making permanent statements to all who would be interested enough to inquire that he worshiped the God of Heaven Who had made a covenant of grace with him. He also called on the name of the Lord. The people of Babel wanted to make a name for themselves and God promised to make Abram's name great. But what really counted with Abram was the name of the Lord. Publicly and joyfully extolling His worth and stating his dependence upon His strong name were natural expressions of faith.

When I was preaching through Genesis a man told me that he had become excited about being involved in church after many years' absence. When I asked what had made the difference he said, "I love Genesis!" I was surprised and asked, "What do you like about it?" and he replied, "I like the stories about all those guys like Abram and Jacob because they're all worse than me and it makes me feel so good!" I agreed with him that Abram was not perfect but he was a man of faith, and that we should not gloat over his failures but learn from his mistakes and emulate his strong dependence on the faithful God. You'll be glad to know that my friend eventually came to call on Abram's God.

CHAPTER THIRTEEN

Facing Up to Reality

Genesis 13:1–18

13:1 Then Abram went up from Egypt, he and his wife and all that he had, and Lot with him, to the South.

2 Abram *was* very rich in livestock, in silver, and in gold.

3 And he went on his journey from the South as far as Bethel, to the place where his tent had been at the beginning, between Bethel and Ai,

4 to the place of the altar which he had made there at first. And there Abram called on the name of the LORD.

5 Lot also, who went with Abram, had flocks and herds and tents.

6 Now the land was not able to support them, that they might dwell together, for their possessions were so great that they could not dwell together.

7 And there was strife between the herdsmen of Abram's livestock and the herdsmen of Lot's livestock. The Canaanites and the Perizzites then dwelt in the land.

8 So Abram said to Lot, "Please let there be no strife between you and me, and between my herdsmen and your herdsmen; for we *are* brethren.

9 "*Is* not the whole land before you? Please separate from me. If *you take* the left, then I will go to the right; or, if *you go* to the right, then I will go to the left."

10 And Lot lifted his eyes and saw all the plain of Jordan, that it *was* well watered everywhere (before the LORD destroyed Sodom and Gomorrah) like the

garden of the LORD, like the land of Egypt as you go toward Zoar.

11 Then Lot chose for himself all the plain of Jordan, and Lot journeyed east. And they separated from each other.

12 Abram dwelt in the land of Canaan, and Lot dwelt in the cities of the plain and pitched *his* tent even as far as Sodom.

13 But the men of Sodom *were* exceedingly wicked and sinful against the LORD.

14 And the LORD said to Abram, after Lot had separated from him: "Lift your eyes now and look from the place where you are—northward, southward, eastward, and westward;

15 "for all the land which you see I give to you and your descendants forever.

16 "And I will make your descendants as the dust of the earth; so that if a man could number the dust of the earth, *then* your descendants also could be numbered.

17 "Arise, walk in the land through its length and its width, for I give it to you."

18 Then Abram moved *his* tent, and went and dwelt by the terebinth trees of Mamre, which *are* in Hebron, and built an altar there to the LORD.

Gen. 13:1–18

Abram was a man of faith. That does not mean he was a man who lived in a fantasy world. He was very much in touch with reality, as are all men and women of faith, despite the popular misconceptions of some people. When faith fails, men and women of faith face up to that reality and act accordingly.

FACING UP TO FAILURE

Abram's actions in Egypt which led to his deportation and humiliation had to be faced. He *"was very rich in livestock, in silver, and in gold"* (Gen. 13:2), and presumably therefore he was a success in the eyes of many. But he had to evaluate his life on spiritual principles rather than on purely secular considerations. So it is good to notice that he traveled from Egypt, through the Negev, to *"Bethel, to the place where his tent had been at the beginning, between Bethel and Ai, to the place of the altar which he had made there at first"* (vv. 3, 4). Once failure has been recognized it needs to be rectified and the best way to do that is to return to basics, review the situation, and renew any commitments which may have been compromised. So *"Abram called on the name of the Lord"* (v. 4). He was refreshed in spirit as he remembered how the Lord had called him in Ur, shown him the land, and promised one day it would be his. But even though the failure of Egypt had been addressed there were still other problems to face and other tests to survive.

FACING UP TO FRICTION

Abram now had to confront the unpalatable fact that the land of promise did not appear to be living up to its promise. *"Lot also, who went with Abram, had flocks and herds and tents. Now the land was not able to support them, that they might dwell together, for their possessions were so great that they could not dwell together"* (vv. 5, 6). God had prospered him and had promised him the land, but the problem he now had to deal with was that what God appeared to be doing did not fit what God appeared to be providing. This was another test of faith which was made more severe by the *"strife between the herdsmen of Abram's livestock and the herdsmen of Lot's livestock"* (v. 7). One obvious solution would have been for them to decide that they had made a genuine mistake and to move on to greener pastures. But Abram could not do that because he believed that God was behind his move into this piece of real estate, and so other solutions had to be found. Perhaps he was tempted to think that the problems would go away if they were left alone! But Abram said to Lot, *"Please let there be no strife between you and me . . . for we are brethren"* (v. 8).

When strife comes along something needs to be done, and Abram showed what and how. He took the initiative, directly addressed the issue, appealed to what they had in common, and stated clearly his desire for resolution. It is doubtful if all those things, admirable as they were, would have achieved a solution, but Abram did not leave things there. *"Is not the whole land before you? Please separate from me. If you take the left, then I will go to the right; or if you go to the right, then I will go to the left"* (v. 9). Abram, the senior member of the party, the one to whom the promise had been made, the one who received the call to leave Ur and proceed to the place of God's appointing, could have told his younger relative either to shape up or ship out! He refrained from such an action, and humbly made a concession which he trusted would resolve the issue. Abram has much to teach us!

You've heard the expression, "Where there's a will there's a way," but have you ever been to a family gathering after a funeral and wondered if it would not be better to say, "Where there's a will there's a problem"? Wherever people live in close proximity to each other there will inevitably be friction whether it is in the family, the business, or the church.

Unfortunately our skills at handling friction do not always match up to our skills in creating problems. Because of this there is a tendency to leave tensions unresolved, and this often means that they get worse. Some people deny that there is anything wrong and settle for a repressed anger which bodes ill for their future. Others admit only too freely that something is wrong, but they admit it to the wrong people, thereby compounding the problem. Their aim is directed more to seeking approval of their own behavior from a supportive person rather than a desire to rectify a bad situation with an offended or offensive person. There has to be the right kind of confrontation if there is to be harmony. One thing I have learned from many years in the ministry is that before you can adequately confront you must earn the right to do so by proving to the confrontee that you genuinely have his or her interest at heart. Without this there is probably little that you can achieve except to make matters worse. There must also be a willingness to back down yourself because confrontations that make one person a winner by manufacturing a loser out of the other person rarely achieve the desired result.

FACING UP TO FACTS

Men and women of faith should never be afraid of facing facts! It would have been difficult for Abram to avoid some of the more obvious ones. He had to come to terms with the fact that some situations will not work out. From a purely practical point of view there was no way that Abram and Lot, with all their resources, could live in the same area. The land just could not handle both of them, and no amount of spiritualizing or wishful thinking would change that fact.

Another unpleasant fact is that some people will disappoint you. Abram had invested a lot of time in Lot and had given him a great chance to improve his lot. You could say Lot's lot had improved a whole lot! But there is no evidence that Lot reciprocated Abram's generosity or even protested that Abram was the one who had the right to choose first and that he, Lot, would take what was left. But Lot looked long and hard at what was offered, *"saw all the plain of Jordan, that it was well watered everywhere . . . like the garden of the Lord"* (v. 10), and chose what he figured was to his own best advantage, even though we read somewhat ominously that the region he chose was populated by men who were *"exceedingly wicked and sinful against the Lord"* (v. 13).

But through it all Abram remembered the most important fact— that God's call was irrevocable, that God's purposes do not change, and that the Lord was totally committed to completing what He had started in Abram's life. Abram faced up to this, and in characteristic fashion, *"moved his tent . . . and built an altar"* (v. 18). His faith was intact and though he was a little sadder he was undoubtedly a whole lot wiser. Reality is not always pleasant but it is always present. Reality is not an enemy of faith but it can be a great opportunity for faith to show its true colors.

CHAPTER FOURTEEN

Getting Involved

Genesis 14:1–24

14:1 And it came to pass in the days of Amraphel king of Shinar, Arioch king of Ellasar, Chedorlaomer king of Elam, and Tidal king of nations,

2 *that* they made war with Bera king of Sodom, Birsha king of Gomorrah, Shinab king of Admah, Shemeber king of Zeboiim, and the king of Bela (that is, Zoar).

3 All these joined together in the Valley of Siddim (that is, the Salt Sea).

4 Twelve years they served Chedorlaomer, and in the thirteenth year they rebelled.

5 In the fourteenth year Chedorlaomer and the kings that *were* with him came and attacked the Rephaim in Ashteroth Karnaim, the Zuzim in Ham, the Emim in Shaveh Kiriathaim,

6 and the Horites in their mountain of Seir, as far as El Paran, which *is* by the wilderness.

7 Then they turned back and came to En Mishpat (that *is,* Kadesh), and attacked all the country of the Amalekites, and also the Amorites who dwelt in Hazezon Tamar.

8 And the king of Sodom, the king of Gomorrah, the king of Admah, the king of Zeboiim, and the king of Bela (that *is,* Zoar) went out and joined together in battle in the Valley of Siddim

9 against Chedorlaomer king of Elam, Tidal king of nations, Amraphel king of Shinar, and Arioch king of Ellasar—four kings against five.

10 Now the Valley of Siddim *was full of* asphalt pits; and the kings of Sodom and Gomorrah fled;

some fell there, and the remainder fled to the mountains.

11 Then they took all the goods of Sodom and Gomorrah, and all their provisions, and went their way.

12 They also took Lot, Abram's brother's son who dwelt in Sodom, and his goods, and departed.

13 Then one who had escaped came and told Abram the Hebrew, for he dwelt by the terebinth trees of Mamre the Amorite, brother of Eshcol and brother of Aner; and they *were* allies with Abram.

14 Now when Abram heard that his brother was taken captive, he armed his three hundred and eighteen trained *servants* who were born in his own house, and went in pursuit as far as Dan.

15 He divided his forces against them by night, and he and his servants attacked them and pursued them as far as Hobah, which *is* north of Damascus.

16 So he brought back all the goods, and also brought back his brother Lot and his goods, as well as the women and the people.

17 And the king of Sodom went out to meet him at the Valley of Shaveh (that *is*, the King's Valley), after his return from the defeat of Chedorlaomer and the kings who *were* with him.

18 Then Melchizedek king of Salem brought out bread and wine; he *was* the priest of God Most High.

19 And he blessed him and said:
"Blessed be Abram of God Most High,
Possessor of heaven and earth;

20 And blessed be God Most High,
Who has delivered your enemies into your
hand."
And he gave him a tithe of all.

21 Now the king of Sodom said to Abram, "Give me the persons, and take the goods for yourself."

22 But Abram said to the king of Sodom, "I have raised my hand to the LORD, God Most High, the Possessor of heaven and earth,

23 "that I *will take* nothing, from a thread to a sandal strap, and that I will not take anything that *is* yours, lest you should say, 'I have made Abram rich'—

24 "except only what the young men have eaten,
and the portion of the men who went with me: Aner,
Eshcol, and Mamre; let them take their portion."

Gen. 14:1–24

Perhaps Abram breathed a sigh of relief when his nephew Lot took his flocks and herds and headed down to the plains although he may well have had reservations about the region he was entering. On the other hand Lot probably was well satisfied with the deal he had made with Abram. But his triumph was not to last long because the political instability of the area boiled over into a nasty little war.

There was nothing unusual about this because the political structure of the area invited turmoil. There were many small cities ruled by kings whose resources were limited which meant that stronger kings periodically overthrew the weaker and lumped them together in confederacies which subsequently rebelled. Depending on the seriousness of the uprising the larger king might need to call in his allies to help bring his vassal states to heel, and so the seemingly endless turmoil went on. But when God determined to give the land to Abram, He was not arbitrarily robbing Peter to pay Paul. He was giving the stricken area a chance to operate on a new basis of peace and harmony. This, of course, is what He always offers the human race, but if history teaches us anything it teaches us that man is not too quick to learn that God's rule brings peace whereas man's genius not infrequently creates trouble and strife.

The kings of Sodom and Gomorrah and three other neighboring cities were dominated for twelve years by Chedorlaomer, the king of Elam. They decided that twelve years was quite enough and in the thirteenth year rebelled only to have Chedorlaomer and his allies take the opportunity to attack them and to extend their dominions into the surrounding areas. A battle was fought in *"the Valley of Siddim (that is, the Salt Sea)"* (Gen. 14:3) with the result that *"the kings of Sodom and Gomorrah fled; some fell there, and the remainder fled to the mountains"* (v. 10). Along with the booty they took from the defeated cities they *"also took Lot, Abram's brother's son who dwelt in Sodom, and his goods, and departed"* (v. 12). The fall of the cities and particularly the plight of Lot presented Abram with yet another challenge.

137

ABRAM'S INVOLVEMENT WITH SODOM

The people of Sodom, where Lot had chosen to live, were characterized by spiritual depravity and moral degeneration before this disaster, but now they had become socially deprived of freedom and property not to mention justice and in some cases even life itself. The options of response presented to Abram are the same options with which God's people have always been confronted—isolation, identification, or involvement. It would have been easy to rationalize an isolationist position. The people were corrupt; they deserved judgment. They had rebelled, so they deserved punishment. Anyway it was none of Abram's business, and as far as Lot was concerned he had made his bed and now he could lie in it. Furthermore, if Abram went to the aid of these dreadful people his own reputation might suffer. The problem with this position, however, was that blatant injustice would not be countered, suffering would not be alleviated, and Abram's own flesh and blood would be permanently estranged from him. Isolation was out of the question. Identification was equally out of the question. There was no way that Abram could even consider accepting the philosophy of Sodom, adopting its lifestyle, and becoming a part of its structures. He had made one major move from Ur to identify with the living God, and he was not about to take a giant step backward into a similar situation.

So that left involvement which stopped short of identification. He was struggling with the problem with which God's people have always struggled: How to be in the world but not of it. To be neither in it nor of it is the stuff of which many religious systems have been made. To be in it and of it is the stuff of which many a testimony to the unique power of God has been lost. Abram acted promptly. Calling together his allies and mobilizing his own resources, he marched after the triumphant Chedorlaomer, the crestfallen Lot, and the other captives. Using sound military strategy, *"he and his servants attacked them and pursued them as far as Hobah, which is north of Damascus"* (v. 15). That this was no minor achievement can be seen from the distances covered, the scope of the defeat, and the obvious delight with which Abram was greeted on his return by the kings of Sodom, Salem, and other cities. The king of Sodom showed his appreciation by making Abram an offer, *"Give me the persons, and take the goods for yourself"* (v. 21). But Abram promptly showed that he had a different way of operating and said, in effect, that he had promised the Lord he would not touch anything that belonged to the king of Sodom so that he would never be able to say, *"I have made Abram rich"* (v. 23). That honor belonged, as Abram well knew, to God alone. In case we are tempted to think that Abram was being a little impractical we should note that he made an exception for those who had helped him in the expedition stating, *"except only what the young men have eaten, and the portion of the men who went with me"* (v. 24). There is much to learn from Abram's handling of involvement with the Sodoms of this world.

ABRAM'S INVOLVEMENT WITH SALEM

If Abram treated the king of Sodom with a marked degree of circumspection, he had no reservations about Melchizedek, the king of Salem. The meaning of Salem is "peace," and it is ironic that this city, which we know as Jerusalem, should have had such a long and bitter history of warfare and bloodshed. But on this occasion Melchizedek was rejoicing in the cessation of hostility and wished to share in the joy of the victor. He *"brought out bread and wine; he was the priest of God Most High. And he blessed him and said: / Blessed be Abram of God Most High, / Possessor of heaven and earth; / And blessed be God Most High, / Who has delivered your enemies into your hand. / And he gave him a tithe of all"* (vv. 18–20). Abram gladly received this gracious gift of food for himself and his hungry soldiers. The king who was also a priest then blessed Abram in the name of El Elyon. It is important to note that in a time when religious knowledge had been corrupted, as we saw was the case in Ur, the people of Salem had a clear understanding of the *"possessor of heaven and earth"* Whom they knew as El Elyon—*God Most High.* Abram warmly received the blessing as is evidenced by his reference to his Lord as El Elyon (see Gen. 14:22) and by the fact that he gave a tithe to the kingly priest as an expression of gratitude both to God and His servant. It is important to note that tithing is not something that appeared on the scene in the law of Moses but was commonly practiced long before Moses was born. It is difficult, therefore, to understand where some modern Christians have gotten the idea that tithing is "legalistic." Although Melchizedek, whose name means "King of righteousness," makes such a brief appearance on the biblical stage it is impossible to overlook his importance, not only because of the relationship he had with Abram, but more significantly because of the way both David (see Ps. 110:4) and the writer of the Epistle to the Hebrews view him as a type of Christ—the kingly priest (see Heb. 7).

Abram showed by his relations to the two kings how God's people need to tread carefully in the matter of involvements. Isolation protected by insulation which some people confuse with sanctification is not the answer. Identification which leaves no room for differentiation serves only to confuse. Involvement without compromise is not easy, but it is necessary and Abram shows us how it is done.

CHAPTER FIFTEEN

The Promises of God

Genesis 15:1–21

15:1 After these things the word of the LORD came to Abram in a vision, saying, "Do not be afraid, Abram. I *am* your shield, your exceedingly great reward."

2 But Abram said, "LORD GOD, what will You give me, seeing I go childless, and the heir of my house *is* Eliezer of Damascus?"

3 Then Abram said, "Look, You have given me no offspring; indeed one born in my house is my heir!"

4 And behold, the word of the LORD *came* to him, saying, "This one shall not be your heir, but one who will come from your own body shall be your heir."

5 Then He brought him outside and said, "Look now toward heaven, and count the stars if you are able to number them." And He said to him, "So shall your descendants be."

6 And he believed in the LORD, and He accounted it to him for righteousness.

7 Then He said to him, "I *am* the LORD, who brought you out of Ur of the Chaldeans, to give you this land to inherit it."

8 And he said, "LORD GOD, how shall I know that I will inherit it?"

9 So He said to him, "Bring Me a three-year-old heifer, a three-year-old female goat, a three-year-old ram, a turtledove, and a young pigeon."

10 Then he brought all these to Him and cut them in two, down the middle, and placed each piece opposite the other; but he did not cut the birds in two.

11 And when the vultures came down on the carcasses, Abram drove them away.

12 Now when the sun was going down, a deep sleep fell upon Abram; and behold, horror *and* great darkness fell upon him.

13 Then He said to Abram: "Know certainly that your descendants will be strangers in a land *that is* not theirs, and will serve them, and they will afflict them four hundred years.

14 "And also the nation whom they serve I will judge; afterward they shall come out with great possessions.

15 "Now as for you, you shall go to your fathers in peace; you shall be buried at a good old age.

16 "But in the fourth generation they shall return here, for the iniquity of the Amorites *is* not yet complete."

17 And it came to pass, when the sun went down and it was dark, that behold, there appeared a smoking oven and a burning torch that passed between those pieces.

18 On the same day the LORD made a covenant with Abram, saying:

"To your descendants I have given this land, from the river of Egypt to the great river, the River Euphrates—

19 "the Kenites, the Kenezzites, the Kadmonites,

20 "the Hittites, the Perizzites, the Rephaim,

21 "the Amorites, the Canaanites, the Girgashites, and the Jebusites."

Gen. 15:1–21

Even though Abram enjoyed a special relationship with God he was not exempt from the circumstances of life and he was not immune to the reactions common to man. Apparently he was so thoroughly upset by the events which led to his military expedition on behalf of his nephew, Lot, that the Lord found it necessary to remind him of some of the great promises upon which their relationship was built. He told His nervous servant, *"Do not be afraid, Abram. I am your shield, your exceedingly great reward"* (Gen. 15:1).

THE PROMISES OF GOD BANISH FEAR

The promise to Abram that He would be His shield was particularly appropriate in that it came *"after these things"* (v. 1), that is, immediately after Abram had shown that he had no desire for alliances with the king of Sodom or his kind. Abram was being asked to believe that having the Lord acting as his shield was a much better proposition than relying on the support and strength of the kings of the region. There is good reason to translate the latter part of the Lord's statement, "your reward shall be very great," in which case Abram was also being asked to believe that his faith would ultimately be vindicated. Abram did not respond with a passive acceptance of the vision but rather with a question which betrayed the anguish of his heart and a desire for certainty. *"But Abram said, 'Lord God, what will You give me, seeing I go childless, and the heir of my house is Eliezer of Damascus?'"* (v. 2). Abram feared that in some way the promise that all the families of the earth would be blessed through him did not necessarily mean that he would be the father of a child. He confronted the thought that perhaps the Lord was going to fulfill this promise through the perfectly acceptable practice of regarding a servant as the heir of a childless man. This was not what Abram had in mind and he said so in no uncertain terms. It is helpful to note the nature of Abram's faith. It was not without elements of fear and uncertainty, and it was not untouched by reservations and questions. It is also encouraging to remember the way in which the Lord patiently helped His servant deal with his fears.

THE PROMISES OF GOD PROMOTE FAITH

The Lord does not always answer His servants as specifically as they question Him, but in this instance He did. *"And behold, the word of the Lord came to him, saying, 'This one shall not be your heir, but one who will come from your own body shall be your heir'"* (v. 4). This promise did not indicate to Abram who the mother would be and, as subsequent events showed, Abram was still not fully conversant with all that the Lord had in mind for him and his family. But when the Lord told him to *"Look now toward heaven, and count the stars if you are able to number them,"* he obeyed and then was told, *"So shall your descendants be"* (v. 5). The result was startling not only in that Abram believed what he was told, but *"He believed in the Lord, and He counted it to him for righteousness"* (v. 6). John Calvin, commenting on this verse, wrote, "None of us would be able to conceive the rich and hidden doctrine which this verse contains, unless Paul had borne his torch for us." He was referring particularly to the apostle's exposition and application of this verse in his treatment of the faith which leads to justification in Romans 4:1–25. This truth is pivotal to any statement of the gospel of Christ because it answers one of the oldest and most important questions known to man, "How then can man be righteous before God?" (Job 25:4). Paul added in his Epistle to the Galatians that "the Scripture, foreseeing that God would justify the Gentiles by faith, preached the gospel to Abraham beforehand, saying, 'In you all the nations shall be blessed.' So then those who are of faith are blessed with believing Abraham" (Gal. 3:8, 9). James weighed in with his contribution by quoting the same passage from Genesis, making the important point that "faith without works is dead" (James 2:20). These New Testament applications of Genesis 15:6 show how profoundly God was speaking to Abram and through him to all who would believe down through the ages.

Some people have wondered aloud why God should declare someone righteous, that is forgive their sin and fit them for heaven, just because they believed they were going to become a father! But this is to miss the point. God was stimulating faith through His word so that Abram would learn to trust the Lord for all that he was unable to do for himself. In exactly the same way God still proclaims His truth through His word in order that men and women might believe Him and trust Him to be all that they could ever wish for in time and eternity.

The Promises of God Unveil the Future

Abram was well aware of the Lord's call out of Ur and of His promise that He would inherit the land of Canaan. When he was reminded of these things, however, he said, *"Lord God, how shall I know that I will inherit it?"* (Gen. 15:8). The Lord's response was to direct Abram to set the stage for an ancient ritual wherein parties to a covenant would walk between the divided parts of sacrificed animals with a view to dramatically indicating that they themselves would rather be torn in two like the animals than renege on their agreement. When Abram had made the preparations and chased the invading vultures away he fell into a deep sleep *"and behold, horror and great darkness fell upon him"* (v. 12). Even though the promise of God was full of light and life there was a sense in which it would only be fulfilled through much horror and not a little darkness. Eternal life is certainly a gift, but the gift bears a terrible and awesome price for the Giver. Neither were Abram's descendants to enter into their place of blessing without pain and trial. The Lord said to Abram, *"Know certainly that your descendants will be strangers in a land that is not theirs, and will serve them, and they will afflict them four hundred years. And also the nation whom they serve I will judge; afterward they shall come out with great possessions"* (vv. 13, 14). It would be difficult to imagine a clearer prediction of the events of the captivity in Egypt and the subsequent exodus. Whether Abram regarded the promise of his own demise with delight or dismay we are not told!

If Abram wondered why there was to be a delay of "four hundred years" or to "the fourth generation" we are not told, but modern man tends to wonder about such things. In the first place Abram could not possibly subdue the land with his own limited resources. But there was a much more profound reason for the delay. The Lord explained, *"In the fourth generation they shall return here, for the iniquity of the Amorites is not yet complete"* (v. 16). In other words God knew that the people of Canaan could not be judged by Him through His people without there being proper reason for such judgment. He was not arbitrarily deciding to kick the Amorites out so that His favorites could take their place. His people were going to be the means to achieving His divine ends, but His divine ends were going to be impeccably just. Moreover, the Lord Who knows the end from the beginning knew exactly how long it would take these people to become how bad. A sobering reminder of the sovereign knowledge and will of God! Abram awoke to see *"a smoking oven and a burning torch that passed between those pieces"* (v. 17). The description of this theophany is certainly strange but not too far removed from the more familiar images of God appearing in the cloud by day and the pillar of fire by night.

The Lord also promised that the people descended from Abram would possess the land of His choice and He even gave geographic details of its extent stating specifically that it would stretch *"from the river of Egypt to the great river, the River Euphrates"* (v. 18). Rarely during its checkered history did Israel occupy all the regions of which the Lord spoke. There are some well-known members of Israel's Parliament who look to this and similar prophecies for a rationale for their policies of annexation and development by settlement in what others call the Occupied Territories. But others point out that during the golden days of David's reign the prediction was fulfilled while still others look for a future fulfillment when the Messiah shall return. Whatever the truth may be, the fact remains that the promises made by God to Abram stimulated his faith, calmed his fears, and gave him a hope for the future. We should not easily forget that we too are Abram's sons if we believe in the same Lord of the promises, bearing in mind that in Christ we have much more to go on than Abram ever had!

It may be objected that Abram was promised a whole lot of things that he would never see but which his descendants would enjoy. Therefore, the promises were probably not too exciting for him. With our modern Western emphasis on the individual this is a perfectly understandable objection, but to Abram this would not pose a problem because the Eastern perceptions were different from ours. The Old Testament scholar H. Wheeler Robinson introduced a term, "corporate personality," to describe the Eastern ability to recognize that individuals are not islands but are part of a community which can be blessed or cursed through individual actions. Robinson probably went too far in his exposition of this theme in that he came close to ignoring the clear teaching in the Old Testament which shows the Hebrews understood individual responsibility as well as corporate solidarity. It may be appropriate to point out that our individualistic society may have slipped into the opposite ditch of ignoring the corporate ramifications of individual actions. It may be helpful to realize that while we stand in horror and amazement every time an "innocent" hostage is taken in the Middle East that the perpetrators of the action do not regard them as "innocent" because in their reckoning every American is "guilty" of everything that America has done. This concept of corporate solidarity may be hard for us to swallow, but on the other hand we have no difficulty recognizing that when Ray Kroc invented "McDonald's" he introduced the whole of American society solidly into the era of fast foods. Whether this was a corporate blessing or a corporate curse we must determine individually!

CHAPTER SIXTEEN

Making Mistakes

Genesis 16:1–16

16:1 Now Sarai, Abram's wife, had borne him no *children*. And she had an Egyptian maidservant whose name was Hagar.

2 So Sarai said to Abram, "See now, the LORD has restrained me from bearing *children*. Please, go in to my maid; perhaps I shall obtain children by her." And Abram heeded the voice of Sarai.

3 Then Sarai, Abram's wife, took Hagar her maid, the Egyptian, and gave her to her husband Abram to be his wife, after Abram had dwelt ten years in the land of Canaan.

4 So he went in to Hagar, and she conceived. And when she saw that she had conceived, her mistress became despised in her eyes.

5 Then Sarai said to Abram, "My wrong *be* upon you! I gave my maid into your embrace; and when she saw that she had conceived, I became despised in her eyes. The LORD judge between you and me."

6 So Abram said to Sarai, "Indeed your maid *is* in your hand; do to her as you please." And when Sarai dealt harshly with her, she fled from her presence.

7 Now the Angel of the LORD found her by a spring of water in the wilderness, by the spring on the way to Shur.

8 And He said, "Hagar, Sarai's maid, where have you come from, and where are you going?" She said, "I am fleeing from the presence of my mistress Sarai."

9 The Angel of the LORD said to her, "Return

to your mistress, and submit yourself under her hand."

10 Then the Angel of the LORD said to her, "I will multiply your descendants exceedingly, so that they shall not be counted for multitude."

11 And the Angel of the LORD said to her:
"Behold, you *are* with child,
And you shall bear a son.
You shall call his name Ishmael,
Because the LORD has heard your affliction.

12 He shall be a wild man;
His hand *shall be* against every man,
And every man's hand against him.
And he shall dwell in the presence of all his
    brethren."

13 Then she called the name of the LORD who spoke to her, You-Are-the-God-Who-Sees; for she said, "Have I also here seen Him who sees me?"

14 Therefore the well was called Beer Lahai Roi; observe, *it is* between Kadesh and Bered.

15 So Hagar bore Abram a son; and Abram named his son, whom Hagar bore, Ishmael.

16 Abram *was* eighty-six years old when Hagar bore Ishmael to Abram.

Gen. 16:1–16

The Lord used the process of elimination in His dealings with Abram concerning the remarkable promise that his descendants would be as numerous as the stars of heaven. At first Abram was afraid that Eliezer, his servant, was going to be his heir. But the Lord said that was not the case, but that the heir would be a natural son of Abram. That in itself was remarkable because of Abram's advanced age. Sarai had a dual problem in that she was elderly and also barren. So using her natural reasoning skills she put two and two together and finished up with three! It is encouraging, in a perverse sort of way, to see that even a spiritual man of Abram's stature was capable of making mistakes. This in itself should help us to deal realistically with our own blunders and help us to be taught from his experience that mistakes are not without their consequences.

MAKING MISTAKES

"So Sarai said to Abram, 'See now, the Lord has restrained me from bearing children. Please, go in to my maid; perhaps I shall obtain children by her.' And Abram heeded the voice of Sarai" (Gen. 16:2). If this arrangement sounds strange to us we should not overlook the fact that in our modern wisdom we have introduced a similar system called, euphemistically, "surrogate motherhood." Sarai's idea was not altogether without merit in that her suggestion was apparently normal custom, and could certainly be justified on "common sense" grounds. She and her husband had been promised descendants ten years previously and nothing seemed to be happening using the normal methods! But it was not long until the error of judgment became obvious.

At the risk of utilizing 20/20 hindsight, a gift given to the most stupid of people, we can identify why the mistake was made. We should note that the desire for the child was so great that other considerations were apparently subordinated to this desire. Added to this was a degree of impatience which clouded their judgment although they had waited ten years. It is possible also to see how the acceptance of conventional wisdom could have crowded out the unique statements and interventions of their unconventional Lord. All honest people who have confronted their own mistakes have probably recognized similar causes for their bad choices.

I have often cringed when parents, displaying more candor than tact, have introduced their children to me with such remarkable statements as, "This is Tommy, and this is Tammy and here is Timmy, our little mistake!" Timmy could be excused for wondering whether he really amounted to much! The result of Abram and Hagar's liaison had plenty of opportunities to harbor similar sentiments.

MAKING MISTAKES WORSE

Alexander Pope reminded us that "to err is human" and we all know that "to make matters worse" is also a human specialty. Bad attitudes often serve to exacerbate bad situations. Hagar, the servant girl, as soon as she realized she was pregnant, was unable to resist the temptation to look down on her less accomplished mistress.

"When she saw that she had conceived, her mistress became despised in her eyes" (v. 4). Perhaps she had been made to feel inferior at the hands of Sarai, and when the opportunity to get even presented itself she grasped it with both hands. Sarai's reaction was no more noble. Sensing the hostility from Hagar she turned on her husband and said, *"My wrong be upon you! I gave my maid into your embrace; and when she saw that she had conceived, I became despised in her eyes. The Lord judge between you and me"* (v. 5). With thinly disguised anger Sarai talked about justice but showed that she was really interested in getting even! Caught between two feuding women Abram hardly covered himself with glory, telling his wife, *"Indeed your maid is in your hand; do to her as you please"* (v. 6). Sarai took her opportunity and dealt so harshly with the young pregnant woman that she ran away into the wilderness and neither Abram nor Sarai did anything about it. Abram's attempt to deal with the situation by hoping it would go away served only to make matters worse.

MAKING SOMETHING OUT OF MISTAKES

There is no telling where this tragic story would have ended if the Lord had not intervened. *"Now the Angel of the Lord found her by a spring of water in the wilderness, by the spring on the way to Shur"* (v. 7). Modern society would do well to recognize the Lord's concern for the unborn child. Apparently Sarai had to learn that getting rid of an unwanted pregnancy was not acceptable to the Lord Who recognized Hagar's plight and intervened on her behalf. She was told by the angel of the Lord, *"Return to your mistress, and submit yourself under her hand"* (v. 9). This tough-sounding instruction was tempered by the gracious promise of the Lord, *"I will multiply your descendants exceedingly, so that they shall not be counted for multitude"* (v. 10). Predictions concerning the attitudes and lifestyle of the unborn child were added including a delightful statement concerning his name, Ishmael, which means "God hears." That Hagar was deeply moved by her meeting with the Lord in the wilderness becomes apparent when we note that she called the well "Beer Lahai Roi" which means, "Well of the One Who lives and sees me." Having been used, mistreated, and rejected by her superiors she was overwhelmed by the thought that the Lord Himself cared for her and had plans for her and her unborn son which would have worldwide repercussions. Even though she was well on the way back to her native Egypt, and had no idea what awaited her in Abram's household, she returned on the basis of the word from the Lord. In so doing she started to make something positive out of the mistakes she had made.

Abram and Sarai were also required to alter their attitudes to the young woman in order that they might receive her back into their household. Perhaps it was the reminder that the Lord is called, among other things, *You-Are-the-God-Who-Sees*" (v. 13), which served to bring them to a recognition of the things that they had done so badly. Nothing is more likely to encourage men and women to rectify their errors than the reminder that the Lord is not unmindful of what they have done and requires an accounting from each one.

At the ripe old age of eighty-six Abram received the gift of a son who would perpetuate his name. Although he would later discover that he had jumped the gun on the Lord's plans, Abram nevertheless rejoiced in his boy whose very name, Ishmael—"God hears"—was a constant reminder to him that he was to live in the conscious enjoyment and under the caring gaze of the Lord his God. This would help him not to make other mistakes in the future. We do well to learn from this man of God.

CHAPTER SEVENTEEN

Covenant

Genesis 17:1–27

17:1 When Abram was ninety-nine years old, the LORD appeared to Abram and said to him, "I *am* Almighty God; walk before Me and be blameless.

2 "And I will make My covenant between Me and you, and will multiply you exceedingly."

3 Then Abram fell on his face, and God talked with him, saying:

4 "As for Me, behold, My covenant is with you, and you shall be a father of many nations.

5 "No longer shall your name be called Abram, but your name shall be Abraham; for I have made you a father of many nations.

6 "I will make you exceedingly fruitful; and I will make nations of you, and kings shall come from you.

7 "And I will establish My covenant between Me and you and your descendants after you in their generations, for an everlasting covenant, to be God to you and your descendants after you.

8 "Also I give to you and your descendants after you the land in which you are a stranger, all the land of Canaan, as an everlasting possession; and I will be their God."

9 And God said to Abraham: "As for you, you shall keep My covenant, you and your descendants after you throughout their generations.

10 "This *is* My covenant which you shall keep, between Me and you and your descendants after you: Every male child among you shall be circumcised;

11 "and you shall be circumcised in the flesh of

your foreskins, and it shall be a sign of the covenant between Me and you.

12 "He who is eight days old among you shall be circumcised, every male child in your generations, he who is born in your house or bought with money from any foreigner who is not your descendant.

13 "He who is born in your house and he who is bought with your money must be circumcised, and My covenant shall be in your flesh for an everlasting covenant.

14 "And the uncircumcised male child, who is not circumcised in the flesh of his foreskin, that person shall be cut off from his people; he has broken My covenant."

15 Then God said to Abraham, "As for Sarai your wife, you shall not call her name Sarai, but Sarah *shall be* her name.

16 "And I will bless her and also give you a son by her; then I will bless her, and she shall be *a mother of* nations; kings of peoples shall be from her."

17 Then Abraham fell on his face and laughed, and said in his heart, "Shall *a child* be born to a man who is one hundred years old? And shall Sarah, who is ninety years old, bear *a child?*"

18 And Abraham said to God, "Oh, that Ishmael might live before You!"

19 Then God said: "No, Sarah your wife shall bear you a son, and you shall call his name Isaac; I will establish My covenant with him for an everlasting covenant, *and* with his descendants after him.

20 "And as for Ishmael, I have heard you. Behold, I have blessed him, and will make him fruitful, and will multiply him exceedingly. He shall beget twelve princes, and I will make him a great nation.

21 "But My covenant I will establish with Isaac, whom Sarah shall bear to you at this set time next year."

22 Then He finished talking with him, and God went up from Abraham.

23 So Abraham took Ishmael his son, all who were born in his house and all who were bought with his money, every male among the men of Abraham's

house, and circumcised the flesh of their foreskins that very same day, as God had said to him.

24 Abraham *was* ninety-nine years old when he was circumcised in the flesh of his foreskin.

25 And Ishmael his son *was* thirteen years old when he was circumcised in the flesh of his foreskin.

26 That very same day Abraham was circumcised, and his son Ishmael;

27 and all the men of his house, born in the house or bought with money from a foreigner, were circumcised with him.

Gen. 17:1–27

THE CONCEPT OF THE COVENANT

"When Abram was ninety-nine years old, the Lord appeared to Abram and said to him, 'I am Almighty God; walk before Me and be blameless. And I will make My covenant between Me and you . . .'" (Gen. 17:1, 2). In the nineteenth century, Old Testament scholars believed that the people of God were much the same as the tribal people amongst whom they lived and their God was seen as being nothing more than another tribal deity. The fact that the people of God held that they had a special relationship with their God was attributed to a later "ethical" refinement in their development which was then added retrospectively. It was rather like saying that Hannibal couldn't possibly have had any elephants and therefore to suggest that he took them over the Alps was clearly a later tradition added to the historical account of his military exploits! If these scholars had been right it would have been ridiculous to believe that Jehovah had personal dealings with His people in the way that Genesis describes the relationship between Abram and Jehovah. And the idea of a covenant would have been regarded as totally inappropriate. However, more recent study and research of the ancient Hittites have shown marked similarities between their suzerainty treaties and the covenants recorded in the Decalogue. A suzerain was a dominant power who having overcome another power would then arrive at an agreement by which their relationship would be established. The greater would guarantee the well-being of the lesser while the lesser would make responsive guarantees of loyalty and service. It is delightful to note

how the covenants God made with His people originated in His loving, caring heart and were designed to introduce man to His gracious presence and protection.

A covenant (Hebrew, *běrîth*) could also be a pledge of friendship like the one which existed between David and Jonathan (see 1 Sam. 23:18); a trade agreement as in the case of Ben Hadad and Ahab (see 1 Kings 20:34); or the special marriage covenant (see Prov. 2:16, 17). In the military treaties there was, of course, a clear sense of superiority and inferiority, while in the other covenants there was more of a sense of equality. The covenant Jehovah chose to make with Abram was clearly based on His sovereignty, but at the same time it had elements of equality in the sense that Abram was known as the friend of God. But overarching equality and inequality was the sense of integrity which was fundamental to any concept of covenant. Having already pledged His integrity to Abram concerning the possession of the land (see Gen. 15:18), the Lord reaffirmed another aspect of the covenant—which He had already introduced (see Gen. 12:1–3)—the promise of progeny and worldwide blessing.

THE CONTENT OF THE COVENANT

It is significant that the covenant was introduced with a revelation by God of His name. This may not seem of great importance to us but in Eastern thought to reveal the name was to reveal the person and to invite intimacy. Perhaps the British can understand this easier than Americans in that they are much more reluctant to reveal their first names to people unless they have known them for at least twenty-five years, while Americans often start a conversation with, "Hi, I'm Bill!" I have noticed, however, that some air hostesses instead of wearing a name tag saying, "Cindy" chose a more guarded "Ms. Smith," thereby retaining some degree of distance from possible familiarity which they do not desire.

"I am Almighty God" translates the Hebrew "El Shaddai" (*Ēl-Šaddaî*). Scholars have experienced difficulty identifying the exact meaning of the name but are generally agreed that it refers to God's all-sufficient power and might, particularly in contrast to man's weakness and vulnerability. The great news to Abram was that such a God wished to relate intimately to him and had the power in

Himself to do all that He was committing Himself to do. This was the unshakable basis upon which the covenant would operate.

The details of the covenant can be divided readily into two sections introduced by the phrases *"As for Me"* (v. 4) and *"As for you"* (v. 9). The first section detailed God's commitments under the covenant. The latter outlined His expectations from His covenant partner.

El Shaddai committed Himself to giving Abram the land (nothing new about that); He promised to grant him progeny (this too was not new); but then He added the most important part, *"I will establish My covenant between Me and you and your descendants after you in their generations, for an everlasting covenant, to be God to you and your descendants after you"* (v. 7). Abram was to discover that far outweighing any consideration such as property or progeny was the remarkable truth that El Shaddai, in all His power, was personally knowable and was committed to a humble man living in the wild regions of Canaan. Moreover this great God was committed to being eternally that which He was promising to be to Abram in time. In addition this promise was available to all who would come from Abram's loins—a promise applied by Paul to all who would believe in Christ down through the ages (see Gal. 3:9).

Sarai, who had not figured largely in the drama up until this point was then brought center stage and, to Abram's astonishment, El Shaddai said, *"I will bless her and also give you a son by her; then I will bless her, and she shall be a mother of nations; kings of peoples shall be from her"* (Gen. 17:16). Abram's response was as understandable as it was inappropriate. He *"fell on his face and laughed, and said in his heart, 'Shall a child be born to a man who is one hundred years old? And shall Sarah, who is ninety years old, bear a child?'"* (v. 17). He recovered quickly and suggested that as he already had one son, Ishmael; perhaps God would work out His purposes through him thereby saving all manner of embarrassment. I don't think he wanted to take the news to his ninety-year-old wife! But the Lord was adamant, adding that the child yet to be conceived would be called Isaac and that the covenant would relate to him and emphatically would not relate to Ishmael. This in no way suggested that Ishmael and his descendants were to be estranged from God's blessing of eternal salvation, but did state that God had exercised His sovereign prerogative, choosing that His purposes for all mankind would be worked out through Abram's son, Isaac, rather than Abram's son, Ishmael. Clearly the thin red line of descent through which the bruiser of the serpent would come could not stretch through both sons and God decided which one it would be. But He had also decided that Ishmael was to be a greatly significant man too. To Abram the Lord said, *"And as for Ishmael, I have heard you. Behold, I have blessed him, and will make him fruitful, and will multiply him exceedingly. He shall beget twelve princes, and I will make him a great nation"* (v. 20). The divine side of the covenant was firmly in place.

El Shaddai expected some practical responses. They were outlined, in principle, as follows, *"walk before Me and be blameless"* (v. 1). The Hebrew word translated *"blameless"* means "whole" and was sometimes used to describe an animal provided for sacrifice, meaning that it should be without blemish. But when applied to people it meant that their approach to God should be "whole (hearted)." It does not mean sinless perfection, which is as big a relief to us as it would have been to Abram had he ever been misled by the word!

This wholeheartedness was to be demonstrated by both Abram and Sarai in their willingness to accept a change of name, which as we saw above, would have special significance to them. Abram was to become Abraham—*"for I have made you a father of many nations"* (v. 5)—and regarding his wife he was told, *"You shall not call her name Sarai, but Sarah shall be her name"* (v. 15). Sarah means "Princess," and while there is no major difference in meaning in Sarah's name change the fact that it was changed would be a statement in itself and would present opportunities to explain its significance.

"And God said to Abraham, 'As for you, you shall keep My covenant . . . This is My covenant which you shall keep . . . Every male child among you shall be circumcised; and you shall be circumcised in the flesh of your foreskins, and it shall be a sign of the covenant between Me and you'" (vv. 9–11). At ninety-nine years of age Abraham was to subject himself to a painful ritual which while not unknown in the regions in which he lived was certainly something that he had not found at all necessary before. In addition his son Ishmael who was thirteen, his men servants, and even those who were slaves in his household were to undergo circumcision and thereby demonstrate in their bodies their relationship of privilege with El Shaddai. This

ritual was to be taken so seriously that those who declined to participate were to be cut off from their people and were not parties to the covenant. The ceremony in itself, while having profound significance in that it bestowed "*a sign of the covenant*" (v. 11), was to be an outward and visible sign of an inward and spiritual grace. The covenant was clearly one of grace appropriated by faith, but at the same time the faith had to be manifested in obedience and circumcision was ample evidence of that obedience.

In later years the prophets would lash out at the empty ritualism into which the spiritual experience of the people of God had degenerated (see Jer. 4:4) and Paul writing to his fellow Jews was at great pains to show that "he is not a Jew who is one outwardly, nor is circumcision that which is outward in the flesh; but he is a Jew who is one inwardly; and circumcision is that of the heart, in the Spirit, and not in the letter" (Rom. 2:28, 29).

THE CONSEQUENCES OF THE COVENANT

So Abraham went ahead and did all that the Lord had told him to do. He believed and it was reckoned to him for righteousness; he obeyed and in so doing the believing became apparent and the covenant was sealed in the heart of God and man while man in his body bore the evidence that he was the beneficiary of the grace of El Shaddai. Abraham had entered into a relationship which would only be surpassed by a subsequent, new, and better covenant sealed in the blood of Christ into which countless thousands in earth's four corners have entered. Like Abraham we stand in grace and rejoice therein. But Abraham also found that there was an appropriate posture for those whose lives are enriched by El Shaddai. He "*fell on his face, and God talked with him*" (Gen. 17:3). No more suitable response to the covenant-making and covenant-keeping God has ever been devised to this day.

CHAPTER EIGHTEEN

Big Questions about God

Genesis 18:1–33

18:1 Then the LORD appeared to him by the terebinth trees of Mamre, as he was sitting in the tent door in the heat of the day.

2 So he lifted his eyes and looked, and behold, three men were standing by him; and when he saw *them*, he ran from the tent door to meet them, and bowed himself to the ground,

3 and said, "My LORD, if I have now found favor in Your sight, do not pass on by Your servant.

4 "Please let a little water be brought, and wash your feet, and rest yourselves under the tree.

5 "And I will bring a morsel of bread, that you may refresh your hearts. After that you may pass by, inasmuch as you have come to your servant." They said, "Do as you have said."

6 So Abraham hurried into the tent to Sarah and said, "Quickly, make ready three measures of fine meal; knead *it* and make cakes."

7 And Abraham ran to the herd, took a tender and good calf, gave *it* to a young man, and he hastened to prepare it.

8 So he took butter and milk and the calf which he had prepared, and set *it* before them; and he stood by them under the tree as they ate.

9 Then they said to him, "Where *is* Sarah your wife?" So he said, "Here, in the tent."

10 And He said, "I will certainly return to you according to the time of life, and behold, Sarah your wife shall have a son." (Sarah was listening in the tent door which *was* behind him.)

11 Now Abraham and Sarah were old, well advanced in age; *and* Sarah had passed the age of childbearing.

12 Therefore Sarah laughed within herself, saying, "After I have grown old, shall I have pleasure, my lord being old also?"

13 And the LORD said to Abraham, "Why did Sarah laugh, saying, 'Shall I surely bear *a child*, since I am old?'

14 "Is anything too hard for the LORD? At the appointed time I will return to you, according to the time of life, and Sarah shall have a son."

15 But Sarah denied *it*, saying, "I did not laugh," for she was afraid. And He said, "No, but you did laugh!"

16 Then the men rose from there and looked toward Sodom, and Abraham went with them to send them on the way.

17 And the LORD said, "Shall I hide from Abraham what I am doing,

18 "since Abraham shall surely become a great and mighty nation, and all the nations of the earth shall be blessed in him?

19 "For I have known him, in order that he may command his children and his household after him, that they keep the way of the LORD, to do righteousness and justice, that the LORD may bring to Abraham what He has spoken to him."

20 And the LORD said, "Because the outcry against Sodom and Gomorrah is great, and because their sin is very grave,

21 "I will go down now and see whether they have done altogether according to the outcry against it that has come to Me; and if not, I will know."

22 Then the men turned away from there and went toward Sodom, but Abraham still stood before the LORD.

23 And Abraham came near and said, "Would You also destroy the righteous with the wicked?

24 "Suppose there were fifty righteous within the city; would You also destroy the place and not spare *it* for the fifty righteous that were in it?

25 "Far be it from You to do such a thing as this, to slay the righteous with the wicked, so that the righteous should be as the wicked; far be it from You! Shall not the Judge of all the earth do right?"

26 So the LORD said, "If I find in Sodom fifty righteous within the city, then I will spare all the place for their sakes."

27 Then Abraham answered and said, "Indeed now, I who *am but* dust and ashes have taken it upon myself to speak to the LORD:

28 "Suppose there were five less than the fifty righteous; would You destroy all of the city for *lack of* five?" So He said, "If I find there forty-five, I will not destroy *it*."

29 And he spoke to Him yet again and said, "Suppose there should be forty found there?" So He said, "I will not do *it* for the sake of forty."

30 Then he said, "Let not the LORD be angry, and I will speak: Suppose thirty should be found there?" So He said, "I will not do *it* if I find thirty there."

31 And he said, "Indeed now, I have taken it upon myself to speak to the LORD: Suppose twenty should be found there?" So He said, "I will not destroy *it* for the sake of twenty."

32 Then he said, "Let not the LORD be angry, and I will speak but once more: Suppose ten should be found there?" And He said, "I will not destroy *it* for the sake of ten."

33 So the LORD went His way as soon as He had finished speaking with Abraham; and Abraham returned to his place.

Gen. 18:1–33

Abraham had been learning a lot about God's plans for his life, but it is not clear how much Sarah knew. At first he thought that his servant would be his heir, but he was put straight on that one and told specifically that his heir would be a natural son. So he had a son by his wife's servant but was then told that he would have a natural son by his own wife. Abraham believed that but his wife had to believe it too, for obvious reasons. And therein lay a problem which was addressed when Abraham and Sarah received some very special visitors. At first Abraham did not recognize them, but he was most hospitable and treated them with the utmost respect which was just as well as things turned out! The conversation with the visitors was most interesting, not least because of the intriguing questions about God which were raised.

A QUESTION OF DIVINE ABILITY

We are not told at what stage of the visit Abraham realized that he was entertaining the Lord Himself accompanied by angels, all in human form. If he recognized the identity of his visitors early in the encounter then his bowing down, his solicitous care, and his warm welcome were most appropriate. On the other hand, if he acted so courteously and generously to total strangers he not only "unwittingly entertained angels" (Heb. 13:2) but he also discovered firsthand the truth that what is done generously to one of the Lord's people is done to the Lord Himself (see Matt. 25:40). His hospitality extended to a fine meal which he hastily mobilized his wife and a young servant to prepare. During the meal the visitors asked, *"'Where is Sarah your wife?' So he said, 'Here in the tent'"* (Gen. 18:9). In actual fact she was hiding behind the tent flap listening to the conversation from which she, as a woman, was barred. She discovered what many an eavesdropper has discovered—eavesdropping has its own occupational hazards! She heard something she was not expecting to hear! *"Sarah your wife shall have a son"* (v. 10). She was incredulous and *"laughed within herself, saying, 'After I have grown old, shall I have pleasure, my lord being old also?'"* (v. 12). Evidently her laughter was not as discreet as her eavesdropping because *"the Lord said to Abraham, 'Why did Sarah laugh, saying, 'Shall I surely bear a child, since I am old?'"* (v. 13). Suddenly exposed, Sarah acted reflexively and lied, *"I did not laugh"* (v. 15).

In that she was ninety years of age and barren to boot one has to have considerable sympathy for Sarah's response and perhaps even grudgingly admit that at least she could laugh about it! But there is a factor that must not be overlooked. The Lord Himself asked the $64,000 question, *"Is anything too hard for the Lord?"* (v. 14). This question does not belong in the same category as "Can God build a stone so big that He cannot move it?" because so often that kind of question is not altogether serious. The Lord Himself asked the question as a challenge to Sarah and Abraham's faith. It related to their acknowledgment of divine ability and is a question that needs to be addressed in all ages.

When my father was a young preacher he asked this question in a Sunday school class and one of the kids in all seriousness said he knew of something that was too hard for the Lord. When asked what it was he responded, "He couldn't make my brother's mouth any bigger without moving his ears!" The ability of God is not limitless because He has chosen to set limits upon it. If baby brother's mouth really was as big as big brother suggested then big brother was right, in the same way that he could have said God cannot make a two-sided triangle or a square circle. God's power is clearly limited by His will and by His character. He cannot lie and He cannot be unfaithful to His promises. But He is powerful enough to do all that He wills to do and adequate enough to accomplish all that He intends to accomplish.

Jeremiah understood this when he purchased land in Anathoth at the same time that he was prophesying that the land would be destroyed, and the people would be led away into captivity. His apparently inconsistent behavior was a direct result of his conviction that the purchase was the Lord's will, that he was acting in obedience, that the Lord would restore the fortunes of the people and return them to the land and therefore he could state unequivocally, "There is nothing too hard for You" (Jer. 32:17).

God's people in all ages have been confronted with the question, "Is anything too hard for the Lord?" and those who have known His mind and have sought His honor have answered with great confidence, "There is nothing too hard for You."

A QUESTION OF DIVINE STRATEGY

The visitors, having concluded their meal and finished their business with Abraham and Sarah, began to take their leave. Abraham, ever courteous, went with them and as they stood looking over the plains toward Sodom, "the Lord said, 'Shall I hide from Abraham what I am doing?'" (Gen. 18:17). This question which apparently the Lord was addressing to Himself is of great interest to us as it was undoubtedly to Abraham. It deals with the whole question of whether God has a strategy and if He will share it with His people and in fact involve them in its outworking. The Lord answered His own question by going on to speak about the special relationship which He enjoyed with Abraham, *"For I have known him, in order that he may command his children and his household after him, that they keep the way of the Lord, to do righteousness and justice, that the Lord may bring to Abraham what He has spoken to him"* (v. 19). The answer to the question was, and still is, "Yes." God still speaks to His people about the concerns of His heart, tells them what He proposes to do, and enrolls them in the corps which will be instrumental in bringing His purposes to pass.

The pressing concern at that moment was the condition of Sodom which had strayed far from the justice and righteousness to which the Lord and His servant Abraham were committed. Something had to be done about Sodom, the Lord was going to do it, and Abraham was going to be involved. The Lord spoke about the *"outcry against it that has come to Me"* (v. 21) and indicated that He proposed to investigate the situation in order to deal with Sodom appropriately. We do not know whether this outcry came from the surrounding peoples or whether the anguished cry of those who were suffering from Sodom's sin was indicated, but we do know of the Lord's concern and His commitment to action. And Abraham was cognizant of all that the Lord was doing. Not surprisingly he *"still stood before the Lord"* (v. 22). No doubt he was discovering that the delights of friendship had introduced him to the privilege of partnership, but that also meant he shared the burden of stewardship. He was God's man and there was no escape from that privileged and burdensome position because the Lord had chosen not to keep Abraham in the dark about His plans.

A QUESTION OF DIVINE INTEGRITY

Abraham sensed the seriousness of Sodom's impending judgment. His concern showed in his prayer to the Lord. *"Would You also destroy the righteous with the wicked?"* (v. 23). This was unthinkable and he expressed himself in a question which if it had not been addressed in the most humble and reverential tones could have been impertinent, *"Shall not the Judge of all the earth do right?"* (v. 25). He then engaged in a dialogue with the Lord which at first sight is reminiscent of an American tourist trying to beat down an Arab shopkeeper in the bazaars of the Old City of Jerusalem. He got a guarantee from the Lord that if there were fifty righteous people in Sodom the city would not be destroyed for their sake, but he recognized that he was overestimating the spiritual condition of Sodom. He brought down his figure by increments until the Lord promised that if there were ten righteous Sodom would be saved from judgment. The Lord had proved once again that His commitment to righteousness was inviolate. That if His servant was capable of moral integrity the Lord Himself was no stranger to rectitude and could indeed be trusted always to do what is right.

There are many questions about good and evil. There are many problems concerning inequality and iniquity. There is no doubt that often the wicked flourish and the righteous suffer. Some people have allowed their hurts to turn to cynicism which in turn has dragged them into the cold pit of unbelief. They say things like, "If God is good He is not God. If God is God He is not good." Better to rest on the assurance that the Lord is righteous, that our concepts of righteousness originated with Him, and that we should trust Him to be all that He professes to be even though we might wonder which way He is going at times in much the same way that Abraham worried about His intentions concerning Sodom. But the safeguard in all our uncertainties is the attitude of an Abraham who asked his hard questions in a spirit which could not be faulted. He was careful to preface his remarks with suitably humble words like, *"Indeed now, I who am but dust and ashes have taken it upon myself to speak to the Lord"* (v. 27). It is hard to imagine more profound or significant questions about God and it is encouraging to note that the Scriptures do not ignore them but address them in such a way that God's people need never be afraid to ask them just so long as they will keep their hearts and minds tender to the Lord and open to the answers He is committed to provide.

CHAPTER NINETEEN

The Significance of Sodom

Genesis 19:1–38

19:1 Now the two angels came to Sodom in the evening, and Lot was sitting in the gate of Sodom. When Lot saw *them,* he rose to meet them, and he bowed himself with his face toward the ground.

2 And he said, "Here now, my lords, please turn in to your servant's house and spend the night, and wash your feet; then you may rise early and go on your way." And they said, "No, but we will spend the night in the open square."

3 But he insisted strongly; so they turned in to him and entered his house. Then he made them a feast, and baked unleavened bread, and they ate.

4 Now before they lay down, the men of the city, the men of Sodom, both old and young, all the people from every quarter, surrounded the house.

5 And they called to Lot and said to him, "Where are the men who came to you tonight? Bring them out to us that we may know them *carnally.*"

6 So Lot went out to them through the doorway, shut the door behind him,

7 and said, "Please, my brethren, do not do so wickedly!

8 "See now, I have two daughters who have not known a man; please, let me bring them out to you, and you may do to them as you wish; only do nothing to these men, since this is the reason they have come under the shadow of my roof."

9 And they said, "Stand back!" Then they said, "This one came in to stay *here,* and he keeps acting as a judge; now we will deal worse with you than with

them." So they pressed hard against the man Lot, and came near to break down the door.

10 But the men reached out their hands and pulled Lot into the house with them, and shut the door.

11 And they struck the men who *were* at the doorway of the house with blindness, both small and great, so that they became weary *trying* to find the door.

12 Then the men said to Lot, "Have you anyone else here? Son-in-law, your sons, your daughters, and whomever you have in the city—take *them* out of this place!

13 "For we will destroy this place, because the outcry against them has grown great before the face of the LORD, and the LORD has sent us to destroy it."

14 So Lot went out and spoke to his sons-in-law, who had married his daughters, and said, "Get up, get out of this place; for the LORD will destroy this city!" But to his sons-in-law he seemed to be joking.

15 When the morning dawned, the angels urged Lot to hurry, saying, "Arise, take your wife and your two daughters who are here, lest you be consumed in the punishment of the city."

16 And while he lingered, the men took hold of his hand, his wife's hand, and the hands of his two daughters, the LORD being merciful to him, and they brought him out and set him outside the city.

17 So it came to pass, when they had brought them outside, that he said, "Escape for your life! Do not look behind you nor stay anywhere in the plain. Escape to the mountains, lest you be destroyed."

18 Then Lot said to them, "Please, no, my lords!

19 "Indeed now, your servant has found favor in your sight, and you have increased your mercy which you have shown me by saving my life; but I cannot escape to the mountains, lest some evil overtake me and I die.

20 "See now, this city *is* near *enough* to flee to, and it *is* a little one; please let me escape there (*is* it not a little one?) and my soul shall live."

21 And he said to him, "See, I have favored you concerning this thing also, in that I will not overthrow this city for which you have spoken.

22 "Hurry, escape there. For I cannot do anything until you arrive there." Therefore the name of the city was called Zoar.

23 The sun had risen upon the earth when Lot entered Zoar.

24 The the LORD rained brimstone and fire on Sodom and Gomorrah, from the LORD out of the heavens.

25 So He overthrew those cities, all the plain, all the inhabitants of the cities, and what grew on the ground.

26 But his wife looked back behind him, and she became a pillar of salt.

27 And Abraham went early in the morning to the place where he had stood before the LORD.

28 Then he looked toward Sodom and Gomorrah, and toward all the land of the plain; and he saw, and behold, the smoke of the land which went up like the smoke of a furnace.

29 And it came to pass, when God destroyed the cities of the plain, that God remembered Abraham, and sent Lot out of the midst of the overthrow, when He overthrew the cities in which Lot had dwelt.

30 Then Lot went up out of Zoar and dwelt in the mountains, and his two daughters were with him; for he was afraid to dwell in Zoar. And he and his two daughters dwelt in a cave.

31 Now the firstborn said to the younger, "Our father is old, and there is no man on the earth to come in to us as is the custom of all the earth.

32 "Come, let us make our father drink wine, and we will lie with him, that we may preserve the lineage of our father."

33 So they made their father drink wine that night. And the firstborn went in and lay with her father, and he did not know when she lay down or when she arose.

34 It happened on the next day that the firstborn said to the younger, "Indeed I lay with my father last night; let us make him drink wine tonight also, and you go in and lie with him, that we may preserve the lineage of our father."

35 Then they made their father drink wine that night also. And the younger arose and lay with him, and he did not know when she lay down or when she arose.

36 Thus both the daughters of Lot were with child by their father.

37 The firstborn bore a son and called his name Moab; he *is* father of the Moabites to this day.

38 And the younger, she also bore a son and called his name Ben-Ammi; he *is* the father of the people of Ammon to this day.

Gen. 19:1–38

Of the three "men" who visited Abraham One has already been identified as the Lord but now the other two are identified, *"Now the two angels came to Sodom in the evening, and Lot was sitting in the gate of Sodom"* (Gen. 19:1). In much the same way as Abraham greeted them Lot warmly received them, treated them respectfully, and offered hospitality to them. Lot had chosen Sodom as his place of residence and the fact that he sat in the gate showed that he had achieved some measure of success in his chosen domicile. But despite the presence of a righteous, influential man like Lot, Sodom was under a cloud of divine displeasure. We need to be clear about the conditions in the city.

SODOM'S SOCIETY

Sodom was a beautiful place "well watered everywhere . . . like the garden of the Lord" (Gen. 13:10). It offered its inhabitants a life of considerable luxury and hedonistic enjoyment. The Lord said of her, "She and her daughter had pride, fullness of food, and abundance of idleness; neither did she strengthen the hand of the poor and needy. And they were haughty and committed abomination before Me; therefore I took them away as I saw fit" (Ezek. 16:49, 50). The description of the Lord Jesus showed that there was an air of normalcy about the life of many of its inhabitants, "They ate, they drank, they bought, they sold, they planted, they built" (Luke 17:28) but Peter used very strong language about both the people and the place. In his exposé of this richly endowed city and its people, he said that God had intervened in their affairs by "turning the cities of Sodom and Gomorrah into ashes, condemned them to destruction, making them an example to those who afterward would live ungodly" and describing their activities as "the filthy conduct of the wicked" which "tormented" (2 Pet. 2:6–8) the few righteous people in the city. The reason for this powerful indictment was that the people of the city were blatant about their sin in that they carried on their unspeakable behavior in the midst of everyday life as if it was perfectly acceptable and normal which in their opinion it was! Isaiah said that his contemporaries were like the people of Sodom in that, "The look on their countenance witnesses against them, and they declare their sin as Sodom; they do not hide it. Woe to their soul!" (Isa. 3:9).

SODOM'S SIN

The demands of the townspeople that Lot's two visitors should be sent out to them that they might *"know them"* (Gen. 19:5) has been interpreted by some as meaning that the visitors had arrived without their credentials being checked. But it is difficult to see why Lot should have been so concerned about his guests' safety, why he should have offered his daughters as sex objects, and why he should have risked life and limb in the mob which was beating down his door if it was just a matter of checking passports! There seems to be little reason to doubt that what the men of Sodom had in mind was the kind of sexual activity to which Sodom has lent its name and which was not only roundly condemned at the time of this incident but was punishable with death in the Law (see Lev. 20:13) and was treated to the greatest censure by the writers of the New Testament (see Rom. 1:26, 27; 1 Tim. 1:8–11).

Lot's offer of his daughters to the mob which was bent on gang rape is incomprehensible to modern ears. Attempts have been made to show that this may have been a customary procedure in Sodom's culture. If that is the case one can only respond by recognizing the decay of the culture and the erosion of Lot's ethical standards through long exposure to it. Without the dramatic intervention of the visitors it is unlikely that any of the inhabitants of Lot's house would have survived that sad night, but *"they struck the men who were at the doorway of the house with blindness, both small and great, so that they became weary trying to find the door"* (Gen. 19:11). Capitalizing on the time they had bought, the visitors began to check on Lot's extended family in light of the fact that they proposed to destroy the city, saying *"the Lord has sent us to destroy it"* (v. 13).

It is instructive to note the responses of Lot's family to the promised judgment. The sons-in-law thought Lot was joking when he told them, *"Get up, get out of this place; for the Lord will destroy this city!"* (v. 14). Perhaps they did not take Lot seriously because he seemed in no hurry to leave town himself. His wife and daughters were not enthusiastic about leaving their home despite its squalor and the sordidness from which they had so narrowly escaped on the previous night. In fact, the visitors had to drag the reluctant Lot, his wife, and their daughters out of the city in the nick of time. They urged him, *"Escape for your life! Do not look behind you nor stay anywhere in the plain. Escape to the mountains, lest you be destroyed"* (v. 17). But Lot was reluctant to do even that, citing some unspoken fear of living in the mountains—a fear that evidently was greater than his fear of divine judgment!

Sodom's sin was overt in the midst of its attractive normalcy. But it had exacted a terrible toll on the righteous soul of Lot. Without succumbing to its grossest forms Lot had become imbued with the spirit of Sodom, his wife disregarded the command concerning looking back, and the daughters showed clearly that they had been deeply affected by the sexual laxity of the city in which they had done their growing up. What had started out as a choice to live in comfort and pleasantness enjoying the fat of the land had become a nightmare for Lot and his family. Lot had flirted with Sodom and found himself seduced by her and but for the grace of God he would have been destroyed with her and by her.

SODOM'S SIGNIFICANCE

Sodom and Gomorrah have become bywords even in secular vocabulary. They stand for cities that have become morally reprehensible and to the reverent heart speak of the inevitability of divine judgment for sin. Their destruction was so complete that even to this day there is no certain knowledge as to their whereabouts, although there is no doubt about their general location. The Lord Jesus used Sodom as an example of the righteous judgment of God, stating to the inhabitants of Capernaum, "it shall be more tolerable for the land of Sodom in the day of judgment than for you" (Matt. 11:24). Ruth Graham, after she had read the manuscript of one of Billy's books which dealt with the moral climate of the USA, is reputed to have said, "If God does not judge America He will need to apologize to Sodom!" Sodom speaks loud and clear to the cities of the modern world about the patience, mercy, and righteousness of God which must never be abused. Sodom's hold on Lot's wife cost her her life. Warned not to look back she did anyway and was overtaken in the fallout of the explosive destruction of the city. *She became a pillar of salt"* (Gen. 19:26). It is common knowledge that the region of the Dead Sea, which is unusually rich in all manner of mineral deposits, is situated on top of one of the major faults in the earth's surface making it particularly vulnerable to earthquakes and volcanic eruptions. Bearing this in mind it is not too difficult to imagine what probably happened to Mrs. Lot as she paused to look longingly at that which God condemned. *"Remember Lot's wife"* (Luke 17:32) is still one of the most salutary reminders to those who are tempted to look back from the path they have chosen to follow in response to the gracious call of their God.

The gradual erosion of Lot's life appears to be directly related to his time in Sodom. The city appeared to influence him more than he was able to influence the city. This is sadly demonstrated in the pathetic picture with which the chapter ends. Afraid to go to the mountains, as directed, he asked for and received special permission to stay in Zoar. But this did not work out because he was afraid to stay there too. So he and his daughters made their way into the wild country of the mountains—a far cry from the early days in the land of Ur, the special days with Abraham, and the promising days in the beautiful lands of the plain! Eventually the old man succumbed to the scheming of his unscrupulous daughters, drank himself into a stupor, and engaged in incestuous relations which were to produce offspring from whom would come long chapters of even sadder history.

Meanwhile Abraham continued to walk before the Lord. As he *"went early in the morning to the place where he had stood before the Lord"* (Gen. 19:27) he saw *"the smoke of the land which went up like the smoke of a furnace"* (v. 28). Abraham had experienced his difficulties but he was standing firm even as Lot was being rescued by the skin of his teeth, and when Lot's life finally disintegrated the man of God was going on quietly from strength to strength. It is no secret what a Sodom can do to a careless man and his family.

CHAPTER TWENTY

The Danger of Underestimating

Genesis 20:1–18

20:1 And Abraham journeyed from there to the South, and dwelt between Kadesh and Shur, and stayed in Gerar.

2 Now Abraham said of Sarah his wife, "She *is* my sister." And Abimelech king of Gerar sent and took Sarah.

3 But God came to Abimelech in a dream by night, and said to him, "Indeed you *are* a dead man because of the woman whom you have taken, for she *is* a man's wife."

4 But Abimelech had not come near her; and he said, "Lord, will You slay a righteous nation also?

5 "Did he not say to me, 'She *is* my sister'? And she, even she herself said, 'He *is* my brother.' In the integrity of my heart and innocence of my hands I have done this."

6 And God said to him in a dream, "Yes, I know that you did this in the integrity of your heart. For I also withheld you from sinning against Me; therefore I did not let you touch her.

7 "Now therefore, restore the man's wife; for he *is* a prophet, and he will pray for you and you shall live. But if you do not restore *her*, know that you shall surely die, you and all who *are* yours."

8 So Abimelech rose early in the morning, called all his servants, and told all these things in their hearing; and the men were very much afraid.

9 And Abimelech called Abraham and said to him, "What have you done to us? How have I offended you, that you have brought on me and on my kingdom a

great sin? You have done deeds to me that ought not to be done."

10 Then Abimelech said to Abraham, "What did you have in view, that you have done this thing?"

11 And Abraham said, "Because I thought, surely the fear of God *is* not in this place; and they will kill me on account of my wife.

12 "But indeed *she is* truly my sister. She *is* the daughter of my father, but not the daughter of my mother; and she became my wife.

13 "And it came to pass, when God caused me to wander from my father's house, that I said to her, 'This *is* your kindness that you should do for me: in every place, wherever we go, say of me, "He *is* my brother."'"

14 Then Abimelech took sheep, oxen, and male and female servants, and gave *them* to Abraham; and he restored Sarah his wife to him.

15 And Abimelech said, "See, my land *is* before you; dwell where it pleases you."

16 Then to Sarah he said, "Behold, I have given your brother a thousand *pieces* of silver; indeed this vindicates you before all who *are* with you and before everybody." Thus she was rebuked.

17 So Abraham prayed to God; and God healed Abimelech, his wife, and his female servants. Then they bore *children;*

18 for the Lord had closed up all the wombs of the house of Abimelech because of Sarah, Abraham's wife.

Gen. 20:1–18

Ever since Eve underestimated the serpent, human beings have been making the same mistake. Goliath underestimated David, the Israelites underestimated Ai, Chamberlain underestimated Hitler, and the Americans underestimated the Vietnamese. In all these cases the results were serious. Abraham had a marked tendency to underestimation and in his case the results could have been far more serious than they were. The difference was divine intervention.

UNDERESTIMATING PERSONAL CHARACTERISTICS

They say you can't teach an old dog new tricks and seeing that Abraham by this time was 100 years old perhaps it is not surprising that his personal characteristics were well established—both good and bad. He had never been able to conquer a deep-rooted fear that his beautiful wife would catch somebody's eye, and they would get rid of him in order to have her. Some scholars have seen this story as a duplicate of the one recorded in chapter 12 but in light of the fact that all humans are known to have a remarkable capacity for failing to learn by mistakes there seems to be no reason why we should not accept the story as a sad repetition of a familiar weakness.

This streak of fear in Abraham is even more noteworthy when we remember his fearless approach to life in so many other dimensions. He had not been afraid to launch out in faith from Ur. He had been anything but fearful when he chased the kings who had captured Lot. He had even been bold enough to challenge God in his intercession for Sodom. But when it came to his own fears concerning his wife his Achilles' heel continued to be exposed. Sadly, he had not carefully calculated this weakness and as a result had not made proper compensation for it.

There was also a disconcerting tendency on Abraham's part to take a cavalier attitude to the truth when it suited his purposes. After he had been caught in his subterfuge he explained the situation to Abimelech as follows, *"when God caused me to wander from my father's house, that I said to her, 'This is your kindness that you should do for me: in every place, wherever we go, say of me, "He is my brother"'"* (Gen. 20:13). Kidner points out that he said literally, "when the gods caused me to wander," an expression which not only failed to testify to the uniqueness of his relationship with Jehovah but also implied that there was something less than beneficial about what "the gods" had caused to happen in his life. Abraham was perilously close to using the common excuse, "the devil made me do it!", thereby exonerating himself.

Another weakness showed in this incident. When Abraham said to Abimelech, *"I thought, surely the fear of God is not in this place"* (v. 11), he exhibited a certain high-mindedness which was not at all becoming in the circumstances. It was he whose morality was questionable, not the Philistines'. The words of the Lord Jesus

177

spoken so much later would have applied, "How can you say to your brother, 'Let me remove the speck from your eye'; and look, a plank is in your eye?" (Matt. 7:4).

UNDERESTIMATING SPIRITUAL CONSIDERATIONS

There are three spiritual considerations which appear to have escaped Abraham's reckoning—spiritual exhaustion, spiritual amnesia, and spiritual myopia. It is not uncommon to find spiritual exhaustion following some spiritual high point. Anticlimax can come swiftly on the heels of spiritual climax. After his remarkable experience of prayer and victory in the Sodom affair Abraham promptly lapsed into old patterns of behavior which were strangely incompatible with what had just taken place. Elijah had a similar experience after the confrontation on Carmel with the priests of Baal and countless saints have learned to be on their guard against a spiritual letdown in their own lives. Spiritual amnesia is dangerous when it allows an Abraham to forget about the promises of God particularly as they relate to his wife's role in the divine plan for the nations. If Sarah had disappeared into the lives of the Philistines what would have become of the promised son for whom they had waited so long? Under pressure it is not unusual for spiritual forgetfulness to take over with dire consequences. Abraham was also suffering from spiritual myopia. His shortsightedness was such that he who had been so concerned that God should deal justly with Sodom and its inhabitants now appeared to be totally unaware that he himself was showing no concern whatsoever for the inhabitants of Gerar in general and their king Abimelech in particular. Abraham's vision was filled with his own concerns; his perspective was warped to the shape of his own paranoia. It is a serious matter to underestimate the human potential for spiritual miscalculation.

UNDERESTIMATING SPECIAL CIRCUMSTANCES

We do not know why Abraham chose to travel into the Negev but it was probably related to the needs of his flocks and herds. However, he had to be conversant with the particular dangers of living in different environments. He had his own experience of living in Egypt to consider, and his recent observation of what happened to Lot in Sodom should have been warning enough to tread lightly. Coleridge was right when he said, "If men could learn from history, what lessons it might teach us!"

UNDERESTIMATING PRACTICAL CONSEQUENCES

When Abimelech discovered that he was the victim of Abraham and Sarah's conniving he was understandably upset, not only because he had incurred divine displeasure, but because he and his people had suffered considerable loss of face. He quite rightly protested that he had been misled by both Abraham and his wife and objected strenuously when he thought that God was going to judge him for his deed, saying, *"In the integrity of my heart and innocence of my hands I have done this"* (Gen. 20:5). Calling everyone together he explained to them what had happened and then turned to Abraham and asked, *"What have you done to us? How have I offended you, that you have brought on me and on my kingdom a great sin? You have done deeds to me that ought not to be done"* (v. 9). Abraham had not calculated on the possible loss of face for Abimelech. Neither had he given much thought to the possibility of Sarah's loss of virtue or his own loss of credibility. He must have felt uncomfortable when, after he had been exposed, the Lord introduced him to Abimelech as, *"a prophet, and he shall pray for you and you shall live"* (v. 7).

But the greatest miscalculation in terms of practical consequences had to do with the possible loss of the special son who was promised and whom Abraham and Sarah were so anxious to welcome into the world. It should not be forgotten that when fear comes in the door rational thought, spiritual insight, and moral integrity are sometimes all too anxious to beat a hasty retreat. Abraham once again reminds us that actions have consequences and it is wise to "look before you leap"!

UNDERESTIMATING DIVINE CONTROL

Once again the theme of God's sovereignty in the affairs of men takes center stage. Abraham had drastically miscalculated and without the dramatic intervention of the Almighty all manner of evil could and would have resulted. *"But God came to Abimelech in a dream by night, and said to him, 'Indeed you are a dead man because of the woman whom you have taken, for she is a man's wife'"* (v. 3). The king of Gerar had not *"come near her"* (v. 4), had been misled, and therefore protested his innocence to which the Lord replied, *"Yes, I know that you did this in the integrity of your heart. For I also withheld you from sinning against Me; therefore I did not let you touch her"* (v. 6). Abraham's carefully laid plans had run into the roadblock of divine control for which he would eventually be immensely grateful! With a delightful touch of irony the Lord told Abimelech that Abraham would pray for him, which he eventually did, with the result that *"God healed Abimelech, his wife, and his female servants. Then they bore children; for the Lord had closed up all the wombs of the house of Abimelech because of Sarah, Abraham's wife"* (vv. 17, 18). The Lord was undoubtedly in control and if there was any doubt about it in Abraham's mind it was dispelled when *"Abimelech took sheep, oxen, and male and female servants, and gave them to Abraham; and he restored Sarah his wife to him"* (v. 14). In addition he was told to settle wherever he wished and Sarah walked away with a present of a thousand pieces of silver!

It is possible to miscalculate in many areas of life but there is no greater miscalculation than the one that assumes either that God is disinterested in human affairs or is incapable of intervention.

CHAPTER TWENTY-ONE

A Time for Every Purpose

Genesis 21:1–34

21:1 And the LORD visited Sarah as He had said, and the LORD did for Sarah as He had spoken.

2 For Sarah conceived and bore Abraham a son in his old age, at the set time of which God had spoken to him.

3 And Abraham called the name of his son who was born to him—whom Sarah bore to him—Isaac.

4 Then Abraham circumcised his son Isaac when he was eight days old, as God had commanded him.

5 Now Abraham was one hundred years old when his son Isaac was born to him.

6 And Sarah said, "God has made me laugh, *and* all who hear will laugh with me."

7 She also said, "Who would have said to Abraham that Sarah would nurse children? For I have borne *him* a son in his old age."

8 So the child grew and was weaned. And Abraham made a great feast on the same day that Isaac was weaned.

9 And Sarah saw the son of Hagar the Egyptian, whom she had borne to Abraham, scoffing.

10 Therefore she said to Abraham, "Cast out this bondwoman and her son; for the son of this bond-woman shall not be heir with my son, *namely* with Isaac."

11 And the matter was very displeasing in Abraham's sight because of his son.

12 But God said to Abraham, "Do not let it be displeasing in your sight because of the lad or because of your bondwoman. Whatever Sarah has said to

you, listen to her voice; for in Isaac your seed shall be called.

13 "Yet I will also make a nation of the son of the bondwoman, because he *is* your seed."

14 So Abraham rose early in the morning, and took bread and a skin of water; and putting *it* on her shoulder, he gave *it* and the boy to Hagar, and sent her away. Then she departed and wandered in the Wilderness of Beersheba.

15 And the water in the skin was used up, and she placed the boy under one of the shrubs.

16 Then she went and sat down across from *him* at a distance of about a bowshot; for she said to herself, "Let me not see the death of the boy." So she sat opposite *him*, and lifted her voice and wept.

17 And God heard the voice of the lad. Then the angel of God called to Hagar out of heaven, and said to her, "What ails you, Hagar? Fear not, for God has heard the voice of the lad where he *is*.

18 "Arise, lift up the lad and hold him with your hand, for I will make him a great nation."

19 Then God opened her eyes, and she saw a well of water. And she went and filled the skin with water, and gave the lad a drink.

20 So God was with the lad; and he grew and dwelt in the wilderness, and became an archer.

21 He dwelt in the Wilderness of Paran; and his mother took a wife for him from the land of Egypt.

22 And it came to pass at that time that Abimelech and Phichol, the commander of his army, spoke to Abraham, saying, "God *is* with you in all that you do.

23 "Now therefore, swear to me by God that you will not deal falsely with me, with my offspring, or with my posterity; but that according to the kindness that I have done to you, you will do to me and to the land in which you have dwelt."

24 And Abraham said, "I will swear."

25 Then Abraham rebuked Abimelech because of a well of water which Abimelech's servants had seized.

26 And Abimelech said, "I do not know who has

done this thing; you did not tell me, nor had I heard
of it until today."

27 So Abraham took sheep and oxen and gave them
to Abimelech, and the two of them made a covenant.

28 And Abraham set seven ewe lambs of the flock
by themselves.

29 Then Abimelech asked Abraham, "What *is the
meaning of* these seven ewe lambs which you have set
by themselves?"

30 And he said, "You will take *these* seven ewe
lambs from my hand, that they may be my witness
that I have dug this well."

31 Therefore he called that place Beersheba, because the two of them swore an oath there.

32 Thus they made a covenant at Beersheba. So
Abimelech rose with Phichol, the commander of his
army, and they returned to the land of the Philistines.

33 Then *Abraham* planted a tamarisk tree in Beersheba, and there called on the name of the LORD, the
Everlasting God.

34 And Abraham stayed in the land of the Philistines
many days.

Gen. 21:1–34

After many dramatic events, delays, and roller-coaster experiences, *"the Lord visited Sarah as He had said, and the Lord did for Sarah
as He had spoken. For Sarah conceived and bore Abraham a son in his
old age. . . . And Abraham called the name of his son . . . Isaac"*
(Gen. 21:1–3). Once again the Lord had proved Himself faithful to
His word. Repeatedly He had promised a dramatic intervention in
the affairs of His children and relentlessly He had carried out His
purposes sometimes despite the well-meaning efforts and not so
well-meaning attitudes of Abraham and Sarah. The baby had safely
arrived and, in addition to naming him, *"Abraham circumcised his son
Isaac when he was eight days old, as God had commanded him"* (v. 4).
The deeply spiritual aspects of this event cannot be overlooked as
we note that everything was done as the Lord had spoken, in the
light of what He had promised, and because He had commanded.
But Sarah's spirituality did not preclude her from some very down-
to-earth celebrating! In fact, it was her laughter which played a major role in the naming of the boy, for Isaac means "laughter."

A TIME TO LAUGH

Long before the wisest man who ever lived penned Ecclesiastes, Abraham and Sarah discovered that "to everything there is a season, a time for every purpose under heaven" including "a time to heal . . . a time to laugh; a time to mourn" (Eccles. 3:1–4). Sarah's laughter, when she heard the news of the impending birth from her position behind the tent flap, while understandable was regarded as impermissible by the Lord. She tried to deny that she had laughed rather than admit that sometimes laughter can be the reaction of incredulity and disbelief. It is doubtful if the elderly lady would have been severely censured for incredulous laughter given the circumstances but it was made clear to her that disbelief and denial of disbelief are not acceptable to the Lord. But now her laughter was totally different. It was the laughter of delight, the overflowing emotion of gratitude and excitement and as such it was appropriate and acceptable.

When my first son was born I was out of town on business but naturally I returned home post haste. So post was my haste that I found myself overtaking a police car in a built-up restricted area with a grin on my face that wouldn't wash off! When I arrived at the hospital and was reunited with my wife and introduced to my son I am told that I held the little bundle tightly (like a rugby ball that I was afraid to fumble) and laughed and laughed. It was not that he was particularly funny looking or that the situation was particularly funny but the only suitable emotional response that I was capable of at that moment was uncontrollable laughter. I know how Sarah felt because I too knew, at that moment, something of the unique delight of holding a special gift from the Lord. God certainly made us with mouths that smile and all kinds of facial muscles which when working properly produce evidence of delight and celebration. He is a God of joy and knows not only how to rejoice over His children with gladness but also rejoices over us with singing (see Zeph. 3:17).

Unfortunately, Sarah's smile froze on her face one day because she saw Ishmael, Abraham's son by Hagar, the Egyptian girl, mocking her darling Isaac. This she was not prepared to accept as she was obviously far from happy about having Hagar and the boy in the family setting in the first place. Whether or not Ishmael was just being a typical nasty big brother engaging in adolescent misbehavior (the word "mocking" is related to "laughing") we do not know but we do know that Sarah's response indicated that she did not regard Isaac as a laughing matter at all! *Therefore she said to Abraham, 'Cast out this bondwoman and her son; for the son of this bondwoman shall not be heir with my son, namely with Isaac'"* (Gen. 21:10). The time to laugh had given way to something else nowhere near as pleasant.

A TIME TO MOURN

Abraham was horrified by Sarah's antagonism and hostility toward the boy Ishmael. Ishmael was Abraham's son, but he was not Sarah's son and even though she had made the arrangement by which he was born there would never beat in Sarah's heart the same love that throbbed in Abraham's veins. Surprisingly, however, the Lord said to Abraham, *"Do not let it be displeasing in your sight because of the lad or because of your bondwoman. Whatever Sarah has said to you, listen to her voice; for in Isaac your seed shall be called"* (v. 12). No doubt Abraham struggled with the perception that the Lord was taking Sarah's side in this conflict until he was reminded that while the promised seed would come through Isaac the Lord still had plans for Ishmael who was just as much Abraham's son as Isaac. The Lord said to him, *"Yet I will also make a nation of the son of the bondwoman, because he is your seed"* (v. 13). With a heavy heart the old man made preparations to send off his firstborn son with the woman who for many years had been part of his household. He was not the only one grieving because it was not long before Hagar and Ishmael ran out of water and faced imminent death in the wilderness. Having placed the boy under the scant shade of a shrub, *"she sat opposite him, and lifted her voice and wept"* (v. 16). The boy, while understandably afraid and weak, did not waste his time under the bush. He cried out to the Lord and He intervened and through His angel said, *"What ails you, Hagar? Fear not, for God has heard the voice of the lad where he is. Arise, lift up the lad and hold him with your hand, for I will make of him a great nation"* (vv. 17, 18). Abraham mourning for his loss, Hagar mourning her impending death and bereavement, and Ishmael crying out in anguish combine to present a picture of our world which knows so much about the time to mourn yet so often has few resources to meet tragedy when it comes. They need an experience not unlike Hagar's, *"then God opened her eyes, and she saw a well of water. And she went and filled the skin with water, and gave the lad a drink. So God was with the lad"* (vv. **19, 20**). Isaiah stated magnificently what the Lord has always promised to those who will hear His voice:

> The Lord has anointed Me . . .
> To comfort all who mourn,
> To console those who mourn in Zion,
> To give them beauty for ashes,
> The oil of joy for mourning.
>
> *Isa. 61:1–3*

On more than one occasion the Lord Jesus did exactly that for those whose paths crossed His and today He still works through His body the church to accomplish similarly delightful divine ends. It might be appropriate to mention at this juncture that Paul's application of this story in Gal. 4:21–31 should not be understood in such a way as to suggest that the progeny of Ishmael are outside the offer of divine grace any more than those who are the natural children of Isaac are automatically the recipients of saving grace.

A TIME TO HEAL

The old problem of grazing rights raised its ugly head soon after Abraham had bidden a reluctant farewell to his son. Abimelech with whom he had had previous problems came to see him one day, greeted him most courteously, *"God is with you in all that you do"* (Gen. 21:22), and then asked Abraham for a specific undertaking of loyalty and friendship in light of the generous way in which he had chosen to resolve their earlier confrontation. Abraham agreed but took the opportunity to point out that some of Abimelech's men had seized one of his wells. It appears that this may have been a long-standing complaint but Abimelech said, *"I do not know who has done this thing; you did not tell me, nor had I heard of it until today"* (v. 26). Clearly there were all the makings of a typical feud between the two men but they were both too wise to allow that to happen. The situation needed to be healed, not heated.

It is instructive to note that they confronted each other with their complaints. They both listened respectfully to what the other had to say, answers were given, and then a formal covenant agreement was drawn up which was probably "sealed" with the blood of sacrificed animals. Abraham offered and Abimelech accepted seven ewe lambs as a token of their agreement, the well was named Beersheba (a word which is related to "swear as in a covenant"), a special tree was planted, and Abraham called on *the Lord, the Everlasting God* (v. 33). They understood that there is a time to heal. Similar steps when used wisely today at points of conflict can still produce harmony in the place of discord and cooperation where previously there was only confrontation.

CHAPTER TWENTY-TWO

Faith's High Point

Genesis 22:1–24

22:1 Now it came to pass after these things that God tested Abraham, and said to him, "Abraham!" And he said, "Here I am."

2 Then he said, "Take now your son, your only *son* Isaac, whom you love, and go to the land of Moriah, and offer him there as a burnt offering on one of the mountains of which I shall tell you."

3 So Abraham rose early in the morning and saddled his donkey, and took two of his young men with him, and Isaac his son; and he split the wood for the burnt offering, and arose and went to the place of which God had told him.

4 Then on the third day Abraham lifted his eyes and saw the place afar off.

5 And Abraham said to his young men, "Stay here with the donkey; the lad and I will go yonder and worship, and we will come back to you."

6 So Abraham took the wood of the burnt offering and laid *it* on Isaac his son; and he took the fire in his hand, and a knife, and the two of them went together.

7 But Isaac spoke to Abraham his father and said, "My father!" And he said, "Here I am, my son." Then he said, "Look, the fire and the wood, but where *is* the lamb for a burnt offering?"

8 And Abraham said, "My son, God will provide for Himself the lamb for a burnt offering." So the two of them went together.

9 Then they came to the place of which God had told him. And Abraham built an altar there and

placed the wood in order; and he bound Isaac his son and laid him on the altar, upon the wood.

10 And Abraham stretched out his hand and took the knife to slay his son.

11 But the Angel of the LORD called to him from heaven and said, "Abraham, Abraham!" So he said, "Here I am."

12 And He said, "Do not lay your hand on the lad, or do anything to him; for now I know that you fear God, since you have not withheld your son, your only *son*, from Me."

13 Then Abraham lifted his eyes and looked, and there behind *him was* a ram caught in a thicket by its horns. So Abraham went and took the ram, and offered it up for a burnt offering instead of his son.

14 And Abraham called the name of the place, The-LORD-Will-Provide; as it is said *to* this day, "In the Mount of the LORD it shall be provided."

15 Then the Angel of the LORD called to Abraham a second time out of heaven,

16 and said: "By Myself I have sworn, says the LORD, because you have done this thing, and have not withheld your son, your only *son*—

17 "in blessing I will bless you, and multiplying I will multiply your descendants as the stars of the heaven and as the sand which *is* on the seashore; and your descendants shall possess the gate of their enemies.

18 "In your seed all the nations of the earth shall be blessed, because you have obeyed My voice."

19 So Abraham returned to his young men, and they rose and went together to Beersheba; and Abraham dwelt at Beersheba.

20 Now it came to pass after these things that it was told Abraham, saying, "Indeed Milcah also has borne children to your brother Nahor:

21 "Huz his firstborn, Buz his brother, Kemuel the father of Aram,

22 "Chesed, Hazo, Pildash, Jidlaph, and Bethuel."

23 And Bethuel begot Rebekah. These eight Milcah bore to Nahor, Abraham's brother.

24 His concubine, whose name was Reumah, also
bore Tebah, Gaham, Thahash, and Maachah.
Gen. 22:1–24

If the progress of Abraham's faith could have been drawn on a piece of graph paper it would have looked like the Himalayas, with many staggering pinnacles of trust interspersed with deep valleys of doubt. But towering over the other incidents was Everest, or to put it more accurately Mt. Moriah! What took place there stands throughout human history as one of the great demonstrations of man's faith in a faithful God.

THE INCIDENT AS A TEST

"Now it came to pass after these things that God tested Abraham, and said to him, '. . . Take now your son, your only son Isaac, whom you love, and go to the land of Moriah, and offer him there as a burnt offering on one of the mountains of which I shall tell you'" (Gen. 22:1, 2). Some have seen this story as evidence that Abraham had embraced some of the awful practices of the Canaanite culture but the Scripture states unequivocally *"that God tested Abraham"* (v. 1). Modern man, if he believes in God, has a tendency to think of the God in Whom he believes as a benevolent figure Whose main concern is to make man feel good about himself. This God is regarded as something like the recreational director on a cruise ship whose task is to give everyone a good time with no expense spared. The idea that God might initiate a test is therefore foreign to many people both outside and inside the Kingdom. But James put it in perspective when he wrote, "My brethren, count it all joy when you fall into various trials, knowing that the testing of your faith produces patience. But let patience have its perfect work, that you may be perfect and complete, lacking nothing" (James 1:2, 3). Faith is matured through the experience of stressful testing in much the same way that the cardiovascular system is strengthened through exercise and the muscles are developed by pumping iron. James made another major contribution to our understanding when, using the Moriah incident as an example, he explained that, "faith by itself, if it does not have works, is dead" (James 2:17). Faith is not lived out in a vacuum. It operates in the tensions of

190

life and often demonstrates itself more fully by its responses to the furnace of affliction than the warm shallow waters of ease and prosperity. For faith to become visible it has to perform, or as James said, "Show me your faith without your works, and I will show you my faith by my works" (James 2:18). The Lord was providing Abraham with the most awesome stage upon which his faith could not only be strengthened but also displayed.

The human aspects of the story are compelling in the extreme. Abraham's natural paternal love was probably more intense than most if only because Isaac had been so long promised, so wonderfully born, and so miraculously presented to this man in his old age. The expression *"your only son"* (Gen. 22:2) must have hurt deeply in light of the fact that Abraham had only recently said a reluctant, sad farewell to Ishmael who was now being regarded as nonexistent as far as the immediate events were concerned. Abraham was being asked to evaluate his faith in terms of his natural affections and no loving human being can take such testing lightly. The social aspects of the case could not be disregarded. If Abraham became known as the man who, in his old age, had callously murdered his own son and had given peculiar religious reasons for doing such a thing it would be reasonable to assume that he would have been regarded by his contemporaries as some kind of freak. Knowing Sarah as we now do, it takes little imagination to guess what her reactions would have been.

But these concerns pale alongside the spiritual ramifications of what Abraham was being asked to do. Wrapped up in Isaac were the promises of God to Abraham regarding his own succession but more importantly regarding the salvation of the race. God had revealed to Abraham the unique significance of this young boy and he knew that for the promises of God to be fulfilled the life of Isaac had to be preserved. The dilemma was obvious. The promise of God required that Isaac should live while the command of God demanded that he should die. Abraham was suddenly confronted with that most awesome of problems—a self-contradictory God! Unbelief stumbles over such problems while mature faith waits to see how the distant recesses of the wisdom of God hidden from human reason and understanding will be made known. But the waiting can be excruciating and many people, rather than bear the pain, simply abandon the faith.

There are numerous small details in this story which highlight the faith of the old man. Abraham was told to go to the general region of Moriah with no more specific instructions than *"offer him there as a burnt offering on one of the mountains of which I shall tell you"* (v. 2). On the strength of that he made preparations. There was no quibbling about details! With these limited instructions he *"rose early in the morning . . . and arose and went to the place of which God had told him"* (v. 3). There was no delayed response on Abraham's part. Three days the old man and his young son traveled together. The younger puzzled, the old man troubled. But they pressed on. There was no partial obedience in Abraham now; his faith though troubled was firm. This is clearly shown in the conversations which took place during the journey. To the young men he said, *"Stay here with the donkey; the lad and I will go yonder and worship, and we will come back to you"* (v. 5). Only Abraham knew the significance of what he was saying. He was promising that the youngster who was about to die would also return with him. The writer of the Hebrews epistle explains "By faith Abraham, when he was tested, offered up Isaac . . . concluding that God was able to raise him up, even from the dead, from which he also received him in a figurative sense" (Heb. 11:17–19). To the questioning youngster who wanted to know how they could sacrifice without a sacrificial animal he replied with amazing confidence, *"My son, God will provide for Himself the lamb for a burnt offering"* (Gen. 22:8).

The testing of Abraham's faith shows that his was no reckless abandonment to irrational behavior. Nor was it an uncaring, callous procession along the pathway of careless irresponsibility. Abraham's faith was relentlessly locked in to the premise that God was faithful and that as He had promised to do certain things. Anything that would get in the way of His ultimate purpose had to be removed and in all probability when the issues were truly faced only God Himself would be able to remove the obstacles. Therefore he pressed on not always knowing how or why or where or when but always knowing Who! Abraham reminds believers in all generations that faith in a faithful God will stretch them to the limits of their physical, emotional, social, intellectual, and spiritual beings but the stretching will serve only to expand their capacity to know God and in that knowing to discover the vast potential of life lived by faith.

I have a friend who is a devoted Christian. She is single and perfectly happy to be single although not at all averse to being married if the right person should come along. She spends no time at all looking, but believes that in the course of a life of service that God will bring someone along in the context of that service if He so chooses. A few years ago a wonderful man came into her life. He was distinguished, respected, successful, and committed to the Lord's service. All who knew about the burgeoning relationship were ecstatic. But I had a major problem because I was aware of a circumstance in the gentleman's life which in my opinion disqualified him from marrying the young lady. I had to tell her although I did not relish the thought. Her reaction was prompt and superb. She told me that she would love to be married to the gentleman but if the circumstance I had outlined was true then she did not have freedom to do so because of God's law and the relationship would therefore be terminated and all thought of marriage dismissed.

In unrelenting obedience her trust in the Lord came through. She believed God had told her to take a knife to a precious thing in her life and she did it. Her Mt. Moriah experience may not have held all the pain of Abraham's but it showed similar obedient faith.

THE INCIDENT AS A TRIUMPH

Having arrived on the top of Mt. Moriah, which incidentally was also to become the site of Solomon's Temple and accordingly a most sacred place to the Jews, and years later the site of the Mosque of Omar (a place revered by the followers of Islam), Abraham busied himself building the altar and preparing for sacrifice still not at all sure what was going to happen. But he was absolutely sure that the faithful God was about to do something. Then to the amazement of Isaac the old man grabbed him, bound him, and threw him on the altar. Bearing in mind the age of Abraham and that Isaac was a teenager at the time one can reasonably assume that there was a degree of trustful acquiescence on the part of the boy. As Abraham stood over the boy with knife raised high, heart breaking, and faith stretched to unspeakable limits God spoke, *"Do not lay your hand on the lad, or do anything to him; for now I know that you fear God, since you have not withheld your son, your only son, from Me"* (v. 12). Once again God had intervened and this time there was no disputing that it was a triumph of divine timing. This was the ultimate in brinks-manship! Not a minute too soon God had acted, but not a minute too late either! Abraham had to be taken to that point to see what was in his heart, not only for God to see, but also for Abraham to see for himself, not to mention what Isaac saw from his uncomfortable posi-tion on the altar as potential sacrifice.

"Then Abraham lifted his eyes and looked, and there behind him was a ram caught in a thicket by its horns. So Abraham went and took the ram, and offered it up for a burnt offering instead of his son" (v. 13). A triumph of divine provision! Little did Abraham know that when he had told Isaac that God would provide He would do it in such grand fashion. The impact was so great that, *"Abraham called the name of the place, The-Lord-Will-Provide; as it is said to this day, 'In the Mount of the Lord it shall be provided'"* (v. 14). Faith puts people in positions where they can observe God's dazzling abilities in terms of trium-phant timing and providing. Like people who pay exorbitant fees to charter a plane that will fly them high above the pollution so they can see Halley's comet arrive in orbit right on time God's people through faith place themselves in the exact place where God will deliver exactly what is needed at exactly the right time in exactly the right manner. Paul stated it well when, talking of the Incarnation, he said, *"But when the fulness of time had come, God sent forth His Son, born of a woman, born under the law, to redeem those who were under the law"* (Gal. 4:4, 5).

Having gained Abraham's full attention the Lord took the oppor-tunity to point out once again that His plans had not changed and that *"in blessing I will bless you, and multiplying I will multiply your descendants as the stars of the heaven . . . . In your seed all the nations of the earth shall be blessed, because you have obeyed my voice"* (Gen. 22:17, 18). A triumph of communication!

THE INCIDENT AS A TYPE

While it is clear that typology is part of revelation and therefore that the interpretation of types is a valid means of communicating the truth, we should be careful not to be too exuberant in our per-ceptions of types or too creative in our interpretations thereof. With that in mind we may see in Isaac a type of the Suffering Son Who willingly submitted Himself unreservedly to the Father's will. In Abraham we have a poignant picture of the Father Who "did not spare His own Son, but delivered Him up for us all" (Rom. 8:32) and in the ram a type of the Lamb Who died as a substitute for the sins of the world.

When I was a boy I heard a preacher say, "I have five sons and I would not offer up any one of them for any one of you! But God had only one Son and He offered Him freely for the sins of a world that did not even heed His action nor desire His grace." I have not forgotten that and when I look at Abraham's action I see something equally unforgettable! Truly a high point of faith!

CHAPTER TWENTY-THREE

Coping with Death

Genesis 23:1–20

23:1 Sarah lived one hundred and twenty-seven years; *these were* the years of the life of Sarah.

2 So Sarah died in Kirjath Arba (that *is,* Hebron) in the land of Canaan, and Abraham came to mourn for Sarah and to weep for her.

3 Then Abraham stood up from before his dead, and spoke to the sons of Heth, saying,

4 "I *am* a foreigner and a visitor among you. Give me property for a burial place among you, that I may bury my dead out of my sight."

5 And the sons of Heth answered Abraham, saying to him,

6 "Hear us, my lord: You *are* a mighty prince among us; bury your dead in the choicest of our burial places. None of us will withhold from you his burial place, that you may bury your dead."

7 Then Abraham stood up and bowed himself to the people of the land, the sons of Heth.

8 And he spoke with them, saying, "If it is your wish that I bury my dead out of my sight, hear me, and meet with Ephron the son of Zohar for me,

9 "that he may give me the cave of Machpelah which he has, which *is* at the end of his field. Let him give it to me at the full price, as property for a burial place among you."

10 Now Ephron dwelt among the sons of Heth; and Ephron the Hittite answered Abraham in the presence of the sons of Heth, all who entered at the gate of his city, saying,

11 "No, my lord, hear me: I give you the field and

the cave that *is* in it; I give it to you in the presence of the sons of my people. I give it to you. Bury your dead!"

12 Then Abraham bowed himself down before the people of the land;

13 and he spoke to Ephron in the hearing of the people of the land, saying, "If you *will give it,* please hear me. I will give you money for the field; take *it* from me and I will bury my dead there."

14 And Ephron answered Abraham, saying to him,

15 "My lord, listen to me; the land is *worth* four hundred shekels of silver. What *is* that between you and me? So bury your dead."

16 And Abraham listened to Ephron; and Abraham weighed out the silver for Ephron which he had named in the hearing of the sons of Heth, four hundred shekels of silver, currency of the merchants.

17 So the field of Ephron which *was* in Machpelah, which *was* before Mamre, the field and the cave which *was* in it, and all the trees that *were* in the field, which *were* within all the surrounding borders, were deeded

18 to Abraham as a possession in the presence of the sons of Heth, before all who went in at the gate of his city.

19 And after this, Abraham buried Sarah his wife in the cave of the field of Machpelah, before Mamre (that *is,* Hebron) in the land of Canaan.

20 So the field and the cave that *is* in it were deeded to Abraham by the sons of Heth as property for a burial place.

Gen. 23:1–20

After a long and eventful life Sarah died at the ripe old age of 127. Abraham's handling of this traumatic event is helpful because it shows the man of faith coping with one of the greatest challenges of life—the death of a deeply loved and cherished partner. Sarah's death cannot have been totally unexpected given her great age but Abraham grieved nevertheless. They had lived together for many years and seen many dramatic, divine interventions in their lives, but this only served to make Abraham's sense of loss more acute.

THE EXPERIENCE OF DYING

The thought of aging and dying is not pleasant and accordingly people try to avoid thinking about it. Perhaps this is why as many as 50 percent of Americans die without making a will. Great efforts are made to hold back the ravages of aging—diminished physical strength, deteriorating beauty, lapses of memory, loss of hearing and hair, and all kinds of other nasty things. But Nautilus equipment, hair pieces, and plastic surgery notwithstanding, the issue of mortality has to be faced. As a surgeon friend reminded me recently, "It has been proven conclusively that life is one hundred percent fatal." Accepting this without in any way succumbing to morbid despair is a sign of maturity which believers particularly can reasonably be expected to demonstrate. I know of no better expression of a proper attitude than that of the apostle Paul who wrote, "Therefore we do not lose heart. Even though our outward man is perishing, yet the inward man is being renewed day by day" (2 Cor. 4:16).

THE EXPERIENCE OF DEATH

Abraham set about the task of dealing with death as soon as Sarah passed away. He approached his neighbors and said, *"I am a foreigner and a visitor among you. Give me property for a burial place among you, that I may bury my dead out of my sight"* (Gen. 23:4). The poignant expression *"my dead"* expresses something of the burden of death which Abraham felt and the necessity for the burial to be "out of sight" spoke to the necessity of prompt action because of the rapid deterioration of the body once death had taken over. The gruesomeness of death has to be faced but not only at the physical level. Scripture teaches that death, which is the wages of sin (see Rom. 6:23), leads not only to physical separation from loved ones but also spiritual separation from God and eventual eternal separation from His glory. The Christian, of course, is party to the great news of Christ's resurrection and overwhelming victory over death. But while Abraham had a vital faith in the God who had justified him by faith he did not express the buoyant hope of the New Testament believer or even the sentiments of the psalmist, who wrote "I

198

will dwell in the house of the Lord forever" (Ps. 23:6). We can only imagine something of his burden as he went about the practical details of arranging the burial of Sarah. The sons of Heth amongst whom he was living in the region of Hebron were sympathetic to him in his bereavement but they did not miss the opportunity to look out for their own interests even as they were showing great courtesy to the old man. Abraham had freely admitted that he was *a foreigner and a visitor* in their midst and as such he had no rights to own property. For the sons of Heth to have sold him a burial site would have been to establish a precedent which they might later regret. This supports their apparent desire to meet his needs without deeding property to him. Abraham, astute as ever, pointed out a particular plot which he wanted and even though he was given offers he could not refuse he managed to refuse them and came away with the site he wanted at a price he apparently found reasonable. He not only had his place to bury Sarah but he also now owned property in the land the Lord has promised him. It should not go unnoticed that the decision to bury Sarah in Hebron also pointed out Abraham's commitment to remain in the land of promise until all that the Lord had promised had come to pass. Even when confronting death Abraham showed that life must go on.

The Experience of Bereavement

Different cultures have different ways of handling the grief which accompanies bereavement, but it is clear that Abraham was perfectly free to express his grief. He *came to mourn for Sarah and to weep for her* (Gen. 23:2). The people of the East recognize that grief, which is a sense of loss, shock, desolation, and sometimes even guilt, needs to be expressed. They even go to the extent of having professional mourners available where necessary. It is interesting to remember, however, that the people who "wept and wailed loudly" at the bedside of Jairus's daughter "ridiculed Him" within minutes when He asked them, "Why make this commotion and weep? The child is not dead but sleeping" (Mark 5:39, 40). Their phoniness was showing! When bereavement is handled well, grief is expressed but not extended, while the memory of the departed one is held dear even

199

while the one left behind presses on with the life yet to be lived. Acceptance of loss is a matter of practical necessity; adjustment to the new status is a realistic goal. For Christians there is always the added dimension of hope which makes it impossible for them to sorrow "as those who have no hope" (1 Thess. 4:13). So Sarah was laid to rest and Abraham was encouraged to go on living the life of faith which had carried him through yet another of life's pressure points.

CHAPTER TWENTY-FOUR

Commitment

Genesis 24:1–67

24:1 Now Abraham was old, well advanced in age; and the LORD had blessed Abraham in all things.

2 So Abraham said to the oldest servant of his house, who ruled over all that he had, "Please, put your hand under my thigh,

3 "and I will make you swear by the LORD, the God of heaven and the God of the earth, that you will not take a wife for my son from the daughters of the Canaanites, among whom I dwell;

4 "but you shall go to my country and to my family, and take a wife for my son Isaac."

5 And the servant said to him, "Perhaps the woman will not be willing to follow me to this land. Must I take your son back to the land from which you came?"

6 But Abraham said to him, "Beware that you do not take my son back there.

7 "The LORD God of heaven, who took me from my father's house and from the land of my family, and who spoke to me and swore to me, saying, 'To your descendants I give this land,' He will send His angel before you, and you shall take a wife for my son from there.

8 "And if the woman is not willing to follow you, then you will be released from this oath; only do not take my son back there."

9 So the servant put his hand under the thigh of Abraham his master, and swore to him concerning this matter.

10 Then the servant took ten of his master's camels and departed, for all his master's goods *were in* his hand. And he arose and went to Mesopotamia, to the city of Nahor.

11 And he made his camels kneel down outside the city by a well of water at evening time, the time when women go out to draw *water.*

12 Then he said, "O LORD God of my master Abraham, please give me success this day, and show kindness to my master Abraham.

13 "Behold, here I stand by the well of water, and the daughters of the men of the city are coming out to draw water.

14 "Now let it be that the young woman to whom I say, 'Please let down your pitcher that I may drink,' and she says, 'Drink, and I will also give your camels a drink'—*let* her *be the one* You have appointed for Your servant Isaac. And by this I will know that You have shown kindness to my master."

15 And it happened, before he had finished speaking, that behold, Rebekah, who was born to Bethuel, son of Milcah, the wife of Nahor, Abraham's brother, came out with her pitcher on her shoulder.

16 Now the young woman *was* very beautiful to behold, a virgin; no man had known her. And she went down to the well, filled her pitcher, and came up.

17 And the servant ran to meet her and said, "Please let me drink a little water from your pitcher."

18 So she said, "Drink, my lord." Then she quickly let her pitcher down to her hand, and gave him a drink.

19 And when she had finished giving him a drink, she said, "I will draw *water* for your camels also, until they have finished drinking."

20 Then she quickly emptied her pitcher into the trough, ran back to the well to draw *water,* and drew for all his camels.

21 And the man, wondering at her, remained silent so as to know whether the LORD had made his journey prosperous or not.

22 So it was, when the camels had finished drinking,

that the man took a golden nose ring weighing half a shekel, and two bracelets for her wrists weighing ten *shekels* of gold,

23 and said, "Whose daughter *are* you? Tell me, please, is there room *in* your father's house for us to lodge?"

24 So she said to him, "I *am* the daughter of Bethuel, Milcah's son, whom she bore to Nahor."

25 Moreover she said to him, "We have both straw and feed enough, and room to lodge."

26 Then the man bowed down his head and worshiped the LORD.

27 And he said, "Blessed *be* the LORD God of my master Abraham, who has not forsaken His mercy and His truth toward my master. As for me, being on the way, the LORD led me to the house of my master's brethren."

28 So the young woman ran and told her mother's household these things.

29 Now Rebekah had a brother whose name *was* Laban, and Laban ran out to the man by the well.

30 So it came to pass, when he saw the nose ring, and the bracelets on his sister's wrists, and when he heard the words of his sister Rebekah, saying, "Thus the man spoke to me," that he went to the man. And there he stood by the camels at the well.

31 And he said, "Come in, O blessed of the LORD! Why do you stand outside? For I have prepared the house, and a place for the camels."

32 Then the man came to the house. And he unloaded the camels, and provided straw and feed for the camels, and water to wash his feet and the feet of the men who *were* with him.

33 *Food* was set before him to eat, but he said, "I will not eat until I have told about my errand." And he said, "Speak on."

34 So he said, "I *am* Abraham's servant.

35 "The LORD has blessed my master greatly, and he has become great; and He has given him flocks and herds, silver and gold, male and female servants, and camels and donkeys.

36 "And Sarah my master's wife bore a son to my master when she was old; and to him he has given all that he has.

37 "Now my master made me swear, saying, 'You shall not take a wife for my son from the daughters of the Canaanites, in whose land I dwell;

38 'but you shall go to my father's house and to my family, and take a wife for my son.'

39 "And I said to my master, 'Perhaps the woman will not follow me.'

40 "But he said to me, 'The LORD, before whom I walk, will send His angel with you and prosper your way; and you shall take a wife for my son from my family and from my father's house.

41 'You will be clear from this oath when you arrive among my family; for if they will not give *her* to you, then you will be released from my oath.'

42 "And this day I came to the well and said, 'O LORD God of my master Abraham, if You will now prosper the way in which I go,

43 'behold, I stand by the well of water; and it shall come to pass that when the virgin comes out to draw *water*, and I say to her, "Please give me a little water from your pitcher to drink,"

44 'and she says to me, "Drink, and I will draw for your camels also,"—*let* her *be* the woman whom the LORD has appointed for my master's son.'

45 "But before I had finished speaking in my heart, there was Rebekah, coming out with her pitcher on her shoulder; and she went down to the well and drew *water*. And I said to her, 'Please let me drink.'

46 "And she made haste and let her pitcher down from her *shoulder*, and said, 'Drink, and I will give your camels a drink also.' So I drank, and she gave the camels a drink also.

47 "Then I asked her, and said, 'Whose daughter *are* you?' And she said, 'The daughter of Bethuel, Nahor's son, whom Milcah bore to him.' So I put the nose ring on her nose and the bracelets on her wrists.

48 "And I bowed my head and worshiped the LORD,

and blessed the LORD God of my master Abraham, who had led me in the way of truth to take the daughter of my master's brother for his son.

49 "Now if you will deal kindly and truly with my master, tell me. And if not, tell me, that I may turn to the right hand or to the left."

50 Then Laban and Bethuel answered and said, "The thing comes from the LORD; we cannot speak to you either bad or good.

51 "Here is Rebekah before you; take her and go, and let her be your master's son's wife, as the LORD has spoken."

52 And it came to pass, when Abraham's servant heard their words, that he worshiped the LORD, bowing himself to the earth.

53 Then the servant brought out jewelry of silver, jewelry of gold, and clothing, and gave them to Rebekah. He also gave precious things to her brother and to her mother.

54 And he and the men who were with him ate and drank and stayed all night. Then they arose in the morning, and he said, "Send me away to my master."

55 But her brother and her mother said, "Let the young woman stay with us a few days, at least ten; after that she may go."

56 And he said to them, "Do not hinder me, since the LORD has prospered my way; send me away so that I may go to my master."

57 So they said, "We will call the young woman and ask her personally."

58 Then they called Rebekah and said to her, "Will you go with this man?" And she said, "I will go."

59 So they sent away Rebekah their sister and her nurse, and Abraham's servant and his men.

60 And they blessed Rebekah and said to her:

"Our sister, may you become
The mother of thousands of ten thousands;
And may your descendants possess
The gates of those who hate them."

61 Then Rebekah and her maids arose, and they rode on the camels and followed the man. So the servant took Rebekah and departed.

62 Now Isaac came from the way of Beer Lahai Roi, for he dwelt in the South.

63 And Isaac went out to meditate in the field in the evening; and he lifted his eyes and looked, and there, the camels *were* coming.

64 Then Rebekah lifted her eyes, and when she saw Isaac she dismounted from her camel;

65 for she had said to the servant, "Who *is* this man walking in the field to meet us?" The servant said, "It *is* my master." So she took a veil and covered herself.

66 And the servant told Isaac all the things that he had done.

67 Then Isaac brought her into his mother Sarah's tent; and he took Rebekah and she became his wife, and he loved her. So Isaac was comforted after his mother's *death.*

Gen. 24:1–67

Abraham, who by this time was *"well advanced in age,"* still had work to do. He had lived a full and eventful life. He was well placed in that *"the Lord had blessed Abraham in all things"* (Gen. 24:1). But now he had to turn his attention to the future. The Lord had proved Himself faithful throughout Abraham's long life but in order for the divine purposes to be fulfilled Isaac, his son, had to move in the train of God's blessing. Abraham recognized that the choice of a wife was crucial. To a society that has produced "The Dating Game" for our entertainment and computerized dating for our enlightenment, the idea of Abraham sending out his servant to look for a wife for his son is strange indeed. But this was normal practice for a people who believed that healthy, stable marriages require more than physical attraction and romantic and sentimental feelings to make them work. They understood that commitment was at the heart of the matter. While we have no desire to advocate a return to the principles of courtship practiced by the patriarchs and still practiced in many societies we do believe that we need to emphasize in our relationships the things that they found important, which we may have tended to neglect. And commitment needs to head the list.

A COMMITMENT TO PROVIDENCE

Abraham required his senior servant to *"swear by the Lord, God of heaven and the God of the earth"* (v. 3) that he would search for a wife for Isaac, but she must not be a Canaanite and she must be from Abraham's family who still resided in Mesopotamia. The procedure of placing the hand under the thigh was evidently not uncommon as we know that Jacob and Joseph did a similar thing (see Gen. 47:29). There is a strong suggestion of deep intimacy and concern for the reproduction of future generations in the rite, and this, coupled with the requirement that he swear before God, would serve only to impress upon the servant the extreme seriousness of his mission. What he was about to do would have ramifications for the nations of the world and while he would have no conception of the significance of his task he was certainly aware that his master was commissioning him before God and he, himself, was doing what God required of him. All those who serve masters of any kind would do well to remember that there is divine significance in the most menial of tasks and that all should be done "as unto the Lord."

Having received instructions to return to Mesopotamia the servant asked a very reasonable question—*"Perhaps the woman will not be willing to follow me to this land. Must I take your son back to the land from which you came?"* (Gen. 24:5). Abraham's response was swift and unequivocal, *"Beware that you do not take my son back there"* (v. 6). And his reasoning was that the Lord Who had brought him out of Mesopotamia into the land of promise intended to settle Abraham's descendants in the land and therefore there should not even be a thought of returning to the old country and thereby turning their backs on what God had promised. Perhaps the practical-minded servant, who realized he would be called upon to make some hard decisions, was wondering how all this was going to work. But Abraham gave him the clue, *"He will send His angel before you, and you shall take a wife for my son from there"* (v. 7). Abraham's absolute conviction that God would act was, of course, related to his unshakable commitment to the plan that God had outlined to him. He had come too far in his walk with the Lord to doubt that God would not have His own special way of doing what was necessary. His God was too good and too great to allow anything to go wrong at this juncture.

There is, however, a delightful blend of trust in divine intervention and practical attention to detail in this story. Abraham fully recognized that the young lady might not be enthusiastic about going to a land she has never seen to marry a man she has never met so he told his servant, *"and if the woman is not willing to follow you, then you will be released from this oath"*; but he insisted, *"only do not take my son back there"* (v. 8).

The servant loaded up his ten camels and took off in the direction of the land Abraham had left so many years ago. Presumably he knew the area where Abraham's kith and kin were to be found but he could have been forgiven if he felt that finding the right woman for Isaac was rather like finding the proverbial needle in the haystack. But at this point his commitment to the Lord and the assurance of His guidance came through. Going to the center of activity, the well, at the time the young ladies would be on view (the evening watering time for the animals), he stationed himself in a strategic place and prayed a strategic prayer, to the effect that he would ask a young lady to give him a drink and if she answered, *"Drink, and I will also give your camels a drink"* (v. 14), he would assume that she was the one! It should be remembered that a camel can drink up to 25 gallons of water at a lick and she was therefore offering to do a monumental job of backbreaking labor for a total stranger. The old servant knew he was looking for a girl with a willing heart and a strong back. More importantly he was looking for the Lord to guide, not through some coincidental serendipity, but through an ordering of events which would outline His direction. The answer came *"before he had finished speaking"* (v. 15). Rebekah stood before him beautiful, suitable, and eager to help. Her heavy volunteer work was done with a degree of enthusiasm which left the servant wondering at her. Still unsure whether she was the one, he offered her presents, inquired about her family, found everything fitted perfectly, and did what all men do who are committed to the God Who is committed to them—he *"bowed down his head and worshiped the Lord. And he said, 'Blessed be the Lord God of my master Abraham, who has not forsaken His mercy and His truth toward my master. As for me, being on the way, the Lord led me'"* (vv. 26, 27). The key word *"mercy"* is the familiar covenant word *hesed*, clear evidence that the servant knew he was dealing with a God Who was, and is, committed to leading His covenant people to the place and people of His choice.

A COMMITMENT TO PRINCIPLE

Life is so full of decisions that it is imperative that men and women should know how to make good decisions. Many decisions are made purely on the basis of "seat of the pants" intuition. Inspired, or uninspired, guesses at what appears to be the best thing to do are often the order of the day, but not infrequently disorder is the result. It is better if people can learn to establish solid principles upon which their lives are based and then decisions can be made in that context. For instance, if an investor has decided that he will never invest in gold then he won't have to spend a lot of time wondering whether or not to speculate on what appears to be a propitious opportunity to make a quick buck. His established principle has already provided the context for a practical decision. God's people are committed to principles which they believe are rooted in their relationship with Him. It is helpful to note the commitment to principle exhibited in the lives of the major players in the drama before us.

Abraham's unflinching commitment to the principle of separation has already been noted. There was no way that he was prepared to depart from the clearly defined principle that his descendants through whom the promised One would come should not have any connection with the people of Canaan. Adherence to this principle made life much more simple for Abraham in that he knew where not to send his servant to look for a bride. Similar restrictions placed by the Lord on contemporary believers require similar commitment which will not only save them from serious mistakes but will also free them to live in the way He would have them live (see 2 Cor. 6:14).

The model senior servant, whom many people think was Eliezer who would have been heir if Isaac had not been born, was also a man of commitment. He was a man who knew the meaning of integrity. When Abraham asked him to promise before the Lord there was no doubt in either man's mind that the promise would be kept. In days when a promise was a promise and a pledge was a pledge life was considerably more simple and more satisfying. In our modern world there is great opportunity for the believer who is committed to integrity and is willing to show it by eschewing some of the more questionable practices which may be regarded by others as "good business sense." Like the servant of Abraham, the man of integrity who has a sense of commitment to doing what he says he will do and saying exactly what he means to do will become a highly valued member of society.

Rebekah, besides being beautiful and industrious (how could Isaac be so lucky!), was a young woman committed to the principle of chastity. Without going into detail, but clearly making an important point, the Scripture describes her as, *"very beautiful to behold, a virgin; no man had known her"* (Gen. 24:16). While the word "know" is used in the Old Testament in ways similar to our usage it should be noted that in this context, and many others, "to know" means "to have sexual intercourse with." We should not allow this ancient usage to slip by unnoticed because it reminds us that casual sex is far removed from the divine intention. Sexual experience is to be part of the mutual knowing of two persons whose lives are spent in the ongoing discovery of what constitutes their personality and their uniqueness. To divorce sexual activity from this commitment to ongoing discovery, appreciation, enrichment, and enjoyment is not only to debase sex but also to insult the sexual partner. How much of this was known by the young lady living in Mesopotamia centuries ago, we have no way of knowing, but she clearly understood the place and the value of chastity and had stood firm in this regard. Modern men and women may laugh at those who "save themselves for the right person" but strangely when they find the right person themselves they often regret that the person they found has not operated on the principle of chastity. They could learn from Rebekah not only how to slake the thirst of ten camels by hauling 250 gallons of water out of a well but also the much more difficult task of handling the legitimate thirsts and hungers of the body in such a way that they are not satisfied illegitimately.

A COMMITMENT TO PERFORMANCE

The girl hurried home. Her brother Laban, as subsequent chapters will reveal, was not a man to be unimpressed with a display of wealth and *"when he saw the nose ring, and the bracelets on his sister's wrists, and when he heard the words of his sister Rebekah . . . he went to the man . . . and he said, 'Come in, O blessed of the Lord!'"* (vv. 30, 31).

Generous hospitality was extended to Abraham's man and his beasts but he said, *"I will not eat until I have told about my errand"* (v. 33). The story was told, the request was made, the simple challenge was presented, and the response came as Laban and his father, Bethuel, said, *"This thing comes from the Lord; we cannot speak to you either bad or good. Here is Rebekah before you; take her and go, and let her be your master's son's wife, as the Lord has spoken"* (vv. 50, 51). Yet again the servant worshiped in response to the great workings of the Lord, he sealed the agreement with suitable gifts, and after a long, full day fell asleep rejoicing in the Lord's grace and the goodness of the people who had welcomed him so warmly. The next morning he wanted to be on his way but Rebekah's family, not at all unreasonably, asked if they couldn't delay a few days before leaving. But the man was ready to go and said, *"Do not hinder me, since the Lord has prospered my way; send me away so that I may go to my master"* (v. 56). Rebekah was given the opportunity to make the final decision, opted to leave right away, and so they left, with a traditional blessing ringing in their ears which none could have guessed would be so dramatically fulfilled.

Abraham's servant is a wonderful reminder to those who tend to let things slip that when something needs to be done it gets done because people make a commitment to action and don't let things get in the way. He did not hesitate to dispense with a meal when more important things were at hand. He would not even let perfectly legitimate and reasonable requests come between him and the task which he had undertaken. He would probably be branded with the title "workaholic" today, but perhaps he knew something about commitment to performance that is too easily overlooked.

A Commitment to People

Sometimes in the world of principles and performance the forgotten entities are people. This happens in businesses which have goals to meet no matter how exhausted their workers. It sometimes occurs in churches where adherence to principle becomes the anvil on which a sensitive soul is broken and shattered. Commitment to people must stand shoulder to shoulder with other commitments. The servant's commitment to his master Abraham needs no elucidation.

The remarkable commitment of Rebekah to a man she had never seen purely on the basis of the Lord's direction in her life is unparalleled. But another character, who would be around for a long time, appeared at this stage in the story. Deborah was her name and she had been deeply involved in Rebekah's life since infancy, and would be faithfully at her side through the many painful years that stretched ahead.

The caravan made its way homeward and at Beer Lahai Roi Isaac who was "meditating" in the cool of the evening greeted the servant, listened to the wonderful story of God's leading, and then saw for the first time the beautiful young lady who was to be his wife. Simply the story states, *"and he took Rebekah and she became his wife, and he loved her. So Isaac was comforted after his mother's death"* (v. 67). There is no greater commitment to people than that of husband and wife who, in love, step out into life together to be to each other all that God intended. Happy is the couple that knows and practices such commitment. But what heartache awaits those who think they have found a better way!

CHAPTER TWENTY-FIVE

From Womb to Tomb

Genesis 25:1–34

25:1 Abraham again took a wife, and her name *was* Keturah.

2 And she bore him Zimran, Jokshan, Medan, Midian, Ishbak, and Shuah.

3 Jokshan begot Sheba and Dedan. And the sons of Dedan were Asshurim, Letushim, and Leummim.

4 And the sons of Midian *were* Ephah, Epher, Hanoch, Abidah, and Eldaah. All these *were* the children of Keturah.

5 And Abraham gave all that he had to Isaac.

6 But Abraham gave gifts to the sons of the concubines which Abraham had; and while he was still living he sent them eastward, away from Isaac his son, to the country of the east.

7 This *is* the sum of the years of Abraham's life which he lived: one hundred and seventy-five years.

8 Then Abraham breathed his last and died in a good old age, an old man and full *of years*, and was gathered to his people.

9 And his sons Isaac and Ishmael buried him in the cave of Machpelah, which *is* before Mamre, in the field of Ephron the son of Zohar the Hittite,

10 the field which Abraham purchased from the sons of Heth. There Abraham was buried, and Sarah his wife.

11 And it came to pass, after the death of Abraham, that God blessed his son Isaac. And Isaac dwelt at Beer Lahai Roi.

12 Now this *is* the genealogy of Ishmael, Abraham's

son, whom Hagar the Egyptian, Sarah's maidservant, bore to Abraham.

13 And these *were* the names of the sons of Ishmael, by their names, according to their generations: The firstborn of Ishmael, Nebajoth; then Kedar, Adbeel, Mibsam,

14 Mishma, Dumah, Massa,

15 Hadar, Tema, Jetur, Naphish, and Kedemah.

16 These *were* the sons of Ishmael and these *were* their names, by their towns and their settlements, twelve princes according to their nations.

17 These *were* the years of the life of Ishmael: one hundred and thirty-seven years; and he breathed his last and died, and was gathered to his people.

18 (They dwelt from Havilah as far as Shur, which *is* east of Egypt as you go toward Assyria.) He died in the presence of all his brethren.

19 This *is* the genealogy of Isaac, Abraham's son. Abraham begot Isaac.

20 Isaac was forty years old when he took Rebekah as wife, the daughter of Bethuel the Syrian of Padan Aram, the sister of Laban the Syrian.

21 Now Isaac pleaded with the LORD for his wife, because she *was* barren, and the LORD granted his plea, and Rebekah his wife conceived.

22 But the children struggled together within her; and she said, "If *all is* well, why *am I like* this?" So she went to inquire of the LORD.

23 And the LORD said to her:

"Two nations *are* in your womb,
Two peoples shall be separated from your body;
One people shall be stronger than the other,
And the older shall serve the younger."

24 So when her days were fulfilled *for her* to give birth, indeed *there were* twins in her womb.

25 And the first came out red. *He was* like a hairy garment all over; so they called his name Esau.

26 Afterward his brother came out, and his hand took hold of Esau's heel; so his name was called Jacob. Isaac *was* sixty years when she bore them.

27 So the boys grew. And Esau was a skillful hunter, a man of the field; but Jacob was a mild man, dwelling in tents.

28 And Isaac loved Esau because he ate *of his* game, but Rebekah loved Jacob.

29 Now Jacob cooked a stew; and Esau came in from the field, and he *was* weary.

30 And Esau said to Jacob, "Please feed me with the same red *stew,* for I *am* weary." Therefore his name was called Edom.

31 But Jacob said, "Sell me your birthright as of this day."

32 And Esau said, "Look, I *am* about to die; so what *is* this birthright to me?"

33 Then Jacob said, "Swear to me as of this day." So he swore to him, and sold his birthright to Jacob.

34 And Jacob gave Esau bread and stew of lentils; then he ate and drank, arose, and went his way. Thus Esau despised *his* birthright.

Gen. 25:1-34

The experiences of earthly existence originate in the womb and terminate in the tomb. Both womb and tomb present great fascination and mystery to modern man, not to mention the great questions raised about what happens in between.

MAN IN THE TOMB

"This is the sum of the years of Abraham's life which he lived: one hundred and seventy-five years. Then Abraham breathed his last and died in a good old age, an old man and full of years, and was gathered to his people" (Gen. 25:7, 8). Abraham was not taken by surprise when death came calling. Seeing that he was 175 years of age at the time this should not be surprising although it is surprising how often people are unprepared to face death even when they have had every indication that it is coming. Abraham's will was simple in the extreme—*"Abraham gave all that he had to Isaac"* (v. 5)—and at first sight would appear to set the stage for the usual scenario, "Where there's a will, there's a quarrel!" But Abraham had already given gifts to his numerous other sons and had sent them out of the special land and off toward the east. This was not altogether a matter of favoritism. It should be seen as another statement by Abraham that Isaac

was the one through whom God's purposes would be worked out both in the promised land and through the promised people.

Having already purchased a family tomb in which Sarah was buried and made his will Abraham was technically prepared to die. But we need to note that he *"died in a good old age"* (v. 8) which implies, according to Calvin, "a good conscience and a serene and tranquil mind." This old man was also *"full of years"* (v. 8), meaning that he was well satisfied with the life that he had lived and he was ready to move on to other things.

"Gathered to his people" (v. 8), a phrase which we do not use, probably refers, however indistinctly, to the hope in which he died. Whatever Abraham knew about life after death we need not be in doubt because of Christ's resurrection and the promise of eternal life to all those who die in faith.

The death of Abraham also brought together the two half-brothers, Isaac and Ishmael. They had long been estranged but it is good to know that their estrangement could be terminated so that they could cooperatively treat their deceased father with the respect that was his due. It is a sad commentary on human relations that not infrequently it takes a tragedy before people will admit how much they need each other! So Abraham left the scene and his two older sons were left to contemplate life ahead of them. Abraham had made an indelible mark on human history and these two men would also play great roles in human affairs. Both would be the fathers of great peoples; both would be significantly blessed by God; but Isaac was the one through whom the special purposes of God would be fulfilled. The thread of divine intention was still intact.

Man in the Womb

At first sight it seems strange that immediately before the account of Abraham's death we are told that he took another wife called Keturah. We should not necessarily assume that Abraham and Keturah married and had children after the death of Sarah. It is more likely that Keturah was a concubine (see v. 6) who functioned in much the same way as Hagar during the lifetime of Sarah. Alternatively we would need to assume that the old gentleman discovered a new lease on life and started suddenly to reproduce children. In light of the fact

that the chapter also gives details of Ishmael's children and introduces the subject of Isaac's posterity we should assume that the emphasis is on finalizing the account of Abraham's life by showing once
again the thread of succession through which the promised One
would come. As is customary in Genesis this was done by briefly
introducing those wings of the family not involved and highlighting
those which were crucial to the ongoing story.

While our modern world debates such subjects as the status of the
fetus, the time when conception actually takes place, the rights of the
mother and those of the unborn, Genesis gives some interesting insights into life in the womb. *"Now Isaac pleaded with the Lord for his
wife, because she was barren; and the Lord granted his plea, and Rebekah
his wife conceived"* (v. 21). While the emotional aspect of reproduction
is sharply presented in Isaac's pleading, and the physical aspect is
assumed, it is the spiritual aspect which is emphasized. The conception of Isaac's children is directly related to prayer and is attributed to
the action of the Lord. That Rebekah understood this is seen in her
inquiry of the Lord as soon as she had problems in her pregnancy.
*"But the children struggled together within her; and she said, 'If all is
well, why am I like this?' So she went to inquire of the Lord"* (v. 22). The
answer she received must have been somewhat unnerving:

> *Two nations are in your womb,*
> *Two peoples shall be separated from your body;*
> *One people shall be stronger than the other,*
> *And the older shall serve the younger* (v. 23).

This is our introduction to the twins, Esau and Jacob. Before they
were born the Lord had predicted what would happen in their lives.
This should not be interpreted with the kind of fatalism which says,
"There you are! God has it all planned before we are even born so
there's nothing we can do about anything. How can God hold anybody responsible for his or her life when He had planned it all before
he or she was born?" The parallel truth of human responsibility must
always be brought alongside any teaching on divine sovereignty. This
account should be treated with the most profound reverence because
at the least it shows that the Lord is aware of, and concerned about,
and involved in, the very existence of those as yet unborn. The un-
borns were struggling with each other before they were born and this

217

was a preview of the way they would behave toward each other throughout their lives. Some would interpret this as a suggestion that human personality is well on the way to being formed even in the womb, while others would be a little more reticent on the subject. But all would have to admit that the mysteries of life in the womb are profound and wonderful and may never be fully understood despite the phenomenal advances in medical science. This should always lead to a deep sense of wonder and reverence when dealing with the mysteries of the womb.

Isaac and Rebekah were married twenty years before their sons were born and that is probably all to the good in light of the struggles they would experience with their children! Even their birth was un-usual—*"the first came out red. He was like a hairy garment all over; so they called his name Esau. Afterward his brother came out, and his hand took hold of Esau's heel; so his name was called Jacob"* (vv. 25, 26). It is doubtful if anyone would have called Esau a beautiful baby from this unflattering description which suggests he looked like a red, wooly sweater (even his name is close to the word for "hairy"!). And Jacob's name, which described his holding of his twin's foot at birth, while it was related to the idea of God being at our heels, as a guard, came to mean someone who had a tendency to supplant, to trip, or to cheat. The twins had arrived on the scene and the scene would never be the same again.

MAN IN THE MIDDLE

Between womb and tomb there is a lot of living to be done. And it can be done well or badly; it can produce triumph or tragedy. This is brought out clearly in the experiences of the brothers. Their instincts and interests were clearly defined. *"Esau was a skillful hunter, a man of the field; but Jacob was a mild man, dwelling in tents"* (v. 27). What led to the development of the personalities of these men we are not told but an ominous potential for discord is easily discernible. Had the twins not struggled in the womb they probably would have started soon afterward given their major differences and the fact that *"Isaac loved Esau because he ate of his game, but Rebekah loved Jacob"* (v. 28). But the differences in interests reached deeper than indoor versus outdoor living. Esau appreciated Jacob's famous stew and not only because it was as red as his complexion. After a particularly strenuous hunting trip from which he arrived home exhausted and possibly starving he requested some stew and when Jacob offered to trade some for Esau's birthright his impatient and ill-considered answer was, *"Look, I am about to die; so what is this birthright to me?"* (v. 32). A deal was struck and the result was that *"Esau despised his birthright"* (v. 34) while his twin brother showed that he was not at all averse to driving any kind of bargain to get what he wanted. The one was cool and calculating, the other hot-blooded and flippant. The Epistle to the Hebrews calls Esau a "profane person" (Heb. 12:16). Kidner succinctly states, "If Jacob is ruthless here, Esau is feckless."

The birthright, which was so important to Jacob and of such insignificance to Esau that he rated it lower than a dish of stew, was related to the concept that the firstborn was the head of the family and responsible for the well-being of its members' spiritual and material well-being. There were, of course, advantages as well as responsibilities. The firstborn son received the status of the father and also a "double portion" of the inheritance (see Deut. 21:15–17). This meant that considerable prestige, power, and property were involved in the birthright as well as the pressures of caring for the family or tribe. Perhaps Jacob was involved in a power play or perhaps he was showing concern that Esau was not going to do the job properly. We do not know but we do know that Esau showed his colors early in life and continued to live the way he had started. Jacob, however, despite having more than his fair share of faults, did in later years show a willingness to learn and a readiness to change. The Esaus of this world tread a selfish and self-indulgent path to destruction, while the rocky roads of the Jacobs do at least climb higher, leading on to better things.

It is interesting to note that the unusual trading of the birthright recorded in this chapter was not an isolated event. The clay tablets which were discovered in the NE Iraqi city of Nuzi in the late 1920s have shed considerable added light on the patriarchal period because they recount independently what life was like at that time. Esau's transaction is seen in even worse light when we note that one of the Nuzi tablets tells of a similar trade, but the man in question at least regarded his birthright as worth "three sheep"!

CHAPTER TWENTY-SIX

Pressure Points

Genesis 26:1–35

26:1 There was a famine in the land, besides the first famine that was in the days of Abraham. And Isaac went to Abimelech king of the Philistines, in Gerar.

2 Then the LORD appeared to him and said: "Do not go down to Egypt; live in the land of which I shall tell you.

3 "Dwell in this land, and I will be with you and bless you; for to you and your descendants I give all these lands, and I will perform the oath which I swore to Abraham your father.

4 "And I will make your descendants multiply as the stars of heaven; I will give to your descendants all these lands; and in your seed all the nations of the earth shall be blessed;

5 "because Abraham obeyed My voice and kept My charge, My commandments, My statutes, and My laws."

6 So Isaac dwelt in Gerar.

7 And the men of the place asked about his wife. And he said, "She *is* my sister"; for he was afraid to say, "*She is* my wife," *because he thought,* "lest the men of the place kill me for Rebekah, because she *is* beautiful to behold."

8 Now it came to pass, when he had been there a long time, that Abimelech king of the Philistines looked through a window, and saw, and there was Isaac, showing endearment to Rebekah his wife.

9 Then Abimelech called Isaac and said, "Quite obviously she *is* your wife; so how could you say,

'She *is* my sister'?" Isaac said to him, "Because I said, 'Lest I die on account of her.'"

10 And Abimelech said, "What *is* this you have done to us? One of the people might soon have lain with your wife, and you would have brought guilt on us."

11 So Abimelech charged all *his* people, saying, "He who touches this man or his wife shall surely be put to death."

12 Then Isaac sowed in that land, and reaped in the same year a hundredfold; and the LORD blessed him.

13 The man began to prosper, and continued prospering until he became very prosperous;

14 for he had possessions of flocks and possessions of herds and a great number of servants. So the Philistines envied him.

15 Now the Philistines had stopped up all the wells which his father's servants had dug in the days of Abraham his father, and they had filled them with earth.

16 And Abimelech said to Isaac, "Go away from us, for you are much mightier than we."

17 Then Isaac departed from there and pitched his tent in the Valley of Gerar, and dwelt there.

18 And Isaac dug again the wells of water which they had dug in the days of Abraham his father, for the Philistines had stopped them up after the death of Abraham. He called them by the names which his father had called them.

19 Also Isaac's servants dug in the valley, and found a well of running water there.

20 But the herdsmen of Gerar quarreled with Isaac's herdsmen, saying, "The water *is* ours." So he called the name of the well Esek, because they quarreled with him.

21 Then they dug another well, and they quarreled over that *one* also. So he called its name Sitnah.

22 And he moved from there and dug another well, and they did not quarrel over it. So he called its name Rehoboth, because he said, "For now the LORD has made room for us, and we shall be fruitful in the land."

23 Then he went up from there to Beersheba.

24 And the LORD appeared to him the same night and said, "I *am* the God of your father Abraham; do not fear, for I *am* with you. I will bless you and multiply your descendants for My servant Abraham's sake."

25 So he built an altar there and called on the name of the LORD, and he pitched his tent there; and there Isaac's servants dug a well.

26 Then Abimelech came to him from Gerar with Ahuzzath, one of his friends, and Phichol the commander of his army.

27 And Isaac said to them, "Why have you come to me, since you hate me and have sent me away from you?"

28 But they said, "We have certainly seen that the LORD is with you. So we said, 'Let there now be an oath between us, between you and us; and let us make a covenant with you,

29 'that you will do us no harm, since we have not touched you, and since we have done nothing to you but good and have sent you away in peace. You *are* now the blessed of the LORD.'"

30 So he made them a feast, and they ate and drank.

31 Then they arose early in the morning and swore an oath with one another; and Isaac sent them away, and they departed from him in peace.

32 It came to pass the same day that Isaac's servants came and told him about the well which they had dug, and said to him, "We have found water."

33 So he called it Shebah. Therefore the name of the city *is* Beersheba to this day.

34 When Esau was forty years old, he took as wives Judith the daughter of Beeri the Hittite, and Basemath the daughter of Elon the Hittite.

35 And they were a grief of mind to Isaac and Rebekah.

Gen. 26:1–35

Because he was Abraham's son and heir Isaac was born with the equivalent of a silver spoon in his mouth. He was born to privilege but this does not mean he was exempt from pressure. In fact, in his case it would appear that the higher the privilege, the heavier the pressure!

POLITICAL PRESSURE

Politics and economics are bosom companions. Like his father before him Isaac was confronted with a famine situation and he soon discovered that he had his hands full when it came to feeding his flocks, running his business, and caring for his family in the midst of adverse circumstances. So he *"went to Abimelech king of the Philistines, in Gerar. Then the Lord appeared to him and said: 'Do not go down to Egypt; live in the land of which I shall tell you'"* (Gen. 26:1, 2). Apparently he approached the Philistine king to see what he could do to help but then considered the possibility of traveling down to Egypt because he thought he could get a better deal there. In all probability Egypt could offer him more than the impoverished land in which he and the Philistines were living but while he was weighing the pros and cons the Lord gave him some straightforward instructions, forbidding him to enter into a relationship with the Egyptians. This presented him with a pressure-packed decision because he was being asked to trade immediate solutions to a serious problem for a promise which was nowhere near as tangible. He knew he and his family could not eat promises but the Lord told him, *"Dwell in this land, and I will be with you and bless you; for to you and your descendants I give all these lands, and I will perform the oath which I swore to Abraham you father"* (v. 3). The choice was straightforward—he could throw in his lot with Abimelech king of the Philistines, Pharaoh and the Egyptians, or the Lord. From the comfort of an armchair or a padded pew the decision is easy, but for Isaac with a growling stomach and starving dependents the decision was much more difficult. He showed he was his father's son and chose to stand by the One who had repeatedly proved Himself faithful in the past. It has never been easy for the people of God to know how to apply faith in the Lord when matters of economic viability and political stability are involved.

PSYCHOLOGICAL PRESSURE

Isaac was not only a son of privilege; he also had a beautiful wife! The men of Gerar had noticed this too but they did not know that she was his wife because he had said, *"'She is my sister'; for he was afraid to say, 'She is my wife,' because he thought, 'lest the men of the place kill me for Rebekah'"* (v. 7). So he lived under the constant psychological pressure of fear for his life compounded by the knowledge that he was living a lie and in danger of being exposed as a cheat and deceiver. Any reader of Genesis who, at this point, has a distinct feeling of "deja vu" should be forgiven because Isaac's father had done exactly the same thing on two occasions. This probably explains why Abimelech showed his great displeasure after he had seen Isaac and Rebekah being somewhat indiscreet in public. Realizing that he had been duped he said, quite understandably, *"Quite obviously she is your wife; so how could you say, 'She is my sister'? . . . What is this you have done to us?"* (vv. 9, 10). We can sense something of the pressure he was under when we note that his deception had been going on for a long time (see v. 8). Some commentators and scholars have suggested that there may have been some kind of mixup resulting in the same tale being told three times. This may be plausible but it hardly allows for the careful statement, *"There was a famine in the land, besides the first famine that was in the days of Abraham"* (v. 1). In addition it should be noted that there are enough differences in the story to show that a different event is being described and, of course, we should not overlook the fact that the son of Abraham quite probably had learned some bad traits from his father as well as the admirable qualities already demonstrated in this series of events.

PERSONAL PRESSURE

Whichever way you look things seemed to go well for Isaac. Alongside his great start in life and his beautiful wife he also had a remarkable business sense. It is intriguing to read that immediately after a serious famine *"Isaac sowed in that land, and reaped in the same year a hundredfold; and the Lord blessed him. The man began to prosper, and continued prospering until he became very prosperous"* (v. 12). But once again he ran into problems because the neighbors did not appreciate his success. He had to live in the midst of people who despised him and his success. That the problem was theirs did not in any way alleviate the sense of alienation which he undoubtedly felt. Everyone, however successful, likes to be liked and longs to be accepted. Doubtlessly, Isaac was no exception.

In addition to this he had all kinds of trouble with his wells because the Philistines had taken to the unpleasant tactic of filling them up with earth. This was not designed to help him feel welcome and eventually he got the message that he was not appreciated and the only thing the Philistines wanted from him was the space he vacated. Tensions came to a head when *"Abimelech said to Isaac, 'Go away from us, for you are much mightier than we'"* (v. 16). He was left with no alternative but to pack up and head out to the valley of Gerar. Apparently he quickly set about establishing himself and his enterprises and he and his men re-dug the filled up wells, renamed them to remind themselves of their great heritage, and hopefully settled down to a comfortable and prosperous life. But it was not to be. "Deja vu" struck again. A running feud developed between his herdsmen and those of the valley and no matter how many wells he dug and how much water he discovered it seemed that everything he did precipitated another fight. Doggedly he stuck to his task and eventually they *"dug another well, and they did not quarrel over it. So he called its name Rehoboth, because he said, 'For now the Lord has made room for us, and we shall be fruitful in the land'"* (v. 22).

He did receive some encouragement when Abimelech and some friends came over from Gerar. He greeted them coolly, saying, *"Why have you come to me, since you hate me and have sent me away from you?"* But they replied, *"We have certainly seen that the Lord is with you. So we said, 'Let there now be an oath between us, between you and us; and let us make a covenant with you'"* (vv. 27, 28). There is no doubt that their action was self-serving but it was an encouragement, nevertheless, to a man who had known more than his share of pressure and rejection. His response was immediate and warm, the covenant was sealed with a joyous feast, and to add to the excitement his men arrived with news of the new well they had developed and which they named "Shebah." At last things were really going well for Isaac. But wait!

PARENTAL PRESSURE

Isaac's troubles followed him home. Many a man can empathize with Isaac. After a killing day at the office he had finally closed on a crucial deal, got news of a new venture, and wanted nothing more than to go home and celebrate in the peace and tranquillity of his own special retreat, only to find trouble on the home front. It was Esau. He had decided to go off and marry a couple of Hittite women who *were a grief of mind to Isaac and Rebekah"* (v. 35). That he was forty years of age at the time did not alleviate the grief that they felt. Despite all the evidence to the contrary Isaac still regarded his older son as the potential head of the family who would succeed him both as practical and spiritual leader of all that God had committed to Abraham's son. But Esau was not made of the right stuff and only grief and shame would follow him and those who held him dear. Isaac knew pressure and but for a rugged faith and a dogged perseverance would probably have succumbed in much the same way that many people today wilt under the burden of the day. The Bible is wonderfully realistic about its heroes, showing not only their successes but their failures and highlighting not only their blessings but also the bruises they collected along the way.

CHAPTER TWENTY-SEVEN

All in the Family

Genesis 27:1–46

27:1 Now it came to pass, when Isaac was old and his eyes were so dim that he could not see, that he called Esau his older son and said to him, "My son." And he answered him, "Here I am."

2 Then he said, "Behold now, I am old. I do not know the day of my death.

3 "Now therefore, please take your weapons, your quiver and your bow, and go out to the field and hunt game for me.

4 "And make me savory food, such as I love, and bring *it* to me that I may eat, that my soul may bless you before I die."

5 Now Rebekah was listening when Isaac spoke to Esau his son. And Esau went to the field to hunt game and to bring *it*.

6 So Rebekah spoke to Jacob her son, saying, "Indeed I heard your father speak to Esau your brother, saying,

7 'Bring me game and make savory food for me, that I may eat it and bless you in the presence of the LORD before my death.'

8 "Now therefore, my son, obey my voice according to what I command you.

9 "Go now to the flock and bring me from there two choice kids of the goats, and I will make savory food from them for your father, such as he loves.

10 "Then you shall take *it* to your father, that he may eat *it*, and that he may bless you before his death."

11 And Jacob said to Rebekah his mother, "Look, Esau my brother *is* a hairy man, and I *am* a smooth-*skinned* man.

12 "Perhaps my father will feel me, and I shall seem to be a deceiver to him; and I shall bring a curse on myself and not a blessing."

13 But his mother said to him, "*Let* your curse *be* on me, my son; only obey my voice, and go, get *them* for me."

14 And he went and got *them* and brought *them* to his mother, and his mother made savory food, such as his father loved.

15 Then Rebekah took the choice clothes of her elder son Esau, which *were* with her in the house, and put them on Jacob her younger son.

16 And she put the skins of the kids of the goats on his hands and on the smooth part of his neck.

17 Then she gave the savory food and the bread, which she had prepared, into the hand of her son Jacob.

18 So he went to his father and said, "My father." And he said, "Here I am. Who *are* you, my son?"

19 Jacob said to his father, "I *am* Esau your first-born; I have done just as you told me; please arise, sit and eat of my game, that your soul may bless me."

20 But Isaac said to his son, "How *is it* that you have found *it* so quickly, my son?" And he said, "Because the LORD your God brought *it* to me."

21 Then Isaac said to Jacob, "Please come near that I may feel you, my son, whether you *are* really my son Esau or not."

22 So Jacob went near to Isaac his father, and he felt him and said, "The voice *is* Jacob's voice, but the hands *are* the hands of Esau."

23 And he did not recognize him, because his hands were hairy like his brother Esau's hands; so he blessed him.

24 Then he said, "*Are* you really my son Esau?" He said, "I *am.*"

25 He said, "Bring *it* near to me, and I will eat of my son's game, so that my soul may bless you." So he

brought *it* near to him, and he ate; and he brought him wine, and he drank.

26 Then his father Isaac said to him, "Come near now and kiss me, my son."

27 And he came near and kissed him; and he smelled the smell of his clothing, and blessed him and said:

> "Surely, the smell of my son
> *Is* like the smell of a field
> Which the LORD has blessed.

28 Therefore may God give you
> Of the dew of heaven,
> Of the fatness of the earth,
> And plenty of grain and wine.

29 Let peoples serve you,
> And nations bow down to you.
> Be master over your brethren,
> And let your mother's sons bow down to you.
> Cursed *be* everyone who curses you,
> And blessed *be* those who bless you!"

30 Now it happened, as soon as Isaac had finished blessing Jacob, and Jacob had scarcely gone out from the presence of Isaac his father, that Esau his brother came in from his hunting.

31 He also had made savory food, and brought it to his father, and said to his father, "Let my father arise and eat of his son's game, that your soul may bless me."

32 And his father Isaac said to him, "Who *are* you?" So he said, "I *am* your son, your firstborn, Esau."

33 Then Isaac trembled exceedingly, and said, "Who? Where *is* the one who hunted game and brought *it* to me? I ate all *of it* before you came, and I have blessed him—*and* indeed he shall be blessed."

34 When Esau heard the words of his father, he cried with an exceedingly great and bitter cry, and said to his father, "Bless me—me also, O my father!"

35 But he said, "Your brother came with deceit and has taken away your blessing."

36 And *Esau* said, "Is he not rightly named Jacob? For he has supplanted me these two times. He took

away my birthright, and now look, he has taken away my blessing!" And he said, "Have you not reserved a blessing for me?"

37 Then Isaac answered and said to Esau, "Indeed I have made him your master, and all his brethren I have given to him as servants; with grain and wine I have sustained him. What shall I do now for you, my son?"

38 And Esau said to his father, "Have you only one blessing, my father? Bless me—me also, O my father!" And Esau lifted up his voice and wept.

39 Then Isaac his father answered and said to him:

"Behold, your dwelling shall be of the fatness of
    the earth,
And of the dew of heaven from above.
40 By your sword you shall live,
And you shall serve your brother;
And it shall come to pass, when you become
    restless,
That you shall break his yoke from your neck."

41 So Esau hated Jacob because of the blessing with which his father blessed him, and Esau said in his heart, "The days of mourning for my father are at hand; then I will kill my brother Jacob."

42 And the words of Esau her older son were told to Rebekah. So she sent and called Jacob her younger son, and said to him "Surely your brother Esau comforts himself concerning you *by intending* to kill you.

43 "Now therefore, my son, obey my voice: arise, flee to my brother Laban in Haran.

44 "And stay with him a few days, until your brother's fury turns away,

45 "until your brother's anger turns away from you, and he forgets what you have done to him; then I will send and bring you from there. Why should I be bereaved also of you both in one day?"

46 And Rebekah said to Isaac, "I am weary of my life because of the daughters of Heth; if Jacob takes a wife of the daughters of Heth, like these *who are* the daughters of the land, what good will my life be to me?"

Gen. 27:1–46

The story of Isaac's family is all too familiar. Starting out well, full of glorious promise, it degenerated into a shambles. What happened and how it came to pass is clearly explained in this chapter and careful study of it proves beneficial to all who take seriously the divine structure of the family.

How Are Families Founded?

Any structure which is to stand needs solid foundations. Isaac's family was sound in this regard which is more than can be said for many families which eventually disintegrate. Despite the good start, however, his family fell apart. This, in itself, is a salutary reminder that when it comes to building a family, nothing should be taken for granted. There are two important factors about Isaac's family which should be carefully noted. First, there was "A marriage made with care" and, second, there were "children bathed in prayer." The careful and prayerful preparations for the marriage of Isaac and Rebekah have already been studied. At this juncture it will suffice simply to remind ourselves that the marriage was based on the clearly defined principles of knowing and obeying God's revealed will and trusting Him to make it known. The story of Eliezer's journey bears ample testimony to this fact. In addition there was a clearly stated commitment behind the marriage. Rebekah was asked bluntly if she was willing to go with Eliezer into the unknown and marry the man she had never met, to which she replied affirmatively without hesitation, and as soon as she met her husband-to-be he affirmed his love for her. Later their clearly expressed love for each other, which in itself was most commendable, almost got them into trouble because Abimelech saw what was going on and tumbled to the ruse to which he had been subjected.

As for the children we have specific details of the prayers which their parents had expressed on their behalf. Isaac had "pleaded with the Lord for his wife, because she was barren; and the Lord granted his plea, and Rebekah his wife conceived" (Gen. 25:21). One wonders what Isaac thought about his "pleading" in later years when he had the benefit of 20/20 hindsight! Rebekah, too, when she was experiencing marked discomfort during her pregnancy, did not hesitate to "inquire of the Lord" (Gen. 25:22) only to be told by the Lord in a specific prophetic utterance that she was carrying twins and that they would become the fathers of great nations. There was no shortage of prayer or of spiritual insight on the part of the parents of the boys. All the ingredients for a successful marriage and family were firmly in place.

WHY DO FAMILIES FAIL?

This is the question asked by countless despairing people and fortunately this story offers some answers. The prevailing atmosphere of the home was one of intrigue, and therein lay a major part of the problem. This family was made up of people committed to their own ends which were to be achieved by any and all means irrespective of who might be abused in the process. The Lord had stated clearly before the twins were born that the elder would serve the younger (see Gen. 25:23). But apparently Isaac was not prepared to accept this piece of divine determination. He instructed Esau, *"make me savory food, such as I love, and bring it to me that I may eat, and that my soul may bless you before I die"* (Gen. 27:4). He was determined that the blessing should belong to Esau. We do not know if Isaac and Rebekah were aware that the birthright had been traded by Esau to his brother but it is hard to imagine how such an event could have been kept secret. The blessing and the birthright belonged together and so to accept and administer the blessing when it no longer applied was a fundamentally dishonest action on the part of father and son.

Rebekah, like her late mother-in-law, had become skilled at the art of eavesdropping, so she was *"listening when Isaac spoke to Esau his son"* (v. 5). She promptly went to Jacob, her favorite son, and instituted a scheme designed to outwit and deceive her husband and her elder son. Families are intended to support each other, not scheme against each other. Loving is the key word not lying! Members of a family learn to complement rather than compete. But unfortunately none of these distinctions were made in this household.

The scheme may seem ludicrous in its naïvete but the results were devastating. Coupled with an atmosphere of intrigue there was a prevailing attitude of indifference. Isaac by this time was in poor shape. *"His eyes were so dim that he could not see"* (v. 1) and he said rather plaintively, *"Behold now, I am old. I do not know the day of my death"* (v. 2). Under such conditions one could reasonably expect that the old blind man would have been cared for by a loving family. But his condition was a matter of total indifference to those who professed to love him. The tendencies of both sons had been clearly manifested up to this point and their weaknesses were no secret. Under those circumstances young people are usually encouraged by their elders to be on their guard and steps are taken to assist them in combating the temptations to which they might succumb. The weakness of the cold, calculating Jacob was seen by his mother as an asset rather than a liability and the tendency of Esau to be hasty and superficial was seen as a golden opportunity to manipulate him for personal advantage.

Matters of simple decency were of no significance and integrity was regarded as being a luxury which no one could afford. So the charade took place. Esau went hunting. Rebekah went scheming. Jacob dressed up and the old man sat in his tent being conned. Isaac was not altogether out of it and he was suspicious that something was going on which he could not quite understand. Perhaps living in his family had taught him to be suspicious most of the time! He was surprised that the choice food he had ordered was prepared so quickly. He knew that Esau had to hunt it, prepare it, and serve it and he had never experienced such quick service before. But Jacob with the worse kind of piety answered his query, *"How is it that you have found it so quickly, my son?"*, with the amazing lie, *"Because the Lord your God brought it to me"* (v. 20). Still suspicious, old Isaac said, *"Please come near, that I may feel you, my son, whether you are really my son Esau or not"* (v. 21). But, of course, Rebekah had planned for such an eventuality and the goat skins on Jacob's smooth skin served to fool the old man into thinking he was touching his other son whose hirsute exterior made him resemble a red sweater. It is a sad commentary on the atmosphere of distrust which prevailed that Isaac was still unsure. He said, *"The voice is Jacob's voice, but the hands are the hands of Esau"* (v. 22), but he went ahead with the blessing anyway. There was an underlying flippancy about Isaac which may have been predicted in his name "Laughter," projected in his careless and inappropriate public fondling of his wife and promoted in his relationship with Esau who was made of similar stuff. But it finally got him into severe trouble. The great event in which he was fooled and humiliated was an event in which he relied entirely on his senses—every one of which betrayed him! He felt the hairy arms and guessed wrong. He smelled the earthy smell of the clothes his son wore and was wrong again. He listened to the voice and his ears fooled him. His sight was already gone and when he tasted the stew he thought he knew what he was eating but his taste buds let him down too! Such is the lot of the man who lives trivially and ignores the word that the Lord has spoken and the oaths that have been solemnly sworn.

It is hard to imagine how the beautiful young woman who left Nahor in Mesopotamia to marry Isaac could have turned into the scheming, unprincipled, bitter woman seen in this incident. She had become totally dedicated to her own ends even to the point of feeling that she could humiliate her own husband and blatantly manipulate her own sons. Setting father against son and brother against brother did not worry her at all. The end justified the means in her book. Pity the family with such a mother!

Both sons failed to distinguish themselves too. Jacob was a stranger to principle, Esau unrelated to priority. Like his scheming mother Jacob was prepared to do "whatever it takes"; like his trivial father Esau was happy to live in the area of self-gratification. The consequences of the nefarious activities of the family were quickly apparent. *"Isaac trembled exceedingly"* (v. 33) when he realized what had transpired. The blessing had been given and could not be retracted. The deed was done and it was not the deed he wanted done. He had been mercilessly fooled! Esau *"cried with an exceedingly great and bitter cry"* (v. 34) and said of his twin brother, *"Is he not rightly named Jacob? For he has supplanted me these two times. He took away my birthright, and now look, he has taken away my blessing!"* (v. 36). Esau's somewhat convoluted recollection of what had actually transpired does not detract from the feeling of indignation and revulsion with which he responded to the actions of his mother and brother. Deep in his heart something snapped and he said, *"The days of mourning for my father are at hand; then I will kill my brother Jacob"* (v. 41). Rebekah, ever the alert and resourceful woman, heard what was going on, quickly told Jacob, and instructed him to leave home and put as much distance as possible between himself and his brother, saying, *"flee to my brother Laban in Haran. And stay with him a few days, until*

*your brother's fury turns away . . . and he forgets what you have done
to him"* (vv. 43–45). A few days? Did she really think that the whole
sordid episode would be forgotten in a few days or was she up to her
old tricks trying to convince Jacob that all would be easily manipu-
lated? Notice that her outlook was not that confession of wrong
should be made and reconciliation on the basis of forgiveness should
be sought. She just wanted everything forgotten so that she could
enjoy the fruits of her conniving without the inconvenience of
putting any wrong right! Moreover, her approach to Isaac was not
one of honesty. She put on another act, pretended that she was distressed about Jacob picking up with some of the women his brother
was associating with, and implied that Jacob ought to go away for a
little while! What Isaac was thinking about during this episode is
anyone's guess!

Meanwhile Jacob was hardly covering himself with glory! He
packed his bags and headed east as fast as he could go, leaving
father and brother to their rage and his mother to whatever would
be meted out to her. Perhaps he had reason to believe from past
experience that she could handle herself, but even so his looking out
for himself was indicative of what lay in his heart. This family,
which started out so well, is a powerful witness to the possibilities
of disintegration and disaster which can readily overtake any com-
munity of people which fails to order its lives on the clear-cut outlines of divine principles. Such is the wickedness of the human heart
that given an unhealthy atmosphere and unwholesome attitudes
there is no limit to the harm that even family members can do to
each other and there is no saying to what extent the damage may
spread. Isaac's sad family is a powerful testimony to the necessity
not only to start well but to continue steadfastly!

When Do Families Flourish?

Families flourish when father and mother give God glory by living
according to the principles laid down from the very beginning of
human history. When man and woman regard each other as being
truly made in the image of God, commissioned to subdue the earth
together, with the husband functioning as head and the wife in reality being all that is meant by the expression "helpmeet," there is a

stable basis for marriage and family. It may not be profitable to second guess Isaac's relationship with Rebekah but it does seem that he was less than a compelling leader of the family and Rebekah was conversely a very capable woman. Unfortunately her considerable organizational abilities went sour and became manipulative while Isaac's status was hardly undergirded by his performance. So while she was going sour he was going stale! Perhaps they should have been able to see this and help each other.

Meanwhile the boys had lost all respect for their parents with very good reason. Children are taught to respect their parents but respect has to be earned eventually. At first young children have no option but to obey and like it but as time goes by they have more say in their lives and then the respect factor becomes much more crucial. If a solid, loving relationship has not been built in the early days it is highly unlikely there will be a healthy relationship in later days. When young people grow up they discover their parents are not perfect. Unless an underlying respect for the parents has been forged which allows them to remain significant in the children's eyes having allowed for the deficiencies, disillusionment and disgust may result. Then disintegration is highly probable and the family will either fragment and go its individual ways or remain together in a frigid atmosphere of suspicious toleration. I suspect this is what happened to Isaac and Rebekah, Esau and Jacob.

There is one profound factor which must not be overlooked in this pathetic story. Behind the scheming and conniving of man the sovereign Lord was still at work. Despite all the efforts of man to thwart the purposes of God through all manner of mistakes and misdemeanors, Jacob, whom God had said would be the next link in the chain of divine purpose, had arrived in that exact position. Moreover, he was now on his way to the family home where he would eventually find the bride through whom the promised line would be extended. Not for him the women of the Canaan. God would see to that. The lesson behind all of this is that God delights to have His men and women work in glad cooperation with Him, but should they freely choose not to cooperate, they will eventually discover that God works despite their having chosen not to allow Him to work with them! It was ever thus!

CHAPTER TWENTY-EIGHT

Meet the Master

Genesis 28:1–22

28:1 Then Isaac called Jacob and blessed him, and charged him, and said to him: "You shall not take a wife from the daughters of Canaan.

2 "Arise, go to Padan Aram, to the house of Bethuel your mother's father; and take yourself a wife from there of the daughters of Laban your mother's brother.

3 "May God Almighty bless you,
And make you fruitful and multiply you,
That you may be an assembly of peoples;

4 And give you the blessing of Abraham,
To you and your descendants with you,
That you may inherit the land
In which you are a stranger,
Which God gave to Abraham."

5 So Isaac sent Jacob away, and he went to Padan Aram, to Laban the son of Bethuel the Syrian, the brother of Rebekah, the mother of Jacob and Esau.

6 Esau saw that Isaac had blessed Jacob and sent him away to Padan Aram to take himself a wife from there, *and that* as he blessed him he gave him a charge, saying, "You shall not take a wife from the daughters of Canaan,"

7 and that Jacob had obeyed his father and his mother and had gone to Padan Aram.

8 Also Esau saw that the daughters of Canaan did not please his father Isaac.

9 So Esau went to Ishmael and took Mahalath the daughter of Ishmael, Abraham's son, the sister of Nebajoth, to be his wife in addition to the wives he had.

10 Now Jacob went out from Beersheba and went toward Haran.

11 So he came to a certain place and stayed there all night, because the sun had set. And he took one of the stones of that place and put it at his head, and he lay down in that place to sleep.

12 Then he dreamed, and behold, a ladder *was* set up on the earth, and its top reached to heaven; and there the angels of God were ascending and descending on it.

13 And behold, the LORD stood above it and said: "I *am* the LORD God of Abraham your father and the God of Isaac; the land on which you lie I will give to you and your descendants.

14 "Also your descendants shall be as the dust of the earth; you shall spread abroad to the west and the east, to the north and the south; and in you and in your seed all the families of the earth shall be blessed.

15 "Behold, I *am* with you and will keep you wherever you go, and will bring you back to this land; for I will not leave you until I have done what I have spoken to you."

16 Then Jacob awoke from his sleep and said, "Surely the LORD is in this place, and I did not know *it.*"

17 And he was afraid and said, "How awesome *is* this place! This *is* none other than the house of God, and this *is* the gate of heaven!"

18 Then Jacob rose early in the morning, and took the stone that he had put at his head, set it up as a pillar, and poured oil on top of it.

19 And he called the name of that place Bethel; but the name of that city had been Luz previously.

20 Then Jacob made a vow, saying, "If God will be with me, and keep me in this way that I am going, and give me bread to eat and clothing to put on,

21 "so that I come back to my father's house in peace, then the LORD shall be my God.

22 "And this stone which I have set as a pillar shall be God's house, and of all that You give me I will surely give a tenth to You."

Gen. 28:1–22

Isaac's family was in a sorry state. Perhaps the biggest concern for Isaac was Esau's threat on the life of his twin brother, Jacob. Discretion rather than valor was called for and arrangements were quickly made to get Jacob away from the scene. But before he left Isaac blessed him with words which specifically related to Jacob the promises given to Abraham. Among other things Esau was being warned in no uncertain terms not to touch his brother, unless he wanted to run afoul of the purposes of the Lord. Isaac's insistence that Jacob should not marry outside the family structure would also be a rebuke to Esau who had done just that to the intense displeasure of his parents. It is significant that Esau was concerned enough about his parents that he tried to rectify his wrongdoing by taking another wife! This time he chose one of Ishmael's daughters, but it is hard to see how he concluded that by adding another wife to the two he already had, he would undo what he had done. So Jacob left home and headed out from Beersheba with the birthright and the blessing and little else besides his own wits. Or so it seemed!

THE ACTION OF JEHOVAH

At some stage of his lonely journey Jacob settled down for the night, picked a rock for a pillow, and tried to get some sleep. But little did he realize that the Lord had other plans for him that evening. *"He dreamed, and behold, a ladder was set up on the earth, and its top reached to heaven; and there the angels of God were ascending and descending on it"* (Gen. 28:12). The significance of the dream is enhanced when we bear in mind that the Lord Jesus apparently referred to it in His statement to Nathanael, "Most assuredly, I say to you, hereafter you shall see heaven open, and the angels of God ascending and descending upon the Son of Man" (John 1:51). In the dream Jacob was being reminded that the Lord was able and willing to maintain communications with His children even in the most desolate places and lonely times. In the statement to Nathanael the message was elaborated to tell God's people of all ages that the communication par excellence is through the Lord Jesus Himself. The dream must have been encouraging to Jacob but how much more encouraging the word of Jesus has been to the people of God through the ages! As Jacob studied the stairway (a better translation

239

than "ladder"), "*behold, the Lord stood above it and said, 'I am the Lord God of Abraham your father and the God of Isaac; the land on which you lie I will give to you and your descendants'*" (Gen. 28:13). At this stage in our study of Genesis these words have become familiar to us but we should not forget that they were being addressed to Jacob for the first time. No doubt he had often heard the story of the Lord's covenant with Abraham and how it had been repeated to Isaac, but now he was hearing it for himself. In a very special way the God of Abraham and the God of Isaac was introducing Himself as the God of Jacob. The reiteration of the covenant went on in familiar terms to describe the multiplicity of descendants and specifically the blessing which would come through his family to the whole world. But then the Lord moved from generalities to specifics which were of great interest to Jacob. "*Behold, I am with you and will keep you wherever you go, and will bring you back to this land; for I will not leave you until I have done what I have spoken to you*" (v. 15). The personal relationship which was being established as a result of the divine initiative should be carefully noted. The promise of the divine Presence was to be both a source of encouragement and, at times, a source of embarrassment to Jacob as his life unfolded. The divine plan which specifically guaranteed that he would be brought back to the land of promise must have been greatly reassuring, and the implied promises of protection and provision could not have escaped Jacob's notice. Jacob was being confronted by the Lord as never before and he who had shown great capabilities in mastering others was meeting the Master.

THE REACTION OF JACOB

"*Jacob awoke from his sleep and said, 'Surely the Lord is in this place, and I did not know it'*" (v. 16). Different people have different ways of waking up to God but few people ever needed to wake up to Him more than Jacob! His propensities which had been so clearly demonstrated in his home situation and which had led to exile from his own family were custom-made to get him into all kinds of trouble. Without the Lord there would have been little hope for him and yet the Lord in His wisdom had called him to play a significant role in the blessing of the nations. This serves as another reminder that

God's ways are not our ways and another encouraging word to the effect that no one is outside the pale when it comes to the possibilities of a changed life through divine intervention.

Jacob's response to his awakening was most appropriate, *"How awesome is this place! This is none other than the house of God, and this is the gate of heaven!"* (v. 17). The awareness of God in His splendor should always lead to a sense of the awesomeness of God, but this does not always happen. The reason may be that in our modern world we are so preoccupied with ourselves. When we reluctantly turn our attention away from ourselves to God we see Him as a means to self-improvement rather than One to Whom we reverently submit in worship and adoration. The awesomeness of God, however, would be intolerable to human beings had He not devised a way in which He could become accessible. But He is approachable only on His own terms. This is brought out in Jacob's wondering expression, *"This is the gate of heaven"* (v. 17), an expression related to the name "Babel," but with a major difference. In the Babel episode men decided they would reach God by their own efforts, and God soon showed them what He thought about that approach! But in Jacob's experience the Lord took the initiative. Man still has problems with this lesson. God is accessible and available but the gate of heaven is opened from the inside and there is no other entrance.

Something profound had happened in Jacob's heart. He *"rose early in the morning, and took the stone that he had put at his head, set it up as a pillar, and poured oil on top of it. And he called the name of that place Bethel"* (vv. 18, 19). These actions were designed to memorialize the place and to retain it in Jacob's memory as the scene of a deep and lasting commitment to the Lord Who had touched his life at that place. *"Bethel"* means "the house of God" and in so renaming the site Jacob made a lasting statement about the meeting he had had there with the living God.

It is important to note that no temple was erected; no shrine marked the place. The people amongst whom Jacob was living kept their gods in special places and this in itself said something about the limitations of the gods. Jacob's God was not limited to a location or dependent on a human structure to meet his needs. Jehovah was able and willing to meet his wandering child anywhere anytime. This holds true today, and while we recognize the value of certain special places being set aside for the worship and service of the living God, we rejoice that He cannot be contained and He is always reachable. Solomon was overwhelmed with this thought as he dedicated his magnificent new temple. He said, "But will God indeed dwell on the earth? Behold, heaven and the heaven of heavens cannot contain You. How much less this temple which I have built!" (1 Kings 8:27). This constitutes the mystery of our God. Heaven of heavens cannot contain Him and yet His divine Omnipresence means that He dwells with us and through the Holy Spirit is prepared to dwell within us. When God's people have realized this truth their attitude to their work place has changed dramatically. Sometimes even production has been known to increase! Sick and sorrowing people need to be reminded that Bethel is wherever they are at any given moment, and when they appreciate this even their hospital bed will be bathed in light and their room will know the special warmth of His presence.

The depth of Jacob's response to the meeting he had at Bethel with the living God is shown in the words which he uttered to the Lord, *"If God will be with me, and keep me in this way that I am going, and give me bread to eat and clothing to put on, so that I come back to my father's house in peace, then the Lord shall be my God"* (Gen. 28:20, 21). Care should be taken not to misunderstand what he said. A cursory reading may lead to the impression that Jacob tried to make a deal with God, and given his track record this would not have been unexpected. But to believe this is to minimize the depth of his encounter with the Lord. He was not saying, "Alright, God, if You do thus and so, then when You eventually get me back home I'll get religion." Subsequent events show quite clearly that he had a living relationship with the Lord during the long years which elapsed before he returned home, although it must be admitted that the relationship wore thin at times. The promise of the tithe is most interesting because it predates the Law which required this kind of giving and therefore must have been a voluntary act of gratitude on his part. (See also comments at 14:20.) He had his theology squared away when he said, *"of all that You give me I will surely give a tenth to You"* (v. 22). He knew that he would only have what the Lord gave him and therefore anything he gave to the Lord would be a token presentation to the One who had given him everything. It has been said, and unfortunately it may be true, that the last thing to be converted is the pocketbook. With all his faults Jacob showed early in his new experience with the Lord that to understand the grace of God is to respond in grateful acts of benevolence and practical demonstrations of love.

Jacob did not of course experience an immediate and total eradication of the many flaws in his character and nature, as subsequent events portray in devastating detail. But he had met the Master and the Master had started being busy in his life. One cannot help feeling that Jacob was not unaware of his faults and that he would have been one of the first to apply for a bumper sticker to put on his chariot bearing the sign, "P.B.P.W.M.G.H.F.W.M.Y.", which being interpreted is, "Please be patient with me, God hasn't finished with me yet."

CHAPTER TWENTY-NINE

The School of Hard Knocks

Genesis 29:1–35

29:1 So Jacob went on his journey and came to the land of the people of the East.

2 And he looked, and saw a well in the field; and behold, there *were* three flocks of sheep lying by it; for out of that well they watered the flocks. A large stone *was* on the well's mouth.

3 Now all the flocks would be gathered there; and they would roll the stone from the well's mouth, water the sheep, and put the stone back in its place on the well's mouth.

4 And Jacob said to them, "My brethren, where *are* you from?" And they said, "We *are* from Haran."

5 Then he said to them, "Do you know Laban the son of Nahor?" And they said, "We know him."

6 So he said to them, "Is he well?" And they said, "*He is* well. And look, his daughter Rachel is coming with the sheep."

7 Then he said, "Look, *it is* still high day; *it is* not time for the cattle to be gathered together. Water the sheep, and go and feed *them.*"

8 But they said, "We cannot until all the flocks are gathered together, and they have rolled the stone from the well's mouth; then we water the sheep."

9 Now while he was still speaking with them, Rachel came with her father's sheep, for she was a shepherdess.

10 And it came to pass, when Jacob saw Rachel the daughter of Laban his mother's brother, and the sheep of Laban his mother's brother, that Jacob went

near and rolled the stone from the well's mouth, and watered the flock of Laban his mother's brother.

11 Then Jacob kissed Rachel, and lifted up his voice and wept.

12 And Jacob told Rachel that he *was* her father's relative and that he *was* Rebekah's son. So she ran and told her father.

13 Then it came to pass, when Laban heard the report about Jacob his sister's son, that he ran to meet him, and embraced him and kissed him, and brought him to his house. So he told Laban all these things.

14 And Laban said to him, "Surely you *are* my bone and my flesh." And he stayed with him for a month.

15 Then Laban said to Jacob, "Because you *are* my relative, should you therefore serve me for nothing? Tell me, what *should* your wages *be?*"

16 Now Laban had two daughters: the name of the elder *was* Leah, and the name of the younger *was* Rachel.

17 Leah's eyes *were* delicate, but Rachel was beautiful of form and appearance.

18 Now Jacob loved Rachel; so he said, "I will serve you seven years for Rachel your younger daughter."

19 And Laban said, "*It is* better that I give her to you than that I should give her to another man. Stay with me."

20 So Jacob served seven years for Rachel, and they seemed *only* a few days to him because of the love he had for her.

21 Then Jacob said to Laban, "Give *me* my wife, for my days are fulfilled, that I may go in to her."

22 And Laban gathered together all the men of the place and made a feast.

23 Now it came to pass in the evening, that he took Leah his daughter and brought her to Jacob; and he went in to her.

24 And Laban gave his maid Zilpah to his daughter Leah *as* a maid.

25 So it came to pass in the morning, that behold, it *was* Leah. And he said to Laban, "What is this you

have done to me? Was it not for Rachel that I served you? Why then have you deceived me?"

26 And Laban said, "It must not be done so in our country, to give the younger before the firstborn.

27 "Fulfill her week, and we will give you this one also for the service which you will serve with me still another seven years."

28 Then Jacob did so and fulfilled her week. So he gave him his daughter Rachel as wife also.

29 And Laban gave his maid Bilhah to his daughter Rachel as a maid.

30 Then *Jacob* also went in to Rachel, and he also loved Rachel more than Leah. And he served with Laban still another seven years.

31 When the LORD saw that Leah *was* unloved, He opened her womb; but Rachel *was* barren.

32 So Leah conceived and bore a son, and she called his name Reuben; for she said, "The LORD has surely looked on my affliction. Now therefore, my husband will love me."

33 Then she conceived again and bore a son, and said, "Because the LORD has heard that I *am* unloved, He has therefore given me this *son* also." And she called his name Simeon.

34 She conceived again and bore a son, and said, "Now this time my husband will become attached to me, because I have borne him three sons." Therefore his name was called Levi.

35 And she conceived again and bore a son, and said, "Now I will praise the LORD." Therefore she called his name Judah. Then she stopped bearing.

Gen. 29:1–35

The experience at Bethel was only the beginning of Jacob's education. The Lord had gained his attention and had led him to a response of love and commitment. But there was much work to be done on this young man and the Lord was busy putting him in the right place for the work to be done. He sent him to school under the tutelage of his uncle Laban. It was called the school of hard knocks. Many of God's servants have studied in a similar school. Not everyone wishes to be enrolled in such an institution but the

Lord is certainly in favor of putting His people through it. The Duke of Edinburgh, the father of Prince Charles, the present Prince of Wales, surprised many people by insisting that his son should attend a particularly spartan boys' boarding school rather than staying at home to be taught by resident tutors. He felt that a future king should be exposed to the rough and tumble of life in order to get some rough edges smoothed out. The Lord seems to think in similar fashion when He is dealing with the Jacobs of this world.

THE SCHOOL'S FOUNDER

In the Song of Moses which is recorded in Deuteronomy 32:1–43 there is a section about God's dealings with Jacob. There is, of course, a sense in which *"Jacob"* in this context refers to the people of Israel but there are aspects of the song which can also be legitimately applied to Jacob, the individual.

> For the Lord's portion is His people;
> Jacob is the place of His inheritance.
> He found him in a desert land
> And in the wasteland, a howling wilderness;
> He encircled him, He instructed him,
> He kept him as the apple of His eye.
> As an eagle stirs up its nest,
> Hovers over its young,
> Spreading out its wings, taking them up,
> Carrying them on its wings,
> So the Lord alone led him,
> And there was no foreign god with him.
> *Deut. 32:9–12*

Whatever the tough circumstances Jacob was going to encounter during the twenty years he spent in Laban's employ, the Lord was committed to instructing him and keeping him as the apple of His eye. No doubt there were times when Jacob felt like a baby eagle ruffled by its mother until it fell head over heels out of the nest, only to discover the encircling and undergirding wings at the last moment before disaster struck. The words used to describe Jehovah's relationship with Jacob are significant—"found," "encircled," "instructed," "kept," and "led"—because they all speak of the tender

247

care of the Lord for His troublesome child. Yet the care of the Lord did not exempt Jacob from the hard knocks which came his way, some because of his own stupidity and stubbornness, others because of the stupidity and cupidity of others.

There may have been times when Jacob wondered what had happened to the Lord Whom he had met at Bethel. Many of God's children down through the centuries have wondered the same thing, only to discover that the faithful God never allows His children to be tested beyond their God-given capacity and never without there being the promise that they will someday experience the ultimate good to which He is committed.

THE SCHOOL'S CURRICULUM

The first lesson Jacob learned was not at all unpleasant. After a long journey, not without incident as we have seen, he arrived in *"the land of the people of the East"* (Gen. 29:1). He had some idea he would find his relatives in the area but on arriving at a well he made inquiries and discovered not only that they lived in the neighborhood but also that they used the very well at which he was standing and moreover the young lady just arriving on the scene was his cousin, Rachel! Apparently it was love at first sight for Jacob. He immediately wanted to impress Rachel so he suggested to the shepherds that they should move the stone from the well and get the sheep watered. For some unknown reason they were not about to do this so with characteristic enthusiasm and initiative, not to mention brute strength, he moved the stone himself. No doubt Rachel was impressed particularly when he watered the flock for her! Then, to the young lady's surprise, *"Jacob kissed Rachel, and lifted up his voice and wept. And Jacob told Rachel that he was her father's relative and that he was Rebekah's son. So she ran and told her father"* (vv. 11, 12). When Jacob was introduced to the family it was hugs and kisses all around and he must have been delighted by his reception. Laban even went so far as to say with great emotion, *"Surely you are my bone and my flesh"* (v. 14). Some would call it coincidence, others good luck, and others serendipity. But Jacob would learn that this was just like the Lord. The lesson was simple—"God is in control." Truly, as Moses would say much later, *"the Lord alone led him"* (Deut. 32:12).

Laban was an expert at the shady deal. He put Jacob to work for a month before discussing remuneration and then said, *"Because you are my relative, should you therefore serve me for nothing? Tell me, what should your wages be?"* (Gen. 29:15). Jacob, who was not known for missing tricks, answered promptly, *"I will serve you seven years for Rachel your younger daughter"* (v. 18). Laban's enigmatic response may not have been as enthusiastic as Jacob would have wished, *"It is better that I give her to you than that I should give her to another man. Stay with me"* (v. 19). But Jacob was in love. The fateful deal was struck and the labor of love began. Jacob's love was so true and deep that he *"served seven years for Rachel, and they seemed only a few days to him"* (v. 20). Even allowing for a little hyperbole the message is clear. But Jacob, like many people after him, was about to learn another lesson—"the course of true love never did run smooth."

The wedding date was set, the great day arrived, the feasting and celebrating began, and Laban delivered his daughter. But it wasn't until the next morning that Jacob discovered that it was the wrong daughter. To his horror he realized that instead of the beautiful Rachel his bride was her older sister, the less than beautiful Leah! The great trickster had been tricked; the biter bit. Jacob who had conned his father and brother had been conned by his uncle. The lesson was hard but necessary—"every man meets his match."

With understandable indignation Jacob asked Laban, *"What is this you have done to me? Was it not for Rachel that I served you? Why then have you deceived me?"* (v. 25). Laban replied that it was not customary for the younger daughter to marry before her older sister. This piece of information, if it was true, should, of course, have been communicated at least seven years earlier. But Laban had not really committed himself at that juncture and if Jacob had pressed his case further no doubt he would have been told he should have read the fine print! Jacob's query about deception is ironic when we remember that he had made a career out of deception back home; in fact, the only human reason he was away from home was that his deceptive antics had finally caught up with him. But now the school of hard knocks was in session and the lesson was—"you reap what you sow."

The two men reached another agreement. Jacob would wait until the end of the marriage week of celebration and then he would marry Rachel. The condition was that he would work another seven years for her. Laban presumably laughed himself hoarse when he got back to his tent while Jacob probably went to his wife and tried to explain why he did not love her and why he wanted to establish the impossible situation of two wives in one kitchen and sisters to boot! The desperate loneliness and hurt of Leah, the older sister, did not go unnoticed in heaven and by way of consolation, *"When the Lord saw that Leah was unloved, He opened her womb; but Rachel was barren"* (v. 31). The Lord continued to open her womb with great regularity and each time she produced a son. Without exception the names of her sons spoke, in one form or another, of her heartache and unfulfilled desires. In rapid succession Reuben, Simeon, Levi, and Judah were born to Jacob and Leah. But the child that he longed for did not arrive, for Rachel was barren. Jacob, the man who was used to getting his own way, the man who was only interested in winning, was learning another lesson—"there is a limit to man's resources." This was as hard for him to learn as it is hard for modern man to admit. But until it is learned men tend to rely on their own inadequacies only to discover their shortcomings after much pain and sometimes when it is too late. For all his ingenuity Jacob could not make Rachel pregnant, he couldn't make Leah happy, and neither of his wives could make him content. He had met his match, he had reached his limit, he had reaped what he had sown, but he was also in the process of learning that God was still in control.

THE SCHOOL'S GRADUATES

I have a friend who tells me that he had a fine college career—he crammed four years into ten! Jacob attended Laban's Academy for twenty years and at the end of his time there he was still struggling with himself and the lessons which needed to be learned. Some learn more quickly than others because they realize that there is little point in resisting what God is saying. The more quickly this is learned the sooner they get on to other classes. But the longer people take to come to grips with the gracious but firm guiding hand of the Lord in the affairs of life the longer it takes them to mature. Of course there is no such thing as graduation from the school of Christ this side of eternity. And as this school always offers graduate courses in hard knocks there are many opportunities for those who really want to grow!

CHAPTER THIRTY

Relationships

Genesis 30:1–43

30:1 Now when Rachel saw that she bore Jacob no children, Rachel envied her sister, and said to Jacob, "Give me children, or else I die!"

2 And Jacob's anger was aroused against Rachel, and he said, *"Am* I in the place of God, who has withheld from you the fruit of the womb?"

3 So she said, "Here is my maid Bilhah; go in to her, and she will bear *a child* on my knees, that I also may have children by her."

4 Then she gave him Bilhah her maid as wife, and Jacob went in to her.

5 And Bilhah conceived and bore Jacob a son.

6 Then Rachel said, "God has judged my case; and He has also heard my voice and given me a son." Therefore she called his name Dan.

7 And Rachel's maid Bilhah conceived again and bore Jacob a second son.

8 Then Rachel said, "With great wrestlings I have wrestled with my sister, *and* indeed I have prevailed." So she called his name Naphtali.

9 When Leah saw that she had stopped bearing, she took Zilpah her maid and gave her to Jacob as wife.

10 And Leah's maid Zilpah bore Jacob a son.

11 Then Leah said, "A troop comes!" So she called his name Gad.

12 And Leah's maid Zilpah bore Jacob a second son.

13 Then Leah said, "I am happy, for the daughters will call me blessed." So she called his name Asher.

14 Now Reuben went in the days of wheat harvest and found mandrakes in the field, and brought them to his mother Leah. Then Rachel said to Leah, "Please give me *some* of your son's mandrakes."

15 But she said to her, "*Is it* a small matter that you have taken away my husband? Would you take away my son's mandrakes also?" And Rachel said, "Therefore he will lie with you tonight for your son's mandrakes."

16 When Jacob came out of the field in the evening, Leah went out to meet him and said, "You must come in to me, for I have surely hired you with my son's mandrakes." And he lay with her that night.

17 And God listened to Leah, and she conceived and bore Jacob a fifth son.

18 Leah said, "God has given me my wages, because I have given my maid to my husband." So she called his name Issachar.

19 Then Leah conceived again and bore Jacob a sixth son.

20 And Leah said, "God has endowed me *with* a good endowment; now my husband will dwell with me, because I have borne him six sons." So she called his name Zebulun.

21 Afterward she bore a daughter, and called her name Dinah.

22 Then God remembered Rachel, and God listened to her and opened her womb.

23 And she conceived and bore a son, and said, "God has taken away my reproach."

24 So she called his name Joseph, and said, "The LORD shall add to me another son."

25 And it came to pass, when Rachel had borne Joseph, that Jacob said to Laban, "Send me away, that I may go to my own place and to my country.

26 "Give *me* my wives and my children for whom I have served you, and let me go; for you know my service which I have done for you."

27 And Laban said to him, "Please *stay*, if I have found favor in your eyes, *for* I have learned by experience that the LORD has blessed me for your sake."

28 Then he said, "Name me your wages, and I will give *it*."

29 So *Jacob* said to him, "You know how I have served you and how your livestock has been with me.

30 "For what you had before I *came was* little, and it has increased to a great amount; the LORD has blessed you since my coming. And now, when shall I also provide for my own house?"

31 So he said, "What shall I give you?" And Jacob said, "You shall not give me anything. If you will do this thing for me, I will again feed and keep your flocks:

32 "Let me pass through all your flock today, removing from there all the speckled and spotted sheep, and all the brown ones among the lambs, and the spotted and speckled among the goats; and *these* shall be my wages.

33 "So my righteousness will answer for me in time to come, when the subject of my wages comes before you: every one that *is* not speckled and spotted among the goats, and brown among the lambs, will be considered stolen, if *it is* with me."

34 And Laban said, "Oh, that it were according to your word!"

35 So he removed that day the male goats that were speckled and spotted, all the female goats that were speckled and spotted, every one that had *some* white in it, and all the brown ones among the lambs, and gave *them* into the hand of his sons.

36 Then he put three days' journey between himself and Jacob, and Jacob fed the rest of Laban's flocks.

37 Now Jacob took for himself rods of green poplar and of the almond and chestnut trees, peeled white strips in them, and exposed the white which *was* in the rods.

38 And the rods which he had peeled, he set before the flocks in the gutters, in the watering troughs where the flocks came to drink, so that they should conceive when they came to drink.

39 So the flocks conceived before the rods, and

the flocks brought forth streaked, speckled, and
spotted.

40 Then Jacob separated the lambs, and made the
flocks face toward the streaked and all the brown in
the flock of Laban; but he put his own flocks by
themselves and did not put them with Laban's flock.

41 And it came to pass, whenever the stronger
livestock conceived, that Jacob placed the rods before the eyes of the livestock in the gutters, that they
might conceive among the rods.

42 But when the flocks were feeble, he did not put
them in; so the feebler were Laban's and the stronger
Jacob's.

43 Thus the man became exceedingly prosperous,
and had large flocks, female and male servants, and
camels and donkeys.

Gen. 30:1–43

Human beings were not created to live in isolation. They were
designed for relationships. It is therefore impossible for them to
function adequately without healthy involvement in the lives of others. The status and the nature of relationships contribute greatly to
the quality of life. Jacob's life was so full of less than ideal relationships that it is hardly surprising that his life was far from smooth.
His home life was full of tensions resulting from marriage to two
wives, while his work situation was desperate because of his ties to
an unscrupulous boss who was also his father-in-law!

RELATIONSHIPS REFLECT VALUES

The way people treat people is in itself a statement about the
value they place on God. Those who believe that men and women
are created in the divine image treat people quite differently from
those who have no such conception. This is clearly demonstrated in
the different values placed on human life in cultures that have a
Judeo-Christian foundation and those which are built on different
concepts. In personal relationships this is equally true. Those who
believe that the Lord is interested and involved in relationships are
much more careful about the way they treat each other than those

who simply regard people as pawns in a game. Recently, as a pastor, I dealt with a particularly painful schism between believers. In a final reconciliation meeting one of the parties observed, "If we weren't Christians we would never have gone to all this trouble to put things right! But because we are believers we didn't have any option."

Relationships also portray the value we put on individuals. To treat a person badly is the same as saying to a person, "In my book, you are not particularly significant or worthy of my attention and concern." This in turn reflects the value people place on morality. What people feel "ought" to happen at any one time can be most easily demonstrated by how they treat others or perhaps more accurately by how they expect to be treated. Even little children learn very quickly to complain "It's not fair!" when they usually mean that they have lost the advantage over their siblings! But their relationships are showing what they believe is right and fair and that in itself is a moral statement.

If we apply this principle to Jacob's life we come up with some interesting insights into his values. When Rachel prayed with great heartache, *"Give me children, or else I die!"*, his *"anger was aroused against Rachel, and he said, 'Am I in the place of God, who has withheld from you the fruit of the womb?'"* (Gen. 30:1, 2). His response shows something about his frustration with God as well as his intolerance of his wife's hurt and complaint. Meanwhile his treatment of Leah was reprehensible. Granted he had not wanted to marry her in the first place but he did not seem at all loath to have children by her. But when for some reason she became infertile he apparently lost interest in her altogether. She was so humiliated that she had to stoop to the level of saying to him, *"You must come in to me, for I have surely hired you with my son's mandrakes"* (v. 16). He acquiesced to her request and in so doing said something about his evaluation of his wife. Mandrakes, incidentally, are plants related to the deadly nightshade, which the ancients believed were helpful in promoting fertility in infertile women. Neither were Jacob's relations with his father-in-law of the highest caliber. The two men seemed to have had a grudging admiration for each other, possibly because they were tarred with the same brush. But they were also highly competitive and not at all reluctant to use each other to further their own ends.

After Jacob had finished his long-term commitment to Laban in exchange for Laban's daughters he said, *"Send me away, that I may go to my own place and to my country"* (v. 25). There was some natural reluctance on Laban's part because that meant parting with his daughters and grandchildren. But it became clear that they were not his major concern when he suggested that Jacob should not be so hasty! He responded, *"Please stay, if I have found favor in your eyes, for I have learned by experience that the Lord has blessed me for your sake"* (v. 27). In other words Jacob had economic value to him and he was not at all eager to lose such a valuable asset. Jacob did not rate very highly in Laban's book as a person to be cherished, but he was highly regarded as a person to be used. But Jacob in customary fashion saw a chance to make good on this situation so when he was asked to state his wages one more time he replied, *"Let me pass through all your flock today, removing from there all the speckled and spotted sheep, and all the brown ones among the lambs, and the spotted and speckled among the goats; and these shall be my wages"* (v. 32). Laban may or may not have known that there had to be a catch to this apparently innocuous request but he readily agreed. But Jacob had hatched a scheme. It was commonly believed that when animals were breeding the embryo was affected by any strange sight which might confront the mother during pregnancy. Jacob figured out how he could startle the prime sheep and goats into producing a disproportionate number of the speckled and spotted variety, leaving the weak and scraggly progeny to the boss.

Commentators vary in their understanding of what actually happened as a result of Jacob's handling of the breeding season and the resultant abnormally high proportion of *"speckled and spotted"* (and remarkably healthy) animals which were born. Some think that Jacob believed the peeled rods in the feeding trough would do the trick even though they could not possibly have had any effect. In actual fact it was his skill in breeding that was the real reason. Others suggest that there may be biological factors that the ancients were aware of that we in our modern sophistication have not discovered.

A third view assumes that God must have told him to put the rods in the troughs and though there was no intrinsic merit in the rods the act itself was an act of faithful obedience which God was pleased to bless by a miraculous intervention, in much the same way that

He acted in response to Moses and his brass serpent. Whichever interpretation is accepted it should be noted that however it was accomplished Jacob came away from the situation immeasurably more prosperous than he went into it despite the fact that his initial proposal was so loaded in Laban's favor that he regarded it as an offer he couldn't refuse! Surely there is a reminder here that the Lord had once again intervened on his servant's behalf even though there were many things about Jacob that left room for considerable improvement, particularly in the realm of relationships. Whatever the outcome of the deal one is left with the uneasy feeling that Laban was no more to be cherished in Jacob's estimation than Jacob was to be cherished in Laban's!

RELATIONSHIPS REVEAL VICES

There's a common saying in the North of England relating to marriage, "You never know what you've got until you get them home and the door is shut!" This is another way of saying that relationships not only reflect values but they also reveal vices! The unfortunate situation in which the sisters found themselves lent itself to all kinds of tensions which in turn gave every opportunity for the dark side of the women's lives to be revealed. *"Now when Rachel saw that she bore Jacob no children, Rachel envied her sister"* (v. 1). This unhealthy attitude was reflected in Leah's response to her sister. On one occasion she said to her, *"Is it a small matter that you have taken away my husband? Would you take away my son's mandrakes also?"* (v. 15). If their relationship to each other showed their capacity for envy and resentment their attitude to their mutual husband was no better. Their calculating how to get him into bed needs no elucidation on our part. These women were clearly capable of less than honorable activities when it suited their own purposes. One can only guess about the feelings of the slave girls Bilhah and Zilpah when they were coolly and calmly handed over to Jacob by Rachel and Leah respectively simply to function as baby makers. They functioned admirably in this regard and as a result added to the growing number of sons who could call Jacob their father.

It is worth noting that while Jacob was busy with his scheme to produce healthy speckled and spotted animals, Laban was busy getting the speckled and spotted three days' journey away from Jacob's tender mercies. There was no shortage of distrust and suspicion in these men. And it was not at all misplaced!

RELATIONSHIPS REFINE VIRTUES

While all these nasty things were swirling around Jacob's head a lot of little boys, and a little girl, were crawling around his feet. When we study the circumstances in which these children were born and the names they were given, which in a number of cases reflected the circumstances of their birth, it is easy to overlook the fact that there was still a lot of joy in the lives of the mothers at the birth of the children. There was also a lot of love in the heart of Laban for his daughters even though he had a strange way of demonstrating it at times. And Jacob was capable of showing that under his hard-bitten scheming exterior there beat a heart that could feel and care for these little ones.

The hardest heart is so often touched by the smallest child. The toughest exterior cracks at the gurgle of an infant. These are reminders enough that relationships offer innumerable opportunities for the refining of those delightful human capabilities of love and compassion which, so often, lie fallow in the human heart. Possibly more than anything else in life relationships can be the means of mankind acting nobly or insufferably. And it is through relationships that we can learn more about ourselves and each other than in any other area of human experience. It behooves us all to learn from the Jacob and Laban situations and to watch carefully the Jacob, Leah, and Rachel triangle and be warned.

CHAPTER THIRTY-ONE

Settling Differences

Genesis 31:1-55

31:1 Now *Jacob* heard the words of Laban's sons, saying, "Jacob has taken away all that was our father's, and from what was our father's he has acquired all this wealth."

2 And Jacob saw the countenance of Laban, and indeed it *was* not *favorable* toward him as before.

3 Then the LORD said to Jacob, "Return to the land of your fathers and to your family, and I will be with you."

4 So Jacob sent and called Rachel and Leah to the field, to his flock,

5 and said to them, "I see your father's countenance, that it *is* not *favorable* toward me as before; but the God of my father has been with me.

6 "And you know that with all my might I have served your father.

7 "Yet your father has deceived me and changed my wages ten times, but God did not allow him to hurt me.

8 "If he said thus: 'The speckled shall be your wages,' then all the flocks bore speckled. And if he said thus: 'The streaked shall be your wages,' then all the flocks bore streaked.

9 "So God has taken away the livestock of your father and given *them* to me.

10 "And it happened, at the time when the flocks conceived, that I lifted my eyes and saw in a dream, and behold, the rams which leaped upon the flocks *were* streaked, speckled, and gray-spotted.

11 "Then the Angel of God spoke to me in a dream, saying, 'Jacob.' And I said, 'Here I am.'

12 "And He said, 'Lift your eyes now and see, all the rams which leap on the flocks *are* streaked, speckled, and gray-spotted; for I have seen all that Laban is doing to you.

13 'I *am* the God of Bethel, where you anointed the pillar *and* where you made a vow to Me. Now arise, get out of this land, and return to the land of your family.'"

14 Then Rachel and Leah answered and said to him, "Is there still any portion or inheritance for us in our father's house?

15 "Are we not considered strangers by him? For he has sold us, and also completely consumed our money.

16 "For all these riches which God has taken from our father are *really* ours and our children's; now then, whatever God has said to you, do it."

17 Then Jacob rose and set his sons and his wives on camels.

18 And he carried away all his livestock and all his possessions which he had gained, his acquired livestock which he had gained in Padan Aram, to go to his father Isaac in the land of Canaan.

19 Now Laban had gone to shear his sheep, and Rachel had stolen the household idols that were her father's.

20 And Jacob stole away, unknown to Laban the Syrian, in that he did not tell him that he intended to flee.

21 So he fled with all that he had. He arose and crossed the river, and headed toward the mountains of Gilead.

22 And Laban was told on the third day that Jacob had fled.

23 Then he took his brethren with him and pursued him for seven days' journey, and he overtook him in the mountains of Gilead.

24 But God had come to Laban the Syrian in a dream by night, and said to him, "Be careful that you speak to Jacob neither good nor bad."

25 So Laban overtook Jacob. Now Jacob had pitched his tent in the mountains, and Laban with his brethren pitched in the mountains of Gilead.

26 And Laban said to Jacob: "What have you done, that you have stolen away unknown to me, and carried away my daughters like captives *taken* with the sword?

27 "Why did you flee away secretly, and steal away from me, and not tell me; for I might have sent you away with joy and songs, with timbrel and harp?

28 "And you did not allow me to kiss my sons and my daughters. Now you have done foolishly in *so* doing.

29 "It is in my power to do you harm, but the God of your father spoke to me last night, saying, 'Be careful that you speak to Jacob neither good nor bad.'

30 "And now you have surely gone because you greatly long for your father's house, *but* why did you steal my gods?"

31 Then Jacob answered and said to Laban, "Because I was afraid, for I said, 'Perhaps you would take your daughters from me by force.'

32 "With whomever you find your gods, do not let him live. In the presence of our brethren, identify what I have of yours and take *it* with you." For Jacob did not know that Rachel had stolen them.

33 And Laban went into Jacob's tent, into Leah's tent, and into the two maids' tents, but he did not find *them*. Then he went out of Leah's tent and entered Rachel's tent.

34 Now Rachel had taken the household idols, put them in the camel's saddle, and sat on them. And Laban searched all about the tent but did not find *them*.

35 And she said to her father, "Let it not displease my lord that I cannot rise before you, for the manner of women *is* with me." And he searched but did not find the household idols.

36 Then Jacob was angry and rebuked Laban, and Jacob answered and said to Laban: "What *is* my trespass? What *is* my sin, that you have so hotly pursued me?

37 "Although you have searched all my things, what part of your household things have you found? Set *it* here before my brethren and your brethren, that they may judge between us both!

38 "These twenty years I *have been* with you; your ewes and your female goats have not miscarried their young, and I have not eaten the rams of your flock.

39 "That which was torn *by beasts* I did not bring to you; I bore the loss of it. You required it from my hand, *whether* stolen by day or stolen by night.

40 "*There* I was! In the day the drought consumed me, and the frost by night, and my sleep departed from my eyes.

41 "Thus I have been in your house twenty years; I served you fourteen years for your two daughters, and six years for your flock, and you have changed my wages ten times.

42 "Unless the God of my father, the God of Abraham and the Fear of Isaac, had been with me, surely now you would have sent me away empty-handed. God has seen my affliction and the labor of my hands, and rebuked *you* last night."

43 And Laban answered and said to Jacob, "*These* daughters *are* my daughters, and *these* children *are* my children, and *this* flock *is* my flock; all that you see *is* mine. But what can I do this day to these my daughters or to their children whom they have borne?

44 "Now therefore, come, let us make a covenant, you and I, and let it be a witness between you and me."

45 So Jacob took a stone and set it up *as* a pillar.

46 Then Jacob said to his brethren, "Gather stones." And they took stones and made a heap, and they ate there on the heap.

47 Laban called it Jegar Sahadutha, but Jacob called it Galeed.

48 And Laban said, "This heap *is* a witness between you and me this day." Therefore its name was called Galeed,

49 also Mizpah, because he said, "May the LORD watch between you and me when we are absent one from another.

50 "If you afflict my daughters, or if you take *other* wives besides my daughters, *although* no man *is* with us—see, God *is* witness between you and me!'

51 Then Laban said to Jacob, "Here is this heap and here is *this* pillar, which I have placed between you and me.

52 "This heap *is* a witness, and *this* pillar *is* a witness, that I will not pass beyond this heap to you, and you will not pass beyond this heap and this pillar to me, for harm.

53 "The God of Abraham, the God of Nahor, and the God of their father judge between us.' And Jacob swore by the Fear of his father Isaac.

54 Then Jacob offered a sacrifice on the mountain, and called his brethren to eat bread. And they ate bread and stayed all night on the mountain.

55 And early in the morning Laban arose, and kissed his sons and daughters and blessed them. Then Laban departed and returned to his place.

Gen. 31:1–55

For twenty years Jacob and Laban continued their stormy relationship. Jacob said of it, *"I served you fourteen years for your two daughters, and six years for your flock, and you have changed my wages ten times. Unless the God of my father, the God of Abraham and the Fear of Isaac, had been with me, surely now you would have sent me away empty-handed"* (Gen. 31:41, 42). Clearly there was little love lost between the two men and even less trust. Their differences were real and deep.

THE REASONS DIFFERENCES ARISE

There was little hope of a sound relationship between these two men because of their personalities. They were both highly competitive and therefore saw each other as opponents to be beaten rather than blood relatives to be assisted. As a result they were constantly either threatening each other, irritating each other, or misunderstanding each other.

They also suffered from inevitable conflicts of interest. As was common in those areas in the times in which they lived there was only so much grass and water to go around and as their flocks were increasing it was only a matter of time until they began to run afoul of each other because their interests were mutually exclusive and tended therefore to become mutually destructive.

Jacob, whatever his faults, was aware of the activity of the Lord in his life but Laban gave little evidence of sensitivity to such factors. He told his wives, *"I see your father's countenance, that it is not favorable toward me as before; but the God of my father has been with me"* (v. 5). Then he added that their father had been unfair to him, *"but God did not allow him to hurt me"* (v. 7). But quite apart from the practical considerations which seemed to suggest that once again discretion would be the better part of valor for Jacob he was deeply influenced by the call of God which he received. In a dream the Lord showed him first of all that the remarkable increase in the numbers of "streaked, speckled, and gray-spotted" sheep was attributable to the Lord looking out for his interests rather than his own ingenuity, but then the Lord added, *"I am the God of Bethel, where you anointed the pillar and where you made a vow to Me. Now arise, get out of this land, and return to the land of your family"* (v. 13). It is true that the Lord did appear to Laban in a dream and instruct him to be very careful how he dealt with Jacob and he did accede to the divine directive. But there is little evidence of a genuine desire on his part to serve the Lord as was evident in Jacob's experience even if it was sometimes a little hard to identify. This difference in spiritual outlook led to conflict.

The emotional tensions were also very real. Jacob repeatedly complained about the mistreatment he had received from Laban and in a graphic and moving passage relayed his grievances to his father-in-law (see vv. 38–42). But Laban felt no less intensely about Jacob's behavior. When Jacob decided to obey his own instincts as well as the command of the Lord he did it in a less than noble manner. Having obtained his wives' agreement he packed up all his belongings and rounded up his herds and while Laban was out of camp seeing to the sheep shearing he headed for the hills. Whatever we think of Laban and the way he had treated his daughters and their husband, they were still his girls and their children were still his grandchildren and to come home and find that they had all disappeared without any warning was understandably upsetting. In fact, *"Laban said to Jacob, 'What have you done . . . ? Why did you flee away secretly, and steal away from me, and not tell me . . . ? And you did not allow me to kiss my sons and my daughters. Now you have done foolishly in so doing'"* (vv. 26–28).

Jacob's attitude toward his father-in-law could not have been helped by Rachel and Leah, for they were not at all happy about their treatment by their father. They complained, *"Is there still any portion or inheritance for us in our father's house? Are we not considered strangers by him? For he has sold us, and also completely consumed our money"* (vv. 14, 15). To summarize, Jacob thought he had been deceived, Laban was sure he had been deserted, and the daughters were convinced they had been used!

Then there were the ethical differences. While none of the parties seemed to stay awake at night worrying about ethics they seemed to spend time worrying about the ethics, or lack of same, of the other parties. Laban's casual approach to agreements was legendary. Jacob's complaint about him changing wages *"ten times"* should probably not be taken literally as the term was used to suggest a round number possibly like "dozens of times." He seems to have been able to rationalize his behavior to his own satisfaction if to no one else's. Rachel showed something of her father's approach to integrity when she was preparing to depart from her home in a hurry. She found time to think of ways in which she could get even with her father, and when he returned from sheep shearing he found not only that his family had disappeared but also his household gods. Rachel had helped herself to them. Her action may have had spiritual connotations but it is more likely that she had economic advantage in mind because it was believed that possession of the gods was helpful in this regard.

When eventually Laban caught up with Jacob and his slow-moving entourage, he expostulated among other things about the loss of his idols and Jacob, who knew nothing about it, said, *"With whomever you find your gods, do not let him live. In the presence of our brethren, identify what I have of yours and take it with you"* (v. 32). Laban began to search with a will but came up empty only because Rachel had hidden the idols under a camel saddle and sat on it. When her father arrived she made some excuses about the time of the month and asked to be excused if she did not stand up. What she lacked in truthfulness she made up in quick-wittedness.

Laban and Jacob were no strangers to the pressures which are so often related to success and survival. Jacob had become more successful than Laban although Laban had not been hurt either. But the comparisons were not in Laban's favor and that he did not like. Then the continual struggle against the harsh environment in which they lived and the precarious nature of their livelihood and lifestyle meant that unless their relationships were of the highest order there would be inevitable conflict. Spiritual, emotional, ethical, and practical factors all played a role in leading to the differences between the men and their families. Even a casual glance at today's society shows that nothing has changed to any marked degree!

THE RESULTS DIFFERENCES PRODUCE

Fractured relationships are one of the first consequences of differences which are not handled properly. This was clearly the case in the Laban/Jacob saga. But there was also another factor—the fear of reprisal. Jacob was driven to his drastic action because of the human pressure to which he had been subjected as well as the divine call he had received. But when Laban eventually caught him and asked why he had fled he said, *"Because I was afraid, for I said, 'Perhaps you would take your daughters from me by force'"* (v. 31). When the settling of differences becomes a major concern this often leads to strenuous efforts on the part of both parties to prove the rightness of their own position and the error of their adversary's stand. This in turn can produce the possibility of intimidation for those who feel they are about to lose. The energy expended in such endeavors and the waste of time and worry can have only a detrimental effect on the lives of all concerned. The case of Jacob and Laban readily illustrates this point without amplification.

THE RESOLUTION DIFFERENCES DEMAND

The most encouraging part of this sad story is the degree of resolution which Jacob and Laban were able to extricate from the ashes of their relationship. The way this was done merits study. First there was an honest confrontation of the issues. Jacob was able to tell Laban he wanted to leave and why he thought it was necessary.

He expressed his dismay and dissatisfaction at the treatment he had received and was courageous enough to tell Laban, *"God has seen my affliction and the labor of my hands, and rebuked you last night"* (v. 42). It is not unusual for people who get into arguments to claim that the Lord is on their side and not infrequently their protestations can lead to some very confusing conclusions. One is left to wonder how God can be equally in favor of such totally differing points of view! Laban does not seem to contest this notion so perhaps he was beginning to learn at long last that his actions were not meeting with divine approval. At any rate he was being confronted with the issue.

Laban countered by objecting, not so much to Jacob's action as to the manner in which he had done what he had done. This may have been the wily old Laban's way of getting around the issue but there does seem to be some degree of concession on his part. Confrontation and concession are the key ingredients. But it should be noted that it was Laban who was wise enough to introduce the next step. He proposed, *"Now therefore, come, let us make a covenant, you and I, and let it be a witness between you and me"* (v. 44). The suggestion met with immediate response on Jacob's part and although the two men would never be bosom buddies they at least were mature enough to work out a basis of understanding which would allow them to cooperate without being in constant competition. The agreement had both spiritual and practical dimensions. Together they made a heap of stones, ate a meal, and called upon the Lord to watch between them in some very practical ways. Laban, still not too sure about his son-in-law and what he might do to his wives, said, *"If you afflict my daughters, or if you take other wives besides my daughters, although no man is with us—see, God is witness between you and me!"* (v. 50).

This must have been a sobering thought to Jacob and this is exactly what Laban intended it to be. Laban added a very practical concession on his part, *"This heap is a witness, and this pillar is a witness, that I will not pass beyond this heap to you, and you will not pass beyond this heap and this pillar to me, for harm"* (v. 52). At last a semblance of reasonableness began to develop between the men. The agreement was sealed when Jacob made an oath in response to Laban's oath. He swore by *"the Fear of his father Isaac"* (v. 53). Jacob also used this unusual expression in conjunction with other more familiar names for the Lord (see v. 42) so it would appear that

this is a particularly solemn title for the Lord which in the circumstances was most appropriate. He sealed the agreement with oath
and sacrifice, spent the night with Laban on the mountain, and the
next morning the parting was completed. Jacob won his freedom,
Laban got his kisses, and while the two did not live together happily
ever after, they did not spend the rest of their days as they had spent
the last twenty years of their lives. This is an encouraging note for
all those people who feel that the differences they are experiencing
with others are draining their resources and hindering their ability
to get on with the business of living.

CHAPTER THIRTY-TWO

The Main Event

Genesis 32:1–32

32:1 So Jacob went on his way, and the angels of God met him.

2 When Jacob saw them, he said, "This *is* God's camp." And he called the name of that place Mahanaim.

3 Then Jacob sent messengers before him to Esau his brother in the land of Seir, the country of Edom.

4 And he commanded them, saying, "Speak thus to my lord Esau, 'Thus your servant Jacob says: "I have dwelt with Laban and stayed there until now.

5 "I have oxen, donkeys, flocks, and male and female servants; and I have sent to tell my lord, that I may find favor in your sight."'"

6 Then the messengers returned to Jacob, saying, "We came to your brother Esau, and he also is coming to meet you, and four hundred men *are* with him."

7 So Jacob was greatly afraid and distressed; and he divided the people that *were* with him, and the flocks and herds and camels, into two companies.

8 And he said, "If Esau comes to the one company and attacks it, then the other company which is left will escape."

9 Then Jacob said, "O God of my father Abraham and God of my father Isaac, the LORD who said to me, 'Return to your country and to your family, and I will deal well with you':

10 "I am not worthy of the least of all the mercies and of all the truth which You have shown Your servant; for I crossed over this Jordan with my staff, and now I have become two companies.

11 "Deliver me, I pray, from the hand of my brother, from the hand of Esau; for I fear him, lest he come and attack me *and* the mother with the children.

12 "For You said, 'I will surely treat you well, and make your descendants as the sand of the sea, which cannot be numbered for multitude.'"

13 So he lodged there that same night, and took what came to his hand as a present for Esau his brother:

14 two hundred female goats and twenty male goats, two hundred ewes and twenty rams,

15 thirty milk camels with their colts, forty cows and ten bulls, twenty female donkeys and ten foals.

16 Then he delivered *them* to the hand of his servants, every drove by itself, and said to his servants, "Pass over before me, and put some distance between successive droves."

17 And he commanded the first one, saying, "When Esau my brother meets you and asks you, saying, 'To whom do you belong, and where are you going? Whose *are* these in front of you?'

18 "then you shall say, 'They *are* your servant Jacob's. It *is* a present sent to my lord Esau; and behold, he also *is* behind us.'"

19 So he commanded the second, the third, and all who followed the droves, saying, "In this manner you shall speak to Esau when you find him;

20 "and also say, 'Behold, your servant Jacob *is* behind us.'" For he said, "I will appease him with the present that goes before me, and afterward I will see his face; perhaps he will accept me."

21 So the present went on over before him, but he himself lodged that night in the camp.

22 And he arose that night and took his two wives, his two female servants, and his eleven sons, and crossed over the ford of Jabbok.

23 He took them, sent them over the brook, and sent over what he had.

24 Then Jacob was left alone; and a Man wrestled with him until the breaking of day.

25 Now when He saw that He did not prevail against him, He touched the socket of his hip; and

the socket of Jacob's hip was out of joint as He wrestled with him.

26 And He said, "Let Me go, for the day breaks." But he said, "I will not let You go unless You bless me!"

27 So He said to him, "What *is* your name?" He said, "Jacob."

28 And He said, "Your name shall no longer be called Jacob, but Israel; for you have struggled with God and with men, and have prevailed."

29 Then Jacob asked, saying, "Tell *me* Your name, I pray." And He said, "Why *is* it *that* you ask about My name?" And He blessed him there.

30 So Jacob called the name of the place Peniel: "For I have seen God face to face, and my life is preserved."

31 Just as he crossed over Penuel the sun rose on him, and he limped on his hip.

32 Therefore to this day the children of Israel do not eat the muscle that shrank, which *is* on the hip socket, because He touched the socket of Jacob's hip in the muscle that shrank.

Gen. 32:1–32

One night stands out in the eventful life of Jacob. It was the night he added wrestling to his other accomplishments. The bout in which he was involved was no minor incident for he wrestled with the Lord Himself—an exercise in futility if ever there was one and yet one of the most common pursuits known to mankind. The struggle and the eventual outcome of the event proved to be the main event in Jacob's experience to date. Jacob had good reason to be nervous about his return to the land of promise because, while it was not absolutely necessary for him to go near his brother's territory, he recognized it would only be a matter of time until they met and perhaps he felt that the new direction of his life required the repair of the damage from his old life. He was wonderfully reassured, therefore, when, as he *went on his way, the angels of God met him* (Gen. 32:1). We are not told what transpired in the meeting but the result was that he named the place "Mahanaim" which means "Double Camp" and probably reflected his conviction that from this point on he knew that his own camp had been joined by the camp of the Lord's angels. He sent messengers to Esau announcing his return. They were instructed to behave in such a manner that his brother would understand that his intentions were peaceable. The news they brought on their return was not at all reassuring. They said, *"We came to your brother Esau, and he also is coming to meet you, and four hundred men are with him"* (v. 6). Jacob was understandably *"greatly afraid and distressed"* (v. 7) and promptly devised a strategy which divided his people and his herds with a view to cutting his losses should his brother attack him. Thus began Jacob's dark night of the soul.

THE NIGHT OF STRUGGLE

At some point in the dark night Jacob had another idea. He would send a generous gift to Esau in a manner most likely to impress his skeptical and belligerent brother. Using his favorite method of dividing in order to conquer he split the present of sheep and goats into three separate parties which would approach Esau at suitable intervals. He carefully instructed the shepherds to draw attention to his generosity. Then at strategic moments he dispatched his wives, maidservants, and sons (presumably Dinah went along too although she does not rate a mention!) after the presents trusting that the softening up process would have taken effect.

The result of all this activity was that Jacob was left alone with his fears and his thoughts, so he did a very wise thing, he turned to prayer. Whether he felt the need for solitude or whether it was simply the outcome of everybody else leaving at his command we do not know. He anchored his prayer firmly in his understanding of his God, referring to Him as, *"God of my father Abraham and God of my father Isaac, the Lord who said to me, 'Return to your country and to your family, and I will deal well with you'"* (v. 9). His sense of God's faithful dealing with his family over the years and his personal experiences of the Lord's call were the bases on which he felt free to pray even though he suffered under no illusions about his own worthiness to approach the Lord. He made particular reference to the way the Lord had blessed him saying, *"I crossed over this Jordan with my staff, and now I have become two companies"* (v. 10) and then, reminding the Lord of His great promise to make his descendants

272

as numerous as *"the sand of the sea, which cannot be numbered for multitude"* (v. 12), he made a most moving appeal for protection for himself and his family. There is much to learn from the way Jacob prayed and whatever else we may feel about his obvious short-comings there is no doubt that his lifestyle had afforded him both the opportunity and necessity to learn to pray.

Jacob was particularly vulnerable at that moment. He was ashamed as he thought of the way he had lived despite God's grace so vividly brought to his memory by the differing circumstances under which he was crossing the river Jordan compared to his crossing twenty years earlier. He was afraid for his life and the life of his loved ones and he was alone in the awful aloneness of those who suddenly feel the inadequacy of human effort to deal with the vicissitudes of life. Ashamed, afraid, and alone a man is open to divine intervention as perhaps at no other time.

In the darkness of the night and the loneliness of his solitude *"Jacob was left alone; and a Man wrestled with him until the breaking of day"* (v. 24). While the account does not state at what point the identity of his assailant was revealed to Jacob he said at the end of the incident, *"I have seen God face to face, and my life is preserved"* (v. 30). It is worth noting that despite the many experiences Jacob had known with God there was still an element of resistance to God's rule in his life portrayed by the graphic picture of him wrestling with the Man. His prayer had shown an element of reliance but the prevailing attitude underlying it was resistance. His language had been the language of dependence but there was evidence of a latent defiance in the way he fought the grip of God on his life. And instead of the submission to the purposes of God which would be necessary if he was to enter into all that the Lord had planned for him there was evidence of the self-assertion which had gotten him into trouble not a few times previously.

THE MOMENT OF TRUTH

"Now when He saw that He did not prevail against him, He touched the socket of his hip; and the socket of Jacob's hip was out of joint as He wrestled with him" (v. 25). Anyone who has dislocated a little finger or a big toe can imagine what kind of pain Jacob must have

experienced. Only those who know anything about wrestling can begin to imagine what he must have gone through in that excruciating moment.

The drastic nature of God's action reminds us that there is a limit beyond which He is not prepared to go in His dealings with mankind. The Lord Jesus taught this to His disciples when He told them to shake the dust of a city off their feet if the inhabitants were not prepared to hear and heed the Word of the Lord. He reflected this in His dealings with Herod and Pilate, when He apparently determined that both men had more than enough information on which to act and to which to respond. Perhaps He perceived that He did not prevail against them. To discover that God is not be trifled with is to arrive at the moment of truth which seems to elude many people who fondly imagine they are free to respond as and when they will with impunity.

The finality of the subtle but powerful touch of God on Jacob's life must have been unnerving. Suddenly he realized that his wrestlings were puny and that when God chose to reveal the true nature and extent of His power he was powerless to withstand. This lesson would be taught and learned and forgotten by the children of Israel for centuries to come, despite the fact that their father had learned it the hard way. Their striving and wrestlings with their God would be evidence of their imagined self-sufficiency and arrogant waywardness which would always end in chaos and exile. The prophets would warn them endlessly but rarely would they listen until the mighty power of their God was revealed in judgment and then for many of them it was too late. The moment of truth had dawned when the power of God was released in Jacob's life. As he lay on his back with the weight of his assailant heavy upon him, utterly powerless to move, the moment of truth concerning the true nature of Jacob's finiteness dawned. There had always been a reliance on his wits, his ingenuity, and his cool, determined commitment to coming out on top. But now he had met his match. One would have thought that Jacob's dealings with Laban would have taught him that even he had his limits. But while the truth may have begun to dawn it did not come to a full realization until he sank exhausted and defeated under the mighty hand of God. Donald Grey Barnhouse used to say, "The way to up is down. And the way to down is up." By that he meant that God is committed to bringing down those who exalt themselves but is equally committed to exalting those who will humble themselves under His hand. Jacob was busy learning what everybody who is earnest about spiritual life must learn either the hard way or the easy way.

THE HOUR OF DECISION

When Jacob's submission was complete the Man said, *"Let Me go, for the day breaks. But he said, 'I will not let You go unless You bless me!'"* (v. 26). Jacob, who like all men could not look on the unveiled glory of the divine face and survive, needed to be protected from the vision that would be his should the Lord be seen in the light of day. Hence the request for Jacob to let Him go. But Jacob's defiance had suddenly turned to reliance. He who had until a few moments ago been trying to do without the Lord as much as possible had realized how impossible it was for him to function without the Lord and the thought of trying was appalling to him. He would not and he could not let Him go!

His request for a blessing was beautifully described by Hosea:

> In his strength he struggled with God.
> Yes, he struggled with the Angel and prevailed;
> He wept, and sought favor from Him.
>
> *Hosea 12:3, 4*

The contrast between the struggling in his own strength and his weeping and seeking after favor from the Lord amply document the decision that had taken place in the heart of Jacob. But it was not quite so simple. The Lord *"said to him, 'What is your name?' He said, 'Jacob'"* (Gen. 32:27). Many of the names in the Old Testament bore great significance because they were a reflection either of the aspirations of the parents for their child or else a statement of the perceived characteristics and nature of the young person. Jacob was no exception and therefore the request for his name was tantamount to a request for an admission of who and what he really was. The answer probably came with reluctance, without bravado or

braggadocio. To admit to being Jacob was to admit to being a sup-
planter who had obtained both blessing and birthright by less than
the most honorable methods. Jacob decided to come clean about
himself in the same way he had decided to admit having arrived at
the end of his own resources.

THE DAY OF BLESSING

The Lord then uttered the wonderful words, *"Your name shall no
longer be called Jacob, but Israel; for you have struggled with God and
with men, and have prevailed"* (v. 28). The new name "Israel," which
comes from a verb related to the idea of "striving, persevering, and
overcoming," joined to "El" refers specifically to God overcoming
and persevering but in this context appears to draw special attention
to Jacob's ability to strive and prevail. Perhaps the conjunction of the
ideas of God prevailing and Jacob overcoming are intended to remind us that Jacob in his new name would be continually reminded
that man only overcomes as he knows the overcoming power of God
in him and through him. When Israel asked for the name of his
conqueror he was given no direct answer, but he knew that it was
the Lord with Whom he had been dealing and Who before leaving
blessed him as requested.

Israel's conviction about what had happened was memorialized by
him naming the place Peniel—"the face of God"— because as he
said, *"I have seen God face to face, and my life is preserved"* (v. 30). The
striking picture of the sun rising on the once self-sufficient Jacob as
he limped on his way—the proud bearer of his new name—should
never be forgotten. God had dealt graciously with His servant and
there would never be a day as long as he lived that Israel would
forget that his strength had come from his surrender. As he sank low
on one hip and rose strongly on the other each step was a statement
about the night he learned that "the way to up is down and the way
to down is up!"

Incidentally, the ban on eating *"the muscle that shrank"* (v. 32) is
nowhere repeated in the Old Testament but the Talmudists have regarded it as a law to be revered and even prescribed "several stripes"
if the law should be broken. Strict Jews still adhere to the ruling and

kosher slaughter requires the careful removal of the "nervus ischiadicus" as well as the draining of the blood before the meat can be eaten. Whatever the exact origin and reason for the tradition may be there is no doubt that it will serve as a reminder of the momentous evening when Jacob was transformed because he finally realized who was really in charge. All of us need to bear Jacob's lesson constantly in mind!

CHAPTER THIRTY-THREE

Repairing the Damage

Genesis 33:1–20

33:1 Now Jacob lifted his eyes and looked, and there, Esau was coming, and with him were four hundred men. So he divided the children among Leah, Rachel, and the two maidservants.

2 And he put the maidservants and their children in front, Leah and her children behind, and Rachel and Joseph last.

3 Then he crossed over before them and bowed himself to the ground seven times, until he came near to his brother.

4 But Esau ran to meet him, and embraced him, and fell on his neck and kissed him, and they wept.

5 And he lifted his eyes and saw the women and children, and said, "Who *are* these with you?" So he said, "The children whom God has graciously given your servant."

6 Then the maidservants came near, they and their children, and bowed down.

7 And Leah also came near with her children, and they bowed down. Afterward Joseph and Rachel came near, and they bowed down.

8 Then Esau said, "What *do* you *mean by* all this company which I met?" And he said, "*These are* to find favor in the sight of my lord."

9 But Esau said, "I have enough, my brother; keep what you have for yourself."

10 And Jacob said, "No, please, if I have now found favor in your sight, then receive my present from my hand, inasmuch as I have seen your face as

though I had seen the face of God, and you were pleased with me.

11 "Please, take my blessing that is brought to you, because God has dealt graciously with me, and because I have enough." So he urged him, and he took *it.*

12 Then Esau said, "Let us take our journey; let us go, and I will go before you."

13 But Jacob said to him, "My lord knows that the children *are* weak, and the flocks and herds which are nursing *are* with me. And if the men should drive them hard one day, all the flock will die.

14 "Please let my lord go on ahead before his servant. I will lead on slowly at a pace which the livestock that go before me, and the children, are able to endure, until I come to my lord in Seir."

15 And Esau said, "Now let me leave with you *some* of the people who *are* with me." But he said, "What need is there? Let me find favor in the sight of my lord."

16 So Esau returned that day on his way to Seir.

17 And Jacob journeyed to Succoth, built himself a house, and made booths for his livestock. Therefore the name of the place is called Succoth.

18 Then Jacob came safely to the city of Shechem, which *is* in the land of Canaan, when he came from Padan Aram; and he pitched his tent before the city.

19 And he bought the parcel of land, where he had pitched his tent, from the children of Hamor, Shechem's father, for one hundred pieces of money.

20 Then he erected an altar there and called it El Elohe Israel.

Gen. 33:1–20

Some people, at certain times of their lives, feel a compelling need to be reconciled to those from whom they have been estranged. John Lennon of Beatles fame was reportedly most anxious to rediscover his family roots and was trying to reestablish some kind of family relationship at the time of his brutal murder on the streets of New York City.

Jacob could easily have saved himself the anguish of meeting his brother Esau. He didn't have to go through his brother's territory to get back to his homeland but he undoubtedly felt some kind of obligation to try and put things right between them. While he did not know Christ's teaching about "first be reconciled to your brother" (Matt. 5:24), he showed sensitivity to the necessity for this kind of action.

But he may well have wondered about the wisdom of his action when *"Jacob lifted his eyes and looked, and there, Esau was coming, and with him four hundred men"* (Gen. 33:1). True to form he moved quickly to make the best of a bad situation. He divided up his children among their respective mothers and sent them toward Esau in a formation that must have indicated to them how they rated in Jacob's eyes. The maidservants and their sons went first, followed by Leah and her children and finally Rachel with Joseph. That must have been comforting for Rachel and Joseph but hardly encouraging for the others! But his scheming was soon to appear trivial and unnecessary because Esau took him completely by surprise and in so doing displayed some elements of forgiveness and reconciliation which modern society would do well to learn and practice.

WILLINGNESS TO ADMIT GUILT

Jacob finally confronted his brother but in markedly different circumstances and in a totally different attitude than their last encounter. At that time Jacob had been out to outwit and deceive his brother but now he *"bowed himself to the ground seven times, until he came near to his brother"* (v. 3). After their last encounter Esau had stated publicly that as soon as his father was safely dead and buried he would take it upon himself to kill Jacob. The depth of Esau's anger and hatred which had been provoked by Jacob's trickery was a fearsome thing to behold and the fact that it existed between two brothers was even more disconcerting. Jacob had good reason to expect the worst *"But Esau ran to meet him, and embraced him, and fell on his neck and kissed him, and they wept"* (v. 4).

While no words of actual admission of guilt are recorded the actions of the brothers speak volumes. Jacob's cringing approach to his brother with slow steps interspersed with prostrations was indicative of his total sense of humiliation. He was guilty of all manner of activities against his brother and he was ready at last to admit it. Most people find it hard to admit they were wrong but a man of Jacob's temperament and personality would probably find it doubly difficult. But to his credit he did what was right and thereby showed that the wrestling with the Lord had not been in vain. His submission was shown in his uncharacteristic submissiveness to the one he had wronged. Much heartache and pain would be banished from modern society if a similar attitude could be manifested on the part of those who have misbehaved.

READINESS TO ACCEPT APOLOGY

Reconciliation requires those who have done wrong to admit it and those who have been wronged to accept the apology. Without both parties being willing to participate appropriately nothing is achieved. Whenever the wrongdoer admits wrong and seeks forgiveness there is something about the human heart that wants to milk the situation for everything possible. One eminent American whose writings and sayings have been widely disseminated and equally widely embraced has gone on record as having taught his children, "Don't get mad; get even!" Others find it practically impossible to resist the temptation to rail on the repentant one with long-winded and self-righteous statements of their own rectitude in the situation while others have drunk so long and deeply of the waters of resentment that they find it impossible to break free from their addiction to bitterness.

Esau, to his credit, avoided all these attitudes. His response was most gracious and demonstrative. It is probable that the Lord Jesus had this story in mind when He related the famous reunion of the prodigal son and his father even to the extent of saying that he, like Esau, *"fell on his neck and kissed him"* (v. 4). Esau was intrigued by all the people belonging to Jacob's party who had come to him in their various bands, driving their herds and presenting their gifts, so he asked his brother, *"'What do you mean by all this company which I met?' And he said, 'These are to find favor in the sight of my lord'"* (v. 8). But Esau needed no presents to persuade him to accept the apology and he had as many flocks and herds as he needed so he declined the offer and it was only after Jacob pleaded with him that he accepted the gifts as a token of his acceptance of his brother.

OPENNESS TO ADMINISTER FORGIVENESS

In the emotion of the moment it is easy to weep and hug and say things that on further reflection may prove harder to implement than was thought at first. Esau gave no indication of this because he warmly suggested to Jacob that they continue their journey together. *"But Jacob said to him, 'My lord knows that the children are weak, and the flocks and herds which are nursing are with me. And if the men should drive them hard one day, all the flock will die. Please let my lord go on ahead before his servant'"* (vv. 13, 14). The response was perfectly reasonable but knowing Jacob there was always the possibility that he was being less than candid. He said he would make his way slowly to Seir but in actuality he traveled to Succoth where he settled down for a period of time, built a house and cattle sheds, and in so doing showed that he was not fully responding to the Lord's instructions to return to the land of Canaan. Subsequently he moved on to Shechem and the years rolled by without him doing what he had promised to Esau. Whether he intended to make his peace and then make his exit from Esau's life we do not know. All we can be sure of is that reconciliation was effected and perhaps they were wise enough to recognize as Confucius said, "No mountain big enough for two tigers!" Whatever the reason for Jacob's refusal, the effect of Esau's offer was clear indication of his readiness to forgive and to show that his forgiveness was real by a change of heart and attitude. No more threats on the life of his brother, only a desire to live peaceably with his brother. This was perhaps Esau's noblest moment.

CHAPTER THIRTY-FOUR

Violence

Genesis 34:1–31

34:1 Now Dinah the daughter of Leah, whom she had borne to Jacob, went out to see the daughters of the land.

2 And when Shechem the son of Hamor the Hivite, prince of the country, saw her, he took her and lay with her, and violated her.

3 His soul was strongly attracted to Dinah the daughter of Jacob, and he loved the young woman and spoke kindly to the young woman.

4 So Shechem spoke to his father Hamor, saying, "Get me this young woman as a wife."

5 And Jacob heard that he had defiled Dinah his daughter. Now his sons were with his livestock in the field; so Jacob held his peace until they came.

6 Then Hamor the father of Shechem went out to Jacob to speak with him.

7 And the sons of Jacob came in from the field when they heard *it;* and the men were grieved and very angry, because he had done a disgraceful thing in Israel by lying with Jacob's daughter, a thing which ought not to be done.

8 But Hamor spoke with them, saying, "The soul of my son Shechem longs for your daughter. Please give her to him as a wife.

9 "And make marriages with us; give your daughters to us, and take our daughters to yourselves.

10 "So you shall dwell with us, and the land shall be before you. Dwell and trade in it, and acquire possessions for yourselves in it."

11 Then Shechem said to her father and her brothers, "Let me find favor in your eyes, and whatever you say to me I will give.

12 "Ask me ever so much dowry and gift, and I will give according to what you say to me; but give me the young woman as a wife."

13 But the sons of Jacob answered Shechem and Hamor his father, and spoke deceitfully, because he had defiled Dinah their sister.

14 And they said to them, "We cannot do this thing, to give our sister to one who is uncircumcised, for that *would be* a reproach to us.

15 "But on this *condition* we will consent to you: If you will become as we *are*, if every male of you is circumcised,

16 "then we will give our daughters to you, and we will take your daughters to us; and we will dwell with you, and we will become one people.

17 "But if you will not heed us and be circumcised, then we will take our daughter and be gone."

18 And their words pleased Hamor and Shechem, Hamor's son.

19 So the young man did not delay to do the thing, because he delighted in Jacob's daughter. He *was* more honorable than all the household of his father.

20 And Hamor and Shechem his son came to the gate of their city, and spoke with the men of their city, saying:

21 "These men *are* at peace with us. Therefore let them dwell in the land and trade in it. For indeed the land *is* large enough for them. Let us take their daughters to us as wives, and let us give them our daughters.

22 "Only on this *condition* will the men consent to dwell with us, to be one people: if every male among us is circumcised as they *are* circumcised.

23 "*Will* not their livestock, their property, and every animal of theirs *be* ours? Only let us consent to them, and they will dwell with us."

24 And all who went out of the gate of his city heeded Hamor and Shechem his son; every male was circumcised, all who went out of the gate of his city.

25 Now it came to pass on the third day, when they

were in pain, that two of the sons of Jacob, Simeon and Levi, Dinah's brothers, each took his sword and came boldly upon the city and killed all the males.

26 And they killed Hamor and Shechem his son with the edge of the sword, and took Dinah from Shechem's house, and went out.

27 The sons of Jacob came upon the slain, and plundered the city, because their sister had been defiled.

28 They took their sheep, their oxen, and their donkeys, what *was* in the city and what *was* in the field,

29 and all their wealth. All their little ones and their wives they took captive; and they plundered even all that *was* in the houses.

30 Then Jacob said to Simeon and Levi, "You have troubled me by making me obnoxious among the inhabitants of the land, among the Canaanites and the Perizzites; and since I *am* few in number, they will gather themselves together against me and kill me. I shall be destroyed, my household and I."

31 But they said, "Should he treat our sister like a harlot?"

Gen. 34:1–31

The history of mankind is a sad story of violence. From the earliest times man has opposed man, brother has found himself in conflict with brother. One need look no further than the world's first two brothers to find a murderer and a victim. For many years it was fondly believed that man was improving and would eventually eradicate the world's ills. But the First World War was as damaging to that theory as it was to individual lives. Then along came the Second World War which was responsible for an average of one million deaths per month. Instead of ending all wars those two major confrontations introduced a period in which over twenty million people lost their lives in the space of forty years. The threat of nuclear holocaust and indiscriminate terrorist activity have done nothing to encourage the belief that man has recovered from his frightening penchant for violence. In fact, at the time of writing the most popular movies are those which depict explicit violence on a grand scale often allied to a misbegotten nationalistic spirit. Violence is here to stay and it has much to say about the condition of the human heart.

THE ROOTS OF VIOLENCE

The extremes of the political right and the political left do not often find themselves in agreement. But they both advocate the use of force and violence to further their ends. Revolutionary forces justify their violent acts because they regard them as the only means to overthrow the political structures which they perceive as being corrupt and irredeemable. Forces of the right respond by insisting that their principles and liberties are to be defended by all means, including violence.

Evolutionary theorists see violence as an inevitable factor in the development of the human race. To the optimists among them this is a potentially positive factor producing healthy aggression and competitive spirit which further human well-being, but their pessimistic brethren see it as a destructive factor which causes them concern.

Psychology suggests that violence is the outworking of the inner tensions which are part and parcel of the human make-up. If these tensions are resolved by external acts of mayhem the result is destruction for anybody or anything unfortunate enough to be in the wrong place at the wrong time. On the other hand if the tensions are internalized the result is self-destruction. There is ample evidence to suggest that both things are happening all too frequently in our world.

Anthropologists see the changes in cultures producing stress to which individuals react in self-defense and if it becomes acute enough they can become violent. The most ordinary person if he gets frightened enough may resort to unprecedented acts of violence as was evidenced by the Midwestern farmer who came to the end of his tether, took down his gun, and blew away his banker, his family, and himself.

Biblical theology, however, states that mankind's violence is related to the rejection of God, the substitution of self, and the resultant release of all manner of sinful dynamics which produce alienation from both God and man, the disintegration of society, the introduction of lust and greed, and the loss of self-control. All these factors came into play in the ongoing story of Jacob and his family.

THE RESULTS OF VIOLENCE

Jacob had been told to return to Bethel and he almost did. But his almost was his undoing because he stopped just short in Shechem, and there a terrible thing befell the family. Dinah caught the attention of a young man in the royal family who when he *"saw her, he took her and lay with her, and violated her"* (Gen. 34:2). In all fairness to the young man he apparently did desire to make her his wife but his action was a violation of her maidenhood and the principles of the people to whom she belonged. His violence was destructive of her dignity as a woman and a perversion of love. God had ordained human sexuality for conjugal love and human reproduction but He had also made it clear that it was to be enjoyed only within the confines of marriage. Anything else was a violation of sacred principle.

The young man spoke to his father who in turn approached Jacob asking for a marriage to be arranged. No doubt Jacob was favorably impressed by the prospect of a very profitable alliance which such a marriage would foster. The offer presented to him was, *"So you shall dwell with us, and the land shall be before you. Dwell and trade in it, and acquire possessions for yourselves in it"* (v. 10). Whether he would have succumbed to the tantalizing offer, swallowed his concerns about his daughter, and ignored the command to return to Bethel and thereby have done violence to many things he professed to hold dear, became a moot point when the brothers of Dinah found out about the rape. They *"were grieved and very angry, because he had done a disgraceful thing in Israel by lying with Jacob's daughter, a thing which ought not to be done"* (v. 7). They were unmoved by Shechem's offer, *"Ask me ever so much dowry and gift, and I will give according to what you say to me; but give me the young woman as a wife"* (v. 12). Sounding very pious and perhaps falling back on ancient marriage custom, they said that a marriage could not be arranged unless the men of Shechem were circumcised. Surprisingly, *"their words pleased Hamor and Shechem, Hamor's son. So the young man did not delay to do the thing, because he delighted in Jacob's daughter"* (vv. 18, 19). But Jacob's sons had acted deceitfully and *"it came to pass on the third day, when they were in pain, that two of the sons of Jacob, Simeon and Levi, Dinah's brothers, each took his sword and came boldly upon the city and killed all the males"* (v. 25). Whatever may be said about the righteous indignation of Dinah's brothers when they heard about her rape, nothing good can be said of their violent action both in the violation of truth and trust and in the more heinous violation of the sanctity of life.

The other brothers, who apparently did not participate in the massacre, were not averse, however, to participating in what they felt were the fruits of their brothers' labors. They *came upon the slain, and plundered the city . . . . All their little ones and their wives they took captive; and they plundered even all that was in the houses"* (vv. 27–29). Perhaps they had scruples about the violating of human life but they had no such scruples about violating property and violating the sensitivities of women who had just lost their men and children who had just lost their fathers. Even the homes of these unhappy people were not spared. Such was the violent nature of the sons of Jacob.

The reaction of their father is most instructive. He said to them, *"You have troubled me by making me obnoxious among the inhabitants of the land . . . and since I am few in number, they will gather themselves together against me and kill me. I shall be destroyed, my household and I"* (v. 30). His concerns were understandable and legitimate but his apparent lack of concern for the nature and significance of his sons' action was most disconcerting. He was more concerned about saving his own skin than he was in dealing with sons who had done such a dreadful deed. He could have said that they had troubled him by doing what they had done but instead he simply stated that they had troubled him because they had made life more difficult for him. Perhaps his lack of concern for integrity and dignity, life and property was reflected in the attitudes of his totally unrepentant sons who replied, *"Should he treat our sister like a harlot?"* (v. 31). The answer, of course, was "No"; the unasked question was "Should you have treated these people with such callous indifference and violence?"

THE RESPONSE TO VIOLENCE

Jacob's response to the violence of his family was total noninvolvement with a willingness to overlook it and use the situation to his own advantage. There is little that can be said in favor of such an attitude. Simeon and Levi responded to violence with more violence, showing once again that violence begets violence in a never-ending cycle. In contrast to their father's noninvolvement they were totally involved. The other brothers, however, were selectively involved. Not for them the violence of the sword but the violence of a scavenging hyena picking over the remains of another's violence was perfectly permissible. Shechem violated nobody's right to life, took no one's property, but he did violate a woman's body and do damage to her dignity. He was *"more honorable than all the household of his father"* (v. 19), so it would appear unlikely that he would have indulged in the kind of deceit and bloodshed of Jacob's sons. His violence was the violence of passion and lust which led to a young woman's ruin and in the end to the destruction of his city and its menfolk.

The problem of violence will not be solved by more violence. Neither will total uninvolvement do anything to halt the progress of those who choose to make the lives of others a thing of terror and horror. The problem confronting people of all ages and particularly God's people is, "What exactly should be my response to the violence which is so prevalent in the society of which I am a part and which I have helped to make?"

Abortion is clearly one of the most emotive, controversial topics of the day. Those who are primarily concerned with the "quality of human life" often rationalize the aborting of the fetus under certain circumstances, while those who concentrate on "the sanctity of human life" do not feel the freedom to terminate a pregnancy. Feelings have run so high in some quarters that abortion clinics have been destroyed through bombings and the people concerned, when apprehended, have justified their actions as a legitimate violent response to the violence of abortion. Others equally concerned about the abortion issue have publicly disavowed such methods of protest but have actively taken steps in the political arena to make their opinions and convictions known. Others have felt this was not enough and have organized regular "rescue missions" where they picket the centers where abortions take place and actively try to meet the young pregnant women and seek to dissuade them from terminating the pregnancy while at the same time offering assistance in a Crisis Pregnancy Center and eventually in counsel and practical help. One of my friends told me last week that she had recently been able to save two babies in one day's picketing. These approaches serve to show that in this one issue great care should be taken to identify the violence around us and then to determine what is the most appropriate response.

CHAPTER THIRTY-FIVE

Spiritual Renewal

Genesis 35:1-29

35:1 Then God said to Jacob, "Arise, go up to Bethel and dwell there; and make an altar there to God, who appeared to you when you fled from the face of Esau your brother."

2 And Jacob said to his household and to all who *were* with him, "Put away the foreign gods that *are* among you, purify yourselves, and change your garments.

3 "Then let us arise and go up to Bethel; and I will make an altar there to God, who answered me in the day of my distress and has been with me in the way which I have gone."

4 So they gave Jacob all the foreign gods which *were* in their hands, and *all* the earrings which *were* in their ears; and Jacob hid them under the terebinth tree which *was* by Shechem.

5 And they journeyed, and the terror of God was upon the cities that *were* all around them, and they did not pursue the sons of Jacob.

6 So Jacob came to Luz (that *is,* Bethel), which *is* in the land of Canaan, he and all the people who *were* with him.

7 And he built an altar there and called the place El Bethel, because there God appeared to him when he fled from the face of his brother.

8 Now Deborah, Rebekah's nurse, died, and she was buried below Bethel under the terebinth tree. So the name of it was called Allon Bachuth.

9 Then God appeared to Jacob again, when he came from Padan Aram, and blessed him.

10 And God said to him, "Your name is Jacob; your name shall not be called Jacob anymore, but Israel shall be your name." So He called his name Israel.

11 Also God said to him: "I am God Almighty. Be fruitful and multiply; a nation and a company of nations shall proceed from you, and kings shall come from your body.

12 "The land which I gave Abraham and Isaac I give to you; and to your descendants after you I give this land."

13 Then God went up from him in the place where He talked with him.

14 So Jacob set up a pillar in the place where He talked with him, a pillar of stone; and he poured a drink offering on it, and he poured oil on it.

15 And Jacob called the name of the place where God spoke with him, Bethel.

16 Then they journeyed from Bethel. And when there was but a little distance to go to Ephrath, Rachel labored in childbirth, and she had hard labor.

17 Now it came to pass, when she was in hard labor, that the midwife said to her, "Do not fear; you will have this son also."

18 And so it was, as her soul was departing (for she died), that she called his name Ben-Oni; but his father called him Benjamin.

19 So Rachel died and was buried on the way to Ephrath (that is, Bethlehem).

20 And Jacob set a pillar on her grave, which is the pillar of Rachel's grave to this day.

21 Then Israel journeyed and pitched his tent beyond the tower of Eder.

22 And it happened, when Israel dwelt in that land, that Reuben went and lay with Bilhah his father's concubine; and Israel heard about it.

Now the sons of Jacob were twelve:

23 the sons of Leah were Reuben, Jacob's firstborn, and Simeon, Levi, Judah, Issachar, and Zebulun;

24 the sons of Rachel were Joseph and Benjamin;

25 the sons of Bilhah, Rachel's maidservant, were Dan and Naphtali;

26 and the sons of Zilpah, Leah's maidservant, were

Gad and Asher. These *were* the sons of Jacob who were born to him in Padan Aram.

27 Then Jacob came to his father Isaac at Mamre, or Kirjath Arba (that *is,* Hebron), where Abraham and Isaac had dwelt.

28 Now the days of Isaac were one hundred and eighty years.

29 So Isaac breathed his last and died, and was gathered to his people, *being* old and full of days. And his sons Esau and Jacob buried him.

Gen. 35:1-29

Bethel held a unique attraction and significance for Jacob. It was there that the Lord had appeared to him when he was running away from his irate brother. While there were many ups and downs in Jacob's life he never totally forgot the events which had transpired there. The return visit proved to be most appropriate because it afforded an opportunity for some necessary spiritual renewal.

WHY IS SPIRITUAL RENEWAL NECESSARY?

Spiritual renewal is necessary because human memory is faulty. When Jacob first passed through Bethel the Lord had promised him, "Behold, I am with you and will keep you wherever you go, and will bring you back to this land; for I will not leave you until I have done what I have spoken to you" (Gen. 28:15). In the intervening years the Lord had been faithful to His servant and as he stood once again at Bethel, Jacob could not fail to recognize that He had indeed brought him back to the land of promise. In the business of his life Jacob needed a place of retreat to remember what the Lord had promised and had indeed brought to pass.

At the same time Jacob was reminded of the things he had promised the Lord. He had said, "If God will be with me, and keep me in this way that I am going, and give me bread to eat and clothing to put on, so that I come back to my father's house in peace, then the Lord shall be my God" (Gen. 28:20, 21). The return to Bethel provided the opportunity for Jacob to deliver on his promise.

Recently a young couple came to see me whose marital problems were apparently leading to a divorce. After a long and not particularly fruitful conversation they left my office. But some time later when I went through the sanctuary in which they were married and where for four years they had worshiped together I found them sitting together deep in conversation. Their return to the place of commitment was having more impact on them than all our discussion and debate.

Spiritual renewal is also necessary because human commitment is fickle. Jacob's commitment to the Lord had worn thin at the edges. When he was told to return to Bethel he realized this to be the case so he said to his household and to all who were with him, *"Put away the foreign gods that are among you, purify yourselves, and change your garments. Then let us arise and go up to Bethel"* (Gen. 35:2, 3). He was obviously aware of the presence of the gods but had chosen not to do anything about them until he was confronted again with his exclusive commitment to the Lord. Then and only then did he deal with the issue which he had treated with benign neglect.

Renewal is also necessary because human fortunes change. When Jacob made his original commitment he was young and fancy free. Now he was no longer young and he was responsible for a very large family whose fortunes depended to a large extent on his actions. By this time he had two wives, two concubines, eleven sons, and one daughter, not to mention considerable assets. Many people make profound commitments when they are young and free from responsibilities, but as the years pass by and the responsibilities increase it is not uncommon for the commitments to be overlooked and ignored. Renewal is also appropriate because human life is so fleeting. This came home to Jacob when *"Deborah, Rebekah's nurse, died, and she was buried below Bethel"* (v. 8). The death of this faithful and aged lady was followed shortly by another tragic passing. *"Rachel labored in childbirth, and she had hard labor. . . . So Rachel died and was buried on the way to Ephrath (that is, Bethlehem)"* (vv. 16–19). As if these two reminders of human finitude were not enough Jacob's father Isaac *"breathed his last and died, and was gathered to his people, being old and full of days. And his sons Esau and Jacob buried him"* (v. 29). The "daily round and common task" can become so demanding and compelling that they lead to casualness about spiritual and eternal matters. But when death comes calling, priorities are often quickly rearranged. It is far better to be spiritually fresh in order to meet life's tragedies than to meet them ill-prepared and then try to salvage something from a wasted life.

How Is Spiritual Renewal Experienced?

Jacob needed to get back to basics. Like the football coach who found it necessary to call his defeated team together in the locker room and say to them, "Gentlemen, this is a football!", the Lord called Jacob back to Bethel to start near the beginning. He found it necessary to remind him of His presence, so *"God appeared to Jacob again . . . and blessed him"* (v. 9). Then he reminded him, *"Your name is Jacob; your name shall not be called Jacob anymore, but Israel shall be your name"* (v. 10). After that He reiterated His promise: *"The land which I gave Abraham and Isaac I give to you; and to your descendants after you I give this land"* (v. 12). With all these familiar things going on around him it was not surprising that Jacob responded by doing similar things to those he had done in his original Bethel experience. He *"set up a pillar in the place where He talked with him, a pillar of stone; and he poured a drink offering on it, and he poured oil on it. And Jacob called the name of the place where God spoke to him, Bethel"* (vv. 14, 15). There is a tendency for God's people to seek new and exciting experiences when often what they really need is a renewal of the original basic understandings and ingredients which initiated their experience of the Lord.

Jacob also needed to get rid of barriers. As we have already seen, the foreign gods had made deep incursions into the life of Jacob's family. To be true to the Lord they had to do something about the things that were antithetical to Him. Jacob addressed the issues, gave instructions, and the people responded by handing over to him, *"all the foreign gods which were in their hands, and all their earrings which were in their ears; and Jacob hid them under the terebinth tree which was by Shechem"* (v. 4). He was required to deal with the things which were a blatant contradiction to his professed allegiance. He needed to rid himself of those things which would produce conflict in his walk with the Lord, and he had to address the factors which would serve only to contaminate his soul. Without this type of action there would be no lasting renewal.

WHEN IS SPIRITUAL RENEWAL POSSIBLE?

The most sure way of maintaining spiritual freshness is by daily devotion. This is a discipline which, when adhered to, deals with matters which are relatively insignificant before they get out of hand. Regular participation in public worship is another divinely approved way of walking closely in fellowship with the Lord. Consistent fellowship with God's people on a level where deep and personal care and sharing are possible also contributes greatly to ongoing renewal. But in addition to all these regular factors most of God's people point to Bethel experiences where special events took place in special places. This type of experience leaves impressions which are deeply etched on the heart and mind of the participant.

It should be noted that despite the renewal Jacob's troubles were not over! The actions of his sons at Shechem had done nothing to enhance his image among his neighbors. He had suspected that he would be "obnoxious among the inhabitants of the land" (Gen. 34:30) and apparently his fears were well justified because, as they traveled, *"the terror of God was upon the cities that were all around them"* (Gen. 35:5). While this saved them a lot of trouble it did nothing for their relationships, and less for their reputations. Reuben did not help either. While his father was busy with other things Reuben took the opportunity to *"lay with Bilhah his father's concubine; and Israel heard about it"* (v. 22).

Spiritual renewal never exempted the people of God from the consequences of their own actions or the actions of those whose lives are interwoven with them. But spiritual renewal does equip people to be strong enough to handle all that comes their way in a world where sin abounds.

CHAPTER THIRTY-SIX

The Bitter Root

Genesis 36:1–43

36:1 Now this *is* the genealogy of Esau, who is Edom.

2 Esau took his wives from the daughters of Canaan: Adah the daughter of Elon the Hittite; Aholibamah the daughter of Anah, the daughter of Zibeon the Hivite;

3 and Basemath, Ishmael's daughter, sister of Nebajoth.

4 Now Adah bore Eliphaz to Esau, and Basemath bore Reuel.

5 And Aholibamah bore Jeush, Jaalam, and Korah. These *were* the sons of Esau who were born to him in the land of Canaan.

6 Then Esau took his wives, his sons, his daughters, and all the persons of his household, his cattle and all his animals, and all his goods which he had gained in the land of Canaan, and went to a country away from the presence of his brother Jacob.

7 For their possessions were too great for them to dwell together, and the land where they were strangers could not support them because of their livestock.

8 So Esau dwelt in Mount Seir. Esau *is* Edom.

9 And this *is* the genealogy of Esau the father of the Edomites in Mount Seir.

10 These *were* the names of Esau's sons: Eliphaz the son of Adah the wife of Esau, and Reuel the son of Basemath the wife of Esau.

11 And the sons of Eliphaz were Teman, Omar, Zepho, Gatam, and Kenaz.

12 Now Timna was the concubine of Eliphaz, Esau's son, and she bore Amalek to Eliphaz. These *were* the sons of Adah, Esau's wife.

13 These *were* the sons of Reuel: Nahath, Zerah, Shammah, and Mizzah. These were the sons of Basemath, Esau's wife.

14 These were the sons of Aholibamah, Esau's wife, the daughter of Anah, the daughter of Zibeon. And she bore to Esau: Jeush, Jaalam, and Korah.

15 These *were* the chiefs of the sons of Esau. The sons of Eliphaz, the firstborn *son* of Esau, were Chief Teman, Chief Omar, Chief Zepho, Chief Kenaz,

16 Chief Korah, Chief Gatam, *and* Chief Amalek. These *were* the chiefs of Eliphaz in the land of Edom. They *were* the sons of Adah.

17 These *were* the sons of Reuel, Esau's son: Chief Nahath, Chief Zerah, Chief Shammah, and Chief Mizzah. These *were* the chiefs of Reuel in the land of Edom. These *were* the sons of Basemath, Esau's wife.

18 And these *were* the sons of Aholibamah, Esau's wife: Chief Jeush, Chief Jaalam, and Chief Korah. These *were* the chiefs *who descended* from Aholibamah, Esau's wife, the daughter of Anah.

19 These *were* the sons of Esau, who is Edom, and these *were* their chiefs.

20 These *were* the sons of Seir the Horite who inhabited the land: Lotan, Shobal, Zibeon, Anah,

21 Dishon, Ezer, and Dishan. These *were* the chiefs of the Horites, the sons of Seir, in the land of Edom.

22 And the sons of Lotan were Hori and Hemam. Lotan's sister *was* Timna.

23 These *were* the sons of Shobal: Alvan, Manahath, Ebal, Shepho, and Onam.

24 These *were* the sons of Zibeon: both Ajah and Anah. This *was the* Anah who found the water in the wilderness as he pastured the donkeys of his father Zibeon.

25 These *were* the children of Anah: Dishon and Aholibamah the daughter of Anah.

26 These *were* the sons of Dishon: Hemdan, Eshban, Ithran, and Cheran.

27 These *were* the sons of Ezer: Bilhan, Zaavan, and Akan.

28 These *were* the sons of Dishan: Uz and Aran.

29 These *were* the chiefs of the Horites: Chief Lotan, Chief Shobal, Chief Zibeon, Chief Anah,

30 Chief Dishon, Chief Ezer, and Chief Dishan. These *were* the chiefs of the Horites, according to their chiefs in the land of Seir.

31 Now these *were* the kings who reigned in the land of Edom before any king reigned over the children of Israel:

32 Bela the son of Beor reigned in Edom, and the name of his city *was* Dinhabah.

33 And when Bela died, Jobab the son of Zerah of Bozrah reigned in his place.

34 When Jobab died, Husham of the land of the Temanites reigned in his place.

35 And when Husham died, Hadad the son of Bedad, who attacked Midian in the field of Moab, reigned in his place. And the name of his city *was* Avith.

36 When Hadad died, Samlah of Masrekah reigned in his place.

37 And when Samlah died, Saul of Rehoboth-*by*-the-River reigned in his place.

38 When Saul died, Baal-Hanan the son of Achbor reigned in his place.

39 And when Baal-Hanan the son of Achbor died, Hadar reigned in his place; and the name of his city *was* Pau. His wife's name *was* Mehetabel, the daughter of Matred, the daughter of Mezahab.

40 And these *were* the names of the chiefs of Esau, according to their families and their places, by their names: Chief Timnah, Chief Alvah, Chief Jetheth,

41 Chief Aholibamah, Chief Elah, Chief Pinon,

42 Chief Kenaz, Chief Teman, Chief Mibzar,

43 Chief Magdiel, and Chief Iram. These *were* the chiefs of Edom, according to their dwelling places in the land of their possession. Esau *was* the father of the Edomites.

Gen. 36:1–43

Many years have elapsed since Esau appeared on the scene, "red and like a hairy garment." They have been action-packed years and most of the action has been related to his brother Jacob. Esau usually has been on the receiving end of his brother's quick wits and indifferent morality and the years have held many sorrows for him. Now the unfolding story of Genesis must move on, and like many before him Esau moves out of the spotlight to make way for other characters through whom God worked out His eternal purposes. But before he makes his exit a full record of his genealogy is preserved for posterity. This may not be of great interest to most people but the details serve to remind us that the impact of this man was felt long and often in the centuries after his death. The descendants of Jacob, the children of Israel would find relentless and persistent opposition down through the years from none other than the descendants of Esau. "The evil that men do lives after them" referred to Caesar but it could equally have been written about Esau. But he was not without his nobler moments and Scripture reminds us that he has some important things to teach us.

Esau's Experience

His attitude toward his birthright spoke volumes about the priorities of his life. For him material matters far outweighed spiritual concerns. A sensual smell and the satisfying of a raging hunger were far more important to him than the long-lasting privileges and responsibilities of the firstborn. So he despised his birthright. It is true that he regretted his action in retrospect but his efforts to regain what he had so carelessly traded were to no avail.

He showed little concern for his family when he chose to marry women from the Hittite tribe. He may have tried to rectify this error in a later marriage, but the damage had been done. His hatred of Jacob was deep and damaging and while he did show great restraint and warmth when they finally met after twenty years their brotherly relationship was never what it could and should have been. It seems that he was prone to rash, careless actions which on reflection he regretted and tried to rectify but which he could never adequately undo. The reason presumably was that at heart he was fundamentally a "profane person" (Heb. 12:16). The tensions of his personality were such that without the guarding and guiding grace of God operating within he was often a pitiful victim of the whims and caprices of his own nature.

After it was determined that the land of promise was not big enough for both brothers, *"Esau dwelt in Mount Seir. Esau is Edom . . . the father of the Edomites in Mount Seir"* (Gen. 36:8, 9). Years later when the children of Israel were enroute from Egypt to Canaan under Moses they respectfully asked permission from their cousins, the Edomites, to pass through their land. They were careful to give assurances of their good intentions and promises to pay for anything they might consume on the way. The response of Edom was, "You shall not pass through my land, lest I come out against you with the sword" (Num. 20:18). Edom had not changed during the generations succeeding Esau their father!

Amalek (see Gen. 36:12) was another of Esau's descendants who carried on the family tradition. While we are not certain that the tribe bearing his name was actually descended from him there is good reason to believe that they were perpetuating the antagonism of Esau against Jacob as they relentlessly bore down on the children of Israel, on occasion handing them resounding defeats (see Num. 14:45).

If ever there was any doubt about the Lord's attitude to Esau's descendants' actions against Israel they were dispelled by the prophet Obadiah who, speaking out against the Edomites, said:

> Behold, I will make you small among the nations;
> You shall be greatly despised.
> . . . Oh, how Esau shall be searched out!
> How his hidden treasures shall be sought after!
> . . . For violence against your brother Jacob,
> Shame shall cover you,
> And you shall be cut off forever.
>
> *Obad. 2, 6, 10*

It is surely no coincidence that the age old antagonism between Esau and Jacob should be perpetuated into the time of Christ. When Jesus stood before Herod He was standing in the line of Jacob before a man who stood firmly in the line of Esau, for Herod was an

Idumaean (the Greek equivalent of Edomite). It was left to this descendant of Esau to heap the ultimate shame on the Son of God. Luke records, "Then Herod, with his men of war, treated Him with contempt and mocked Him, arrayed Him in a gorgeous robe, and sent Him back to Pilate. That very day Pilate and Herod became friends with each other, for before they had been at enmity with each other" (Luke 23:11, 12).

Esau's Example

We should be careful not to dismiss lightly these indications that the ancient hostility of the brothers was perpetuated down through the generations. In fact, the writer to the Hebrews makes a very powerful point by way of application in this regard. "Pursue peace with all people, and holiness, without which no one will see the Lord: looking carefully lest anyone fall short of the grace of God; lest any root of bitterness springing up cause trouble, and by this many become defiled" (Heb. 12:14, 15). The analogy of the bitter root and its spreading influence is so clear that it needs no exposition and when applied to the baleful influence of Esau on his successors serves as a solemn warning to people of all generations to ensure that they make peace and pursue holiness lest they too have an impact for ill far beyond anything they ever imagined.

CHAPTER THIRTY-SEVEN

Boys Will Be Men

Genesis 37:1–36

37:1 Now Jacob dwelt in the land where his father was a stranger, in the land of Canáan.

2 This *is* the history of Jacob. Joseph, *being* seventeen years old, was feeding the flock with his brothers. And the lad *was* with the sons of Bilhah and the sons of Zilpah, his father's wives; and Joseph brought a bad report of them to his father.

3 Now Israel loved Joseph more than all his children, because he *was* the son of his old age. Also he made him a tunic of *many* colors.

4 But when his brothers saw that their father loved him more than all his brothers, they hated him and could not speak peaceably to him.

5 Now Joseph had a dream, and he told *it* to his brothers; and they hated him even more.

6 So he said to them, "Please hear this dream which I have dreamed:

7 "There we were, binding sheaves in the field. Then behold, my sheaf arose and also stood upright; and indeed your sheaves stood all around and bowed down to my sheaf."

8 And his brothers said to him, "Shall you indeed reign over us? Or shall you indeed have dominion over us?" So they hated him even more for his dreams and for his words.

9 Then he dreamed still another dream and told it to his brothers, and said, "Look, I have dreamed another dream. And this time, the sun, the moon, and the eleven stars bowed down to me."

10 So he told *it* to his father and his brothers; and

his father rebuked him and said to him, "What *is* this dream that you have dreamed? Shall your mother and I and your brothers indeed come to bow down to the earth before you?"

11 And his brothers envied him, but his father kept the matter *in mind.*

12 Then his brothers went to feed their father's flock in Shechem.

13 And Israel said to Joseph, "Are not your brothers feeding *the flock* in Shechem? Come, I will send you to them." So he said to him, "Here I am."

14 Then he said to him, "Please go and see if it is well with your brothers and well with the flocks, and bring back word to me." So he sent him out of the Valley of Hebron, and he went to Shechem.

15 Now a certain man found him, and there he was, wandering in the field. And the man asked him, saying, "What are you seeking?"

16 So he said, "I am seeking my brothers. Please tell me where they are feeding *their flocks.*"

17 And the man said, "They have departed from here, for I heard them say, 'Let us go to Dothan.'" So Joseph went after his brothers and found them in Dothan.

18 Now when they saw him afar off, even before he came near them, they conspired against him to kill him.

19 Then they said to one another, "Look, this dreamer is coming!

20 "Come therefore, let us now kill him and cast him into some pit; and we shall say, 'Some wild beast has devoured him.' We shall see what will become of his dreams!"

21 But Reuben heard *it,* and he delivered him out of their hands, and said, "Let us not kill him."

22 And Reuben said to them, "Shed no blood, *but* cast him into this pit which *is* in the wilderness, and do not lay a hand on him"—that he might deliver him out of their hands, and bring him back to his father.

23 So it came to pass, when Joseph had come to his brothers, that they stripped Joseph *of* his tunic, the tunic of *many* colors that *was* on him.

24 Then they took him and cast him into a pit. And the pit *was* empty; *there was* no water in it.

25 And they sat down to eat a meal. Then they lifted their eyes and looked, and there was a company of Ishmaelites, coming from Gilead with their camels, bearing spices, balm, and myrrh, on their way to carry *them* down to Egypt.

26 So Judah said to his brothers, "What profit *is there* if we kill our brother and conceal his blood?

27 "Come and let us sell him to the Ishmaelites, and let not our hand be upon him, for he *is* our brother *and* our flesh." And his brothers listened.

28 Then Midianite traders passed by; so *the brothers* pulled Joseph up and lifted him out of the pit, and sold him to the Ishmaelites for twenty *shekels* of silver. And they took Joseph to Egypt.

29 Then Reuben returned to the pit, and indeed Joseph *was* not in the pit; and he tore his clothes.

30 And he returned to his brothers and said, "The lad *is* no *more;* and I, where shall I go?"

31 So they took Joseph's tunic, killed a kid of the goats, and dipped the tunic in the blood.

32 Then they sent the tunic of *many* colors, and they brought *it* to their father and said, "We have found this. Do you know whether it *is* your son's tunic or not?"

33 And he recognized it and said, *"It is* my son's tunic. A wild beast has devoured him. Without doubt Joseph is torn to pieces."

34 Then Jacob tore his clothes, put sackcloth on his waist, and mourned for his son many days.

35 And all his sons and all his daughters arose to comfort him; but he refused to be comforted, and he said, "For I shall go down into the grave to my son in mourning." Thus his father wept for him.

36 Now the Midianites had sold him in Egypt to Potiphar, an officer of Pharaoh *and* captain of the guard.

Gen. 37:1–36

Youth work can be at one and the same time exhilarating and frustrating. When as a youth worker I used to become frustrated with

some of my charges I was often reminded by my friend and col-
league, Ian Thomas, "Don't forget, Stuart, boys will be boys, but just
be patient and boys will be men!" It was always helpful to be reminded of this, particularly at times when it appeared that some of
the boys were more likely to become gorillas! Boys are simply men
under construction and what they will become is to a large extent
determined by what goes into their early building. For this reason
the story of Joseph is particularly helpful, because we not only have
a detailed record of him as a mature man, but we are also given
considerable information relating to his life as a teenager. The factors which went into his early development are worthy of note.

THE INSTILLATION OF WORTHY PRINCIPLES

Our first glimpse of Joseph is significant. *"Joseph, being seventeen
years old, was feeding the flock with his brothers"* (Gen. 37:2). He had
been put to work at an early age, as was customary in his culture.
Joseph's responsibility was to work with the sons of Jacob's concubines as a *"lad"* which suggests that he was an assistant to these men
who themselves did not rank very high in the family pecking order.
Like many people before and since Joseph had his problems at work.
He did not help himself when he *"brought a bad report of them to his
father"* (v. 2). Evidently he had a commitment to truth which served
to override the natural reticence a young man would have against
bearing tales about his brothers to their father and employer. Perhaps he had learned that "honesty is the best policy" from watching
the mess his own father got into with Laban and Esau. While Joseph
was only a young boy at the time of these incidents he was quite old
enough to know that his father had been less than straightforward
and, as a result, he had gotten himself into all kinds of trouble!

In that he exposed what he regarded as *"bad"* shows that he had
learned certain principles about what is good and what isn't. He was
about eleven years of age when his sister Dinah was raped and the
resultant massacre took place. The sense of shame which his father
experienced and expressed after that incident quite probably worked
its way into his consciousness despite his youth.

Joseph was given to dreams through which he believed that the
Lord was speaking to him. This fundamental principle of faith had

been nurtured in his young life but had probably been underlined when his father took the whole family back to Bethel having instructed everyone to do away with his foreign gods. This dramatic action by his father would not go unnoticed by the young teenager who was so close to his dad.

One day Joseph announced to his brothers that he had dreamed that they were all working together in a field when the sheaves of corn started to bow down to each other. Their interest and anger were piqued when he suggested that their sheaves were bowing to his, and they bluntly asked, *"Shall you indeed reign over us? Or shall you indeed have dominion over us?"* (v. 8). They already disliked him intensely. The result of this further revelation was *"they hated him even more for his dreams and for his words"* (v. 8). Subsequently he had another dream on a similar theme and he said *"this time, the sun, the moon, and the eleven stars bowed down to me"* (v. 9). Having already offended his brothers, he now managed through this announcement to offend his father who said to him, *"What is this dream that you have dreamed? Shall your mother and I and your brothers indeed come to bow down to the earth before you?"* (v. 10). The young man may have been short on tact but he was no stranger to truth.

Commitment to the principles of truth, good, right, faith, and work were deeply entrenched in Joseph's life by the time he had reached seventeen years of age. These attributes were to serve him well in the ensuing traumatic events of his life.

THE INEVITABILITY OF VARIOUS PRESSURES

Young people need acceptance more than the average person. To be rejected by their peers is the most devastating thing that can happen to them. That is why so many of them will engage in activities against their better judgment rather than risk being ostracized by the group. Some of them would prefer to fry their brains on drugs, knowing the dangers, rather than risk the disapproval of the "friends" who would introduce them to such destructive influences. Joseph was at the age when he, too, needed to be accepted, but it is important to notice that this was not to be his lot because he had a prior commitment to things which militated against his acceptance.

The measure of the rejection by his peers became clear when he journeyed, at his father's request, to meet his brothers in Dothan. *"Now when they saw him afar off, even before he came near them, they conspired against him to kill him"* (v. 18). Their early hatred and envy had now become obsessive and the cold, calculated plan to commit premeditated murder was put into operation.

This desperate action was probably related to another set of factors outside Joseph's control but which also served to put him under pressure. His father had made no secret of the fact that he *"loved Joseph more than all his children, because he was the son of his old age. Also he made him a tunic of many colors"* (v. 3). There is some doubt about the correct translation of the Hebrew at this point and that accounts for the discrepancies in some versions concerning what exactly Joseph was required to wear by his father. The RSV has "robe with sleeves" but the information that David's daughter Princess Tamar wore the same garment "for the king's virgin daughters wore such apparel" (2 Sam. 13:18) shows that whatever its shape and style it was magnificent and was intended to show that the wearer was privileged and should be appropriately acknowledged.

It would be reasonable to expect that Jacob would have learned from his own family background that favoritism is not only out of place in a family but it is also fatal to family harmony and well-being. But he had not learned and so Joseph was required to walk around wearing a magnificent *"tunic"* which spoke of favoritism and engendered hostility. When parents insist on spoiling their children they make it very difficult for those same children to grow up mature and complete. Joseph had to deal with negative peer pressure as well as unhelpful parental pressure.

In addition he was no stranger to the sharp pressure of pain and bereavement. His mother died shortly after old Deborah passed away and just before his grandfather Isaac "breathed his last." But all these events paled in significance when compared to the unbelievably stressful experiences at Dothan. Due to the intervention of Reuben, who had a plan to save his young brother, Joseph's life was spared, and the plans of the brothers were altered. But nevertheless *"they stripped Joseph of his tunic, the tunic of many colors that was on him. Then they took him and cast him into a pit. And the pit was empty; there was no water in it"* (Gen. 37:23, 24). Incredibly at that point *"they sat down to eat a meal"* (v. 25).

To the pain of rejection and hatred was added now the anguish of desertion and unrelieved cruelty. But there was more to come. At that moment traders from Midian appeared on the scene and Judah suggested that rather than kill him they should trade him. *"So the brothers pulled Joseph up and lifted him out of the pit, and sold him to the Ishmaelites for twenty shekels of silver. And they took Joseph to Egypt"* (v. 28). Reuben who had not been party to these plans returned to find the pit empty, was told of the change of plans, and evidently went along with a particularly cruel scheme to convey to Jacob that his favorite son had been killed. *"They took Joseph's tunic, killed a kid of the goats, and dipped the tunic in the blood. . . . they brought it to their father and said, 'We have found this. Do you know whether it is your son's tunic or not?'"* (vv. 31, 32). The old man, as expected, recognized the tunic, assumed the worst, and *"mourned for his son many days. . . . and he said, 'For I shall go down into the grave to my son in mourning'"* (vv. 34, 35). Meanwhile Joseph was on his way to Egypt where he was subsequently traded to *"Potiphar, an officer of Pharaoh and captain of the guard"* (v. 36).

THE INTRICACIES OF DIVINE PLANS

It would be impossible to fully understand either the making of Joseph or the significance of his story without recognizing the profound factor of the Lord's involvement in the proceedings. The Lord had promised the land of Canaan to Abraham but He had added, "Know certainly that your descendants will be strangers in a land that is not theirs, and will serve them, and they will afflict them four hundred years" (Gen. 15:13). Then having told Abraham that he would die before all this transpired He encouraged the patriarch by saying, "But in the fourth generation they shall return here, for the iniquity of the Amorites is not yet complete" (Gen. 15:16). Abraham at that stage was not strong enough to take over the land and the Amorites were not bad enough to have it taken from them. But by the time the fourth generation came along both problems would be solved. In the meantime the people of promise had to live somewhere and the Lord in His wisdom chose Egypt. But He also planned a great deliverance for them which necessitated getting them into Egypt before He could get them out! To get them in He chose Joseph.

He sent a man before them—
Joseph—who was sold as a slave.
They hurt his feet with fetters,
He was laid in irons.
Until the time that his word came to pass,
The word of the Lord tested him.

Ps. 105:17-19

Stephen, the first Christian martyr, when he addressed those who would shortly usher him without ceremony into eternity said, "the patriarchs, becoming envious, sold Joseph into Egypt. But God was with him and delivered him out of his troubles, and gave him favor and wisdom in the presence of Pharaoh, king of Egypt" (Acts 7:9, 10). Stephen's forthrightness on that occasion was no more appreciated than was Joseph's truthfulness when he spoke out to his brothers. Stephen was killed; Joseph was spared. The only reason for both events being that the sovereign Lord knew what He was doing and intended to do it right on time.

The story of Joseph serves to show how the mysterious workings of the Lord are threaded through all the machinations and schemes of mankind and He will ultimately triumph and His purposes will eventually prevail. Joseph understood this, even as a teenager, and accordingly he had the necessary fortitude to endure to the end.

CHAPTER THIRTY-EIGHT

The Chain of Events

Genesis 38:1–30

38:1 It came to pass at that time that Judah departed from his brothers, and visited a certain Adullamite whose name *was* Hirah.

2 And Judah saw there a daughter of a certain Canaanite whose name *was* Shua, and he married her and went in to her.

3 So she conceived and bore a son, and he called his name Er.

4 She conceived again and bore a son, and she called his name Onan.

5 And she conceived yet again and bore a son, and called his name Shelah. He was at Chezib when she bore him.

6 Then Judah took a wife for Er his firstborn, and her name *was* Tamar.

7 But Er, Judah's firstborn, was wicked in the sight of the LORD, and the LORD killed him.

8 And Judah said to Onan, "Go in to your brother's wife and marry her, and raise up an heir to your brother."

9 But Onan knew that the heir would not be his; and it came to pass, when he went in to his brother's wife, that he emitted on the ground, lest he should give an heir to his brother.

10 And the thing which he did displeased the LORD; therefore He killed him also.

11 Then Judah said to Tamar his daughter-in-law, "Remain a widow in your father's house till my son Shelah is grown." For he said, "Lest he also die like

his brothers." And Tamar went and dwelt in her father's house.

12 Now in the process of time the daughter of Shua, Judah's wife, died; and Judah was comforted, and went up to his sheepshearers at Timnah, he and his friend Hirah the Adullamite.

13 And it was told Tamar, saying, "Look, your father-in-law is going up to Timnah to shear his sheep."

14 So she took off her widow's garments, covered *herself* with a veil and wrapped herself, and sat in an open place which *was* on the way to Timnah; for she saw that Shelah was grown, and she was not given to him as a wife.

15 When Judah saw her, he thought she *was* a harlot, because she had covered her face.

16 Then he turned to her by the way, and said, "Please let me come in to you"; for he did not know that she *was* his daughter-in-law. So she said, "What will you give me, that you may come in to me?"

17 And he said, "I will send a young goat from the flock." So she said, "Will you give *me* a pledge till you send *it?*"

18 Then he said, "What pledge shall I give you?" So she said, "Your signet and cord, and your staff that *is* in your hand." Then he gave *them* to her, and went in to her, and she conceived by him.

19 So she arose and went away, and laid aside her veil and put on the garments of her widowhood.

20 And Judah sent the young goat by the hand of his friend the Adullamite, to receive *his* pledge from the woman's hand, but he did not find her.

21 Then he asked the men of that place, saying, "Where is the harlot who *was* openly by the roadside?" And they said, "There was no harlot in this *place.*"

22 So he returned to Judah and said, "I cannot find her. Also, the men of the place said there was no harlot in this *place.*"

23 Then Judah said, "Let her take *them* for herself, lest we be shamed; for I sent this young goat and you have not found her."

24 And it came to pass, about three months after,

that Judah was told, saying, "Tamar your daughter-in-law has played the harlot; furthermore she *is* with child by harlotry." So Judah said, "Bring her out and let her be burned!"

25 When she *was* brought out, she sent to her father-in-law, saying, "By the man to whom these belong, I *am* with child." And she said, "Please determine whose these *are*—the signet and cord, and staff."

26 So Judah acknowledged *them* and said, "She has been more righteous than I, because I did not give her to Shelah my son." And he never knew her again.

27 Now it came to pass, at the time for giving birth, that behold, twins *were* in her womb.

28 And so it was, when she was giving birth, that *the one* put out *his* hand; and the midwife took a scarlet *thread* and bound it on his hand, saying, "This one came out first."

29 Then it happened, as he drew back his hand, that his brother came out unexpectedly; and she said, "How did you break through? *This* breach *be* upon you!" Therefore his name was called Perez.

30 Afterward his brother came out who had the scarlet *thread* on his hand. And his name was called Zerah.

Gen. 38:1–30

Having introduced us to Joseph and led us into the story of his desperate plight Genesis promptly interrupts the story to recount a sad tale relating to his brother, Judah. At first sight this interruption might appear unfortunate and arbitrary, but reflection shows that it is carefully placed in the record both to show Joseph's life in stark contrast to what was normative and also to show the ways in which the Lord was continuing to work toward His stated purpose.

LINKS IN THE CHAIN

When the Lord promised Eve at the time of the Fall that her seed would bruise the serpent's head He promptly set in motion a series of events which would continue until the final victory of Messiah in the eternal future. Abraham became a major link in the chain of the Lord's activity. As we have seen the next link was Isaac, not Ishmael, followed by Jacob, not Esau. It would be natural to assume that either Reuben, the firstborn son of Jacob, or Joseph, his outstanding son, would be the next link in the chain of divine succession. But that was not to be the case. Judah was the Lord's choice and like some of His other choices it was surprising to say the least!

Compared to the care which Isaac exercised in choosing a bride for Jacob, Judah's approach to marriage was totally irresponsible. *"Judah departed from his brothers, and visited a certain Adullamite whose name was Hirah. And Judah saw there a daughter of a certain Canaanite whose name was Shua, and he married her"* (Gen. 38:1, 2). The Lord had placed a definite prohibition on marriage to a Canaanite, but Judah, assuming he was aware of the ruling, paid no attention to it and did what he wanted to do. The marriage produced three sons one of whom, whose name was Er, married a woman called Tamar. We are not given details of Er's lifestyle but it was *"wicked in the sight of the Lord, and the Lord killed him"* (v. 7). The bluntness of the statement and the lack of detail serve only to point up the dramatic nature of God's intervention in the affairs of man when He decides that it is necessary!

Judah reminded his son Onan, *"Go in to your brother's wife and marry her, and raise up an heir to your brother"* (v. 8). But Onan was not at all enthusiastic about raising a son who would not be his although he was not at all reluctant to engage in sexual activity with his brother's widow. So he became the world's first recorded exponent of "coitus interruptus." Because his name was also lent to the practice of "onanism" this passage has often been interpreted as making a statement about masturbation. It should be noted, however, that Onan's sin for which he too received the ultimate penalty was not onanism or deviant sexual behavior, but simple refusal on his part to perpetuate the line of his brother. His reasons for this were that he *"knew that the heir would not be his"* (v. 9), so he decided to have no part in the procedure although he repeatedly had relations with the widow.

Tamar had every reason to expect that she would be given a husband to replace the one she had lost and the one she never really had, but apparently Judah who had lost two sons who had been related to her was not prepared to risk losing his sole remaining son, Shelah. Remember the line through which the Serpent bruiser would come was at this point precarious and vulnerable. Sensing that Judah was not going to help her, despite his promise that she could marry Shelah eventually, Tamar took matters into her own hands. Judah who had recently lost his wife, who incidentally is never named, finished his period of mourning and went with his friend to a local village to join in the festival related to sheep shearing. Tamar knew he was coming, so, *"she took off her widow's garments, covered herself with a veil and wrapped herself, and sat in an open place which was on the way to Timnah . . . . When Judah saw her, he thought she was a harlot . . . . Then he turned to her by the way, and said, 'Please let me come in to you'; for he did not know that she was his daughter-in-law"* (vv. 14–16). She agreed on promise of payment which he pledged by leaving his seal and his staff, they engaged in intercourse from which she became pregnant, and when Judah was informed he said, *"Bring her out and let her be burned!"* (v. 24).

The ancient double standard has never been better illustrated. The culture felt it was perfectly alright for Judah to have sex with a harlot but totally improper for his daughter-in-law to become pregnant through harlotry. When Tamar was brought out for her execution she asked only that the owner of the seal and the staff should be identified. *"So Judah acknowledged them and said, 'She has been more righteous than I, because I did not give her to Shelah my son'"* (v. 26).

Eventually twin boys were born to Tamar, but not without a touch of drama. One child's hand appeared, a scarlet thread was fastened around the wrist to identify him as the firstborn, but then the other brother preempted him and was born first! Zerah wore the thread but Perez took precedence. The startling truth which attaches to this strange story is that the Lord not only chose Judah but also appointed Perez to be the one through whom the line of descent would be preserved until Messiah should come in the fullness of time (see Matt. 1:3).

LESSONS FROM THE LINKS

The first lesson is that man cannot escape responsibility for his actions. Er and Onan discovered this in the most dramatic fashion as did their father, Judah, in less dramatic terms. They died; he was simply shamed. Man is free to make his choices but he is not free to determine the consequences of his choices. The second lesson is one that reverberates throughout Genesis, namely that the Lord is sovereign. Nothing will thwart His purposes which invariably offer man the opportunity to cooperate in the outworking of His eternal plan. Should man decide not to cooperate, then he alone is the loser for the Lord marches on relentlessly to His ultimate goal.

The third lesson has to do with the remarkable grace of God and the humility of Christ. We are all familiar with the choice that Messiah should be born in a stable rather than a palace but His genealogy portrays even more graphically the humility of Christ. Only five women are mentioned in Matthew's genealogy of Christ. They are Tamar, Rahab, Ruth, Bathsheba (identified only as "her who had been the wife of Uriah" [Matt. 1:6]), and Mary. Tamar posed as a harlot, Rahab was a harlot, Ruth was a Moabitess, Bathsheba was an adulteress, and Mary was regarded as immoral by her contemporaries because they did not believe her story. Perhaps Matthew carefully included these women in order to counter Jewish criticism of his story by showing that God had moved in unusual ways to achieve His ends and had shown that He was not averse to using those who were outside the pale of respectability. Whatever he may have had in mind we cannot escape the fact that the Lord graciously reached out to all manner of people and offered them the chance to be part of what He was doing. He still performs in the same wonderful ways.

CHAPTER THIRTY-NINE

Success

Genesis 39:1–23

39:1 Now Joseph had been taken down to Egypt. And Potiphar, an officer of Pharaoh, captain of the guard, an Egyptian, bought him from the Ishmaelites who had taken him down there.

2 The LORD was with Joseph, and he was a successful man; and he was in the house of his master the Egyptian.

3 And his master saw that the LORD *was* with him and that the LORD made all he did to prosper in his hand.

4 So Joseph found favor in his sight, and served him. Then he made him overseer of his house, and all *that* he had he put under his authority.

5 So it was, from the time *that* he had made him overseer of his house and all that he had, that the LORD blessed the Egyptian's house for Joseph's sake; and the blessing of the LORD was on all that he had in the house and in the field.

6 Thus he left all that he had in Joseph's hand, and he did not know what he had except for the bread which he ate. Now Joseph was handsome in form and appearance.

7 And it came to pass after these things that his master's wife cast longing eyes on Joseph, and she said, "Lie with me."

8 But he refused and said to his master's wife, "Look, my master does not know what *is* with me in the house, and he has committed all that he has to my hand.

9 *"There is* no one greater in this house than I, nor

has he kept back anything from me but you, because you *are* his wife. How then can I do this great wickedness, and sin against God?"

10 So it was, as she spoke to Joseph day by day, that he did not heed her, to lie with her *or* to be with her.

11 But it happened about this time, when Joseph went into the house to do his work, and none of the men of the house *was* inside,

12 that she caught him by his garment, saying, "Lie with me." But he left his garment in her hand, and fled and ran outside.

13 And so it was, when she saw that he had left his garment in her hand and fled outside,

14 that she called to the men of her house and spoke to them, saying, "See, he has brought in to us a Hebrew to mock us. He came in to me to lie with me, and I cried out with a loud voice.

15 "And it happened, when he heard that I lifted my voice and cried out, that he left his garment with me, and fled and went outside."

16 So she kept his garment with her until his master came home.

17 Then she spoke to him with words like these, saying, "The Hebrew servant whom you brought to us came in to me to mock me;

18 "so it happened, as I lifted my voice and cried out, that he left his garment with me and fled outside."

19 So it was, when his master heard the words which his wife spoke to him, saying, "Your servant did to me after this manner," that his anger was aroused.

20 Then Joseph's master took him and put him into the prison, a place where the king's prisoners *were* confined. And he was there in the prison.

21 But the LORD was with Joseph and showed him mercy, and He gave him favor in the sight of the keeper of the prison.

22 And the keeper of the prison committed to Joseph's hand all the prisoners who *were* in the prison; whatever they did there, it was his doing.

23 The keeper of the prison did not look into anything *that was* under *Joseph's* authority, because the

> LORD was with him; and whatever he did, the LORD
> made *it* prosper.
>
> *Gen. 39:1–23*

The story of Joseph must rate as one of the most compelling and attractive narratives in Scripture if not in all literature. Callously betrayed, deserted, and sold like a piece of merchandise by his own brothers, he arrived in Egypt at the age of seventeen without friends and with no visible means of support. *"Potiphar, an officer of Pharaoh, captain of the guard, an Egyptian, bought him from the Ishmaelites who had taken him down there"* (Gen. 39:1). Lesser men would have sunk into despair and defeat in such circumstances but not Joseph! *"The Lord was with Joseph, and he was a successful man . . . . And his master saw that the Lord was with him and that the Lord made all he did to prosper in his hand"* (vv. 2, 3). The expression which catches the eye is, *"he was a successful man."* Few things are of greater interest to modern people than success which can be recognized and verified. "Success," however, can mean "a favorable outcome or result"—an achievement—or more often it can mean "the gaining of wealth, fame, and rank." The Hebrew word used to describe Joseph's experience conveys the former idea. The emphasis is not on his rank, fame, or wealth (although he was not short in any of these departments) but rather on the favorable outcome and achievement of all that he was intended to do.

NOTHING SUCCEEDS LIKE SUCCESS

At a very early age Joseph had been given a sense of what he was to achieve, and when he shared it with his family, he got into trouble. But he did not forget his dreams about the sheaves and the heavenly bodies which had indicated that he would arrive at a position of prominence which even his own wretched brothers would one day acknowledge. This underlying sense of objective, coupled with a consciousness of his close relationship to the Lord, must have been significant factors in the development of his ability to press on regardless of circumstances. The emphasis on *"the Lord"* cannot be overlooked in this account of Joseph's success. *"The Lord was with Joseph,"* *"his master saw that the Lord was with him,"* *"the Lord made all*

318

he did to prosper (be successful) in his hand," "the blessing of the Lord was on all that he had in the house and in the field" (vv. 2–5).

Success requires not only an objective but also suitable criteria of evaluation. One man's success is another man's failure. Jesus hanging on a cross is to most men a loser, but at the moment of His death He cried triumphantly, "Finished." In His own eyes and in the eyes of His Father He was a winner. He had achieved! Joseph's achievements were measurable in material terms. Potiphar was not slow to note that as soon as he put the young man in charge everything in his house and business took off. He was so impressed with Joseph's abilities that he handed over to him the complete running of his household. But it is important to note that the Egyptian interpreted this material achievement in spiritual terms. He was ready to acknowledge that the secret of Joseph's achievement was his relationship to the Lord. It would be a mistake to assume that God's blessing can always be measured in material terms. The Lord Jesus was wonderfully successful but had little to show for it materially; the apostle Paul rates highly in everybody's voting for "Most Valuable Apostle" but he died in a prison with little material comfort besides a cloak and some good reading material.

The key must have been in Joseph's exemplary lifestyle which he related to his spiritual convictions, and the clear articulation of his sense of God-given destiny. In much the same way that John the Baptist was determined not to take credit for his own success, but to point always and only to His Lord, so Joseph managed to convey, even to an Egyptian, that his hope and trust were in the Lord and it was He Who gave him success. Joseph had come a long way from the empty cistern and the future looked bright for the young man who *"was handsome in form and appearance"* (v. 6). Everything was coming up roses for Joseph, but . . .

NOTHING SEDUCES LIKE SUCCESS

The handsome, young man was highly visible and therefore was highly vulnerable. The wife of Potiphar could not fail to be aware of him. She *"cast longing eyes on Joseph, and she said, 'Lie with me'"* (v. 7). Physical attractiveness can provoke lust and desire. It is not necessary for the attractive person to do anything to promote or provoke the desire. In fact that person is often totally unaware of what is going on. This was no doubt the case with Joseph. Other people are drawn to those who have achieved positions of prominence and power. To them physical beauty is not as compelling as the feel and sense of authority and the heady visions it conjures up in the minds of the susceptible and the careless. Joseph was also eminently successful and some people cannot resist getting as close to the successful as possible. Joseph was wide open on all these points. He was a sitting duck.

Men who, like Joseph, have conquered their worlds and tasted conquest find that they have created an appetite for more excitement. The thrill of the chase and the exhilaration of one more victory become the stuff of life for them. This is easily translated into sexual liaisons. If Joseph had succumbed to this seduction he would have simply joined the ranks of thousands of other men in similar circumstances. Moreover, the remarkable freedom which his master had given him could have bred in a lesser man an insatiable appetite for indulgence. Joseph could also have rationalized that if he did not accede to the proposal he might well jeopardize his standing in the household. He may not have been old enough to have learned that "Hell hath no fury like a woman spurned" but he might have suspected it!

His response to the seductive invitation was simple and to the point. *"He refused and said to his master's wife, '. . . How then can I do this great wickedness, and sin against God?'"* (vv. 8–9). It should be noted that this was no isolated event because *"she spoke to Joseph day by day"* (v. 10). The factors which enabled Joseph to take such a stand need to be noted. He was clearly convinced that sexual activity with another man's wife was not only *"great wickedness"* but also a *"sin against God."* At the base of his action was his commitment to solid principle. The person who lacks similar principles is much more likely to succumb to temptation. Second, he clearly stated his position. There was no doubt in Potiphar's wife's mind as to where he stood on the issue, but evidently she thought she could erode his defenses. She failed and there is no doubt that his clear stand made her task much more difficult. Third, he flatly rejected the proposition. His reply allowed no room for debate or discussion. That would have been too dangerous. When passions are high discussions are better postponed. He wisely headed for the exit. Fourth, he did all that he could to avoid being in a compromising position. He not only refused to *"lie with her"* but also *"to be with her"* (v. 10). His duties made it impossible for him to totally isolate himself from her and on one occasion he was trapped by her, with no one else around. She tried to hold him by his clothes and when he tried to get away *"he left his garment in her hand, and fled and ran outside"* (v. 12). When he could not avoid being with her he abandoned all thought of dignity and got out of there as quickly as he could. That is the fifth principle—in situations like that discretion is the better part of valor. Paul told Timothy to *"Flee also youthful lusts"* (2 Tim. 2:22) and his advice is well taken, and not just for youths!

But Joseph's troubles were far from over. The scorned woman screamed for "help," lied to the servants about what had happened, and when her husband returned she said, *"The Hebrew servant whom you brought to us came in to mock me; so it happened, as I lifted my voice and cried out, that he left his garment with me and fled outside"* (Gen. 39:17). It is possible to learn something of the woman's attitude, not only from her illegitimate desire and her lying but also her insulting use of *"Hebrew"* and her disparaging way of talking about her husband to the servants. It is unfortunate that a young man of Joseph's caliber should have been at the mercy of such an unscrupulous and unprincipled person. But it has always been so and it will continue to be so, because God has not excused His people from living in a sinful world. But neither has He deserted them in their struggles, as Joseph soon discovered.

NOTHING SUSTAINS LIKE SUCCESS

Joseph was promptly imprisoned, *"but the Lord was with Joseph and showed him mercy, and He gave him favor in the sight of the keeper of the prison"* (v. 21). His relatively brief but full experience of the Lord had taught him that while he could not expect to be exempted from life's harshness and injustice he could expect the Lord to be merciful and gracious to him in the invidious situation. He could look back on his meteoric rise from minor shepherd to major-domo and recognize the hand of the Lord. True he had been put back in a bad scene through no fault of his own, and true he could have questioned whether or not there was a God of justice but he chose rather to put his roots down deeper in the things to which he was committed. As a result it was not long before he made his mark in the prison although it would be many years before he would understand the remarkable ways in which the Lord had been leading him. Sustained by what he knew had been done, he was strengthened to go on to discover what new wonders God would work in him and through him. This is the secret of true success.

CHAPTER FORTY

Discouragement

Genesis 40:1–23

40:1 It came to pass after these things *that* the butler and the baker of the king of Egypt offended their lord, the king of Egypt.

2 And Pharaoh was angry with his two officers, the chief butler and the chief baker.

3 So he put them in custody in the house of the captain of the guard, in the prison, the place where Joseph *was* confined.

4 And the captain of the guard charged Joseph with them, and he served them; so they were in custody for a while.

5 Then the butler and the baker of the king of Egypt, who *were* confined in the prison, had a dream, both of them, each man's dream in one night *and* each man's dream with its *own* interpretation.

6 And Joseph came in to them in the morning and looked at them, and saw that they *were* sad.

7 So he asked Pharaoh's officers who *were* with him in the custody of his lord's house, saying, "Why do you look *so* sad today?"

8 And they said to him, "We each have had a dream, and *there is* no interpreter of it." So Joseph said to them, "Do not interpretations belong to God? Tell *them* to me, please."

9 Then the chief butler told his dream to Joseph, and said to him, "Behold, in my dream a vine *was* before me,

10 "and in the vine *were* three branches; it *was* as though it budded, its blossoms shot forth, and its clusters brought forth ripe grapes.

11 "Then Pharaoh's cup *was* in my hand; and I took the grapes and pressed them into Pharaoh's cup, and placed the cup in Pharaoh's hand."

12 And Joseph said to him, "This *is* the interpretation of it: The three branches *are* three days.

13 "Now within three days Pharaoh will lift up your head and restore you to your place, and you will put Pharaoh's cup in his hand according to the former manner, when you were his butler.

14 "But remember me when it is well with you, and please show kindness to me; make mention of me to Pharaoh, and get me out of this house.

15 "For indeed I was stolen away from the land of the Hebrews; and also I have done nothing here that they should put me into the dungeon."

16 When the chief baker saw that the interpretation was good, he said to Joseph, "I also *was* in my dream, and there were three white baskets on my head.

17 "In the uppermost basket *were* all kinds of baked goods for Pharaoh, and the birds ate them out of the basket on my head."

18 So Joseph answered and said, "This *is* the interpretation of it: The three baskets *are* three days.

19 "Within three days Pharaoh will lift off your head from you and hang you on a tree; and the birds will eat your flesh from you."

20 Now it came to pass on the third day, *which was* Pharaoh's birthday, that he made a feast for all his servants; and he lifted up the head of the chief butler and of the chief baker among his servants.

21 Then he restored the chief butler to his butlership again, and he placed the cup in Pharaoh's hand.

22 But he hanged the chief baker, as Joseph had interpreted to them.

23 Yet the chief butler did not remember Joseph, but forgot him.

Gen. 40:1–23

By the time he had reached his early twenties Joseph had experienced enough discouragements to last most people a lifetime. But he displayed a remarkable maturity and resilience which bears study and application for all of us who are subjected to people who erode our courage and events which diminish our resources.

SOME REASONS FOR DISCOURAGEMENT

Having approached his imprisonment with a positive attitude and been duly rewarded with trusted prisoner status, Joseph was bound for another setback. Two of Pharaoh's important aides, his butler and his baker, had displeased their master and were incarcerated for their trouble. *"The captain of the guard charged Joseph with them, and he served them"* (Gen. 40:4). This reversal of fortunes which precipitated him abruptly from overseer of the prison to the servant of prisoners was apparently ordered by the captain of the guard— Potiphar. Perhaps he was still consumed with anger against Joseph for his alleged unfaithfulness and betrayal, although the fact that he did not insist on the death penalty may suggest that he had some reasonable doubt about the accuracy of the charges. This kind of thing had been happening to Joseph all his life. His normal procedure seemed to be to take one step forward and two steps back. The added irony was that the setbacks were rarely the result of his actions but rather the interventions of other people in his life. Unfair treatment had become his constant lot. He had been abused by his brothers, falsely accused by his master's wife, unjustly condemned and punished by his master, and now humiliated even in the environment of a prison. He could have written the book on injustice. Apparently the *"dungeon"* (v. 15) in which he was confined was adjacent to Potiphar's house and that in itself would be a constant reminder of how far he had fallen. The psalmist records that "They hurt his feet with fetters, he was laid in irons" (Ps. 105:18). Some scholars question whether he was actually imprisoned, but the text appears to state clearly that he was not only treated unfairly but he was also placed in an environment which was most unpleasant. I know a number of people whose lives appear to be governed by such matters as climate and whose moods are determined by whether the sun is shining. Fortunately Joseph was not susceptible to such frailties or his life would have been intolerable.

One day he noted that his charges were sad and so he asked them,

"Why do you look so sad today?" (Gen 40:7). Apparently it had not occurred to him that some people find being in prison an adequate reason for sadness! The problem was that both men had been dreaming and such was the nature of their dreams and the state of their minds that they were perturbed about what they had dreamed. They were particularly concerned that they could not interpret what they had seen in their visions, but Joseph was equal to the opportunity. He said, *"Do not interpretations belong to God? Tell them to me, please"* (v. 8). The chief butler explained what he had seen and Joseph had no trouble with the interpretation. With God's help he was able to communicate the interpretation which, as he rightly said, belonged to God. The news was good for the butler was released from prison within three days exactly as the dream had indicated and Joseph had said. Joseph did, however, ask the chief butler, *"But remember me when it is well with you, and please show kindness to me; make mention of me to Pharaoh, and get me out of this house"* (v. 14). The request was perfectly reasonable as he added, *"I have done nothing here that they should put me into the dungeon"* (v. 15). But *"the chief butler did not remember Joseph, but forgot him"* (v. 23). Yet another cause for discouragement and disappointment.

Incidentally, when the chief baker saw that his friend received good news he decided to share his own dream. But Joseph had only bad news for him. He did not hide anything from his fellow-prisoner but predicted accurately that according to the dream the baker would be a dead man in three days.

SOME REACTIONS TO DISCOURAGEMENT

The most natural response to discouragement is to complain. There is no evidence that Joseph indulged himself in this regard apart from a possible tinge of self-pity when he spoke to the chief butler. Another response that is all too common is to decide that God is unjust, that being good does not pay, and that honesty is not the best policy and therefore the only thing to do is to join the ranks of those whom you can't beat. None of these reactions hold solutions to the very real problem of discouragement.

Joseph was unshaken in his conviction that the Lord was sovereign. His statement that God interprets dreams suggested that he was convinced that only He knew the future. When he identified the dreams and fearlessly told the truth about them he was showing that he was confident that God was in control. He was so convinced of this that he was prepared to stick his neck out and give a person as significant as the chief baker the unpalatable news of his imminent departure from this life. Down through the centuries God's people have suffered but they have stood firm at this same point—the Lord is sovereign and His plans will ultimately triumph. This conviction has consistently helped the oppressed to rise above their sorrows and dismay when it seemed that they were about to be engulfed in the flood of circumstances.

SOME RESOURCES FOR DISCOURAGEMENT

It is obvious that Joseph also handled his own discouragements by immersing himself in the affairs of others who were also unfortunate. His care for the prisoners around him and his particular concern for the well-being of the butler and the baker are evidence enough of his commitment to help in the alleviation of suffering rather than to concentrate on the nature of his own pain.

In our modern world we have many resources to assist in combatting discouragement which can easily be taken for granted. Paul talked about the "comfort of the Scriptures" (Rom. 15:4). Those who have learned to turn to their pages and to glean from them the promises of God and the reminders of His faithfulness need no reminders of the solace and support they have found therein. But many people turn from the Word of God at the very time they should be turning to it.

The fellowship of believers is also profoundly helpful at times of disappointment. That is why the writer of the Epistle to the Hebrews reminds us, "Let us consider one another in order to stir up love and good works, not forsaking the assembling of ourselves together, as is the manner of some, but exhorting one another, and so much the more as you see the Day approaching" (Heb. 10:24, 25).

But above all for the believer there is the gracious invitation of the Lord Jesus to all "who labor and are heavy laden" (Matt. 11:28) and the promise that in coming to Him they will find rest for their souls.

The amazing thing about Joseph was that he was able to combat his circumstances without many of the aids which would normally be associated with the handling of discouragement. Like many an imprisoned soul since his day he found that communion with the Lord Himself can meet the deepest needs of the human heart, including the ability to combat discouragement.

CHAPTER FORTY-ONE

Living in Two Worlds

Genesis 41:1-57

41:1 Then it came to pass, at the end of two full years, that Pharaoh had a dream; and behold, he stood by the river.

2 Suddenly there came up out of the river seven cows, fine looking and fat; and they fed in the meadow.

3 Then behold, seven other cows came up after them out of the river, ugly and gaunt, and stood by the *other* cows on the bank of the river.

4 And the ugly and gaunt cows ate up the seven fine looking and fat cows. So Pharaoh awoke.

5 He slept and dreamed a second time; and suddenly seven heads of grain came up on one stalk, plump and good.

6 Then behold, seven thin heads, blighted by the east wind, sprang up after them.

7 And the seven thin heads devoured the seven plump and full heads. So Pharaoh awoke, and indeed, *it was* a dream.

8 Now it came to pass in the morning that his spirit was troubled, and he sent and called for all the magicians of Egypt and all its wise men. And Pharaoh told them his dreams, but *there was* no one who could interpret them for Pharaoh.

9 Then the chief butler spoke to Pharaoh, saying: "I remember my faults this day.

10 "When Pharaoh was angry with his servants, and put me in custody in the house of the captain of the guard, *both* me and the chief baker,

11 "we each had a dream in one night, he and I. Each of us dreamed according to the interpretation of his *own* dream.

12 "Now there *was* a young Hebrew man with us there, a servant of the captain of the guard. And we told him, and he interpreted our dreams for us; to each man he interpreted according to his *own* dream.

13 "And it came to pass, just as he interpreted for us, so it happened. He restored me to my office, and he hanged him."

14 Then Pharaoh sent and called Joseph, and they brought him quickly out of the dungeon; and he shaved, changed his clothing, and came to Pharaoh.

15 And Pharaoh said to Joseph, "I have had a dream, and *there is* no one who can interpret it. But I have heard it said of you *that* you can understand a dream, to interpret it."

16 So Joseph answered Pharaoh, saying, "*It is* not in me; God will give Pharaoh an answer of peace."

17 Then Pharaoh said to Joseph: "Behold, in my dream I stood on the bank of the river.

18 "Suddenly seven cows came up out of the river, fine looking and fat; and they fed in the meadow.

19 "Then behold, seven other cows came up after them, poor and very ugly and gaunt, such ugliness as I have never seen in all the land of Egypt.

20 "And the gaunt and ugly cows ate up the first seven, the fat cows.

21 "When they had eaten them up, no one would have known that they had eaten them, for they *were* just as ugly as at the beginning. So I awoke.

22 "Also I saw in my dream, and suddenly seven heads came up on one stalk, full and good.

23 "Then behold, seven heads, withered, thin, *and* blighted by the east wind, sprang up after them.

24 "And the thin heads devoured the seven good heads. So I told *this* to the magicians, but *there was* no one who could explain *it* to me."

25 Then Joseph said to Pharaoh, "The dreams of Pharaoh *are* one; God has shown Pharaoh what He *is* about to do:

26 "The seven good cows *are* seven years, and the seven good heads *are* seven years; the dreams *are* one.

27 "And the seven thin and ugly cows which came up after them *are* seven years, and the seven empty heads blighted by the east wind are seven years of famine.

28 "This *is* the thing which I have spoken to Pharaoh. God has shown Pharaoh what He *is* about to do.

29 "Indeed seven years of great plenty will come throughout all the land of Egypt;

30 "but after them seven years of famine will arise, and all the plenty will be forgotten in the land of Egypt; and the famine will deplete the land.

31 "So the plenty will not be known in the land because of the famine following, for it *will be* very severe.

32 "And the dream was repeated to Pharaoh twice because the thing *is* established by God, and God will shortly bring it to pass.

33 "Now therefore, let Pharaoh select a discerning and wise man, and set him over the land of Egypt.

34 "Let Pharaoh do *this,* and let him appoint officers over the land, to collect one-fifth *of the produce* of the land of Egypt in the seven plentiful years.

35 "And let them gather all the food of those good years that are coming, and store up grain under the authority of Pharaoh, and let them keep food in the cities.

36 "Then that food shall be as a reserve for the land for the seven years of famine which shall be in the land of Egypt, that the land may not perish during the famine."

37 So the advice was good in the eyes of Pharaoh and in the eyes of all his servants.

38 And Pharaoh said to his servants, "Can we find *such a one* as this, a man in whom *is* the Spirit of God?"

39 Then Pharaoh said to Joseph, "Inasmuch as God has shown you all this, *there is* no one as discerning and wise as you.

40 "You shall be over my house, and all my people shall be ruled according to your word; only in regard to the throne will I be greater than you."

41 And Pharaoh said to Joseph, "See, I have set you over all the land of Egypt."

331

42 Then Pharaoh took his signet ring off his hand and put it on Joseph's hand; and he clothed him in garments of fine linen and put a gold chain around his neck.

43 And he had him ride in the second chariot which he had; and they cried out before him, "Bow the knee!" So he set him over all the land of Egypt.

44 Pharaoh also said to Joseph, "I *am* Pharaoh, and without your consent no man may lift his hand or foot in all the land of Egypt."

45 And Pharaoh called Joseph's name Zaphnath-Paaneah. And he gave him as a wife Asenath, the daughter of Poti-Pherah priest of On. So Joseph went out over *all* the land of Egypt.

46 Joseph was thirty years old when he stood before Pharaoh king of Egypt. And Joseph went out from the presence of Pharaoh, and went throughout all the land of Egypt.

47 Now in the seven plentiful years the ground brought forth abundantly.

48 So he gathered up all the food of the seven years which were in the land of Egypt, and laid up the food in the cities; he laid up in every city the food of the fields which surrounded them.

49 Joseph gathered very much grain, as the sand of the sea, until he stopped counting, for *it was* immeasurable.

50 And to Joseph were born two sons before the years of famine came, whom Asenath, the daughter of Poti-Pherah priest of On, bore to him.

51 Joseph called the name of the firstborn Manasseh: "For God has made me forget all my toil and all my father's house."

52 And the name of the second he called Ephraim: "For God has caused me to be fruitful in the land of my affliction."

53 Then the seven years of plenty which were in the land of Egypt ended,

54 and the seven years of famine began to come, as Joseph had said. The famine was in all lands, but in all the land of Egypt there was bread.

55 So when all the land of Egypt was famished,

the people cried to Pharaoh for bread. Then Pharaoh said to all the Egyptians, "Go to Joseph; whatever he says to you, do."

56 The famine was over all the face of the earth, and Joseph opened all the storehouses and sold to the Egyptians. And the famine became severe in the land of Egypt.

57 So all countries came to Joseph in Egypt to buy *grain*, because the famine was severe in all lands.

Gen. 41:1–57

Two years after the butler and the baker were released from prison, Pharaoh began to have disturbing dreams. In one of them he saw seven fat cattle being eaten by seven lean cattle. In the other seven withered heads of grain devoured seven plump heads. As a result of these dreams, *"his spirit was troubled, and he sent and called for all the magicians of Egypt and all its wise men. And Pharaoh told them his dreams, but there was no one who could interpret them for Pharaoh"* (Gen. 41:8). Evidently the dreams and the failure of the magicians to interpret them became a matter of major concern in the court and when the chief butler, Joseph's forgetful former fellow prisoner, became aware of what was going on he remembered Joseph. He said to Pharaoh, *"I remember my faults this day"* (v. 9), and then told of his encounter with the *"young Hebrew man"* (v. 12). He went on to explain his skill in the interpretation of dreams and how his predictions had been totally accurate. Joseph, who was still in prison, was suddenly center stage again. His roller-coaster experience was on the upgrade, but more importantly the remarkable plans of God to get him in a position of prominence in the Egyptian court were at last coming into focus. The early dreams which had encouraged Joseph to believe that he would, one day, hold a position of great importance were starting to make sense.

THE SPIRITUAL WORLD

Joseph was hurriedly summoned into Pharaoh's presence. He shaved (a very non-Hebrew thing to do!), changed his clothing, and came to Pharaoh, who wasted no time telling him about his dreams and the incompetence of his advisors, and saying how he had heard that Joseph was something of an expert in interpretation. Joseph's response was abrupt and pointed. *"It is not in me; God will give Pharaoh an answer of peace"* (v. 16). The English translation does not bring out two important things about his answer. The phrase *"it is not in me"* is one word in Hebrew and suggests a very abrupt, no-frills answer, which coupled with the prominence of *"God"* served to tell Pharaoh in no uncertain terms that his vision needed to be on God and not man.

In the space of one brief sentence consisting of a few words Joseph had set the scene for the next few years of his life and the lives of thousands of people in the Middle East. It is important to note that Joseph's relentless commitment to the Lord had not wavered during the two years in prison. His response to Pharaoh was strikingly similar to the one he gave the butler and the baker when they looked to him to solve their problems (see Gen. 40:8). This is a characteristic of the spiritual world which is hard for those who are not part of it to understand. Paul explained it this way: "the natural man does not receive the things of the Spirit of God, for they are foolishness to him; nor can he know them, because they are spiritually discerned. But he who is spiritual judges all things, yet he himself is rightly judged by no one" (1 Cor. 2:14, 15). By this he did not mean that those who have the Spirit of God are more intelligent than those who do not. But he did mean that the understanding and appreciation of spiritual realities are directly attributable to spiritual life and experience. Joseph was undoubtedly greatly gifted and highly intelligent but it was his spiritual capabilities which were of paramount importance at this moment and Pharaoh and his court could not help but recognize it. It is not often that men and women in high places admit that they are not capable of coping and that they need genuine spirituality to enable them to lead and guide their fellow men in God's world. But when they do reach out it is imperative that there should be a recognizable follower of the Lord at hand.

Joseph listened to Pharaoh's account of the dreams and responded, *"The dreams of Pharaoh are one; God has shown Pharaoh what He is about to do"* (Gen. 41:25). He explained that seven years of plenty were just around the corner, but they would be followed by seven years of such severe famine that the years of plenty would be forgotten and the resources of Egypt would be depleted. It is significant that he punctuated his interpretation with expressions like, *"the thing is established by God, and God will shortly bring it to pass"* (v. 32). Times of great plenty were nothing new to the land of Egypt but times of extended famine were most unusual because the ecology of the land was related to the Nile which was most consistent in its supply. It is a tribute to the credibility of Joseph that he was believed. He possessed the ring of truth!

Having interpreted the dream he had fulfilled his commission. But he did not stop there. He quickly outlined for Pharaoh what needed to be done. *"Now therefore, let Pharaoh select a discerning and wise man, and set him over the land of Egypt"* (v. 33). With remarkable speed and skill he outlined a plan whereby officers would be appointed all over the land, who would be responsible to collect one-fifth of the produce of the bumper crops and store it under Pharaoh's authority as a reserve for the famine years. His dramatic plan was promptly accepted and applauded, which in itself was remarkable. How do you persuade farmers who are having a good year to hand over 20 percent of their crops to the government to meet a famine seven years down the road which they probably do not believe will come? No wonder Pharaoh realized immediately that he needed a special man to undertake a task of such immensity and importance. He did not hesitate. He knew the man he needed and he said, *"Can we find such a one as this, a man in whom is the Spirit of God?"* (v. 38). Pharaoh's amazing statement came out of his polytheistic cultural background but this should not detract from the impact of what he was saying. He clearly recognized that Joseph had a special relationship with the Lord and that in some powerful way the Lord by His Spirit was at work in Joseph's life. This is made clear by what Pharaoh went on to say, *"Inasmuch as God has shown you all this, there is no one as discerning and wise as you"* (v. 39).

The spiritual world which is inhabited by people like Joseph exists in the midst of a secular society. It is extremely difficult for the secularists to understand it and it is not always easy for those who are spiritual to explain it. But one thing is sure. When those who profess to belong to the Lord begin to demonstrate in their lives and testimonies the resources for living which come only from the Spirit of

God, even the most secularized people will note the uniqueness of their lives and given the right set of circumstances will make inquiries about it and in times of stress and strain may even seek the aid of the spiritual person. This means that those who are spiritual should be continually alert to the necessity of maintaining a consistent lifestyle and also a readiness to give a forthright statement of their convictions and a clear articulation of their faith.

THE SECULAR WORLD

The word "secular" has numerous connotations, many of which are not good. But care should be taken to note that the secular world is the world in which even the most spiritual person is called to live. Moreover, the secular world has legitimate concerns about government, education, food distribution, public health, and the protection of citizens, and therefore should be the concern of the spiritual person. But having said that, the secular world, because of its "this world" orientation, is often notorious for its disinterest in, or even antagonism toward, spiritual realities. All too often the secular world sees man rather than God as the center of all things. The secularist frequently acts as if time is the extent of man's experience and that matter is the sole measure of value. Spiritual people must take issue at each point because for them man is not the measure of all things, eternity is a reality which governs the whole of their lives on earth, and they are thoroughly aware that if matter is all there is, then life is clearly deficient.

The secular world has its problems. One of these is the discovery of truth. This can be illustrated from Joseph's experience. With all their considerable emphasis on dreams and their interpretation all the magicians of Egypt could not understand Pharaoh's dreams which were remarkably simple. Joseph had no problem at all in understanding what was happening. Secular persons find many problems desperately confusing because they do not factor in the necessary spiritual dimensions. For instance, the laudable concern about teenage pregnancies which many agencies are expressing is well directed and justified. The spiritual person knows this is at heart a moral problem and while he recognizes that there are no easy answers in a pluralistic society he has no problem recognizing that if biblical standards of sexual morality were to be applied the problem would be solved.

Another immense problem for secular people is knowing what is the right thing to do. This is not to suggest either that spiritual people always know or that they always do what they know. But when Pharaoh was confronted with the specter of the lean cattle eating the fat cattle he was confronting a problem that still faces the leaders of our world. Fat cats (they are abbreviated fat cattle) have been chewing on their lean brothers ever since the days of Pharaoh and before, but recent centuries have introduced movements in society where the lean cats have started to make it clear that they want their piece of the fat cats. These revolutionary movements, fed by radical philosophies, have produced all manner of problems for our societies for which no ready answers have been discovered. Spiritual people who have become alerted to God's views of humanity have discovered answers which, while they cannot be universally applied because of different philosophies, at least point in directions which need to be followed. Joseph knew that the fat years needed to come to the assistance of the lean years and that if they failed to do so they themselves would be consumed. This principle applied to famine in Joseph's day and still applies to many areas of human experience in our day.

Another problem confronting the secular world is the problem of leadership. Like Pharaoh many people are asking, Where can we find "such a man" who can lead with integrity and courage? The answers are not easy to come by in the democratic West because so many factors influence the direction societies take. But there can be little doubt that those who have an ear open to what God is saying and doing need to be in a position to speak loud and clear to the secularist who is asking questions that defy answers and is looking for leadership but is not sure where he wants to go.

THE SPIRITUAL PERSON IN THE SECULAR WORLD

There are at least three possible responses that the spiritual person can make to the challenge of the secular world. The first is intimidation. Some people find the challenge to take a stand against what secular society is doing more than they can handle. They look for a convenient hole and crawl inside hoping that whatever is troubling them will go away. Others find that the attractions of secular life-styles are more compelling than the sacrifices often required of those who confront their society. They find the thought of being different from their peers more than they can face. Perhaps one of the most common feelings is one of inadequacy. The needs and the challenges are so great and the people facing them seem so few and so feeble that the spiritual person can be paralyzed by an overwhelming sense of insignificance and impotence. Fortunately for the people of the Middle East Joseph was not intimidated.

The apostle Paul knew something of the disappointment of seeing those whom he had worked with succumb to the intimidation of the society in which they were endeavoring to minister. In one of the saddest statements of Scripture he wrote to Timothy, "Be diligent to come to me quickly; for Demas has forsaken me, having loved this present world, and has departed for Thessalonica" (2 Tim. 4: 9, 10). I, too, have been saddened to see young people who once were deeply committed to Christ and His cause buckle under the stresses and strains of standing tall for Him on the university campus or failing to be courageous enough in a "dog eat dog" business environment.

The second response is isolation. There is always a temptation for spiritually minded persons to be so spiritually minded that they are no earthly use. Some of them like to keep it that way because they have developed an intense dislike for what they see going on around them and they feel that their major obligation is to protect themselves and those near and dear to them from the dangers of association. Instead of being moved with compassion toward a needy, ugly world they are repelled by it and take flight from it. There was much about the lean cattle that was ugly and mean but Joseph saw them as something to be tackled rather than something to be avoided. However, it must be added that not all those who seek to handle the struggle of being "in the world but not of it" by isolation are doing so out of less than deep and sincere convictions. For instance, there are many parents who feel deeply about the type of education their children are receiving in the public school system and are convinced that the only way that their young people will be adequately trained is if they are placed in a school where the curriculum is what they term "Bible based." The debate on sex education with particular reference to the necessity for instruction on the AIDS virus is an issue which will cause desperate heartache for many parents who cannot imagine their young people being instructed in anal and oral sex, homosexuality, and related subjects in their tender years. Yet at the same time the Surgeon General, Dr. Everett Koop, a convinced evangelical Christian, has been unequivocal about the necessity for this type of education to take place. If it does there will no doubt be a further withdrawal on the part of many.

The third response is the one that Joseph embraced—infiltration. He knew a clear sense of calling to be involved in the aching society of which he was a part and he saw this call as something that emanated from the throne of heaven. To have been less than involved would have meant to be less than obedient. Joseph's sense of calling was coupled with a consuming desire to serve, and even though it led to a position of prominence and power he clearly did not have such things in mind when he stood coolly and calmly before Pharaoh and told him the unpalatable truth of the impending national disaster. Once he had been appointed he wasted no time in taking his stand at the center of the action—a masterpiece of strategic placement in the economy of God and a masterly demonstration of what can be done by one spiritually minded man who takes his opportunities and does not flinch from being God's man in a godless world.

William Wilberforce, the frail and gifted British parliamentarian, is a classic example of a man who like Joseph worked his way into the corridors of power, not for his own advancement, but in order that he might do something about the moral and spiritual condition of his beloved country. On the top of his list was the abolition of slavery and as a result he found himself on the top of the hit list of many influential people who for philosophical and economic reasons were out to stop him. Many tough years elapsed before his work bore fruit, but there is no denying he knew what it was to infiltrate his society for the sake of Christ and through Him the sake of all mankind.

The struggle to find the right balance in what H. Richard Niebuhr in his book, *Christ and Culture,* called "the double wrestle of the church with its Lord and with the cultural society with which it lives in symbiosis"[1] never ends, but Joseph and many like him have much to offer in terms of advice and example.

NOTE

1. H. Richard Niebuhr, *Christ and Culture* (New York: Harper & Row, Pubs., 1951), p. xi.

CHAPTER FORTY-TWO

Leadership

Genesis 42:1-38

42:1 When Jacob saw that there was grain in Egypt, Jacob said to his sons, "Why do you look at one another?"

2 And he said, "Indeed I have heard that there is grain in Egypt; go down to that place and buy for us there, that we may live and not die."

3 So Joseph's ten brothers went down to buy grain in Egypt.

4 But Jacob did not send Joseph's brother Benjamin with his brothers, for he said, "Lest some calamity befall him."

5 And the sons of Israel went to buy *grain* among those who journeyed, for the famine was in the land of Canaan.

6 Now Joseph *was* governor over the land; and it was he who sold to all the people of the land. And Joseph's brothers came and bowed down before him with *their* faces to the earth.

7 Joseph saw his brothers and recognized them, but he acted as a stranger to them and spoke roughly to them. Then he said to them, "Where do you come from?" And they said, "From the land of Canaan to buy food."

8 So Joseph recognized his brothers, but they did not recognize him.

9 Then Joseph remembered the dreams which he had dreamed about them, and said to them, "You *are* spies! You have come to see the nakedness of the land!"

10 And they said to him, "No, my lord, but your servants have come to buy food.

11 "We *are* all one man's sons; we *are* honest *men*; your servants are not spies."

12 But he said to them, "No, but you have come to see the nakedness of the land."

13 And they said, "Your servants *are* twelve brothers, the sons of one man in the land of Canaan; and in fact, the youngest *is* with our father today, and one *is* no more."

14 But Joseph said to them, "It *is* as I spoke to you, saying, 'You *are* spies!'

15 "In this *manner* you shall be tested: By the life of Pharaoh, you shall not leave this place unless your youngest brother comes here.

16 "Send one of you, and let him bring your brother; and you shall be kept in prison, that your words may be tested to see whether *there is* any truth in you; or else, by the life of Pharaoh, surely you *are* spies!"

17 So he put them all together in prison three days.

18 Then Joseph said to them the third day, "Do this and live, *for* I fear God:

19 "If you *are* honest *men*, let one of your brothers be confined to your prison house; but you, go and carry grain for the famine of your houses.

20 "And bring your youngest brother to me; so your words will be verified, and you shall not die." And they did so.

21 Then they said to one another, "We *are* truly guilty concerning our brother, for we saw the anguish of his soul when he pleaded with us, and we would not hear; therefore this distress has come upon us."

22 And Reuben answered them, saying, "Did I not speak to you, saying, 'Do not sin against the boy'; and you would not listen? Therefore behold, his blood is now required of us."

23 But they did not know that Joseph understood *them*, for he spoke to them through an interpreter.

24 And he turned himself away from them and wept. Then he returned to them again, and talked with them. And he took Simeon from them and bound him before their eyes.

25 Then Joseph gave a command to fill their sacks with grain, to restore every man's money to his sack, and to give them provisions for the journey. Thus he did for them.

26 So they loaded their donkeys with the grain and departed from there.

27 But as one *of them* opened his sack to give his donkey feed at the encampment, he saw his money; and there it was, in the mouth of his sack.

28 So he said to his brothers, "My money has been restored, and there it is, in my sack!" Then their hearts failed *them* and they were afraid, saying to one another, "What *is* this *that* God has done to us?"

29 Then they went to Jacob their father in the land of Canaan and told him all that had happened to them, saying:

30 "The man *who is* lord of the land spoke roughly to us, and took us for spies of the country.

31 "But we said to him, 'We *are* honest *men;* we are not spies.

32 'We *are* twelve brothers, sons of our father; one *is* no *more,* and the youngest *is* with our father this day in the land of Canaan.'

33 "Then the man, the lord of the country, said to us, 'By this I will know that you *are* honest *men:* Leave one of your brothers *here* with me, take *food for* the famine of your households, and be gone.

34 'And bring your youngest brother to me; so I shall know that you *are* not spies, but *that* you *are* honest *men.* I will grant your brother to you, and you may trade in the land.'"

35 Then it happened as they emptied their sacks, that surprisingly each man's bundle of money *was* in his sack; and when they and their father saw the bundles of money, they were afraid.

36 And Jacob their father said to them, "You have bereaved me: Joseph is no *more,* Simeon is no *more,* and you want to take Benjamin. All these things are against me."

37 Then Reuben spoke to his father, saying, "Kill my two sons if I do not bring him *back* to you; put him in my hands, and I will bring him back to you."

38 But he said, "My son shall not go down with
you, for his brother is dead, and he is left alone. If
any calamity should befall him along the way in
which you go, then you would bring down my gray
hair with sorrow to the grave."

Gen. 42:1-38

Thirteen years had elapsed since Joseph had left home. He had
known heartbreak and betrayal, success and disappointment. But
nothing compared to his meteoric rise from the dungeon to the position of *"governor over the land"* (Gen. 42:6). The weight of responsibility resting on his thirty-year-old shoulders was immense. How he
handled the situation and what he accomplished are significant because they give insights into his leadership gifts and style. These
insights can prove beneficial because many people suspect that both
the secular world and the church world are deficient in solid leadership. Leadership involves:

THE ACCEPTANCE OF RESPONSIBILITY

The moment God chose to reveal the future to Joseph he became a
partner in the divine plan. This was a privilege but Joseph may have
found it difficult to concentrate on the privilege because he was so
conscious of the responsibility. He said, *"I fear God"* (v. 18), and that
involved a profound sense of being responsible to God for what he
did with the information he had been given and the opportunity
he had been presented. There are some people who have parlayed
privileged business or political information into quick profits for
themselves. Some notorious world leaders have used their privileged
position to denude the resources of their nations while transferring
those same resources into Swiss bank accounts and plush estates
on Long Island and the Caribbean. Joseph demonstrated a mature
sense of responsibility which throws such activities into the dark
relief in which they belong. His dramatic interpretation of the vision
had given him some idea of the appalling physical need which the
famine would produce but he had no idea of the far-reaching consequences of his response to the call to service.

While he was busy putting his nationwide disaster intervention

344

plan into action, his brothers and father were beginning to feel the pinch of famine in their bellies. But more than that they were sinking into the immobilizing depression that hunger brings. The old man, Jacob, seems to have been less affected than his sons because he said to them, *"Why do you look at one another? And he said, 'Indeed I have heard that there is grain in Egypt; go down to that place and buy for us there, that we may live and not die'"* (vv. 1, 2). Apparently none of Joseph's brothers had the resources to provide the leadership necessary for survival. Jacob provided some, but it was Joseph who would be the answer to the need they could not even address. It is noteworthy that in addition to his sense of responsibility to the Lord Joseph also recognized his responsibility to Pharaoh despite the fact that he had great latitude and authority. He had proved himself faithful as a shepherd boy in telling his father the truth. He had shown responsible patterns of behavior far beyond his years in the house of Potiphar, and even in prison when he had been given the chance he had shown that he could be trusted. His apprenticeship was complete and Pharaoh counted him faithful and dependable and he was more than ready to accept any responsibility that came his way.

THE REPUTATION FOR DEPENDABILITY

There is a difference between reputation and character. The former is what people think you are; the latter is what you are. The two may be poles apart. There are those whose reputation is superb whose private lives do not bear looking into, while there are those whose character is unimpeachable but whose reputations have been besmirched by gossip and innuendo. Leaders have to be careful about both character and reputation. With his reputation for dependability well documented Joseph stands in marked contrast to his brothers. When they eventually agreed to travel to Egypt in search of grain their father was adamant about them taking his youngest son Benjamin with them. He said, *"Lest some calamity befall him"* (v. 4). Later, when they returned from Egypt and encouraged him to send Benjamin with them he said, *"You have bereaved me: Joseph is no more, Simeon is no more, and you want to take Benjamin. All these things are against me"* (v. 36). Even when Reuben

345

offered to put his own sons on the line should he fail to return Benjamin, Jacob replied, *"My son shall not go down with you, for his brother is dead, and he is left alone"* (v. 38). The constant referral to the loss of Joseph and Jacob's obvious linkage of this traumatic event with the remaining brothers suggests very strongly that he suspected his sons and he had no intention of allowing them to be in a position of control over his beloved Benjamin. Their reputation was as low as a snake's belly.

From bitter, personal experience Joseph knew that leaders can fall from grace as quickly as they were propelled into their positions of authority and privilege. Having established his reputation, Joseph had to ensure that it was maintained. He had outlined a plan that he said would work and now he was required to show that it would indeed work. He had made predictions; now he had to show that they would be fulfilled. He had stated what he would do, and now he had to deliver. Dependable leaders say what they will do and find ways to do what they say.

The Development of Ability

Are leaders born, or are they made? There may be certain qualities with which potential leaders are born but there can be no doubt that much hard work is necessary to develop the gifts and abilities of leadership. Joseph had developed the ability to communicate. He had identified a problem, analyzed the situation, and come up with a potential solution. His creative juices were flowing but he had to be able to share the vision in such a way that other people would be prepared to buy into it. That he did this in a remarkable manner is evidenced by Pharaoh's prompt response to, and his total support for the plan that Joseph enunciated.

He also exhibited the ability to delegate. We know that he "went throughout all the land of Egypt" (Gen. 41:46) and that his purpose was to appoint officers over the various regions of the country whose responsibility it would be first of all to administer the tax on produce and then later to assist in the distribution of the food reserves. Real leaders must be able to enthuse others about their overall plans in such a way that they will gladly contribute their efforts to the plans' completion.

Leaders also should be able to participate. Gilbert·and Sullivan used their Comic Operas to lampoon First Lords of the Admiralty who had "never been to sea" but who were now "the rulers of the Queen's Navy." There is a legitimate style of leadership that is removed from the action but the most compelling leaders are those who, like Joseph, are involved in the things they expect others to do. It is interesting that when the people called out to Pharaoh for help he told them, "Go to Joseph; whatever he says to you, do" (Gen. 41:55). Later when his brothers arrived in Egypt they had to go to him because he *was governor over the land; and it was he who sold to all the people of the land"* (Gen. 42:6).

Perhaps one of the most elusive requirements of leadership is the ability to motivate. One man's motivation is another man's irritation. The things that enthuse one person, confuse another and defuse the rest. Leaders need to know their people and what will keep them fresh and flourishing.

Joseph's way of handling Pharaoh was obviously different from his procedure for handling his brothers! As soon as he recognized them he realized that they had not recognized him. Then he remembered the dreams of his youth when he had learned that one day his brothers and his father would bow down to him. So he promptly embarked on a plan that would bring his whole family down into Egypt. To do that he had to put some pressure on his brothers who had shown little enthusiasm about anything in recent years. In addition he soon recognized that getting his father to leave the land of promise in his old age would be a formidable task. But he managed to do all these things by using his motivational skills. To move his brothers from apathy to action he used one of the most effective motivational factors known to man. He frightened them out of their wits! He accused them of spying out the land of Egypt. They denied it vehemently. He said they could not leave Egypt unless they brought their youngest brother down and proved that they were telling the truth. To reinforce the point he gave them a three-day sentence in prison, instructed them to go home and return with Benjamin, and ordered Simeon bound and retained until they returned. Under this kind of pressure the brothers began to face up to some things they had long tried to ignore. *"They said to one another, 'We are truly guilty concerning our brother, for we saw the anguish of his soul when he pleaded with us, and we would not hear; therefore this distress has come upon us"* (v. 21). Whatever they had done about their guilt for the last thirteen years they were now beginning to take it out, look at it, and admit what they had done. Unknown to them, of course, Joseph was listening and understanding everything that they said. This was too much for him, *"And he turned himself away from them and wept"* (v. 24). Leaders are allowed to be human. They cry too.

On the way home one of the men opened his grain sack and to his horror discovered his money lying there. He told his brothers and *"their hearts failed them and they were afraid, saying one to another, 'What is this that God has done to us?'"* (v. 28). Joseph had managed, literally, to put the fear of God into his calloused brothers!

THE EXERCISE OF AUTHORITY

Ultimate authority belongs exclusively to God. But He has chosen to delegate this authority to human beings at certain times, for certain tasks under certain conditions. When people recognize that all the authority they possess has been delegated to them and is therefore derived and not intrinsic, they are less likely to abuse their authority. When they assume that their authority is in some way attributable to their intrinsic worth or skill or superiority the possibilities of abuse are frightening.

Joseph's brothers had been thoroughly unnerved by his treatment of them. They told Jacob on their return, *"The man who is lord of the land spoke roughly to us, and took us for spies of the country"* (v. 30). He had certainly moved them but whether or not his methods constituted a breach of his authority we do not have to decide although we can ponder the issue for our own warning and edification. Authority is abused when it is used to intimidate, vindicate, and manipulate. If there was any thought in Joseph's mind of letting his brothers stew in their own juice for a little time because of the way they had made him stew, then he was possibly abusing his authority. If he was unnecessarily heaping pain and terror upon them when they were not in a position to defend themselves then his methods were open to question. And if there was any sense in which he was playing a cat and mouse game with them then his actions were less than honorable. Such is our high regard for this man and what he accomplished under God that these questions may seem out of place. On the other hand, even the greatest leaders with one exception have had their Achilles' heels and we do well to learn from them and guard our own exercise of whatever authority God has loaned to us for the outworking of His purposes.

CHAPTER FORTY-THREE

It's a Changing World

Genesis 43:1–34

43:1 Now the famine *was* severe in the land.

2 And it came to pass, when they had eaten up the grain which they had brought from Egypt, that their father said to them, "Go back, buy us a little food."

3 But Judah spoke to him, saying, "The man solemnly warned us, saying, 'You shall not see my face unless your brother *is* with you.'"

4 "If you send our brother with us, we will go down and buy you food.

5 "But if you will not send *him*, we will not go down; for the man said to us, 'You shall not see my face unless your brother *is* with you.'"

6 And Israel said, "Why did you deal *so* wrongfully with me *as* to tell the man whether you had still *another* brother?"

7 But they said, "The man asked us pointedly about ourselves and our family, saying, '*Is* your father still alive? Have you *another* brother?' And we told him according to these words. Could we possibly have known that he would say, 'Bring your brother down'?"

8 Then Judah said to Israel his father, "Send the lad with me, and we will arise and go, that we may live and not die, both we and you *and* also our little ones.

9 "I myself will be surety for him; from my hand you shall require him. If I do not bring him *back* to you and set him before you, then let me bear the blame forever.

10 "For if we had not lingered, surely by now we would have returned this second time."

11 And their father Israel said to them, "If *it must be* so, then do this: Take some of the best fruits of the land in your vessels and carry down a present for the man—a little balm and a little honey, spices and myrrh, pistachio nuts and almonds.

12 "Take double money in your hand, and take back in your hand the money that was returned in the mouth of your sacks; perhaps it was an oversight.

13 "Take your brother also, and arise, go back to the man.

14 "And may God Almighty give you mercy before the man, that he may release your other brother and Benjamin. If I am bereaved, I am bereaved!"

15 So the men took that present and Benjamin, and they took double money in their hand, and arose and went down to Egypt; and they stood before Joseph.

16 When Joseph saw Benjamin with them, he said to the steward of his house, "Take *these* men to my home, and slaughter an animal and make ready; for *these* men will dine with me at noon."

17 Then the man did as Joseph ordered, and the man brought the men into Joseph's house.

18 Now the men were afraid because they were brought into Joseph's house; and they said, "*It is* because of the money, which was returned in our sacks the first time, that we are brought in, so that he may make a case against us and seize us, to take us as slaves with our donkeys."

19 When they drew near to the steward of Joseph's house, they talked with him at the door of the house,

20 and said, "O sir, we indeed came down the first time to buy food;

21 "but it happened, when we came to the encampment, that we opened our sacks, and there, *each* man's money *was* in the mouth of his sack, our money in full weight; so we have brought it back in our hand.

22 "And we have brought down other money in our hands to buy food. We do not know who put our money in our sacks."

23 But he said, "Peace *be* with you, do not be afraid. Your God and the God of your father has given you treasure in your sacks; I had your money." Then he brought Simeon out to them.

24 So the man brought the men into Joseph's house and gave *them* water, and they washed their feet; and he gave their donkeys feed.

25 Then they made the present ready for Joseph's coming at noon, for they heard that they would eat bread there.

26 And when Joseph came home, they brought him the present which *was* in their hand into the house, and bowed down before him to the earth.

27 Then he asked them about *their* well-being, and said, "*Is* your father well, the old man of whom you spoke? *Is* he still alive?"

28 And they answered, "Your servant our father *is* in good health; he *is* still alive." And they bowed their heads down and prostrated themselves.

29 Then he lifted his eyes and saw his brother Benjamin, his mother's son, and said, "*Is* this your younger brother of whom you spoke to me?" And he said, "God be gracious to you, my son."

30 Now his heart yearned for his brother; so Joseph made haste and sought *somewhere* to weep. And he went into *his* chamber and wept there.

31 Then he washed his face and came out; and he restrained himself, and said, "Serve the bread."

32 So they set him a place by himself, and them by themselves, and the Egyptians who ate with him by themselves; because the Egyptians could not eat food with the Hebrews, for that *is* an abomination to the Egyptians.

33 And they sat before him, the firstborn according to his birthright and the youngest according to his youth; and the men looked in astonishment at one another.

34 Then he took servings to them from before him, but Benjamin's serving was five times as much as any of theirs. So they drank and were merry with him.

Gen. 43:1–34

I know some people who love class reunions! And I know some people who detest them. The former, I suspect, feel that they stack up reasonably well against their peers, while the latter may have the feeling that they are not doing so well in comparison to their class mates. Both types of people are conscious that changes are taking place, some which they like and others which are less than acceptable to them. Because we live in a changing world in which, as Burns said, "Nae man can tether time or tide" we have to learn to handle the changes which life introduces. Jacob, Judah, and Joseph provide good examples for us.

CHANGE WILL BE INEVITABLE

Jacob, who had made a career out of making things happen, was being forced to face the fact that his life situation was changing dramatically. Approximately two years had passed since his sons, minus Simeon, had returned from Egypt with their grain and the money in their sacks. They had been eager to return for more food and to release their captive brother but Jacob would not hear of it. The condition that Benjamin should accompany them was unthinkable to him. But things were happening which even the arch manipulator, Jacob, could not handle. *"Now the famine was severe in the land. And it came to pass, when they had eaten up the grain which they had brought from Egypt, that their father said to them, 'Go back, buy us a little food'"* (vv. 1, 2). He was still not prepared to accept the fact that he could not dictate terms to Pharaoh. In his mind he thought he could have his cake and eat it, or more accurately his corn and keep his son, Benjamin. But his authority had long since left him and he had not adjusted to this new reality.

His son Judah confronted him with the necessity to send Benjamin down to Egypt and he offered to stand surety for the boy in much the same way as Reuben. In typical fashion Jacob responded to this reasoned approach with a self-serving complaint about his own misfortunes saying, *"Why did you deal so wrongfully with me as to tell the man whether you had still another brother?"* (v. 6). He might have been able to get away with this kind of approach for years but times had changed. He heard his son reply, *"Send the lad with me, and we will arise and go, that we may live and not die, both we and you and also our little ones"* (v. 8). While Jacob whined and wheedled, his sons were confronting matters of life and death. While he thought only of his own misfortunes Judah confronted him with the plight of his family including the *"little ones"* and Jacob was forced to listen. Eventually he conceded, and bowed to his son's insistence.

Times were changing for the old man because not only had his authority diminished but his abilities to handle the family and to think clearly were obviously on the wane. It was hard for Jacob to accept the inevitability of change which comes from the passing of time and the changing of circumstances. Times and circumstances had changed but it was the same old Jacob who could not resist giving instructions as to how to handle the difficult negotiations which they faced. His methods had not changed either for he told them to *"carry down a present for the man—a little balm and a little honey, spices and myrrh, pistachio nuts and almonds"* (v. 11). And for good measure he insisted that they should take *"double money"*!

The changes which had taken place in Joseph's life were the opposite of those which his father was experiencing. Joseph's fortunes were waxing as Jacob's were waning. Although the changes he encountered were more pleasant than those of Jacob and therefore easier to handle, they were nevertheless fraught with difficulty and danger. Any young man who was given the opportunity which Joseph was given would be very vulnerable. But handled wisely and maturely, the changes could lead to great opportunities for blessing and help for countless people in need.

Joseph's demeanor showed that he had learned to adapt to the dizzy heights of his new environment. The ease with which he commanded and instructed his servants to fulfill his wishes showed that the ex-shepherd boy had adjusted well to being on top of the heap rather than on the bottom of the totem pole. But nothing showed his ability to change more than his identification with the niceties of Egyptian culture which on some points were far removed from the culture in which he had been born and raised. For instance he adhered to a peculiarly Egyptian seating arrangement for the banquet he gave for his brothers when they returned to Egypt. His servants *"set him a place by himself, and them by themselves, and the Egyptians who ate with him by themselves; because the Egyptians could not eat food with the Hebrews, for that is an abomination to the Egyptians"*

(v. 32). He presumably had to swallow more than his food when he sat down to eat in such a manner!

Old men face the changes that old age brings while the next generation gears up for the new situations which only maturing years afford. Both face the inevitability of change. But for Judah the changes which he faced were not at all related to age; they were related to circumstances. It was Judah who had been squeamish about killing Joseph and who had eased his conscience by the ignoble suggestion that they sell him off to the traders. He had not been all he should have been when he went into the harlot who turned out to be his widowed daughter-in-law but he had admitted the truth when he had been exposed. Judah had matured and circumstances now required him to take the lead. Reuben, the firstborn, had tried and failed, Simeon was otherwise engaged in Egypt, so Judah picked up the slack and took up the matter of dealing with the crisis. He was prepared to face his father with the unpalatable truth, *"if we had not lingered, surely by now we would have returned this second time"* (v. 10). That was telling it like it was! Judah was showing signs of growing up at last!

CHANGE MAY BE UNCOMFORTABLE

"Uncomfortable" may be a less than adequate word to describe the feelings of Jacob as he tried to deal with his rapidly changing world. He was faced with matters he could no longer control, he was realizing that he was no longer in charge, his fears were beginning to rule him, and he was being consumed by dread. When he said, *"If I am bereaved, I am bereaved"* (v. 14), he was speaking like a man on the verge of hopelessness and despair. I have met many people who tread the same path of dread and whose worst fears seem to have been realized and they feel that they can neither cope nor change.

Joseph was most uncomfortable with his changed position because while he held the whip and could do almost anything he wanted, he still had to balance a number of factors in his dealings with his brothers. He had managed to get Benjamin down into Egypt but when he saw him *"his heart yearned for his brother; so [he] made haste and sought somewhere to weep"* (v. 30). His deeply emotional reaction to the reunion with his unsuspecting brothers indicates that at heart

355

he longed for fellowship with them but his circumstances denied him that joy at the present and he had to make do with a relationship which was far less than he desired. In addition his control of the situation did not stretch to the ability to bring his beloved father down to Egypt. This was one thing that he was having great difficulty bringing about.

CHANGE SHOULD BE PROFITABLE

The changes pressed upon Jacob offered a golden opportunity for him to grow in a dimension in which he had often been lacking. Like many a skillful manipulator he had learned to trust his own initiatives and ingenuities. But now he was pressed into a situation where no amount of human effort would suffice. He had reached the end of the line and as he had been forced to do in other similar situations he now had no alternative but to trust. His final instructions to his sons bear this out. He said to them as they set out for Egypt, *"And may God Almighty give you mercy before the man, that he may release your other brother and Benjamin"* (v. 14). The changes Jacob did not like had brought about a change of attitude. From trust in almighty Jacob he had moved to trust in Almighty God, and instead of relying on human manipulation his heart cry was for divine mercy. Any traumatic change which works such wonders in a person's life should be welcomed for its beneficial results.

There was real promise for Judah in his changing circumstances. He now had the chance to do something positive after building a record of less than commendable activities. He had shown signs of nobility when he at least had the grace to acknowledge that the woman he had wronged was more righteous than he was. And when confronted with the horror of a possible murder he had at least averted that, even if he had not gone as far as might have been expected. But now the latent but faint signs of positive factors were given the opportunity to shine through. Change gave him this chance and he took it.

Some people see change as all bad. They distrust everything new and dislike anything that is novel. They experience many miserable moments trying, like King Canute, to hold back the ocean. Others see change as all good. They are fundamentally opposed to all that smacks of tradition and history and approve all things new if for no other reason than they are new. Their lives are often frantic and uncertain because they spend so much time and energy in the search for novelty. A life spent in the pursuit of what is new can get very old in a hurry.

The wisest approach to change is to recognize that a certain amount has to be accepted as inevitable and nothing will change it. Some aspects of change can and should be embraced with delight and enthusiasm and applied positively to life. Some change should be seen as destructive and harmful and resisted with all legitimate means and a clear-sighted view of where trends are leading should be sought at all times. The servant of Joseph who looked after the brothers when they arrived back in Egypt said something which is worth noting.

Two years earlier after their previous visit, when they nervously explained the mystery of the money which had appeared in their sacks he replied, *"Peace be with you, do not be afraid. Your God and the God of your father has given you treasure in your sacks; I had the money"* (v. 23). He was reminding them, perhaps unwittingly, that in the midst of change there is One who changes not. He was indeed their God, but He was also the God of their father. The significance of that remark may not have dawned on them at that emotional moment but for us living in markedly different circumstances the message is clear. The God of one generation is the identical God of succeeding generations and though the generations and their circumstances change, He changes not. That was true in the days of the God of Abraham, Isaac, and Jacob and in our day it is still true because "Jesus Christ is the same yesterday, today, and forever" (Heb. 13:8).

CHAPTER FORTY-FOUR

Putting Things Right

Genesis 44:1–34

44:1 And he commanded the steward of his house, saying, "Fill the men's sacks with food, as much as they can carry, and put each man's money in the mouth of his sack.

2 "Also put my cup, the silver cup, in the mouth of the sack of the youngest, and his grain money." So he did according to the word that Joseph had spoken.

3 As soon as the morning dawned, the men were sent away, they and their donkeys.

4 When they had gone out of the city, *and* were not *yet* far off, Joseph said to his steward, "Get up, follow the men; and when you overtake them, say to them, 'Why have you repaid evil for good?

5 'Is not this *the one* from which my lord drinks, and with which he indeed practices divination? You have done evil in so doing.'"

6 So he overtook them, and he spoke to them these same words.

7 And they said to him, "Why does my lord say these words? Far be it from us that your servants should do such a thing.

8 "Look, we brought back to you from the land of Canaan the money which we found in the mouth of our sacks. How then could we steal silver or gold from your lord's house?

9 "With whomever of your servants it is found, let him die, and we also will be my lord's slaves."

10 And he said, "Now also *let* it *be* according to your words; he with whom it is found shall be my slave, and you shall be blameless."

11 Then each man speedily let down his sack to the ground, and each opened his sack.

12 So he searched. He began with the oldest and left off with the youngest; and the cup was found in Benjamin's sack.

13 Then they tore their clothes, and each man loaded his donkey and returned to the city.

14 So Judah and his brothers came to Joseph's house, and he *was* still there; and they fell before him on the ground.

15 And Joseph said to them, "What deed *is* this you have done? Did you not know that such a man as I can certainly practice divination?"

16 Then Judah said, "What shall we say to my lord? What shall we speak? Or how shall we clear ourselves? God has found out the iniquity of your servants; here we are, my lord's slaves, both we and *he* also with whom the cup was found."

17 But he said, "Far be it from me that I should do so; the man in whose hand the cup was found, he shall be my slave. And as for you, go up in peace to your father."

18 Then Judah came near to him and said: "O my lord, please let your servant speak a word in my lord's hearing, and do not let your anger burn against your servant; for you *are* even like Pharaoh.

19 "My lord asked his servants, saying, 'Have you a father or a brother?'

20 "And we said to my lord, 'We have a father, an old man, and a child of *his* old age, *who is* young; his brother is dead, and he alone is left of his mother's children, and his father loves him.'

21 "Then you said to your servants, 'Bring him down to me, that I may set my eyes on him.'

22 "And we said to my lord, 'The lad cannot leave his father, for *if* he should leave his father, *his father* would die.'

23 "But you said to your servants, 'Unless your youngest brother comes down with you, you shall see my face no more.'

24 "So it was, when we went up to your servant my father, that we told him the words of my lord.

25 "And our father said, 'Go back *and* buy us a little food.'

26 "But we said, 'We cannot go down; if our youngest brother is with us, then we will go down; for we may not see the man's face unless our youngest brother *is* with us.'

27 "Then your servant my father said to us, 'You know that my wife bore me two sons;

28 'and the one went out from me, and I said, "Surely he is torn to pieces"; and I have not seen him since.

29 'But if you take this one also from me, and calamity befalls him, you shall bring down my gray hair with sorrow to the grave.'

30 "Now therefore, when I come to your servant my father, and the lad *is* not with us, since his life is bound up in the lad's life,

31 "it will happen, when he sees that the lad *is* not *with us,* that he will die. So your servants will bring down the gray hair of your servant our father with sorrow to the grave.

32 "For your servant became surety for the lad to my father, saying, 'If I do not bring him *back* to you, then I shall bear the blame before my father forever.'

33 "Now therefore, please let your servant remain instead of the lad as a slave to my lord, and let the lad go up with his brothers.

34 "For how shall I go up to my father if the lad *is* not with me, lest perhaps I see the evil that would come upon my father?"

Gen. 44:1-34

It is hard to imagine the emotional state of the brothers. Back home they had left a famine and a paranoid old father. In Egypt they had encountered the man who had dealt roughly with them on a previous visit. He held their brother in prison and had adamantly refused to sell them more grain without them bringing their youngest brother down to Egypt. They had done so in fear and trembling and when they arrived, not knowing what to expect, they had been treated to a feast in the governor's home. But even though they "drank and were merry" (Gen. 43:34), there were still some things they could not understand. Was it their imagination or did the governor really give Benjamin five times as much food as they were given?

The next morning they had no need to wonder if something was wrong! They loaded up their donkeys and set off for home, but they had only traveled a short distance when they were overtaken by an Egyptian official who said to them, *"Why have you repaid evil for good?"* (Gen. 44:4). Totally confused they denied any impropriety and said that if any of them had stolen property he should be put to death, and the rest of them should be placed in servitude. Search was made and the silver cup which Joseph had ordered planted in Benjamin's sack was discovered. Their interrogators said, *"Is not this the one from which my lord drinks, and with which he indeed practices divination?"* (v. 5).

Whether or not Joseph did practice divination—a practice similar to reading teacups—we do not know. There was a later prohibition against this kind of activity in Israel (see Num. 23:23) but some scholars believe that the expression could mean that Joseph could "divine" that they had stolen his special drinking cup. This translation would help to explain Joseph's remark, *"Did you not know that such a man as I can certainly practice divination?"* (Gen. 44:15), meaning "Did you really think I would be fooled by fellows like you? Did you think I wouldn't know that you had taken the cup?" Whatever the meaning the results were clear: the brothers were devastated. The calculated behavior of Joseph was leading relentlessly to the desired result, the restoration of relationships at the deepest level.

RELATIONSHIPS MUST BE EVALUATED REALISTICALLY

The guilt feelings which had plagued the brothers over the years quickly resurrected. Judah, the spokesman of the group, answered Joseph's query, *"What shall we say to my lord? What shall we speak? Or how shall we clear ourselves? God has found out the iniquity of your servants; here we are, my lord's slaves, both we and he also with whom the cup was found"* (v. 16). In light of the repeated expressions of guilt by the brothers whenever confronted by difficult situations it is appropriate to regard this statement as a reference, not only to the immediate problem, but also to their longstanding feelings of guilt and shame. Approximately twenty-three years had elapsed since they had so dreadfully mistreated their brother but they had never really come to grips with what they had done. They knew they had done evil, they knew that they were accountable, but still they had not taken steps to deal at depth with their sin because they had never been forced to do so. But Joseph was seeing to it that their past was closing in on them.

He also carefully created an opportunity for them to betray Benjamin in much the same way that they had gotten rid of him. Joseph declined to hold them all as slaves. He said, *"Far be it from me that I should do so; the man in whose hand the cup was found, he shall be my slave. And as for you, go up in peace to your father"* (v. 17). All the brothers had to do was agree, abandon Benjamin, grab their sacks, and head for the exit. They knew that they would have a difficult time with Jacob but they had already survived that sort of thing twice, once when they had returned without Joseph and later without Simeon. But consciously or unconsciously they rejected that option. They were beginning to show signs of evaluating their relationships properly thanks to Joseph's firm handling of the situation.

Making people face up to the deficiencies in their relationships and the shortcomings in their lives is never pleasant, but unless it is done by those who love enough to confront, everyone concerned suffers. For instance many families unconsciously aid an alcoholic father to drink himself to death for no other reason than they fail to force him to see correctly. The necessary confrontation by those who love the alcoholic is never easy, rarely without recriminations, and not infrequently most traumatic but always beneficial if rightly handled by all concerned. Joseph was dealing with his brothers in such a manner that there was a real possibility that they would finally deal with their own lives and their former misdemeanors.

RESPONSIBILITY MUST BE ACCEPTED INDIVIDUALLY

Judah stepped forward and made an appeal which was noble and magnanimous. He reminded Joseph of the fears of their father for the safety of Benjamin and tried to explain how the old man would probably die if they returned without him. But then he requested,

"Now therefore, please let your servant remain instead of the lad as a slave to my lord, and let the lad go up with his brothers" (v. 33). In this action Judah showed that he was not interested in evasion. He could easily have been on his way home instead of talking to Joseph. Neither was he concerned about generalization. He chose not to involve everybody in the solution but chose rather to accept the brunt of the burden himself in order that others might benefit. Perhaps he was trying deep down to deal with his own sense of guilt knowing that each one is responsible for his own life and no amount of broad generalization will take the place of personal acceptance of responsibility. It is too easy to evade issues by ducking them or to so generalize that no one admits any responsibility or accepts any accountability. No solutions to relational problems are found that way.

It is worth noting also that Judah's action illustrates the action of the One Who would be known as "the Lion of the tribe of Judah" (Rev. 5:5). Judah's willingness to volunteer for servitude on behalf of his brother, whatever the motivation, was commendable and deeply touching. But our Lord's willingness to be a sacrifice for sin and for a thankless humanity is unspeakably wonderful. The thought of a brother offering freely to subject himself to bondage and deprivation on behalf of another strikes a chord of response in the human heart. Strangely the significantly greater action of the Lord fails to grip the imagination and touch the hearts of many who have heard the message of the one Who, as Paul said, "loved me and gave Himself for me" (Gal. 2:20).

REPENTANCE MUST BE EXPRESSED GENUINELY

When Paul wrote to the Corinthians about repentance he made a clear distinction between "godly sorrow" and "the sorrow of the world" (2 Cor. 7:10). He described their response to him in graphic terms, "What diligence it produced in you, what clearing of yourselves, what indignation, what fear, what vehement desire, what zeal, what vindication! In all things you proved yourselves to be clear in this matter" (2 Cor. 7:11). Judah showed many of these characteristics even before he realized that he was standing before the brother whom he had so despicably treated more than two decades previously. There was evidence that he was genuinely dealing with what he was and what he had done and it only required the full revelation of Joseph's identity to lead to a deeper work of repentance which cleared the way to reconciliation.

Putting Band-Aids on boils is not as traumatic as the proper treatment but neither is it effective! It all depends on whether we want to heal the boil or spare ourselves the trauma of the treatment. Putting things right among those whose relationships have become infected and diseased is not at all dissimilar.

CHAPTER FORTY-FIVE

Joseph's Revelation

Genesis 45:1–28

45:1 Then Joseph could not restrain himself before all those who stood by him, and he cried out, "Make everyone go out from me!" So no one stood with him while Joseph made himself known to his brothers.

2 And he wept aloud, and the Egyptians and the house of Pharaoh heard *it*.

3 Then Joseph said to his brothers, "I *am* Joseph; does my father still live?" But his brothers could not answer him, for they were dismayed in his presence.

4 And Joseph said to his brothers, "Please come near to me." So they came near. Then he said: "I *am* Joseph your brother, whom you sold into Egypt.

5 "But now, do not therefore be grieved or angry with yourselves because you sold me here; for God sent me before you to preserve life.

6 "For these two years the famine *has been* in the land, and *there are* still five years in which *there will be* neither plowing nor harvesting.

7 "And God sent me before you to preserve a posterity for you in the earth, and to save your lives by a great deliverance.

8 "So now *it was* not you *who* sent me here, but God; and He has made me a father to Pharaoh, and lord of all his house, and a ruler throughout all the land of Egypt.

9 "Hurry and go up to my father, and say to him, 'Thus says your son Joseph: "God has made me lord of all Egypt; come down to me, do not tarry.

10 "You shall dwell in the land of Goshen, and you shall be near to me, you and your children,

your children's children, your flocks and your herds, and all that you have.

11 "There I will provide for you, lest you and your household, and all that you have, come to poverty; for *there are* still five years of famine."

12 "And behold, your eyes and the eyes of my brother Benjamin see that *it is* my mouth that speaks to you.

13 "So you shall tell my father of all my glory in Egypt, and of all that you have seen; and you shall hurry and bring my father down here."

14 Then he fell on his brother Benjamin's neck and wept, and Benjamin wept on his neck.

15 Moreover he kissed all his brothers and wept over them, and after that his brothers talked with him.

16 Now the report of it was heard in Pharaoh's house, saying, "Joseph's brothers have come." So it pleased Pharaoh and his servants well.

17 And Pharaoh said to Joseph. "Say to your brothers, 'Do this: Load your animals and depart; go to the land of Canaan.

18 'Bring your father and your households and come to me; I will give you the best of the land of Egypt, and you will eat the fat of the land.

19 'Now you are commanded—do this: Take carts out of the land of Egypt for your little ones and your wives; bring your father and come.

20 'Also do not be concerned about your goods, for the best of all the land of Egypt *is* yours.'"

21 Then the sons of Israel did so; and Joseph gave them carts, according to the command of Pharaoh, and he gave them provisions for the journey.

22 He gave to all of them, to each man, changes of garments; but to Benjamin he gave three hundred *pieces* of silver and five changes of garments.

23 And he sent to his father these *things:* ten donkeys loaded with the good things of Egypt, and ten female donkeys loaded with grain, bread, and food for his father for the journey.

24 So he sent his brothers away, and they departed; and he said to them, "See that you do not become troubled along the way."

25 Then they went up out of Egypt, and came to the land of Canaan to Jacob their father.

26 And they told him, saying, "Joseph *is* still alive, and he *is* governor over all the land of Egypt." And Jacob's heart stood still, because he did not believe them.

27 But when they told him all the words which Joseph had said to them, and when he saw the carts which Joseph had sent to carry him, the spirit of Jacob their father revived.

28 Then Israel said, "*It is* enough. Joseph my son *is* still alive. I will go and see him before I die."

Gen. 45:1-28

It is amazing that Joseph was able to withhold his true identity from his brothers for a period of two years. On more than one occasion he had excused himself from their presence when his emotions threatened to get out of control, but finally he could contain himself no longer. *"He cried out, 'Make everyone go out from me!' So no one stood with him while Joseph made himself known to his brothers"* (Gen. 45:1). The moment had arrived for which he had waited so long and for which he had worked so hard. He needed to reveal himself to his brothers so that they could all live fuller lives. There was much unfinished business which could not be completed until a full disclosure was made.

THE NEED TO RELATE

His brothers were suffering under the delusion that their brother was dead. They had been carrying a load of guilt about his demise for more than two decades and they needed to know the truth of the matter. To say they were surprised at his announcement would be to put it mildly! They *"could not answer him, for they were dismayed in his presence"* (v. 3). No doubt they wondered how this could possibly be true but the fact that this nobleman *"wept aloud, and the Egyptians and the house of Pharaoh heard it"* (v. 2) showed them that this was not an idle tale, or worse, another trap. When the truth finally dawned upon them they were able to understand his unusual behavior and the strange happenings with the sacks, the money, and the divining cup. It was true! The brother they thought they had exterminated had escaped and in some inexplicable manner had risen to the heights in the land of Egypt. Perhaps they remembered their brother's dreams and their indignant rejection of any idea that they would ever bow down to him. But bow down they did! He was not as they thought. He was very much alive and they had assumed him dead.

They themselves were not as they thought either. For years they had assumed that they had escaped all accountability for their behavior but now they stood exposed and their fate lay in the hands of the one they had aggrieved. It was for their own good that they had to face the facts and deal with their sin, but at that moment the revelation of the truth seemed to be the worst possible thing they could have imagined. Little did they realize it was about to lead to the greatest possible blessing they could desire. Ever since the days of Adam man has preferred to cover up his sin rather than confront it, confess it, and be forgiven. In so doing man has robbed himself of the special freedom that forgiveness affords and has damned himself to the bondage of conscience which unpardoned guilt guarantees.

THE NEED TO RECONCILE

Joseph held all the cards and could play them exactly as he wished. His brothers were completely at his mercy and fortunately for them mercy was what he extended. He *said to his brothers, 'Please come near to me.' So they came near. Then he said: '. . . But now, do not therefore be grieved or angry with yourselves because you sold me here; for God sent me before you to preserve life'"* (vv. 4, 5). His attitude was most remarkable in that he refused to impose any blame on them but wanted only to impress upon them that the hand of the Lord had been clearly evident in his life. He wanted them to see that God had sent him to Egypt and that He had done so in order that a great blessing to many people might result. If the brothers had difficulty comprehending these dramatic disclosures it would be understandable. Not only had their long lost brother suddenly reappeared and their long hidden secret been exposed, but Joseph promptly offered forgiveness to them, going to great lengths to encourage them not to grieve or be angry with themselves! This might sound too good to be true but remember that Joseph was coming from a solid conviction that the sovereign Lord had been in control.

The balance of truth which insists on an Almighty One working out His purposes and at the same time teaches that the people through whom He works are free agents has taxed the Lord's people for centuries. Joseph used two phrases which kept both sides of the truth before his brothers and also before us. On the one hand he told them *"you sold me,"* but at the same time he reminded them, *"God sent me."* In no way was their responsibility diminished, but equally in no way had the Lord ever lost control of the situation.

The debate over Calvinism and Arminianism has waxed and waned over the years in the halls of ecclesiastical academia but out in the marketplace of life there are many who have resolved the problem for all practical purposes. They have learned from experience that to ignore the divine sovereignty is arrogance of the first degree but to ignore human accountability is irresponsibility on a grand scale. Theologians will probably never finally figure out the mysteries of the divine will and the part that human decisions play in its outworking. I trust, however, that the Lord will hold a glorious Seminar for us all in Glory when we can ask Him to finally sort these and other thorny subjects. In the meantime perhaps we should join men like Joseph and others whose practical approach to the problem allowed them to continue in deep reverence and dependence while at the same time accomplishing much of significance through hard work and the proper utilization of divine gifts. General William Booth, the founder of the Salvation Army, is a great example. He did not allow himself to be sidetracked in theological debate when he became aware of London's desperate and destitute masses. He put it all together when he insisted, "Work as if everything depended on your work, and pray as if everything depended upon your prayer."

Joseph continued, *"God sent me before you to preserve a posterity for you in the earth, and to save your lives by a great deliverance"* (v. 7). He was referring, of course, to the devastating famine from which they were being delivered but he may have been saying more than he knew, because in the plan of God there would be an even greater deliverance of the children of Israel from Egypt which could not take place without God first sending Joseph to the land of the Pharaohs. The brothers were being invited to explore the wonderful workings of the Lord and moreover to see how an understanding of the Lord can deal with bitterness and put sweetness in its place. He summarized by saying, *"So now it was not you who sent me here, but God"* (v. 8). It is doubtful if guilty men ever heard more pleasant words than those. The victim of their unspeakable wickedness, who held their lives in his hands, was offering them full and free forgiveness. If they had any doubt at all it was dispelled when Joseph *"kissed all his brothers and wept over them, and after that his brothers talked with him"* (v. 15). We are spared the details of their conversation but little imagination is needed to guess that at first they stammered their guilt and then as they grasped the forgiving spirit of their brother, they poured out their gratitude for his mercy and grace.

THE NEED TO RESTORE

A great start had been made in restoring the family of Jacob to its proper condition, but there was still much to be done. Pharaoh was delighted when he heard about Joseph's family and royal instructions were given to the brothers to return home and bring their families down to Egypt. Pharaoh even provided all the necessary transport and assured them, *"do not be concerned about your goods, for the best of all the land of Egypt is yours"* (v. 20).

Knowing his brothers as he did Joseph did not make the mistake of expecting too much from them too quickly. He told them, *"See that you do not become troubled along the way"* (v. 24). He was saying to them, "Don't mess up by getting yourselves into a fight while you're on the way back home. There are more important things to concern you than the sort of things which so easily claim your attention."

Meanwhile Jacob had been waiting in his tent hardly daring to believe that his son Benjamin would return with the food and his older brother Simeon. One day he saw the Egyptian carts and the laden donkeys and Benjamin wearing clothes the like of which he had never seen before. Overjoyed to see his young son he was totally unprepared for what lay ahead. *"They told him, saying, 'Joseph is still alive, and he is governor over all the land of Egypt.' And Jacob's heart stood still, because he did not believe them"* (v. 26). Eventually they were able to convince him and, *"the spirit of Jacob their father revived"* (v. 27). Immediately he promised to go to Egypt as Joseph had arranged and once again the plan of God moved a step nearer completion.

The story of Joseph and his brothers is so moving that it seems almost unreal. But when applied it etches two unforgettable principles on our hearts. First, that God truly is in control and that He will ultimately prevail with or without the cooperation of His erring children. Second, when a man or a woman comes into contact with the immensity of God the result is a heart that pulsates with something of His love to such an extent that extraordinary depths of love and forgiveness flow from that grateful heart.

CHAPTER FORTY-SIX

The God of Surprises

Genesis 46:1–34

46:1 So Israel took his journey with all that he had, and came to Beersheba, and offered sacrifices to the God of his father Isaac.

2 Then God spoke to Israel in the visions of the night, and said, "Jacob, Jacob!" And he said, "Here I am."

3 So he said, "I *am* God, the God of your father; do not fear to go down to Egypt, for I will make of you a great nation there.

4 "I will go down with you to Egypt, and I will also surely bring you up *again*; and Joseph will put his hand on your eyes."

5 Then Jacob arose from Beersheba; and the sons of Israel carried their father Jacob, their little ones, and their wives, in the carts which Pharaoh had sent to carry him.

6 So they took their livestock and their goods, which they had acquired in the land of Canaan, and went to Egypt, Jacob and all his descendants with him.

7 His sons and his sons' sons, his daughters and his sons' daughters, and all his descendants he brought with him to Egypt.

8 Now these *were* the names of the children of Israel, Jacob and his sons, who went to Egypt: Reuben *was* Jacob's firstborn.

9 The sons of Reuben *were* Hanoch, Pallu, Hezron, and Carmi.

10 The sons of Simeon *were* Jemuel, Jamin, Ohad, Jachin, Zohar, and Shaul, the son of a Canaanite woman.

11 The sons of Levi *were* Gershon, Kohath, and Merari.

12 The sons of Judah *were* Er, Onan, Shelah, Perez, and Zerah (but Er and Onan died in the land of Canaan). The sons of Perez were Hezron and Hamul.

13 The sons of Issachar *were* Tola, Puvah, Job, and Shimron.

14 The sons of Zebulun *were* Sered, Elon, and Jahleel.

15 These *were* the sons of Leah, whom she bore to Jacob in Padan Aram, with his daughter Dinah. All the persons, his sons and his daughters, *were* thirty-three.

16 The sons of Gad *were* Ziphion, Haggi, Shuni, Ezbon, Eri, Arodi, and Areli.

17 The sons of Asher *were* Jimnah, Ishuah, Isui, Beriah, and Serah, their sister. And the sons of Beriah *were* Heber and Malchiel.

18 These *were* the sons of Zilpah, whom Laban gave to Leah his daughter; and these she bore to Jacob: sixteen persons.

19 The sons of Rachel, Jacob's wife, *were* Joseph and Benjamin.

20 And to Joseph in the land of Egypt were born Manasseh and Ephraim, whom Asenath, the daughter of Poti-Pherah priest of On, bore to him.

21 The sons of Benjamin *were* Belah, Becher, Ashbel, Gera, Naaman, Ehi, Rosh, Muppim, Huppim, and Ard.

22 These *were* the sons of Rachel, who were born to Jacob: fourteen persons in all.

23 The son of Dan *was* Hushim.

24 The sons of Naphtali *were* Jahzeel, Guni, Jezer, and Shillem.

25 These *were* the sons of Bilhah, whom Laban gave to Rachel his daughter, and she bore these to Jacob: seven persons in all.

26 All the persons who went with Jacob to Egypt, who came from his body, besides Jacob's sons' wives, *were* sixty-six persons in all.

27 And the sons of Joseph who were born to him

in Egypt *were* two persons. All the persons of the house of Jacob who went to Egypt were seventy.

28 Then he sent Judah before him to Joseph, to point out before him *the way* to Goshen. And they came to the land of Goshen.

29 So Joseph made ready his chariot and went up to Goshen to meet his father Israel; and he presented himself to him, and fell on his neck and wept on his neck a good while.

30 And Israel said to Joseph, "Now let me die, since I have seen your face, because you *are* still alive."

31 Then Joseph said to his brothers and to his father's household, "I will go up and tell Pharaoh, and say to him, 'My brothers and those of my father's house, who *were* in the land of Canaan, have come to me.

32 'And the men *are* shepherds, for their occupation has been to feed livestock; and they have brought their flocks, their herds, and all that they have.'

33 "So it shall be, when Pharaoh calls you and says, 'What is your occupation?'

34 "that you shall say, 'Your servants' occupation has been with livestock from our youth even till now, both we *and* also our fathers,' that you may dwell in the land of Goshen; for every shepherd *is* an abomination to the Egyptians."

Gen. 46:1–34

Skeptics insist that God has been manufactured by human ingenuity to meet human inadequacy. He exists only in human imagination to aid man in his struggle to bring meaning and significance to his existence. Scripture flatly contradicts this idea and shows rather that God is the One from Whom all things come and without Whom nothing makes any real sense at all. Therefore fullness of life is found in the discovery of God as He is, rather than in the creation of a God in caricature Who never existed. When human beings accept the fact that they must look to God's revelation of Himself if they desire to find the secrets of their own humanity, they discover that the God Who is, is a God of surprises.

HIS SURPRISING PURPOSES

When Jacob finally came to grips with the stupendous news of Joseph's survival and his position of eminence, he agreed to travel "posthaste" to Egypt. But first he needed to get permission to leave the land of promise so he journeyed *"to Beersheba, and offered sacrifices to the God of his father Isaac"* (v. 1). It is significant that in his haste to see his long lost son he still made time to worship the Lord. But also his return to the place of his father's domain and the offering of sacrifice to the One Who is identified as *"the God of his father"* (v. 1) set the stage for him to hear what he needed to hear. *"God spoke to Israel in the visions of the night, and said, 'Jacob, Jacob!' And he said, 'Here I am.' So He said, 'I am God, the God of your father; do not fear to go down to Egypt, for I will make of you a great nation there'"* (vv. 2, 3).

In the same way that Isaac's life had been rooted in an understanding of the divine purposes promised to his father Abraham, so Jacob's life was based on the conviction that the God of his father was at work in his life bringing about the consummation of His own eternal purpose. But he knew this plan was intimately related to the land of Canaan, and to leave that land could be a step of gravest disobedience and therefore permission was needed even to consider such a move. Jacob's action showed that he was in tune with the purposes of God. The fact that God was going to do a great thing in the land of Canaan but at the same time was moving him out of that land must have given him pause for thought. But Jacob had been around God long enough to learn that He is full of surprises. The Lord continued to assure him, *"I will go down with you to Egypt, and I will also surely bring you up again; and Joseph will put his hand on your eyes"* (v. 4). The promise of His presence in Egypt and the commitment of the Lord to bring him out of Egypt again was most encouraging, but in addition God promised to make him into a great nation *in Egypt!*

This was a new and striking development, and Jacob could not possibly have missed the added information that even though he would die in Egypt (that is the meaning of Joseph putting his hand on Jacob's eyes), at the same time God would bring him out of Egypt. But how could both be true? How could he die in Egypt and return from Egypt? The individual Jacob, or Israel, would finally rest in peace reunited with his family, albeit in a foreign land, but he, in the multitudinous children of his children, the children of Israel, would return to the land of promise. With the assurance that the purposes of God would not be thwarted by his journey into Egypt, Jacob prepared to leave the land of his fathers and the land of his heavenly Father's promises. As he bumped along the wilderness road in his Egyptian cart he had plenty of time to think of the wonderful purposes of God and the surprising ways in which He brings them about.

HIS SURPRISING PRACTICES

Because we live as created beings in the midst of a fabulous creation we often forget to be amazed at the surprising fact that God decided to create in the first place and that if He had not so decided there would be no such things as us, or anything else for that matter! His alone was the creative initiative which when matched by His unique creative capability brought all things into being. This sense of His sovereign creative power is so often lacking in the modern understanding of humanity, but when present in human consciousness it produces a delightful sense of wholeness and fullness in the believing heart. But it can also produce a sense of awesome fear and crushing insignificance in the humbled soul were it not for the matching truth that He is a God Who communicates.

When the Lord spoke in the visions of the night to Jacob in Beersheba, He made it clear that He was aware of, and concerned about, Jacob's dilemma. He was communicating at the most intimate and personal level, calling him both Jacob (a reminder of what he had been) and Israel (an encouraging reminder of what he had become through God's grace). One of the most surprising things about God is that He Who creates on such a vast and complex scale desires to communicate with His children on such a personal and intimate level. Incidentally, some critical scholars have built elaborate interpretative schemes on the use of different names for God and His people in Genesis. They have assumed that the different names were used by different authors, but they have difficulty with verse two where both Jacob and Israel are used. If their theories are to be accepted it would be necessary to assume that this brief verse was therefore the work of two entirely different authors!

The conversation between the Lord and Jacob is touching because it shows surprisingly that the Lord also commiserates with His troubled children. *"Do not fear"* (v. 3) He told Jacob and He has repeated the instructions a million times to His people down through the ages. The reason? *"I will go down with you to Egypt, and I will also surely bring you up again"* (v. 4). He has always been available to bring encouragement to the fearful and confidence to the doubtful.

But He is also the God Who calculates. It would be hard to read the story of Genesis without being gripped by the surprising fact that He chooses to use unreliable people, and the surprising ways in which He uses them. He decided that Joseph was easily the best person for this particular stage of His plan. He also determined that the best place for him was in Egypt, the most suitable position for him was as Vizier of Pharaoh's court, and that the best procedure for getting him there was by using even the reprehensible behavior of the brothers, and the sad occasion of the bitter famine which gripped the land. God has shown through the ages that He will not be blocked in His purposes and He will use whatever is available at any given moment to bring the things of His choosing to pass. We should never become so fearful that things will come unglued that we forget that God will make everything stick together long enough to bring about what He intends. He is truly full of surprises!

HIS SURPRISING PEOPLE

If God's purposes and practices are surprising wait till you meet His people! It is not surprising that He will use a Joseph but people like him are few and far between. People like Jacob and Judah are more common and He uses them too, which is good news for the rest of us. The list of Jacob's descendants who made the journey with him into Egypt serves a number of purposes. But for us, at this juncture, it serves as a reminder that these people who were to be the agents of the divine planning were feeble and failing people. It is not necessary to reiterate the details of the sad events which had surrounded the lives of many of these people, but it is noteworthy that Genesis takes pains to tell the truth about them and at the same time shows the potential of such people when they are held in the hand of God. God uses people who lack spiritual ability for the simple reason that He only has that kind of people available to Him!

The people of God are also surprising because of their lack of numerical superiority. When we consider what God had in mind when He sent Joseph into Egypt and that He promised to make Jacob a great nation in Egypt it is surprising to note that, *"All the persons of the house of Jacob who went to Egypt were seventy"* (v. 27). (Stephen quoted "seventy-five people" [Acts 7:14] but he was presumably including the wives of Jacob's sons who were specifically excluded in the Genesis account.) But God has often demonstrated an apparent preference for working through a small nucleus rather than a large mass. The Lord Jesus addressed His program of world redemption with a handful of the most unlikely disciples chosen from a remarkably small, insignificant location but through them He changed, and is changing, the world.

The Lord also appears to take delight in using those who lack social acceptability. This was certainly the case with Jacob's family. Pharaoh warmly welcomed them to Egypt but not without some degree of reservation. Joseph was sensitive to this, so after his long awaited and deeply emotional reunion with his father, he said, *"So it shall be, when Pharaoh calls you and says, 'What is your occupation?' that you shall say, 'Your servants' occupation has been with livestock from our youth even till now, both we and also our fathers'"* (Gen. 46:33, 34). He then added, *"Every shepherd is an abomination to the Egyptians"* (v. 34). Jacob and his sons may have known this but it is unlikely that they would appreciate it! The brothers had already learned that they, being Hebrews, were an abomination to the Egyptians (see Gen. 43:32) but now they realized they had two strikes against them! As Paul said, "God has chosen the foolish things of the world to put to shame the wise, and God has chosen the weak things of the world to put to shame the things which are mighty; and the base things of the world and the things which are despised God has chosen, and the things which are not, to bring to nothing the things that are, that no flesh should glory in His presence" (1 Cor. 1:27-29).

When God sent His Son into the world He sent Him to a stable as a baby. He has been doing surprisingly different things all along, using the most unlikely people in the most remarkable ways. But through it all the discerning eye can see the wonderful workings of God and glorify Him accordingly. Pity the person who remakes God in his own image, for that person is not only a stranger to the truth but he is also missing all the excitement of discovering what a surprising God is the God of Abraham, Isaac, and Jacob!

CHAPTER FORTY-SEVEN

Life Is a Pilgrimage

Genesis 47:1–31

47:1 Then Joseph went and told Pharaoh, and said, "My father and my brothers, their flocks and their herds and all that they possess, have come from the land of Canaan; and indeed they *are* in the land of Goshen."

2 And he took five men from among his brothers and presented them to Pharaoh.

3 Then Pharaoh said to his brothers, "What *is* your occupation?" And they said to Pharaoh, "Your servants *are* shepherds, both we *and* also our fathers."

4 And they said to Pharaoh, "We have come to dwell in the land, because your servants have no pasture for their flocks, for the famine *is* severe in the land of Canaan. Now therefore, please let your servants dwell in the land of Goshen."

5 Then Pharaoh spoke to Joseph, saying, "Your father and your brothers have come to you.

6 "The land of Egypt *is* before you. Have your father and brothers dwell in the best of the land; let them dwell in the land of Goshen. And if you know *any* competent men among them, then make them chief herdsmen over my livestock.

7 Then Joseph brought in his father Jacob and set him before Pharaoh; and Jacob blessed Pharaoh.

8 Pharaoh said to Jacob, "How old *are* you?"

9 And Jacob said to Pharaoh, "The days of the years of my pilgrimage *are* one hundred and thirty years; few and evil have been the days of the years of my life, and they have not attained to the days of the years of the life of my fathers in the days of their pilgrimage."

10 So Jacob blessed Pharaoh, and went out from before Pharaoh.

11 And Joseph situated his father and his brothers, and gave them a possession in the land of Egypt, in the best of the land, in the land of Rameses, as Pharaoh had commanded.

12 Then Joseph provided his father, his brothers, and all his father's household with bread, according to the number in *their* families.

13 Now *there was* no bread in all the land; for the famine *was* very severe, so that the land of Egypt and the land of Canaan languished because of the famine.

14 And Joseph gathered up all the money that was found in the land of Egypt and in the land of Canaan, for the grain which they bought; and Joseph brought the money into Pharaoh's house.

15 So when the money failed in the land of Egypt and in the land of Canaan, all the Egyptians came to Joseph and said, "Give us bread, for why should we die in your presence? For the money has failed."

16 Then Joseph said, "Give your livestock, and I will give you *bread* for your livestock, if the money is gone."

17 So they brought their livestock to Joseph, and Joseph gave them bread *in exchange* for the horses, the flocks, the cattle of the herds, and for the donkeys. Thus he fed them with bread *in exchange* for all their livestock that year.

18 When that year had ended, they came to him the next year and said to him, "We will not hide from my lord that our money is gone; my lord also has our herds of livestock. There is nothing left in the sight of my lord but our bodies and our lands.

19 "Why should we die before your eyes, both we and our land? Buy us and our land for bread, and we and our land will be servants of Pharaoh; give *us* seed, that we may live and not die, that the land may not be desolate."

20 Then Joseph bought all the land of Egypt for Pharaoh; for every man of the Egyptians sold his field, because the famine was severe upon them. So the land became Pharaoh's.

21 And as for the people, he moved them into the cities, from *one* end of the borders of Egypt to the *other* end.

22 Only the land of the priests he did not buy; for the priests had rations *allotted to them* by Pharaoh, and they ate their rations which Pharaoh gave them; therefore they did not sell their lands.

23 Then Joseph said to the people, "Indeed I have bought you and your land this day for Pharaoh. Look, *here is* seed for you, and you shall sow the land.

24 "And it shall come to pass in the harvest that you shall give one-fifth to Pharaoh. Four-fifths shall be your own, as seed for the field and for your food, for those of your households and as food for your little ones."

25 So they said, "You have saved our lives; let us find favor in the sight of my lord, and we will be Pharaoh's servants."

26 And Joseph made it a law over the land of Egypt to this day, *that* Pharaoh should have one-fifth, except for the land of the priests only, *which* did not become Pharaoh's.

27 So Israel dwelt in the land of Egypt, in the country of Goshen; and they had possessions there and grew and multiplied exceedingly.

28 And Jacob lived in the land of Egypt seventeen years. So the length of Jacob's life was one hundred and forty-seven years.

29 When the time drew near that Israel must die, he called his son Joseph and said to him, "Now if I have found favor in your sight, please put your hand under my thigh, and deal kindly and truly with me. Please do not bury me in Egypt,

30 "but let me lie with my fathers; you shall carry me out of Egypt and bury me in their burial place." And he said, "I will do as you have said."

31 Then he said, "Swear to me." And he swore to him. So Israel bowed himself on the head of the bed.

Gen. 47:1–31

Now that Joseph's family had safely arrived in Egypt they had to be settled along with their considerable flocks and herds. Throughout the years of negotiating Joseph had made all the arrangements for the family while keeping the Pharaoh apprised of the situation. But now he determined it was necessary for the family to be presented at court. *"He took five men from among his brothers and presented them to Pharaoh"* (Gen. 47:2). Joseph had told them of the Egyptian attitude toward shepherds but when they were asked about their occupation they replied without hesitation, as he had instructed them, *"Your servants are shepherds, both we and also our fathers"* (v. 3). Pharaoh responded warmly to their added request for pasture land and apparently thought there might be some advantages for him in their arrival so he commissioned Joseph, *"let them dwell in the land of Goshen. And if you know any competent men among them, then make them chief herdsmen over my livestock"* (v. 6).

Having made suitable arrangements for the family and the flocks Joseph was now eager to introduce his beloved, aged father to Pharaoh. Their encounter, while briefly recorded, is full of interest. The contrast between the young man on the throne and the old man who was virtually a refugee made for a fascinating confrontation. But if Pharaoh was expecting Jacob to be overwhelmed he must have been sorely disappointed. The old pilgrim was definitely underwhelmed by all that he saw and the things that were happening to him.

THE MENTALITY A PILGRIM DEVELOPS

As life expectancy was alarmingly brief in Egypt in those days it is possible that Pharaoh had never seen anyone like the venerable old pilgrim who was ushered into his presence. His opening words were, *"How old are you?"* (v. 8). Jacob replied, *"The days of the years of my pilgrimage are one hundred and thirty years; few and evil have been the days of the years of my life, and they have not attained to the days of the years of the life of my fathers in the days of their pilgrimage"* (v. 9). It is highly probable that Jacob was referring to the nomadic life that he and his fathers had lived, when he talked about a pilgrimage, but it is also possible that he had a broader definition of life in mind. God's people through the ages have been encouraged to regard themselves as pilgrims and when they do they develop a unique approach to life. For example the writer to the Hebrews made special mention of a number of people including Abraham who "confessed that they were strangers and pilgrims on the earth" (Heb. 11:13). This confession had nothing to do with the land that they had left for if that had been the case they could have returned to it. But they were thinking and desiring "a better, that is, a heavenly country" (Heb. 11:16). Perhaps the old pilgrim, Jacob, was telling the young Pharaoh that both he and his fathers had lived lives on earth that were touched with the sense of heaven. They had spent time bathed in the light of eternity. Whether or not this was what Jacob had in mind we cannot be sure, but we do know that for the modern-day believer this is certainly an aspect of life which is most appropriate and necessary.

The apostle Peter expressed similar sentiments to the believers in Asia Minor whom he suspected would shortly be persecuted for their faith. He wrote, "Beloved, I beg you as sojourners and pilgrims, abstain from fleshly lusts which war against the soul, having your conduct honorable among the Gentiles, that when they speak against you as evildoers, they may, by your good works which they observe, glorify God in the day of visitation" (1 Pet. 2:11, 12). His concern was not only the welfare of the believer during times of persecution but also the well-being of the one doing the persecuting. Peter saw the believer's responsibility as a pilgrim to be such as to extend to a concern for the one doing him harm. He had no doubt that when this attitude was evident the persecuting pagan would be put on inquiry by the lifestyle of the believer and accordingly be open to the blessing of God on his life.

The Lord Jesus put the whole matter in perspective when He reminded His disciples that earthly values do tend to be superficial while only heavenly values are substantial. He insisted, "Do not lay up for yourselves treasures on earth, where moth and rust destroy and where thieves break in and steal; but lay up for yourselves treasures in heaven, where neither moth nor rust destroys and where thieves do not break in and steal" (Matt. 6:19, 20). This pilgrim mentality affects the approach to life, death, possessions, and relationships. When this life is regarded as permanent and significant then all that matters is the here and now. But when the life to come is seen as substantial and this life as relatively superficial then the here and now is seen as relatively unimportant in the light of the life to come. The pilgrim mentality is a must for the believer in all ages, not only for the weatherbeaten old timers like Jacob.

When I was a young adolescent growing up in England during World War II I attended a tiny church of which my father was the lay leader. It was not particularly exciting and I was on the verge of trying to decide how I could make what was known in those days as a "strategic withdrawal." One Sunday morning everything changed. Into the service marched an officer of the Royal Artillery. He was ramrod straight; his uniform was "spit and polished"; he was fresh and lively and a convinced and outspoken Christian. He was also the beginning of a new life for me. Over forty years later that same Army officer, Captain H. S. May R. A., is still very much alive, now in his eighties—vigorous, humorous, committed, alert, involved, and thoroughly refreshing. Of all the people I left behind in England when I came to America I hear from him more than any. He listens to my radio broadcasts, critiques them, encourages me, adds his own insights, prays for me, and continues to regale me with stories of God's wonderful workings in his life. One of these days the old Army Captain will slip off into heaven and we will all be so much poorer because he has gone. But he lives so in touch with heaven and so delighted with what it means to be heaven's representative on earth that I rather suspect he may not notice that his pilgrimage is over because the new scene is what he has been preparing for and anticipating for so many years. There's something very special about an old pilgrim who will share all that he has learned on the way.

The Difficulty a Pilgrim Encounters

When Jacob described the days of his pilgrimage as *"few and evil"* he was no doubt thinking of the many tragedies which had accompanied him. Some of the evil had been the direct result of his own misbehavior but many of the things that had happened were completely outside his control. Such is life, and pilgrims have to face it. There are many things that happen for which we must accept full responsibility while there are other events which we must accept as the common lot of sinful people who live among sinners and who together have produced a sinful society full of iniquity and cruelty.

Things were not at all easy for the people whose pilgrimage was being lived out in Egypt during Joseph's jurisdiction. *"There was no bread in the land; for the famine was very severe, so that the land of Egypt and all the land of Canaan languished because of the famine"* (Gen. 47:13). For those people survival itself was a matter of prime significance. But Joseph had foreseen the famine and had laid in the stocks so the people were able to purchase from him, until their money ran out. Then they appealed to him again and were told, *"Give your livestock, and I will give you bread for your livestock, if the money is gone"* (v. 16). To survive the present these wretched people were being required to mortgage their future. They had little choice because unless they found food quickly they would not have a future. After another year spent in the struggle for survival the people arrived at the point where they had neither food nor livestock and so they offered their land and themselves as slaves to Joseph and Pharaoh in exchange for necessary food. The misery of these people is hard to imagine but the extremity of their circumstances does serve to point out that people all over the world suffer similar pressures in principle if not necessarily in the same degree.

Joseph drove a hard bargain. He said, *"Indeed I have bought you and your land this day for Pharaoh. Look, here is seed for you, and you shall sow the land. And it shall come to pass in the harvest that you shall give one-fifth to Pharaoh"* (vv. 23, 24). Given our Western ideals of the freedom of the individual, fundamental human rights, and the non-intervention of government, Joseph's relentless and masterful manipulation of the chronic economic situation to Pharaoh's totalitarian advantage serves at least to raise many eyebrows. Of course, it could be argued that he did not use his advantage to feather his own nest, and he was after all the only person who had been visionary enough to see what was about to happen and capable enough to know what to do about it. Nevertheless his actions do seem to be so opportunistic that some people feel that the later Egyptian antipathy toward the Hebrews was at least partially attributable to this action. It should be borne in mind, however, that it was not at all uncommon in those days for those who were hopelessly in debt to mortgage not only their property but also their families and themselves. We should not forget that the Levitical law made provisions for similar practices but with numerous humanitarian riders that insisted on the principle of redemption (see Lev. 25:25–55). Whatever we think of Joseph's handling of the situation, we cannot avoid recognizing that the people's lives were hanging by a thread and it had taken a Joseph to give them the thread. To a greater or lesser extent all lives are lived in the balance and the pilgrim mentality alone fits people for the difficulties which life inevitably presents.

THE QUALITY A PILGRIM DISPLAYS

In the midst of the confusion and the trauma it is intriguing to note the pilgrim qualities which old Jacob portrayed. When he was introduced to Pharaoh it was he who took the initiative by blessing him and at the end of the interview he repeated the action. We are told, *"So Jacob blessed Pharaoh, and went out from before Pharaoh"* (Gen 47:10). No doubt Jacob's venerable age had something to do with his attitude to Pharaoh but also we should not overlook the fact that those who live before the Lord have a special attitude to those who are in authority. They respect all authority because it is delegated by God, but they live under the Supreme Authority and therefore see human authority as significant but far from ultimate. Accordingly, authority does not hold the same fear for them and there is a certain freedom about the way they approach temporal authority knowing it has its limits which are preordained by God. This spills over into a certain dignity in the bearing of the pilgrim. Once when Dr. Billy Graham had preached at a worship service attended by Her Majesty Queen Elizabeth, he was asked what it felt like to preach before the Queen, and he reputedly answered, "It is an honor to preach before the Queen but whenever I preach the King of kings is present." Jacob had achieved the kind of attitude toward life where he was not easily impressed but neither did he feel any necessity to impress. Pilgrims are like this because they desire the applause of God rather than the applause of men. So when Jacob told Pharaoh that his days had been *"few and evil"* and they had not attained to the life of his fathers, he was being perfectly frank and open about himself because he felt he had nothing to prove and therefore there was nothing to hide. There is a special kind of integrity about pilgrims.

After seventeen years in Goshen which were characterized by remarkably successful farming after the famine, Jacob approached death. He required Joseph to swear to him, *"Please do not bury me in Egypt, but let me lie with my fathers; you shall carry me out of Egypt and bury me in their burial place"* (vv. 29, 30). Joseph readily agreed, *"I will do as you have said"* (v. 30). No doubt Jacob was thinking of the specific promise of the Lord when he had agreed to venture into Egypt in the first place (see Gen. 46:4), but he was also showing that special pilgrim quality of tenacity. He knew that even when he breathed his last there were things that needed to be done that would fulfill the divine plan. He would not have his bones left in Egypt because he was convinced that in the economy of God none of his children belonged there. Canaan was to be their land and he was determined that his remains should be there in the very center of all that God had promised him and his children. It is always good to see old men at the end of their pilgrimage continuing in faith and expectancy. Jacob like his fathers looked for a better country and they did not just mean the land of promise; they looked to all that God had for them. Such is the attitude of all pilgrims.

CHAPTER FORTY-EIGHT

The Ages of Man

Genesis 48:1–22

48:1 Now it came to pass after these things that Joseph was told, "Indeed your father *is* sick"; and he took with him his two sons, Manasseh and Ephraim.

2 And Jacob was told, "Look, your son Joseph is coming to you"; and Israel strengthened himself and sat up on the bed.

3 Then Jacob said to Joseph: "God Almighty appeared to me at Luz in the land of Canaan and blessed me,

4 "and said to me, 'Behold, I will make you fruitful and multiply you, and I will make of you a multitude of people, and give this land to your descendants after you *as* an everlasting possession.'

5 "And now your two sons, Ephraim and Manasseh, who were born to you in the land of Egypt before I came to you in Egypt, *are* mine; as Reuben and Simeon, they shall be mine.

6 "Your offspring whom you beget after them shall be yours; they will be called by the name of their brothers in their inheritance.

7 "But as for me, when I came from Padan, Rachel died beside me in the land of Canaan on the way, when *there was* but a little distance to go to Ephrath; and I buried her there on the way to Ephrath (that is, Bethlehem)."

8 Then Israel saw Joseph's sons, and said, "Who *are* these?"

9 And Joseph said to his father, "They *are* my sons, whom God has given me in this *place.*" And he said, "Please bring them to me, and I will bless them."

10 Now the eyes of Israel were dim with age, *so that* he could not see. Then Joseph brought them near him, and he kissed them and embraced them.

11 And Israel said to Joseph, "I had not thought to see your face; but in fact, God has also shown me your offspring!"

12 So Joseph brought them from beside his knees, and he bowed down with his face to the earth.

13 And Joseph took them both, Ephraim with his right hand toward Israel's left hand, and Manasseh with his left hand toward Israel's right hand, and brought *them* near him.

14 Then Israel stretched out his right hand and laid *it* on Ephraim's head, who *was* the younger, and his left hand on Manasseh's head, guiding his hands knowingly, for Manasseh *was* the firstborn.

15 And he blessed Joseph, and said:

"God, before whom my fathers Abraham and
　Isaac walked,
The God who has fed me all my life long to this
　day,

16 The Angel who has redeemed me from all evil
Bless the lads;
Let my name be named upon them,
And the name of my fathers Abraham and
　Isaac;
And let them grow into a multitude in the midst
　of the earth."

17 Now when Joseph saw that his father laid his right hand on the head of Ephraim, it displeased him; so he took hold of his father's hand to remove it from Ephraim's head to Manasseh's head.

18 And Joseph said to his father, "Not so, my father, for this *one is* the firstborn; put your right hand on his head."

19 But his father refused and said, "I know, my son, I know. He also shall become a people, and he also shall be great; but truly his younger brother shall be greater than he, and his descendants shall become a multitude of nations."

20 So he blessed them that day, saying, "By you Israel will bless, saying, 'May God make you as

Ephraim and as Manasseh!'" And thus he set Ephraim before Manasseh.

21 Then Israel said to Joseph, "Behold, I am dying, but God will be with you and bring you back to the land of your fathers.

22 "Moreover I have given to you one portion above your brothers, which I took from the hand of the Amorite with my sword and my bow."

Gen. 48:1-22

After 147 years of nonstop action Jacob's life was drawing to a close. *"Joseph was told, 'Indeed your father is sick'; and he took with him his two sons, Manasseh and Ephraim"* (Gen. 48:1). This set the stage for another deathbed scene. In some ways it was reminiscent of the one in which Jacob had participated as a young man when his father was dying, but at the crucial points it could not have been more different. The three generations gathered around the bed vividly remind us of the ages of man and the stages through which we must all pass.

JACOB—THE VOICE OF THE PAST

The old man's faculties which had served him so well for so long were now practically worn out. It was only with great effort that he *"strengthened himself and sat up on his bed"* (v. 2) when he heard that visitors were arriving. His memory was also playing the tricks of age. When he spoke of events long gone past he recalled them by the ancient names still stored in his memory (see "Luz" in v. 3), but when he saw his grandsons he said, *"Who are these?"* (v. 8). Yet he spoke with vivid recall about his beloved wife saying, *"When I came from Padan, Rachel died beside me in the land of Canaan on the way, when there was but a little distance to go to Ephrath; and I buried her there on the way to Ephrath (that is, Bethlehem)"* (v. 7). In addition, *"the eyes of Israel were dim with age, so that he could not see"* (v. 10).

The old man might have been weak but he was still his own man! He had his own opinions and he was still committed to making them known. The fact that his son Joseph was the second man in the whole of Egypt did not deter the old pilgrim, in his waning moments, from giving a lecture on the Lord's dealings in his life, and reminding his son, *"I am dying, but God will be with you and bring you back to the land of your fathers"* (v. 21). He had to ensure that there were no doubts in Joseph's mind about his proper place and calling. Old people sometimes wonder about the ways of the younger generations and Jacob may have entertained some thoughts about the possibility that Joseph had found himself a very nice niche in Egypt and might be tempted to stay there. He might be dying but with his long association with the Lord behind him and his unique knowledge of the purposes of God as they related to his family he was anxious to pass on the last piece of information which would lead the succeeding generations down the right path.

He reminded Joseph and his grandsons of their spiritual roots, recounted some spiritual promises, recalled their spiritual heritage, rehearsed his spiritual experience, and then prepared to relay a spiritual blessing. The old man with his feet firmly planted in the past and his heart set on his immediate departure was looking into the future and setting the course for the ones who would follow him. In his own case the blessing which was his by right, even though he was the younger twin, had been received by stealth and trickery. He had grossly abused the failing faculties of his own father, but no such chicanery was evident at the moment of his weakness. History was about to repeat itself in that the younger son was to receive the blessing.

Jacob announced, *"your two sons, Ephraim and Manasseh, who were born to you in the land of Egypt before I came to you in Egypt, are mine; as Reuben and Simeon, they shall be mine"* (v. 5). At first sight this would appear to eliminate Joseph from the sons of Israel but in fact Jacob was ensuring a double place of privilege for the son who meant so much to him. The two grandsons, now adopted by their grandfather, were placed before him, the older to his right, the younger to his left. *"Then Israel stretched out his right hand and laid it on Ephraim's head, who was the younger, and his left hand on Manasseh's head, guiding his hands knowingly, for Manasseh was the first-born"* (v. 14). Joseph, seeing what he thought was an error, moved to correct it but the old man *"refused and said, 'I know, my son, I know'"* (v. 19). He was weak but he wasn't stupid. He was dying but he wasn't dead!

This apparently trivial event was to have far-ranging consequences because it was the elevated Ephraim who would eventually take the place of the deposed Reuben as the leader of the twelve tribes (see 1 Chron. 5:1, 2). The old patriarch was adamant that Joseph should be greatly honored through his sons. It should be noted that Joseph's sons were blessed by their grandfather in the name of their father, Joseph (see Gen. 48:15).

The blessing itself was a poignant reminder of Jacob's experience with the Lord. He recalled that God was the One *"before whom my fathers Abraham and Isaac walked"* (v. 15). This was a reminder of the dominant theme of his life—that the Lord had made a covenant with his family and that through his family eventually all the nations of the world would be blessed. This thought was never far from the minds of the patriarchs because it reminded them not only of His grace but also of their high and holy privilege.

He went on to talk about *"The God who has fed me all my life long to this day"* (v. 15). The word *"fed"* is the shepherd word later used by David in the 23rd Psalm. Both men knew shepherding from personal experience and more importantly both knew the Shepherd intimately. He concluded his triple statement about the Lord, calling Him *"The Angel who has redeemed me from all evil"* (v. 16). By *"Angel"* he meant God as He had appeared to him in human form and he had no difficulty remembering the occasions on which God had intervened to redeem him from evil in the same way that a kinsman redeemer would deliver relatives from indebtedness they could not possibly repay. It was this wonderful Lord whom he had known for many long years Whose blessing he now sought for his son Joseph through his grandsons Ephraim and Manasseh.

JOSEPH—THE MAINSTAY OF THE PRESENT

Joseph, as he stood by the bed of his dying father, presents a picture of the man on whose shoulders the weight of the present rests. Jacob's day in the sun was almost over but life had to go on and it was up to Joseph to see that much of the mechanics of daily living continued. He had to balance out many responsibilities. His office as Vizier, managing the vast resources which had accrued to Pharaoh, must have been heavy and demanding. His two growing sons were of obvious concern to him otherwise he would not have taken them out to Goshen to see their dying grandfather and, of course, his commitment to his father was such that he was ready to leave the affairs of state to be with him in his hour of need.

But like all people who carry loads of responsibility he had to handle his share of frustrations too. With all Egypt bowing down to him he had to bow down to his aged father! With everyone dancing attendance upon him he had to tolerate the contradictions of a dying man! With authority to wield the powers of Pharaoh he had to stand quietly by while his father without so much as asking his permission announced that he was going to adopt his sons and that if Joseph wanted sons who would bear his name he would have to raise some more!

He had also accepted responsibility for seeing that his father would eventually be buried in the land of Canaan and no doubt he was already wondering how things were going to work out with his two sons now that the younger had been placed in ascendancy over the elder. He knew enough family history to know that the possibility of trouble was high. All these responsibilities and frustrations were the stuff of life for him! Many a modern business person will empathize with Joseph.

But he was a man of great resources and there is no indication that he was less than ready for his continued role as leader and provider for many people. His secret was found in the words of his father, *"God will be with you"* (v. 21). He knew these were not empty words for they had been proven true repeatedly in his experience.

EPHRAIM—THE HOPE OF THE FUTURE

The time was coming when the young men would be taking the place of the older men. Ephraim had been wonderfully blessed in preparation for all that lay ahead. He must have had a great sense of history as he knelt by his grandfather's bed and received his blessing. The old man was talking about Abraham and Isaac and his own dealings with God for more than 140 years! He had heard his own father's story about how he had been sold as a slave, promoted, jailed, and promoted to a position second only to Pharaoh. He had watched his father, a man of colossal ability and integrity, operate in tense situations. He had a long history to draw from, a living model to emulate, and more than enough well-documented mistakes of his relatives to learn from. On top of it all he had the strange and wonderful sense that God had chosen him for something significant. Ephraim truly had a lot going for him!

But there is always a danger that youthful enthusiasm will overlook such things and youth will insist on its own way and commit itself to making its own mistakes. This may be unavoidable but there is certainly a lot to be said for the three ages of men getting together and helping each other with their own peculiar burdens. Jacob got the help he needed as he faced death. Joseph was encouraged as he went back to face life and Ephraim was strengthened as, with all the freshness of youth, he faced a future full of promise and opportunity. That is exactly how it should be.

Last Thanksgiving eve my wife and I were fitting an extra leaf in the dining room table to accommodate our kids and their families who were returning for the time of family celebration. A friend who happened to be with us at the time looked at the extra length of the table, the number of chairs we were setting, and said to me "You sure started something, didn't you?" She was joking but I was reminded of the seriousness of what I had started. My grown children who were now busy establishing their young families, my first grandson who was about to take his first steps would soon be gathered around the table and we would have the priceless privilege of sharing the good things of the past and of encouraging each other in our peculiar contemporary situations and then looking to the future with as clear an eye as God would grant. I started my Thanksgiving early that year as I quietly expressed my appreciation to the Lord for all He had allowed me to start and for all the blessings and responsibilities this had introduced into my life.

CHAPTER FORTY-NINE

Appropriate Blessings

Genesis 49:1–33

49:1 And Jacob called his sons and said, "Gather together, that I may tell you what shall befall you in the last days:

2 "Gather together and hear, you sons of Jacob,
And listen to Israel your father.

3 "Reuben, you are my firstborn,
My might and the beginning of my strength,
The excellency of dignity and the excellency of
      power.

4 Unstable as water, you shall not excel,
Because you went up to your father's bed;
Then you defiled *it*—
He went up to my couch.

5 "Simeon and Levi *are* brothers;
Instruments of cruelty *are in* their dwelling
      place.

6 Let not my soul enter their council;
Let not my honor be united to their assembly;
For in their anger they slew a man,
And in their self-will they hamstrung an ox.

7 Cursed *be* their anger, for *it is* fierce;
And their wrath, for it is cruel!
I will divide them in Jacob
And scatter them in Israel.

8 "Judah, you *are he* whom your brothers shall
      praise;
Your hand *shall be* on the neck of your enemies;
Your father's children shall bow down before
      you.

9 Judah *is* a lion's whelp;
　From the prey, my son, you have gone up.
　He bows down, he lies down as a lion;
　And as a lion, who shall rouse him?

10 The scepter shall not depart from Judah,
　Nor a lawgiver from between his feet,
　Until Shiloh comes;
　And to Him *shall be* the obedience of the
　　people.

11 Binding his donkey to the vine,
　And his donkey's colt to the choice vine,
　He washed his garments in wine,
　And his clothes in the blood of grapes.

12 His eyes *are* darker than wine,
　And his teeth whiter than milk.

13 "Zebulun shall dwell by the haven of the sea;
　He *shall become* a haven for ships,
　And his border shall adjoin Sidon.

14 "Issachar is a strong donkey,
　Lying down between two burdens;

15 He saw that rest *was* good,
　And that the land *was* pleasant;
　He bowed his shoulder to bear *a burden*,
　And became a band of slaves.

16 "Dan shall judge his people
　As one of the tribes of Israel.

17 Dan shall be a serpent by the way,
　A viper by the path,
　That bites the horse's heels
　So that its rider shall fall backward.

18 I have waited for your salvation, O LORD!

19 "Gad, a troop shall tramp upon him,
　But he shall triumph at last.

20 "Bread from Asher *shall be* rich,
　And he shall yield royal dainties.

21 "Naphtali *is* a deer let loose;
　He uses beautiful words.

22 "Joseph *is* a fruitful bough,
　A fruitful bough by a well;
　His branches run over the wall.

23 The archers have bitterly grieved him,
　Shot *at him* and hated him.

24 But his bow remained in strength,
   And the arms of his hands were made strong
   By the hands of the Mighty *God* of Jacob
   (From there *is* the Shepherd, the Stone of
      Israel),
25 By the God of your father who will help you,
   And by the Almighty who will bless you
   With blessings of heaven above,
   Blessings of the deep that lies beneath,
   Blessings of the breasts and of the womb.
26 The blessings of your father
   Have excelled the blessings of my ancestors,
   Up to the utmost bound of the everlasting hills.
   They shall be on the head of Joseph,
   And on the crown of the head of him who was
      separate from his brothers.
27 "Benjamin is a ravenous wolf;
   In the morning he shall devour the prey,
   And at night he shall divide the spoil."

28 All these *are* the twelve tribes of Israel, and this *is* what their father spoke to them. And he blessed them; he blessed each one according to his own blessing.

29 Then he charged them and said to them: "I am to be gathered to my people; bury me with my fathers in the cave that *is* in the field of Ephron the Hittite,

30 "in the cave that *is* in the field of Machpelah, which *is* before Mamre in the land of Canaan, which Abraham bought with the field of Ephron the Hittite as a possession for a burial place.

31 "There they buried Abraham and Sarah his wife, there they buried Isaac and Rebekah his wife, and there I buried Leah.

32 "The field and the cave that *is* there *were* purchased from the sons of Heth."

33 And when Jacob had finished commanding his sons, he drew his feet up into the bed and breathed his last, and was gathered to his people.

Gen. 49:1–33

The time had come for Israel to take his leave of this world after 147 years of living life to the full. He had tasted life's sweetest blessings and known its most bitter moments. But one final dramatic scene had to be played out. *"Jacob called his sons and said, 'Gather together, that I may tell you what shall befall you in the last days'"* (Gen 49:1). Dutifully the sons gathered around the old man and he proceeded to speak to each one in turn predicting what would transpire in their future experience.

It should be noted that some scholars are skeptical of the ability of man to predict the future and therefore they see this passage of Scripture as a later piece of writing which, since it was completed after the events had taken place, was given the appearance of a prophetic utterance. The major problem with this view is that the events purportedly predicted took place over such a wide-ranging period of time that they could not have been recorded by one person. This would have required that numerous writings from many sources be collated and given the appearance of a congruent whole. This is obviously not impossible but it can readily be seen that to reject the statement of Scripture about these words being predictive serves only to raise new problems which find no easy solution. It is better to accept the fact that the old man was exercising some good old-fashioned wisdom and foresight mixed with a divine ability to see into the future and warn his children of what lay ahead.

The great event to which all the patriarchs had looked forward was the establishment of Abraham's heirs of the covenant in the land of promise. They knew that they had been placed in Egypt in order that they might become strong enough to overthrow the inhabitants of Canaan and to marshal the resources that they would need to become established in their homeland and now the time was rapidly approaching when the great event would take place. Jacob saw this clearly and many of his statements related not only to his individual sons but to the tribes which would bear their names. As was usually the case with such predictive statements there was a mixture of compliment and complaint, a mix of blessing and cursing.

When we think in terms of blessings we assume the complimentary and encouraging words. But we may have some difficulty distinguishing blessing in some of the things Jacob said to his sons. For example, Simeon and Levi were hardly complimented by their father and there appears to be little cause for celebration on their part in response to what the old man had to say. Unless we bear in mind what presumably Jacob had in mind and that was a good old-fashioned warning to his sons. He had observed them carefully for many years. What he had seen he had carefully filtered through his experience and he had come to some conclusions about these young men. Now he was going to tell them some home truths—some things that their best friend might not tell them but some things that their father needed to tell them. To have a father like that is a blessing and to be told what is going to happen in the future if I continue the way I am going is a blessing indeed.

The Men Who Were Disqualified

Reuben was born to greatness. As the firstborn of Jacob he had inherited special rights and privileges described by his father as *"The excellency of dignity and the excellency of power"* (v. 3). But there was one event in his life which apparently characterized him. Jacob reminded him in the presence of his brothers,

> *Unstable as water, you shall not excel,*
> *Because you went up to your father's bed;*
> *Then you defiled it —*
> *He went up to my couch* (v. 4).

The word translated *"unstable"* is the operative word. It connotes wildness and unruliness and when applied to the metaphor of water suggests an uncontrollable torrent of passion to which he was apparently susceptible and which was expressed most grossly in his incestuous relations with his father's wife. One can almost sense the disgust in Jacob's voice as he turned to the brothers and said, *"He went up to my couch!"* His father's abrupt summary of his future was frightening—*"You shall not excel."* This was not only true of Reuben the man, but also described with great accuracy the fate of the tribe which bore his name.

Turning his attention to the next in line he said,

> *Simeon and Levi are brothers;*
> *Instruments of cruelty are in their dwelling place.*
> *Let not my soul enter into their council;*
> *Let not my honor be united to their assembly* (vv. 5, 6).

400

The old man was referring to the sordid event when the two brothers led the bloody vendetta against Shechem which resulted in the annihilation of the men of the city, the plundering of their homes, and the kidnapping of their wives and children. The violence and viciousness with which they acted was in Jacob's eyes sufficient grounds for saying that he would never want to be placed at their mercy and provoked him to utter the solemn words,

> Cursed be their anger, for it is fierce;
> And their wrath, for it is cruel! (v. 7).

The predicted "scattering" of these two tribes did take place particularly in the case of Simeon but the grace of God was especially evident in Levi's history in that they became the priestly order in Israel. Dan was another son who had failed to live up to his promise and whose descendants would also achieve considerably less than was intended for them.

> Dan shall judge his people
> As one of the tribes of Israel.
> Dan shall be a serpent by the way,
> A viper by the path,
> That bites the horse's heels
> So that its rider shall fall backward (vv. 16, 17).

The name Dan, meaning "judge," gives the clue to what was expected of the man and the tribe but unfortunately there was a treachery about them which made compassionate and fair judgment a rarity. It is interesting to note that Dan is omitted from the list of tribes in Revelation 7:5–8. Many theories have been advanced to explain this and it may be going too far to suggest that it was indicative of a definitive judgment on the tribe. There can be no doubt, however, that Dan failed ignominiously to be Dan in the truest sense of the word.

Jacob's aside, "I have waited for your salvation, O Lord" (Gen. 49:18), may be a reflex response from his own heart as the thought of the viper biting the heel reminded him of a young man whose exploits had proven that his name, Jacob, accurately reflected his own perverse ability to go for the heel and trip people up!

401

THE MEN WHO WERE DISTINGUISHED

Judah was by no means perfect but he had exhibited fine qualities when the opportunity presented itself and as a result had lived up to his name which means "praise." Jacob said of him,

> *Judah, you are he whom your brothers shall praise;*
> *Your hand shall be on the neck of your enemies;*
> *Your father's children shall bow down before you.*
> *Judah is a lion's whelp* (vv. 8, 9).

The robust energy, and the daring initiatives of Judah had won the admiration of the brothers and would continue to do so as his descendants exercised leadership among the tribes. But this leadership was indicative of the Great Leader Who would eventually come from the tribe of Judah.

> *The scepter shall not depart from Judah,*
> *Nor a lawgiver from between his feet,*
> *Until Shiloh comes;*
> *And to Him shall be the obedience of the people* (v. 10).

While the text at this point is somewhat obscure and because interpretations of its meaning vary quite extensively it should be noted that even though there is disagreement on details there has been agreement for centuries that this is a prediction of the arrival of the Messiah. The day would come when the "Lion of the tribe of Judah" (Rev. 5:5) would come from the tribe which was lionlike in its strength and courage. He would be not only King of kings and Lord of lords but Lion of lions! Yet His strength and courage would be demonstrated in His ability to be like a Lamb standing after it had been slain—a striking picture of the crucified but risen Lord (see Rev. 5:6)!

The arrival of the One Who would hold the scepter would introduce an age of blessing and delight. The emphasis in the rest of the oracle on "vine," "grape," and "wine" may not be to everyone's liking but it clearly denotes days of joy and exuberance coming from the abundance of blessing which He would bring. How much Jacob knew about what he was saying we cannot guess but with the benefit of 20/20 hindsight we who have seen the arrival of the Messiah have also tasted of the delights of His blessing and we know what Jacob was talking about! Zebulun and Issachar were to become in the case of the former *"a haven for ships"* and in the case of the latter *"a strong donkey, lying down between two burdens . . . a band of slaves"* (Gen 49:13–15). It is difficult to see exactly how this prediction was fulfilled because their geographical tribal boundaries did not include the coastline and havens. But it is possible that their domination by the area around them led them to become laborers among the seafaring people of the coast. Clearly neither of the men or the tribes would become earthshakers but neither were they heartbreakers for the old man. Perhaps they quietly distinguished themselves by patient labor and steady continuance even in less than ideal circumstances. Similar sentiments were expressed in relation to Gad.

> *Gad, a troop shall tramp on him,*
> *But he shall triumph at last* (v. 19).

The Hebrew at this point is made up to a large extent of puns on the name *"Gad"* but the message is clear. Life will be difficult for Gad but he and his tribe will work through their problems and triumph at last. Asher and Naphtali both received words of approval and encouragement.

> *Bread from Asher shall be rich,*
> *And he shall yield royal dainties* (v. 20).

Asher's geographical location in the land would provide great advantages in terms of trade and commerce. The result would be a high standard of living in pleasant circumstances. The *"royal dainties"* probably refers to the major part the people of Asher would play in providing for King Solomon's palace and household (see 1 Kings 4:7–16).

In marked contrast Naphtali would settle in the highlands: *"Naphtali is a deer let loose; He gives beautiful words"* (Gen. 49:21). The second part of this statement has posed some problems of interpretation and an alternative "he bears beautiful fawns" has been suggested. The emphasis then would be upon this tribe of lively, graceful people living in the rugged part of the land producing generations just like themselves.

Benjamin, the youngest son who had been such a comfort to Jacob in his old age and whose safety was of such concern to the patriarch, does not receive as unqualified an oracle as might have been expected.

> *Benjamin is a ravenous wolf;*
> *In the morning he shall devour the prey,*
> *And at night he shall divide the spoil* (v. 27).

A wolf is nowhere near as attractive metaphorically speaking as a lion although both of them can be nasty if you meet them on a dark night. Judah the lion seems to have the edge on Benjamin the wolf although they would both be similar in their dash and daring, their ruggedness and courage. The difference perhaps is that Benjamin would show aspects of cruelty that would diminish some of his other more attractive characteristics. This seems to have been true in the later history of the tribe (see for example Judges 20).

Jacob's visionary words to his sons show, among other things, that the tribes would have mixed fortunes in the land of promise and their small piece of real estate would yield for them a wide variety of possibilities.

THE MAN WHO WAS DIFFERENT

Jacob's words to his son Joseph are delightful. He spoke of his fruitfulness, his strength, and his blessing.

> *Joseph is a fruitful bough,*
> *A fruitful bough by a well;*
> *His branches run over the wall* (v. 22).

Like a vine with roots deep in the hidden source of refreshment Joseph would grow and flourish. He would not contain his life to himself but like the spreading bough laden with fruit he would reach out over the wall to provide nourishment for others. He had certainly done this so far and Jacob predicted he would continue to do more of the same.

His father went on to reiterate some of the pain he had suffered— a painful reminder of unpleasant days to the brothers standing around the bed! But he explained Joseph's secret source of strength.

> *The arms of his hands were made strong*
> *By the hands of the Mighty God of Jacob*
> *(From there is the Shepherd, the Stone of Israel)* (v. 24).

While there are difficulties in the text at this point there is no ambiguity in the message of Joseph's life of dependence and trust in the power of the Lord in his life.

The listing of blessings which would come Joseph's way are described in wide-ranging terms—*"blessings of heaven above, blessings of the deep . . . blessings of the breasts and the womb . . . Up to the utmost bound of the everlasting hills"* (vv. 25, 26). He who had been separate from his brothers would indeed receive blessings which would excel the blessings of former generations. This certainly was fulfilled for all to see when Ephraim and Manasseh were awarded the prime property in Canaan. Joseph who had suffered and been faithful through it all would discover that the Lord is a debtor to no one and that those who suffer will ultimately be rewarded. Many of the Lord's people have discovered the truth of this through the history of God's dealings with man, and many more have been encouraged to stand tall and strong as a result.

Jacob's blessing of his sons as he lay dying is quoted by the writer to the Hebrews as an illustration of the old man's faith. He was looking ahead to the great things that would happen in coming days as the tribes which would bear his sons' names would inherit the land God had promised to Abraham and his seed. This Jacob firmly believed. He knew that faith is "the evidence of things not seen" (Heb. 11:1). The old man certainly did not go out with a whimper! Having delivered his soul in no uncertain terms to his sons he gave instructions about his impending burial reminding them that he was to be taken to the land of promise and buried alongside Abraham and Sarah, Isaac and Rebekah, and Leah. *"And when Jacob had finished commanding his sons, he drew his feet up into the bed and breathed his last, and was gathered to his people"* (v. 33). So ends the saga of a man whose life was full of the heights and depths of human experience. But he had been the agent of God's activity and strange as it may seem his memory lives on even today, for who can listen to the evening news without hearing on a daily basis the name—Israel?

CHAPTER FIFTY

When Things Get Worse

Genesis 50:1–26

50:1 Then Joseph fell on his father's face, and wept over him, and kissed him.

2 And Joseph commanded his servants the physicians to embalm his father. So the physicians embalmed Israel.

3 Forty days were required for him, for such are the days required for those who are embalmed; and the Egyptians mourned for him seventy days.

4 Now when the days of his mourning were past, Joseph spoke to the household of Pharaoh, saying, "If now I have found favor in your eyes, please speak in the hearing of Pharaoh, saying,

5 'My father made me swear, saying, "Behold, I am dying; in my grave which I dug for myself in the land of Canaan, there you shall bury me.' Now therefore, please let me go up and bury my father, and I will come back.'"

6 And Pharaoh said, "Go up and bury your father, as he made you swear."

7 So Joseph went up to bury his father; and with him went up all the servants of Pharaoh, the elders of his house, and all the elders of the land of Egypt,

8 as well as all the house of Joseph, his brothers, and his father's house. Only their little ones, their flocks, and their herds they left in the land of Goshen.

9 And there went up with him both chariots and horsemen, and it was a very great gathering.

10 Then they came to the threshing floor of Atad, which *is* beyond the Jordan, and they mourned there

with a great and very solemn lamentation. He observed seven days of mourning for his father.

11 And when the inhabitants of the land, the Canaanites, saw the mourning at the threshing floor of Atad, they said, "This *is* a deep mourning of the Egyptians." Therefore its name was called Abel Mizraim, which *is* beyond the Jordan.

12 So his sons did for him just as he had commanded them.

13 For his sons carried him to the land of Canaan, and buried him in the cave of the field of Machpelah, before Mamre, which Abraham bought with the field from Ephron the Hittite as property for a burial place.

14 And after he had buried his father, Joseph returned to Egypt, he and his brothers and all who went up with him to bury his father.

15 When Joseph's brothers saw that their father was dead, they said, "Perhaps Joseph will hate us, and may actually repay us for all the evil which we did to him."

16 So they sent *messengers* to Joseph, saying, "Before your father died he commanded, saying,

17 'Thus you shall say to Joseph: "I beg you, please forgive the trespass of your brothers and their sin; for they did evil to you."' Now, please, forgive the trespass of the servants of the God of your father." And Joseph wept when they spoke to him.

18 Then his brothers also went and fell down before his face, and they said, "Behold, we *are* your servants."

19 Joseph said to them, "Do not be afraid, for *am* I in the place of God?

20 "But as for you, you meant evil against me; *but* God meant it for good, in order to bring it about as *it is* this day, to save many people alive.

21 "Now therefore, do not be afraid; I will provide for you and your little ones." And he comforted them and spoke kindly to them.

22 So Joseph dwelt in Egypt, he and his father's household. And Joseph lived one hundred and ten years.

23 Joseph saw Ephraim's children to the third

generation. The children of Machir, the son of Manasseh, were also brought up on Joseph's knees.

24 And Joseph said to his brethren, "I am dying; but God will surely visit you, and bring you out of this land to the land of which He swore to Abraham, to Isaac, and to Jacob."

25 Then Joseph took an oath from the children of Israel, saying, "God will surely visit you, and you shall carry up my bones from here."

26 So Joseph died, *being* one hundred and ten years old; and they embalmed him, and he was put in a coffin in Egypt.

Gen. 50:1-26

The final chapter of Genesis is remarkable for its contrasts. The early part speaks with some considerable detail of the magnificent funeral for Jacob while Joseph's decease and burial is given in one verse! Times do change and Joseph who had seen more than his share of change apparently saw things change again for him before he died. He was getting a foretaste of the things his descendants would face in the land of Egypt. A day was coming when there would be "a new king over Egypt, who did not know Joseph" (Exod. 1:8). It seems incredible that the man should be forgotten who had led Egypt from disaster to safety and whose ingenuity and industry had protected and solidified the economy of the nation, not to mention the survival of the surrounding nations! But such is life and people like Joseph have to learn how to handle it. And we can all learn from his experience. Centuries later the great apostle would write, "And now abide faith, hope, love, these three; but the greatest of these is love" (1 Cor. 13:13). Joseph knew this long before it was written, and it was his understanding of these things which equipped him for yet another set of changing circumstances.

JOSEPH'S STATEMENT OF FAITH

That Joseph was a man of faith has been thoroughly documented. But there is still more evidence in this closing chapter of his life. This is seen in the way he arranged for his father to be buried, as requested (or commanded!), in the plot of land far away in the land of Canaan. He utilized the resources of Egypt in embalming his father's body and he accepted the gracious offer of the Egyptians to arrange a splendid funeral procession even though it meant them all embarking on a journey of major proportions and organizing an event involving complex logistics. But behind the splendor was a basically simple fact: Joseph believed that the future of his family lay not in splendid Egypt with its pomp and circumstance but in the rugged land of Canaan with all its attendant difficulties and challenges. God had promised his fathers Abraham, Isaac, and Jacob that this would be so and Joseph believed it thoroughly.

Once their father had died the deep-rooted insecurities of the brothers were resurrected. They came to him and said, *"Before your father died he commanded, saying, 'Thus you shall say to Joseph: "I beg you, please forgive the trespass of your brothers and their sin; for they did evil to you."' Now, please, forgive the trespass of the servants of the God of your father"* (Gen. 50:16, 17). That Jacob had not actually said this was obvious to Joseph. The subterfuge which his brothers were engaged in and his brothers' evident lack of trust in him were heart-breaking for him and he wept before them and said, *"Do not be afraid, for am I in the place of God? But as for you, you meant evil against me; but God meant it for good, in order to bring it about as it is this day, to save many people alive"* (vv. 19, 20).

Joseph's commitment of faith to the Lord had been obvious throughout his life and his words at this point were reminiscent of his response to those who thought he could interpret their dreams. He had told them then as he repeated now, "Don't look to me. Look to Him." No one who knew Joseph could ever fail to recognize that he did not trust his own abilities and neither did he hold himself in unrealistically high regard. He knew from whence his strength came and he knew in Whom he alone was secure.

But perhaps the greatest evidence of his faith was his repeated reminder to his brothers that even though they had done him evil the Lord had never lost control and it was He Who had been working out His eternal purposes even in their arrogant and reprehensible behavior. To say this is one thing. To believe it in theory is another. But to relentlessly hold to it in the dark days of betrayal and the lonely years in prison is faith of the highest order. It is imperative that we note Joseph had not moved an inch from this conviction. The faith of his youth continued into his maturity and would continue to be the dynamic force of his life to the very end.

His last recorded words were *"God will surely visit you, and you shall carry up my bones from here"* (v. 25). We need to refer to Hebrews to note the significance placed on these words. "By faith Joseph, when he was dying, made mention of the departure of the children of Israel, and gave instructions concerning his bones" (Heb. 11:22). This man who lived by faith died in faith.

JOSEPH'S SYMBOL OF HOPE

He told his family as he lay dying, *"God will surely visit you"* (Gen. 50:25). In the days to come they would need that assurance for their fortunes which had begun to deteriorate were going to bottom out in abject slavery and cruelty. But Joseph who had known it all personally and had never lost hope knew that those who would follow in his train needed the same kind of certainty that the Lord would be their Visitant. This truth has been the mainstay of generations and must continue to be until the final Day of the Lord in which He will visit this old world in judgment and blessing. But His people must always look for His appearing and live in the light of this glorious hope. Ironically, the symbol of Joseph's hope was a coffin! Those who saw it in the succeeding years knew it was sitting there only until the day of deliverance dawned and the day of march began. In the same way, the symbol of the believer's hope is a cross! Those who look to it see in it the evidence that they can live in hope because the One Who died on that cross rose again and in so doing overcame all that ever defeated a human being. Why then should they fear? What can possibly overthrow the hope bound up in such a victorious triumph and portrayed in such a solemn symbol?

JOSEPH'S SHOW OF LOVE

Love is shown in faithfulness. Joseph's brothers had at various times shown their lack of respect for their father. They had deceived him and hurt him in unimaginable ways. But Joseph had remained constant and those who saw him as he *"fell on his father's face, and wept over him, and kissed him"* (v. 1) knew they were observing a love that was faithful unto death. This was no empty show of emotion because an oath was involved and he showed himself faithful to his promise although the time spent in embalming, mourning, organizing, and traveling must have been demanding. But in his book it was the least he could do because he had promised and love keeps promises.

When his brothers showed their chronic, fearful insecurity his reaction was tender and compassionate. Instead of being angry that they should still not believe him and that they still felt it necessary to deal in an underhanded manner with him, he reached out in a demonstration of fondness and forgiveness which is a model to all of us. He was more concerned with their frailty than with their obvious distrust of his faithfulness. But love understands and makes allowances.

The man whose life had seen such pain and disappointment had one very human delight. He lived long enough to see his grandchildren and to delight in their growth and development. We have followed his life from youth to ripe old age and in so doing we know we have observed one of the greatest men in history—biblical or otherwise.

The journey through Genesis has taken us from Eden to Egypt. Along the way we have met Adam and Abraham and visited Sodom and Salem. Twins have struggled in the womb and men have wrestled with each other and with God. Barrenness and blessedness have passed before our eyes. We have noted the shame of Shechem and the pleasures of Paradise. Famine has raised its ugly head, a flood has wreaked its devastation, and fruitful boughs have leaned gracefully over supportive walls. Eve has been deceived; Dinah has been disgraced. Eyes have blazed with hatred; hearts have overflowed with love. Marriages have sealed young love; covenants have sealed eternal promises. But over it all one theme has arched like a rainbow, and we have no difficulty in identifying the theme because it introduced the book and has never been far from the surface of the narrative. We started with "In the beginning God . . ." (Gen. 1:1) and even though our attention has focused from time to time on different events, people, and places, through it all we have seen the relentless commitment of God to His own eternal and blessed purposes and His unwavering commitment to make Himself known to the race He created and which He loves to the point of ultimate sacrifice. No one knows for sure how many centuries are covered by the story of Genesis but this is all to the good because it reminds us that we are not dealing primarily with centuries of human experience but with a tiny piece of eternity presented to us for our edification and blessing by the One Who inhabits eternity.

After the Battle of Egypt in 1942 Winston Churchill said, "This is not the end. It is not even the beginning of the end. But it is, perhaps, the end of the beginning." Bearing in mind that Genesis speaks of beginnings we do well to remember that having come to the end of Genesis this is not the end, or even the beginning of the end, but it is certainly the end of the beginning!

Bibliography

Aalders, C. C. and Will Heynen. *Genesis.* Bible Study Commentary. 2 vols. Grand Rapids: Zondervan, 1981.

Achtemeier, Paul J. and Elizabeth. *The Old Testament Roots of Our Faith.* Philadelphia: Fortress Press, 1962.

Blocher, Henri. *In the Beginning: The Opening Chapters of Genesis.* Translated by David G. Preston. Downers Grove, IL: Inter-Varsity Press, 1979.

Boice, James M. *Genesis.* Expository Commentary. 2 vols. Grand Rapids: Zondervan, 1985.

Calvin, John. *Genesis.* Geneva Commentary Series. London: The Banner of Truth Trust, 1965.

Carey, George. *I Believe in Man.* London: Hodder & Stoughton, 1977.

Clark, Robert E. *The Universe: Plan or Accident?* Grand Rapids: Zondervan, 1972.

Coder, S. Maxwell and George F. Howe. *The Bible, Science and Creation.* Chicago: Moody Press, 1966.

Douglas, J. D., ed. *The New Bible Dictionary.* Grand Rapids: Wm. B. Eerdmans Pub. Co., 1962.

Dyrness, William A. *Themes in Old Testament Theology.* Downers Grove, IL: Inter-Varsity Press, 1979.

Harrison, Roland R. *Introduction to the Old Testament.* Grand Rapids: Wm. B. Eerdmans Pub. Co., 1969.

Keil, Carl F. and Franz Delitzsch. *Old Testament Commentaries,* vol. 1. Grand Rapids: Wm. B. Eerdmans Pub. Co., 1971.

Kidner, F. Derek. *Genesis.* Tyndale Old Testament Commentary. London: Tyndale Press, 1967.

Leupold, Herbert C. *Exposition of Genesis.* 2 vols. Grand Rapids: Baker Book House, 1942.

Pfeiffer, Charles F. *Old Testament History.* Washington, DC: Canon Press, 1973.

Ramm, Bernard. *The Christian View of Science and Scripture.* London: Paternoster Press, 1955.

Reid, James. *God, the Atom and the Universe.* Grand Rapids: Zondervan, 1968.

Schaeffer, Francis A. *Genesis in Space and Time.* Downers Grove, IL: Inter-Varsity Press, 1972.

Thomas, W. H. Griffith. *Genesis: A Devotional Commentary.* Grand Rapids: Wm. B. Eerdmans Pub. Co., 1946.

Whitcomb, John C., Jr. and H. M. Morris. *The Genesis Flood.* Philadelphia: The Presbyterian and Reformed Pub. Co., 1960.

Youngblood, Ronald F. *Faith of Our Fathers.* Ventura, CA: Regal Books, 1976.

———. *How It All Began.* Bible Commentary for Laymen Series. Ventura, CA: Regal Books, 1980.